D0098306

# The SALT Experience

# The SALT Experience

Thomas W. Wolfe

**Ballinger Publishing Company • Cambridge, Massachusetts**
*A Subsidiary of Harper & Row, Publishers, Inc.*

 This book is printed on recycled paper.

Library of Congress Cataloging in Publication Data

Wolfe, Thomas W.
  The SALT experience.

  Includes bibliographical references and index.
  1. Strategic Arms Limitation Talks. 2. Arms control. I. Title.
JX1974.75.W64      327'.174      78-26779
ISBN 0-88410-079-0

.

Copyright © 1979 by The Rand Corporation. All rights reserved. No part
of this publication may be reproduced, stored in a retrieval system, or
transmitted in any form or by any means, electronic mechanical photo-
copy, recording or otherwise, without the prior written consent of the
publisher.

International Standard Book Number:  0-88410-079-0

Library of Congress Catalog Card Number:  78-26779

Printed in the United States of America

To Rose and Rosalie

For their contributions to this book

# Contents

# Appendix

# List of Figures and Tables

## Figures

## Tables

# Preface

This book is an updated and reorganized version of a Rand study entitled *The SALT Experience: Its Impact on U.S. and Soviet Strategic Policy and Decisionmaking,* R-1686-PR, published in September 1975. The research leading to that report was sponsored by the U.S. Air Force. The updating and conversion of that report into this book was undertaken at the author's initiative. This effort was sponsored by The Rand Corporation.

In updating and broadening the original work for a wider audience, my aim is again that of attempting to gain better understanding of the political and strategic impact of the SALT experience upon U.S.-Soviet relations, and upon the processes of national security decisionmaking in the two countries.

Like any study dealing with issues and relationships that are still evolving, rather than with a finished slice of history, this one must be regarded in some sense as tentative and exploratory. At the same time, since the SALT process has been going on for a decade or longer, there is clearly a challenge to see what lessons it may now hold for us.

Little need be said here about the architecture of the book. Essentially, its chapters cover four major subject areas. The first deals with SALT I, how and why it came about, and the agreements it produced. The second area dealt with is the institutional setting pertinent to SALT-related planning, policy, and negotiating activities of the United States and the Soviet Union, respectively.

A treatment of how the strategic policies and postures of the two superpowers have evolved during the SALT era, and their interaction with the SALT process, constitutes the third main subject area. The fourth, and the largest share of the book, is devoted to the six-year-long pursuit of a SALT II accord under successive American administrations, with the focus upon the substantive issues that arose between the Soviet and American sides and how they were handled.

Finally, the last chapter is given over to some closing reflections on the SALT experience, in which I have allowed my own biases to show through somewhat more than permitted by the attempt earlier in the book to present the various sides of controversial issues—with which the SALT experience abounds—in as evenhanded a manner as I could.

It is not possible to list here all those to whom I owe thanks for advice and intellectual support in the writing of this book. To many friends and acquaintances professionally associated with SALT at one time or another, and who hold a diversity of views with regard to it, I am especially indebted for the sharing of their insights with me. Let me add that the circle of respected professional colleagues from whom I have drawn useful instruction includes some on the Soviet side of the SALT dialogue. I must thank also a number of former or present colleagues at Rand for the invaluable help of one kind or another they have given me: Arnold Horelick, Benjamin S. Lambeth, Frederic S. Nyland, Fritz Ermarth, John C. Hogan, Erma F. Packman, and, not least, Rose E. Gottemoeller, my research assistant, and Rosalie Fonoroff, my secretary, without whom preparation of this book would scarcely have been possible. Needless to say, responsibility for the book's contents is entirely mine.

Washington, D.C.                                         Thomas W. Wolfe

# The SALT Experience

✳ *Chapter 1*

# The SALT I Phase

## HOW SALT BEGAN

SALT remains at this writing an unfinished but ongoing endeavor to regulate the strategic arms competition between the United States and the Soviet Union. Now almost a decade old, and already the longest and most intensive set of Soviet-American negotiations on record, the Strategic Arms Limitation Talks and the several agreements they have produced to date can be regarded as parts of a continuing process that began formally in November 1969, but whose origins probably go back at least about six years earlier to President Lyndon B. Johnson's message of January 21, 1964, to the Eighteen-Nation Disarmament Conference in Geneva. At that time he initially proposed that Washington and Moscow explore "a verified freeze" on strategic offensive and defensive arms as a follow-on to the limited nuclear test ban treaty of the previous year that had been worked out between the Kennedy administration and Nikita Khrushchev.[1]

The Johnson proposal, which called for freezing strategic nuclear systems at then-current levels and for verification by on-site inspection of production facilities, proved unpalatable to the Soviet Union on all counts and was summarily rejected.[2] Nevertheless, because the strategic freeze proposal marked a departure from past comprehensive disarmament approaches and at least stimulated new studies within the Joint Chiefs of Staff and the Arms Control and Disarmament Agency on the complex problems of controlling strategic arms, it has been considered by many analysts as an important early milestone on the road to SALT.[3]

Another American initiative that marked a significant precursory step toward SALT came in January 1967 when President Johnson directed Llewellyn E. Thompson, then returning to Moscow for a second tour as U.S. ambassador, to explore with the Russians as a matter of priority the holding of negotiations to limit ABM deployment. This initiative appears to have grown out of a December 1966 suggestion from Secretary of Defense Robert S. McNamara,[4] who had been resisting pressure from within the Pentagon and Congress to begin deployment of the Nike-X ABM system on the grounds that its deployment would merely stimulate further increases in strategic offensive forces. He also evidently hoped that the Russians—despite having already embarked upon deployment of an AMB system around Moscow—might see it in their own interest to join in mutual ABM curbs.

In a series of private communications in the early months of 1967 between President Johnson and Aleksei Kosygin, chairman of the USSR Council of Ministers, some Soviet interest was in fact shown in holding talks on limiting strategic arms, provided that offensive as well as defensive systems were included, a proviso to which there was quick U.S. agreement.[5] However, as indicated by Johnson's own account, neither in his exchange of letters with Kosygin nor in face-to-face exploration of the subject at Glassboro, New Jersey, in June 1967 in the wake of the Arab-Israeli Six-Day War could he get Kosygin "to name a time or place for serious talks on curbing the missile race."[6] In the president's view, a division of opinion within the Soviet government on whether to enter strategic arms talks may have accounted for Kosygin's negative stance.[7]

President Johnson had stated in his budget message of January 24, 1967, that before the year was out he would reconsider his decision to defer deployment of the Nike-X if discussions with the Soviets on AMB limitation should "prove unsuccessful,"[8] and he had no hankering to be held responsible politically for an "ABM gap."[9] The unyielding attitude displayed by Kosygin at Glassboro was doubtless a factor, therefore, in the U.S. decision—announced with obvious regret by McNamara on September 18—to go ahead with a small-scale deployment of the Sentinel system, an adaptation of the Nike-X.[10]

A third important phase in the pre-1969 genesis of SALT unfolded in the first half of 1968, after it had become known publicly that the United States planned not only to deploy the Sentinel ABM (a system technologically more advanced than the Soviet Galosh system around Moscow) but that a new offensive weapon, MIRV, which would give American ICBMs and SLBMs the capability of delivering multiple, separately targeted warheads, was soon to begin flight tests.[11] During the early months of 1968, when debate within the Soviet government on how to respond to the American proposal for strategic arms talks evidently was coming to a head, further private communications between the president and Kosygin elicited no commitment from the latter, but only word that his government was "studying the question."[12] Toward the end of May 1968, however, a tentative decision apparently was reached in Moscow, and in the following month, both through private messages from Kosygin[13] and a public announcement on June 27 before the Supreme Soviet by Foreign Minister Andrei A. Gromyko, the Soviet Union let it be known that it was ready for "an exchange of opinion" on mutual restrictions of offensive and defensive strategic weapons.[14]

By August 19, Washington and Moscow had agreed privately that SALT would be launched during a visit by Johnson to the Soviet Union in the first ten days of October.[15] Release of this news to the press was scheduled for the morning of August 21, but other events intervened. On August 20, Soviet troops invaded Czechoslovakia, leaving the president little choice but to call off the agreed plans for starting SALT, even though the Russians indicated they would like to go ahead with the talks, ostensibly to soften the unfavorable impact upon world opinion of the armed action against Czechoslovakia.

After the November 1968 elections, Johnson made an effort to revive plans for the talks, suggesting that President-elect Richard M. Nixon accompany him to a summit meeting with the Russians just before Christmas. Nixon, however, declined, serving notice that he would not be bound by the outgoing administration's SALT approach, and, according to Johnson, the Soviet leadership itself now "cooled noticeably" to the idea of entering negotiations with a lame-duck administration.[16] As for the new administration, to which the Soviets made overtures in early 1969 to put the derailed proposal for strategic talks back on the track, its reply was that the U.S. SALT position was under thorough review and no decisions would be made, pending completion of the review and consultation with America's allies.[17] Not until October 25 was the opening date of November 17, 1969, finally set for the first preparatory round of SALT in Helsinki.

Although the proposals, counterproposals, and diplomatic maneuvering summarized above mark some of the main steps along the road to SALT's formal beginning in November 1969, they furnish relatively little insight into the underlying reasons why the United States and the Soviet Union felt impelled to embark upon strategic arms negotiations with each other after more than two decades of intense postwar political, military, and economic rivalry. Perhaps the explanation given the greatest weight, at least in the West, is that despite their rivalries, leaders in both countries had come to a general realization by the mid-sixties that some form of mutual accommodation was mandated by the potential destructiveness of the strategic nuclear arsenals that were being created. Thus, in essence, SALT came about as a response to this formidable mandate, taking the form of a slow and cautious groping for some means of "stabilizing" the strategic force balance.

There are several variations of this basic explanation of why the superpowers opted for SALT. In a perceptive comparison by John Newhouse, for example, SALT has been likened to the Congress of Vienna more than 150 years earlier, both being seen as essentially political negotiations inspired by the need to establish an equilibrium in which the great powers might feel secure—the "stability" to be sought through strategic arms negotiations in SALT representing a kind of nuclear age equivalent of the "general security" that Castlereagh thought it was the business of the Congress of Vienna to establish.[18]

Another variation is that the overall political and power relationship between the United States and the Soviet Union had evolved to a stage in the 1960s that called for some accommodation of both the disparate political interests and the perceived strategic necessities of the two sides. Thus, SALT could be said to have come into being as a major instrumentality for seeking a readjustment of the U.S.-Soviet power relationship and for facilitating the political passage from cold war to detente.[19]

Apart from such broad exegeses concerning the origins of SALT, other factors that contributed in varying degree to bringing it about are also to be noted. The technical evolution of surveillance technology in the 1960s and its potential application to arms control verification, for example, have been singled out as salient factors in making SALT politically feasible. Specifically, reliance upon observation satellites and other surveillance instruments to keep track of deployed strategic systems such as missile launchers could be substituted for intrusive on-site inspection of production and other facilities, permitting contemplated limitation agreements to be monitored unilaterally,[20] and thus easing the verification issue on which most earlier efforts to reach arms control agreements with the secrecy-prone Russians had foundered.[21]

The differing status of both the strategic force posture and programs of the two sides during the sixties, when U.S. initiatives for strategic arms freezes first arose, was another factor that bore significantly upon the genesis of SALT. That decade had found the strategic policies of the United States and the Soviet Union notably out of phase in at least one basic respect. During most of the sixties, Moscow's strategic policy was bent upon a large-scale buildup of Soviet intercontinental strategic forces, following the embarrassment suffered during the Cuban missile crisis of October 1962.[22] By contrast, the main trend of American strategic policy during the same period was to contain the impressive momentum which U.S. strategic programs had acquired toward the end of the Eisenhower and beginning of the Kennedy presidencies, largely as a reaction to the Soviet Sputniks and the so-called missile gap of the late fifties.

In a sense, both of these basic strategic policy trends of the sixties probably were necessary prerequisites for SALT. The Soviet Union, for its part, was in a position that left it essentially uninterested in any U.S. initiatives for strategic arms limitation talks that might call for halting the buildup of Soviet strategic forces before the USSR had attained at least a condition of rough parity with the United States.

Once the two sides approached the status of strategic equals, then negotiations that served to ratify this changed relationship in the eyes of the rest of the world, if accomplishing nothing else, would be politically and strategically tenable for the Soviet Union. Such a status of strategic equality could be rather long in coming through unilateral Soviet efforts, however, unless the United States were to "cooperate," so to speak, in righting the strategic power asymmetry between the two.

For its part, therefore, the United States, while perhaps hoping that through strategic limitation talks the Soviet buildup might be slowed down and the status quo frozen at a point still favoring the U.S. side, nevertheless had to be prepared to constrain the growth of its own strategic forces—in effect, allowing the Russians the opportunity to catch up—if conditions conducive to SALT were to be created.

Although the U.S. policy of strategic constraint during the sixties, of which Secretary McNamara was the principal architect, had neither been expressly adopted to promote the prospect of SALT nor consistently applied toward that end, it did have the effect of giving the Russians a fixed level of U.S. forces against which to plan their own catch-up programs, and thus could be said to have helped in an important way to set the stage for SALT. At the same time, the U.S. constraint policy had a number of other notable effects upon the evolution of SALT.

One aspect of this policy, as pursued by McNamara, was to hold down strategic force size (the number of missile launchers and bombers) by permitting qualitative improvement of strategic delivery systems. Perhaps the most striking example of the tradeoff between force size and offensive missile modernization was the MIRV program, which, together with the ABM issue, was to have significant implications for SALT.

Originally, MIRV had been conceived in the early sixties as a penetration aid to enable American ICBMs and SLBMs to saturate ABM defenses and to serve as a hedge against expected deployment of a Soviet ABM system.[23] It soon became apparent, however, that MIRV technology also promised to increase the U.S. inventory of deliverable warheads without having to deploy additional launchers. Thus, when McNamara found himself in the mid-sixties in need of a rationale to avoid deployment of the additional U.S. missiles for which advocates of larger strategic forces were pressing, the adoption of MIRV provided a convenient cost-effective basis for imposing a fixed ceiling on missile launchers.[24]

There is a certain irony to be noted here. On the one hand, adoption of the MIRV program in the mid-sixties proved useful in McNamara's bureaucratic maneuvering to restrain further growth in the overall size of U.S. strategic forces and therefore served to prepare the way for SALT, at least indirectly, and perhaps more directly as well. On the other hand, the MIRV program was later to bring about a transformation in American missile capabilities that would make the question of limitations on MIRVed missiles one of the more challenging issues to be dealt with in SALT—even though the force-size ceilings established by McNamara in 1964-65 remained essentially intact as the baseline U.S. strategic force for the next decade and beyond.

The strategic logic through which McNamara arrived at a baseline missile force of about 1054 ICBMs and 656 SLBMs for the United States went through several permutations. At the start of the Kennedy administration in 1961, in addition to the principle of assured destruction that had been inherited from the Eisenhower administration, a modified second-strike counterforce concept was also adopted as a basic criterion for force sizing.[25] According to this approach, force levels intermediate between those of a minimum deterrence posture on the one hand and a full first-strike posture on the other would be appropriate and could be measured rather precisely in terms of decreasing marginal effect against Soviet targets. It was essentially this concept which underlay McNamara's well-known Ann Arbor, Michigan, speech of June 1962, which called upon both sides to eschew "city-busting" in favor of attacking military targets in the event of nuclear war.[26]

Emphasis on military targeting tended, however, to become linked with damage-limitation concepts that could stimulate expansion rather than restraint of strategic force levels, as studies of damage-limiting strategies commissioned by McNamara in 1963 suggested.[27] He then began to develop in 1964-1965 the argument that a damage-limiting posture was precluded, not only because of diminishing marginal returns in the effectiveness of bigger strategic programs, but because any U.S. attempt to achieve such a posture would degrade the Soviet assured destruction threat against the United States, and therefore the Russians could be expected to respond with offsetting force increases of their own.[28] McNamara also argued against striving for a damage-limiting posture on the grounds that it would not be worth the effort, in any event, unless coupled with a very large civil defense shelter program, which it appeared the American public was not disposed to accept.

Thereafter, McNamara increasingly narrowed the rationale for strategic forces to the concept of "mutual assured destruction" (MAD), which downgraded counterforce targeting and damage-limitation programs in favor of the capacity to impose assured second-strike retaliation upon the adversary's society while conceding him the same capability against one's own.[29] This was to remain, ostensibly, the basic U.S. strategic rationale for at least the next decade, and one which, in the opinion of some observers, both sides came to recognize as the underlying principle around which SALT was organized.[30]

Whether the Soviet Union as well as the United States had in fact recognized mutual assured destruction as an appropriate conceptual basis for structuring strategic forces and for SALT agreements to limit those forces is a broadly contentious issue that will be taken up later in this study.[31] Here, one further aspect of the effects of the MIRV program upon the origins of SALT remains to be mentioned.

Just as McNamara in 1964-1965 had utilized MIRV logic as a device to put a ceiling on the size of the U.S. strategic offensive arsenal, so he sought a couple of years later, again through MIRV, to constrain strategic defensive capabilities, lest they simply beget larger offensive forces. Specifically, MIRV's potential attributes for overcoming ABM defenses were pressed into service as an argument for delaying a U.S. deployment decision on the Sentinel ABM system when, as mentioned earlier, McNamara and President Johnson were trying in 1967 to get the Soviets to agree to strategic arms limitation talks.[32]

This argument, based on the efficacy of MIRV against ABM, succeeded at the time neither in forestalling a Sentinel deployment decision nor in bringing the Russians to the negotiating table. However, after it appeared in 1968 that the United States was indeed poised to begin ABM deployment, and that MIRV might not be far behind, Soviet assent to SALT was then forthcoming. Whether there was a causal connection here is not demonstrable, but in the view of some, the fact that the United States seemed to be moving closer toward both ABM and MIRV capabilities while the Soviet Union itself had as yet only an inadequate ABM system and no MIRV at all, probably provided a strong incentive for Soviet readiness to begin strategic arms talks: to try to keep the United States from widening the advantages it might derive from these two salient strategic technologies.[33]

Had the SALT negotiations begun in October 1968, as originally agreed before the Soviet intervention in Czechoslovakia, it is difficult to say what would have happened with respect to the American ABM and MIRV programs and the bargaining leverage they appear to have provided. In the ABM case, the incoming Nixon administration in March 1969 proposed changing the Sentinel program into a system for limited ICBM-site defense, renaming it Safeguard, but even this scaled-down program barely squeaked through Congress by a one-vote margin in August 1969, after a heated domestic debate.[34] It seems reasonably plausible that if SALT had gotten under way in the autumn of 1968, ABM deployment in the United States might well have been abandoned before it ever began.

Perhaps the U.S. MIRV program might also have been vulnerable had SALT not been delayed a full year. By the summer of 1968, after an earlier, almost unopposed, development program, resistance to MIRV had begun to jell in some parts of the U.S. government and in arms control circles.[35] The first MIRV test flights went ahead as scheduled on August 16, 1968, to be sure, although if the Czech episode had not occurred just four days later, it is again a possibility that curbs on the U.S. MIRV program might have emerged from SALT before actual deployment began in mid-1970. However, all this remains in the realm of conjecture.[36]

## NEGOTIATIONS: 1969-1972

When the preparatory first round of SALT I opened in Helsinki on November 17, 1969, the Soviet commitment to the negotiations was still tentative, according to Raymond Garthoff,[37] and uncertainty about how seriously substantive questions would be approached also prevailed on the American side.[38] By the time the exploratory session at Helsinki ended a month later, each side seems to have concluded that the other was in fact committed to serious substantive negotiations. It had, however, also become apparent that agreements would not be easily arrived at, owing, among other things, to asymmetries between the two negotiating powers—in political outlook; in the numbers, technical quality, and doctrine of their strategic forces; in their internal policymaking institutions and practices; in relations with their respective allies, and so on.

The two and a half years of SALT I negotiations—seven sessions in all, averaging about three months each and alternating between Helsinki and Vienna—indeed proved difficult and complex. They ended with the first Nixon-Brezhnev summit meeting, in Moscow, at which the ABM Treaty and the Interim Agreement on strategic offensive arms were signed on May 26, 1972, along with a statement on "Basic Principles of Relations" between the United States and the Soviet Union that declared, among other things, that "in the nuclear age there is no alternative to conducting their mutual relations on the basis of peaceful coexistence."[39]

The differences between the two sides that they had sought to reconcile in the process of reaching the SALT I agreements of May 1972 fell into two general categories—those involving negotiating style and approach, and those arising over substantive issues. Illustrative of differences in the first category was the Soviet preference for agreements incorporating broad general restraints on strategic arms and oriented toward achieving strong political impact, as contrasted with the U.S. emphasis on functional and highly specific measures intended to produce militarily meaningful results that would contribute to stabilizing the strategic balance.[40] It should be noted that neither approach was necessarily superior to the other. However, one derivative of the difference between the U.S. functional approach to enhancing strategic stability and the Soviet predilection for broad prescriptive injunctions was that the Soviet approach provided a general umbrella under which they could seek to minimize negotiated tampering with their own force posture and technical preferences.

Also in the category of differing negotiating tactics was the Soviet side's tendency to seek "agreement in principle" before disclosing its specific proposals, in contrast to the American approach of offering a fairly complete and detailed package of proposals.[41] Another difference of style encountered during the SALT I talks was the traditional Soviet dedication to secrecy—carried to the point that the U.S. side found itself obliged to provide most of the factual information pertaining to both U.S. and Soviet strategic forces that was essential to the negotiating process.[42]

In the category of substantive issues, one of the first to arise in SALT I was an argument over what to include in the "strategic forces" that were to be the subject of negotiation. Essentially, the U.S. side preferred to consider only "central" strategic forces—that is, intercontinental delivery systems such as ICBMs, SLBMs, and long-range bombers, and strategic defenses against them. The Russians argued, on the other hand, that U.S. forward-based systems capable of delivering nuclear weapons to Soviet territory must also be included,[43] despite the American contention that such systems were "nonstrategic" and intended as a counter to Soviet medium-range missiles and aircraft targeted against U.S. allies. The FBS issue, as it came to be known, remained one of the unresolved problems of SALT I. It was largely set aside during the last year of the talks, but was to re-emerge later in SALT II.[44]

A second set of substantive issues that dominated much of SALT I centered on ABM and the interrelationship between curbs on ABM and on strategic offensive systems. During the first year of negotiations, after the U.S. had advanced a number of alternative proposals for limitations on both ABM and offensive weapons systems, including MIRV, it became clear that a comprehensive agreement was not in sight.[45] It also became clear that the Soviets were primarily interested at that stage in halting the deployment of Safeguard, the American ABM system, and that toward this end they were prepared to entertain measures that would greatly restrict ABM on both sides.[46]

In December 1970, after a new comprehensive U.S. proposal in August had gotten nowhere,[47] the Soviet Union formally proposed that the negotiators should concentrate on working out an ABM treaty, while leaving the limitation of strategic offensive systems for SALT II.[48] Although originally the United States under the Johnson administration had stressed the need for an ABM freeze as a priority SALT objective, the continuing momentum of the Soviet strategic buildup had altered U.S. perspectives significantly by the end of 1970. Having by then become deeply committed to curtailing the expansion of Soviet offensive forces, especially the SS-9 "heavy" ICBM program, the Nixon administration ruled out any agreement on ABM alone.[49]

The resultant impasse of several months in the formal negotiations[50] was broken in the spring of 1971 by a compromise formula sometimes described as the first major breakthrough in SALT.[51] This compromise was worked out in a set of parallel "back-channel" negotiations between Washington and Moscow that had been initiated by President Nixon in January 1971, and carried on largely by Presidential Assistant Henry Kissinger and Soviet Ambassador A.F. Dobrynin.[52] As announced jointly in the two capitals on May 20, 1971—and up to that time unbeknownst to the U.S. SALT delegation[53]—the two governments pledged that they would concentrate in 1971 on "working out an agreement for the limitation of the deployment of antiballistic missile systems," but that they would also take up "certain measures with respect to the limitation of offensive strategic weapons," pending later negotiations on a more comprehensive and long-term offensive arms agreement.[54]

Although the May 20 formula established a direct link between ABM limitations and the constraints on offensive weapons considered essential by the United States, it did not lead to prompt agreement on either defensive or offensive limitation measures. Nor, for that matter, was agreement immediately forthcoming after Kissinger's precedent-setting visit to Peking in July 1971, which, as John Newhouse notes, had introduced triangular politics into the great-power picture, and perhaps given Moscow new incentive for trying to wrap up a SALT accord.[55]

By early spring of 1972, however, after an exchange of several additional proposals for limits on ABM levels, the negotiations had produced the draft text of an ABM agreement in which differences were narrowed down essentially to defining where each of two ABM complexes permitted each country was to be located.[56] When the Moscow summit began in May 1972, therefore, the key provisions of the ABM Treaty had been basically agreed upon by the SALT delegations in Helsinki.[57]

This was not the case with regard to strategic offensive arms. After the May 20, 1971, announcement, both sides had tabled new offensive limitation proposals, the U.S. in July and the USSR in December of that year,[58] and some elements of what was to become the Interim Agreement (IA) on strategic offensive arms were essentially agreed upon by the spring of 1972. These points—which had been addressed both through the back channel and in the formal negotiations—included the principle of a freeze on ICBM levels that would leave the Soviet Union with approximately a third more ICBMs than the United States,[59] and a duration of five years for the agreement,[60] which would then be replaced by a comprehensive permanent agreement, to be negotiated in SALT II. It was also understood that the omission of such matters as MIRV, FBS, and long-range bombers from the Interim Agreement meant that they would be taken up in SALT II.

But on at least two other important issues about which the United States felt strongly there was continuing disagreement right down to the wire in SALT I. One issue concerned SLBM—the Soviets insisting that SLBMs, in which the United States still held a numerical and qualitative lead, should not be included in the Interim Agreement, while the formal U.S. position came to be equally insistent upon inclusion.[6 1]

The other issue hinged upon missile size and reflected a central American concern over the potential threat to U.S. Minuteman land-based ICBMs that would be posed by a growing force of Soviet heavy missiles with very large payloads or throwweight. The U.S. approach on this issue was three-pronged: (1) to set a sub-limit on numbers of heavy missiles; (2) to define what constituted a heavy missile; and (3) to restrict increases in the size of existing silos, even though other forms of missile "modernization" would be permissible. Since the Soviets had at the time a new but as yet undisclosed fourth generation of ICBMs under development that would be constrained by the proposed limitation, they naturally resisted U.S. efforts to prescribe certain restrictions upon missile modernization.[6 2]

In the case of both the SLBM and missile-size issues, as critics have pointed out, the Soviets may have had some ground for questioning the U.S. positions taken in the formal negotiations between the SALT delegations, in light of ambiguous signals previously received through the back channel, indicating that SLBM launchers need not be included and that missile modernization would not be restricted.[6 3]

The SLBM issue was partly resolved during Kissinger's presummit visit to Moscow in April 1972, when Brezhnev and his colleagues acquiesced to inclusion of SLBMs in the Interim Agreement.[6 4] However, final details on numbers, and provisions for replacing old ICBMs with SLBMs—which represented another American effort to reduce the Soviet land-based missile threat by diverting part of it to sea[6 5]—were worked out only during the last few hectic meetings at the May 1972 summit itself.[6 6] Again, critics have charged that the price paid for Soviet agreement at the last-minute negotiations in Moscow was excessive in terms of allowing the USSR substantially more SLBM launchers and modern submarine platforms than the United States.[6 7]

On the missile-size issue, which had become more vexed than ever after the public disclosure in March 1971 that the Soviets were in the process of building some ninety new silos at SS-9 and SS-11 fields,[6 8] the Soviet side at Vienna in January 1972 somewhat unexpectedly agreed in principle to a heavy missile sublimit.[69] However, this concession failed to resolve the basic issue, inasmuch as the Soviet side persisted in refusing to define what constituted a heavy missile, and it held out for language on silo dimension increases that would allow deployment of new ICBMs having considerably greater throw-weight than the old ICBMs they were to replace.[70] At the May summit in Moscow, the United States was obliged to register its point by offering a unilateral definition of a heavy missile.[71]

As it shaped up after the final negotiating sessions at the May summit, the Interim Agreement on strategic offensive arms set maximum ceilings of 1618 ICBMs for the Soviet Union and 1054 for the United States. Within the ICBM category, heavy missiles of types deployed after 1964 were limited to 313 for the USSR and 54 for the United States.[72] With regard to submarine-launched missiles, the Soviet Union was allowed sixty-two modern nuclear submarines with 950 SLBMs, compared with forty-four submarines and 710 SLBMs for the United States.

Under a complicated tradeoff formula that had been worked out during the summit meeting, the maximum number of SLBMs could be attained only if prescribed numbers of old ICBMs were first turned in—210 by the Soviets and 54 by the Americans. Otherwise, the baseline figures for SLBMs would be 740 and 656, respectively.[73] The net outcome in combined numbers of ICBMs and SLBMs accruing to each if all options were exercised would be 2358 for the Soviet Union and 1710 for the United States. There was no explicit prohibition against mobile, land-based ICBM launchers in the Interim Agreement, as the U.S. side had proposed, but in a unilateral statement the United States indicated that it would consider operational deployment of such missiles "inconsistent" with the objectives of the agreement.[74]

The ABM Treaty, as signed at the May 1972 summit, limited each country to two ABM "deployment areas" of 100 launchers each. This ceiling was later reduced by a July 1974 protocol to the treaty to a single such area, with each party free to choose whether to defend its national capital or an ICBM silo complex.[75] Besides the basic deployment limitations on launchers and radars to preclude the fielding of a nationwide ABM defense system, the treaty included a ban on developing mobile ABM systems, prohibitions to prevent upgrading of air defenses into ABM, and constraints upon converting the potential of "futuristic" technology to ABM purposes.[76]

Both the ABM Treaty and the Interim Agreement explicitly provided for the unimpeded use of "national technical means of verification"—a euphemism for satellite photography and other information collection techniques—as well as for setting up a joint body, the Standing Consultative Commission, to monitor compliance with SALT agreements.[77]

## POLITICAL AND STRATEGIC IMPLICATIONS
## OF THE SALT I ACCORDS

In a political context, perhaps the first point to be made is that despite being political, military, and ideological adversaries, the United States and the Soviet Union had nevertheless managed in the SALT I agreements to take the first steps toward placing negotiated limitations on some of their most important armaments. These first steps, it is true, were probably made easier not only because some of the most difficult issues had been put aside for future consideration, but also because the SALT I accords for the most part amounted essentially to ratifying existing strategic force levels arrived at unilaterally.

Nevertheless, the fact of agreement in itself was politically significant; and if the extent to which the agreements would contribute to accommodation of disparate U.S.-Soviet political interests may appear, in retrospect, to have been overstated, there is still little doubt that the SALT I accords were, as Henry Kissinger put it shortly after their signing, "not merely a technical accomplishment," but "a political event of some magnitude," linked to "a broad understanding about international conduct appropriate to the dangers of the nuclear age."[78]

A second salient point is that while the SALT I agreements could be judged a political success in terms of giving detente a substantial boost, they left important strategic concerns on both sides unassuaged. The American side, for example, came away bothered by the differential quantitative missile levels intended to compensate the Soviet Union for such factors as geographic asymmetries and a notable, but not necessarily permanent, U.S. technological lead. The U.S. aim of constraining the Soviet heavy missile potential, which could threaten survivability of American offensive missiles, also fell short of what had been hoped. In turn, though the Soviet side might derive satisfaction from ABM curbs that would preclude the United States from exploiting a superior ABM technology, its concern to close the qualitative gap in certain other strategic technologies, especially MIRV, had not been met.

A third point of some consequence is that even though the SALT I agreements hardly promised to eliminate Soviet-American strategic competition, they did entail a very considerable political investment in the SALT undertaking by leaders on both sides, creating what might perhaps be called a "SALT imperative." This imperative not only gave both sides a real stake politically in avoiding steps that might derail further negotiations; it also implied in some degree that even unilateral strategic programs permissible within SALT I terms ought not hence forth to appear grossly inconsistent with prospective future agreements.

In a strategic sense, a further interesting effect of the SALT I accords was their resulting impact on the relative weight of defensive and offensive systems in the strategic postures of the two sides. Originally, one of SALT's basic purposes, as seen by its American advocates, had been to constrain ABM deployment in order to remove the incentive for increases in offensive forces. The ABM Treaty of May 1972 did in fact impose sharp limits on ABM, and the Interim Agreement limited ICBM forces numerically to the levels then existing or under construction. However, the latitude remaining on both sides for missile modernization, including MIRV, and for a further SLBM buildup on the Soviet side, meant that the net effect of the SALT I agreements was to weight the officially sanctioned strategic balance even more heavily toward offensive capabilities than had been the case before, suggesting in turn that any new SALT agreements would tend to rest primarily on the conception of balancing off strategic offensive forces against each other.

Still another noteworthy point is that while both sides could be regarded as beneficiaries of the warming trend in Soviet-American relations that was a by-product of—and perhaps also a necessary condition for—the SALT I accords, there were some respects in which the political effects of the agreement seemed to be particularly helpful to Soviet interests. One example lay in "validation" of the proposition that the Soviet Union had finally attained strategic equality with the United States and, in some strategic categories, perhaps surpassed it. Conversely, of course, the implication was that the United States recognized as legitimate the Soviet "right," as a fellow superpower, to receive redress for strategic asymmetries favoring the U.S., and to shorten through negotiations the time required to catch up with the U.S. by unilateral effort alone.

The political impact on Europe of such negotiated strategic equality between the superpowers seemed likely to be especially advantageous from Moscow's standpoint, in view of the tendency of many Europeans to interpret strategic nuclear parity as signaling the end of U.S. nuclear commitment to the defense of Europe. Another example of useful political fallout was that, in the context of a Soviet policy of trying to keep China politically and militarily isolated, the SALT I accords could be seen as a kind of compact with the United States to help ensure against American-Chinese "collusion" at Soviet expense.[79]

Looking back at the kind of reception given the SALT I accords in the United States, it can be said that by and large they enjoyed general public acceptance in 1972 as a useful first step toward heading off a new round of strategic arms competition, and for such positive political effects as helping to reduce international tension and to widen the area of U.S.-Soviet accommodation. Perhaps typical of commentary supporting the results of the Nixon administration's SALT I diplomacy was that of Congressman Gerald R. Ford of Michigan, who said in a speech in Grand Rapids on June 17, 1972: "What it all comes down to is this. We did not give anything away, and we slowed the Soviet momentum in the nuclear arms race."[80]

The merits of SALT I, however, were not universally applauded. In some quarters, the ABM Treaty was acclaimed for its contribution to the "stability of deterrence" and for other exemplary qualities sufficient to justify turning back the "doomsday clock" of *The Bulletin of the Atomic Scientists*,[81] but SALT I as a whole was faulted for not having gone far enough in the direction of such arms control goals as reducing offensive arms, prohibiting MIRV, and imposing controls on qualitative developments.[82] A particular concern voiced by some supporters of the ABM Treaty who gave only qualified endorsement to the Interim Agreement was that the latter might be used to "spur the arms race" by those advocating new offensive programs as "bargaining chips" in further negotiations with the Russians, in which case, as then seen, for example, by Paul Warnke, the "Interim Agreement could prove to be slightly worse than no offensive agreement at all."[83]

Other criticism of the SALT I accords was also to be heard, varying from the assertion that the ABM Treaty had regrettably "institutionalized" a MAD (mutual assured destruction) strategic posture,[84] to claims that the Interim Agreement had given the Soviet Union far too much "headroom" to attain a strategic margin that could pose not only undesirable political consequences for the United States, but military dangers as well. Of all the issues raised in the wake of the May 1972 agreements, it was the issue of Soviet headroom, around which debate over the merits of SALT I largely centered in the United States and in the Congress.

Much of this debate (the detailed flavor of which is summarized in Appendix B) occurred in connection with the steering through Congress in August and September 1972 of a joint congressional resolution approving the SALT I accords, along with an amendment sponsored by Senator Henry M. Jackson of Washington, which stipulated that levels of strategic forces not less than those of the Soviet Union should be sought in the next phase of SALT.[85]

The essence of the headroom issue was the argument that, unlike the ABM Treaty, which affected both sides symmetrically, the Interim Agreement, with its differential numerical ceilings for land-based ICBM launchers and seaborne SLBM forces, would freeze the Soviet numerical advantage in two of the three major categories of strategic delivery forces, while also leaving the Soviet Union free to try to catch up with the United States in such critical technologies as MIRV. Thus, the agreement appeared to give the Soviet Union the opportunity to reduce the leads enjoyed by the United States, but to leave the latter without an opportunity to reduce the Soviet advantages.[86] This, at least in the view of some SALT I critics, meant that the Soviet Union—should it choose to avail itself of all the permissible options—was in a position to develop forces that could pose a greater military threat than existed prior to the agreement, and that might undermine the strategic stability that SALT presumably was meant to ensure.

Another respect in which asymmetry of outcome characterized the SALT I agreements, in the critical view, had to do with the potential Soviet threat to survivability of U.S. deterrent forces. It was ironical that the primary American strategic aim in proposing the SALT talks had been to obtain some kind of ABM ban in order to slow down the defense-offense interaction and to preserve the assured destruction capability of U.S. offensive forces; but that by 1969 the growth of the Soviet SS-9 force had shifted the primary concern of the United States to the survivability of its deterrent forces. Thus, when SALT opened the U.S. priority was to constrain the SS-9 threat, and the major bargaining chip proved to be the Safeguard ABM system, about which the Soviets on their part displayed an evident concern, presumably because of Safeguard's technological potential for development into an area defense capability.

SALT I ended with the United States having cashed in its Safeguard chip, not only assuring the Soviets that the prospect of area defense was largely foreclosed, but also ruling out the possibility of a viable site defense of the U.S. Minuteman force. The key question was: What did the United States get in return to allay its main strategic concern, the survivability of Minuteman?

The United States succeeded in obtaining numerical limits on the SS-9 (that is, on heavy ICBMs), but in the critical view, both failure to get a mutually agreed definition of a heavy ICBM and freedom to modernize could result in qualitatively improved Soviet forces that could threaten the survival of Minuteman. In short, the key tradeoff in the SALT I accords could be said to relieve the Soviets of their central concern about the potential of Safeguard, but not to "solve" the U.S. problem of Minuteman survivability.

On the other side of the argument, perhaps the most compelling strategic case to be made for the central SALT I transaction was that the problem of Minuteman survivability arose primarily out of technological trends that SALT could not, in any event, have controlled; at best, it could only have been expected to delay the day of reckoning.

But if, for whatever reasons, the United States did not receive much in the way of a tradeoff in hard strategic terms from SALT I, then its reward might best be regarded as primarily political and promissory—the possibility that the Soviet Union might henceforth prove to be a more relaxed and tractable adversary, having had strategic parity validated. In the U.S. debate on the merits of SALT I, this was an outcome that could be accepted as adequate, particularly by those inclined in any event to discount the impact of subtle strategic asymmetries upon deterrence and nuclear-age security.

On the other hand, in the view of some critics, various American political assets were likely to suffer depreciation under conditions in which it came to be widely perceived, as a result of an unequal SALT outcome, that U.S. strategic power was on the downgrade, whereas that of the Soviet Union had not yet peaked.[87] Among such potentially frangible assets were: America's international standing with opponents, allies, and neutrals; the resolve of both U.S. decisionmakers and the public during serious crises; and the general national sense of safety in an insecure world.

## SOVIET ASSESSMENT OF THE SALT I OUTCOME

The debate in the United States over the SALT I outcome had no counterpart, publicly at least, in the Soviet Union. Initially, Soviet spokesmen registered great satisfaction with both the SALT I accords and other agreements on Soviet-American cooperation reached at the Moscow summit. In the euphoria of the moment, Premier Kosygin, among others, hailed the SALT accords, expressing the "hope" that they would "go down in history as a major achievement on the road toward curbing the arms race,"[88] and this view was widely seconded by the Soviet press. In addition to helping slow down the strategic arms race and reducing the danger of nuclear war, the Moscow agreements were said to have confirmed the correctness of Soviet policies that combined detente with ideological vigilance and to have been achieved at no cost to the USSR in terms of its military strength and its commitments to "proletarian internationalism."[89]

In Soviet commentary on SALT I, two categories of factors—one described as "objective," the other as "subjective"—were credited with securing a SALT outcome that was said not to "weaken the defense capability of the USSR and its allies to even the slightest degree."[90] In the first category, as stated by G.A. Trofimenko, a prominent Soviet writer on political-military affairs, "The basic objective factor which made these agreements possible consists of the military-economic might of the Soviet Union, and as a result of it, the change in the correlation of forces in the world in favor of socialism in the sociopolitical as well as the military field."[91] According to another, still better known Soviet spokesman, G.A. Arbatov, the category of objective conditions making the SALT accords possible included, in addition to "the increased might of the Soviet Union," a number of objective factors on the U.S. side, such as "American setbacks in Vietnam and such American domestic problems as unemployment, currency difficulties, inflation, and race."[92]

Under the pressure of "objective" conditions, according to Soviet analyses, various "subjective" factors came into play. The most important of these was a change in the attitude of the American leadership, within which, after a "prolonged stubborn struggle on the issue of strategic arms agreements with the USSR," a "realistic line gained the upper hand."[93] The result of this "realistic" shift within the U.S. leadership was that the Nixon administration laid aside "the provocative concept of 'strategic superiority' " for the "concept of 'sufficiency' of strategic arms." In turn, this facilitated a "constructive and businesslike approach" to achieving a strategic arms limitation agreement based on the "principle of equal security."[94]

In none of the voluminous Soviet commentary on SALT I was there any suggestion that the agreements were tilted in Soviet favor. The question of unequal advantage was dealt with by one Soviet radio commentator in the following typical fashion: Senator Jackson and others, he said, "claim that the Moscow accords are an advantage to the Soviet Union, that they supposedly place America in an unequal situation" because "the Soviet Union is allowed a few more land-based ICBMs and missile-launching submarines." But these claims were "groundless." The SALT documents "do not give the one or the other state military superiority. In setting the number of ICBMs and submarines, they take into careful consideration the geographic position of both countries and some other factors." He then went on to add: "Senator Jackson . . . forgets one very important detail—namely, life itself has forced Washington to recognize the military parity of the Soviet Union."[95]

At the same time that the equitable character of the SALT I accords was being defended in the Soviet Union, the United States found itself being admonished against trying to undermine them. Politburo member M.A. Suslov, for example, warned in August 1972 that the Soviet Union would keep a close watch on attempts in the U.S. Congress to attach interpretations that would "distort the spirit and the letter" of the SALT agreements.[96]

Another line of argument, put forward by V.M. Kulish, was that "the reliability of the existing agreements may be considerably reduced if the United States continues its policy aimed at achieving scientific and technological superiority in strategic arms development."[97] It was also asserted by others that "acceleration" of new U.S. strategic programs like the Trident submarine and the B-1 bomber might represent a "cardinal" infraction of the spirit of SALT I, even though they were not specifically covered by the agreements.[98] Curiously enough, these apparent efforts to constrain U.S. strategic programs by invoking the spirit of the SALT I accords stood in some contrast to the declaration of Soviet intent attributed to Secretary General Brezhnev by President Nixon, who said that at the Moscow summit in May 1972: "Mr. Brezhnev made it absolutely clear to me that in those areas that were not controlled by our offensive agreement they were going ahead with their programs."[99]

Although the general assessment of SALT I results in the Soviet Union would suggest that the Soviet side found the outcome to its liking, and that it had acquired a vested interest of sorts in resisting any American attempts to renegotiate the SALT I package on the grounds of unequal advantages to the Soviet Union, there were a few scattered signs of some internal reservations about the accords.

One of these was the admission in a *Pravda* article in mid-June 1972 that the Soviet-American dialogue culminating in the Moscow agreements had gone forward "despite obstructionist actions by rightist and leftist foes of relaxation" and in the face of "occasional direct opposition" from such elements.[100] No names were mentioned, but the supposition that opponents of the talks may have included P.E. Shelest, a reputedly "hardline" Politburo member, was linked to his demotion within the Party hierarchy.[101] The somewhat defensive tone of the *Pravda* article, which stated that the "wise tactical compromises" adopted by the Soviet side in the negotiations should not be regarded as "a sign of weakness," might be interpreted as having been addressed to internal critics of the Soviet position.

Other Soviet commentary also displayed some sensitivity to what was apparently a critical undercurrent within Communist Party circles at home and abroad toward the general advisability of U.S.-Soviet rapprochement at the summit in the face of "tough action by imperialism" in Southeast Asia.[102] In at least one case, there was also what appeared to be a rebuttal, not only to "hardline" criticism from within, but to critics who were "alleging" that the SALT accords did not really signify a step toward disarmament. This rebuttal came from G.A. Arbatov, who wrote that, on the contrary, the SALT agreements were "an important first step," and that such negotiations "concerning the very essence of national security" would have been "inconceivable" not long ago.[103]

Somewhat equivocal hints that the SALT accords may also have been received with less than complete enthusiasm by the Soviet military cropped up in statements by General V.G. Kulikov, then chief of the General Staff, and the late Marshal A.A. Grechko, then minister of defense. The former, in a speech before the Supreme Soviet in August 1972, gave his endorsement of the SALT accords, which he said the United States had been obliged to enter after "soberly evaluating" the "growth of the USSR's military-economic potential."[104] Kulikov then hedged his approval of the agreements by adding: "We are fully aware that they do not signify a change in the nature of imperialism, or renunciation of its aggressive plans."

Marshal Grechko, speaking at a session of the Supreme Soviet, which ratified the ABM Treaty on September 29, 1972, also endorsed the treaty, noting that it would "impede the development of competition between offensive and defensive nuclear/missile weapons."[105] However, Grechko's remarks on the treaty included the following noteworthy comment: "At the same time, it does not place any limits on carrying out research and experimental work directed toward solving the problems of defense of the country against nuclear/missile attack." This statement in itself was literally correct insofar as the ABM Treaty does not bar R&D programs, but the implication that the way remained open to find means for defending the country at large against missile attack was obviously contradictory to the American understanding of the treaty as, in effect, a contract of shared vulnerability that would rule out a countrywide defense.

Whether this implication was in fact intended by Grechko—as a kind of cryptic reservation to the treaty from the military side of the house—cannot be said with any degree of assurance. However, since in terms of both doctrine and practice the strategic defense of the Soviet Union had long been a keystone of the Soviet military outlook, it would seem plausible to suppose that, if any part of the

SALT I package had become a discordant issue within the Soviet establishment, the most likely sore spot was that touched upon by Grechko's inference that the ABM Treaty should not be taken to mean that the search for an effective strategic defense was henceforth foreclosed.

※   *Chapter 2*

# Institutional Setting of the SALT Process: The U.S. Side

During the past decade of strategic arms negotiations, the American and Soviet governments have each worked out their own internal institutional arrangements for conducting the SALT process. Given the dissimilar background and political culture of the respective sides, it can be supposed that these internal arrangements for such matters as the formulation of SALT policy and its integration with other elements of foreign policy and security planning differ considerably in each case.

At the same time that each government has developed its own internal apparatus and practices for managing the SALT process, the two sides also have collaborated in creating a separate category of institutions associated with jointly conducted SALT activities. This category includes the SALT delegations per se, the Standing Consultative Commission, and such quasi-institutional phenomena as the "back-channel" arrangement and the summit meetings, all of which in effect constitute the interface on SALT between the two sides.

The discussion in this chapter will deal with the SALT machinery set up by the United States, and Chapters 3 and 4—also devoted to the institutional setting of SALT—will take up, in turn, the Soviet arrangements for handling SALT, and the back-channel and summit aspects of the SALT process.

## EVOLUTION OF U.S. ORGANIZATIONAL MACHINERY FOR SALT

The U.S. Government's internal machinery for SALT planning and negotiations today is the product of arrangements that have evolved under four different administrations during the lifetime of SALT. In most of the period from 1964 through 1968, when the Johnson administration was going through the preliminary process that eventually led to strategic arms negotiations with the Soviet Union,[1] no particular organizational changes for the support of strategic arms control activities were made within the national security bureaucracy.

Those parts of the bureaucracy concerned with arms control matters in this period were mainly the Arms Control and Disarmament Agency (ACDA), which had been established in 1961, and designated staff elements in the Department of Defense (DOD), the Joint Chiefs of Staff (JCS), the State Department, and CIA. A Committee of Principals, made up of senior national security officials and chaired by the secretary of state, furnished the top-level coordinating mechanism on arms control matters.[2] It received staff support from ACDA through an interagency working group called the Committee of Deputies, chaired by ACDA's Deputy Director, Adrian S. Fisher.

When in the first half of 1967 there had been some possibility that President Johnson's proposal for an ABM moratorium might shortly lead to strategic arms talks with the Russians,[3] the initiative for preparing a U.S. position had been left largely to Secretary of Defense Robert S. McNamara. However, McNamara chose not to mobilize the national security bureaucracy for a major preparatory effort, reportedly because he felt this might create friction with the Joint Chiefs before it was clear that productive negotiations with the Russians could be arranged.[4] Rather, he preferred to enlist a small ad hoc group of officials in whom he had confidence to work out a negotiating position[5]—the need for which subsequently evaporated, at least for the time being, after Glassboro in June 1967.

Again, in the summer of 1968, after the Soviet Union had finally indicated that it was ready to enter strategic arms negotiations and President Johnson had ordered speedy preparation of an agreed U.S. position for the talks prior to the fall elections, the existing interagency machinery—though formally vested with responsibility for coordinating the preparatory effort—once more was in fact largely supplanted by an ad hoc arrangement. In this case, the president had wanted not only a meaningful negotiating package, but one with which the Joint Chiefs would agree, for without their support congressional opposition was assured and a lengthy delay likely in arriving at a U.S. SALT position.[6] Though the Fisher interagency working group staffed by ACDA was the nominal "action" body on SALT, the Joint Chiefs tended, as John Newhouse has put it, to look upon ACDA as "a collection of ritual disarmers,"[7] hence a position drafted at short notice under ACDA's aegis might well have failed to win the Chiefs' confidence.

As it turned out, an ad hoc group set up in the Pentagon in July did much of the work of formulating a set of SALT proposals and informally coordinating them in advance on "both sides of the river," frequently departing from standard procedures in the process. This group had no formal name, but came to be known simply as the "SALT Committee." It was chaired by Morton H. Halperin, deputy to Paul Warnke, then head of the office of International Security Affairs (ISA), and it operated with the direct backing of the new Secretary of Defense, Clark Clifford. Other Pentagon participants in the 1968 SALT-planning exercise included representatives of the office of Systems Analysis (SA), and of the Director of Defense Research and Engineering (DDR&E), as well as a JCS representative, Lieutenant General Royal B. Allison, who had been personally chosen to lend his expertise to the SALT preparations by the chairman of the JCS, General Earle G. Wheeler.

The bureaucratic maneuvering by which the Halperin SALT Committee managed to put together by mid-August 1968 a SALT package that found the Joint Chiefs "on board" need not be examined here,[8] save to note that in part it was probably successful because controversial aspects of the two toughest issues to be dealt with, ABM and MIRV, had been essentially sidestepped. What the agreed SALT package came down to was basically a freeze on long-range offensive missiles mixed with a little regulation of defensive ABMs.[9] The point of interest to this discussion, however, is that even though the "normal" interagency machinery for arms control matters had been bypassed, SALT-related planning was left in the hands of the several governmental agencies concerned with national security matters. The White House itself remained mostly on the sidelines, thus leaving it largely to the processes of bureaucratic bargaining to produce an internal consensus of views for ultimate presentation to the president.

By contrast, the organizational apparatus that evolved within the U.S. government to manage SALT after the advent of the Nixon administration in 1969 was shaped so as to make it fully responsive to centralized White House direction within the National Security Council (NSC) system.[10] As managed by Dr. Henry Kissinger, the new organizational structure was one that would allow the White House to extract information and analysis on policy alternatives from the national security and foreign affairs bureaucracy, while reserving to itself effective decision from amongst a range of options.

The new structure would also provide the instruments for exercising close White House control over the negotiating aspects of the SALT process as well.

In a broad sense, the organizational machinery for central control of SALT can be said to have grown out of the Nixon administration's moves in early 1969 to reinvigorate the National Security Council and to make it a kind of command and control center for the meshing of decisions on interrelated foreign policy and defense issues at the presidential level.[11] In a more specific sense, the inception of particular organizational procedures and the establishment of bodies for dealing with SALT within the NSC system took place in mid-1969, several months before the opening round of negotiations with the Soviet Union began.

At the start of the Nixon term, ACDA, under its new director, Gerard C. Smith, had set up an interagency working group to proceed with preparations for SALT, an initiative that was backed up in March 1969 by NSSM-28, calling for ACDA to supervise a major study of various SALT options, taking account of the strategic, political, and verification aspects of potential limitation agreements.[12] During the next month or two, however, dissatisfaction both in the White House and in the Pentagon with the quality and reliability of the SALT study, particularly its handling of MIRV and verification problems, led to the setting up of two new panels: A special MIRV panel not under ACDA's aegis was established in April, and in June a recommendation was made that a "higher level verification review panel" be created.[13]

The key organizational maneuver leading to White House control over SALT, according to the Newhouse account, was precisely the formal creation of the Verification Panel in July 1969, which Kissinger was to chair and which was modeled after the earlier MIRV Panel, also chaired by him.[14] The creation of the Verification Panel and its backup Working Group (VPWG) for the interagency study of verification problems and the strategic implications of SALT may have come about more by accident than design, but it clearly had several important effects in shaping the U.S. SALT apparatus.

For one thing, it removed the center of initiative for SALT planning from ACDA and established in the White House the central control of SALT that had previously been lacking. Secondly, it placated opposition from the Joint Chiefs of Staff, whose chairman, General Wheeler, had expressed "serious doubt" about the treatment of verification issues in the NSSM-28 study, which had borne the strong imprint of thinking in ACDA.[15] Third, it provided a rather highly structured apparatus for soliciting analytical work on SALT policy alternatives from the national security bureaucracy, including ACDA, while also giving the relevant agencies what has been termed "balanced access" to the analytical process, even if not to the ultimate decisionmaking.[16] Finally, the new system implied that determined political direction from the top down could be expected to make the forging of a policy consensus a less lengthy and arduous process than if the bureaucracies were left to battle it out essentially among themselves.

In this last connection, Kissinger was reported to have said that SALT studies centered in the Verification Panel had "virtually eliminated the narrow adversary approach to arms limitation hitherto practiced within the U.S. government, which used to provoke bitter intramural controversies leading to stultified international negotiations."[17]

Like most institutional arrangements, those established under the Nixon administration to deal with SALT underwent some alteration over the course of time, although on the whole they remained relatively stable and were largely carried over into the period of the Ford presidency. The first changes of note in the Nixon period—apart from the emergence in 1971 of the back-channel line of communications with the Soviet side, which will be examined separately later—came in the year following the conclusion of SALT I in 1972.

These changes involved the naming of a new SALT delegation in March 1973, after the initial session of SALT II had taken place,[18] as well as a wholesale turnover of top personnel in ACDA[19] and a reorientation of ACDA's functions to emphasize research over the direct conduct of negotiations.[20] Among new men appointed to several key posts from which influence on SALT could be wielded were James R. Schlesinger, who became secretary of defense in July 1973; Dr. Fred C. Iklé, who had become director of ACDA three months earlier; and U. Alexis Johnson, who took over as head of the U.S. SALT delegation in early 1973.

None of these changes in the cast of actors, however, had any appreciable effect during the Nixon administration upon the institutional center of power for SALT matters, which remained firmly seated in the Verification Panel under Kissinger's immediate control, even after he assumed a new role—secretary of state—in September 1973, in addition to being the guiding hand behind the NSC in his capacity as presidential assistant for national security.

For a time after the changeover from Nixon to Ford in August 1974, there was some question about how long Kissinger's personal dominance over the U.S. SALT apparatus might continue. Nixon and

Kissinger had established a relationship and a modus operandi that gave the secretary of state wide latitude and generally unquestioned presidential backing across the whole spectrum of strategic and foreign policy matters bearing on SALT. Although the new president hastened to reaffirm heavy reliance on Kissinger,[21] there remained the unknown factor as to whether President Ford's own preferences with regard to the management of SALT would sooner or later begin to diverge from Kissinger's. An alleged, but perhaps overdramatized, bureaucratic power struggle between Kissinger and Schlesinger also added a speculative element to the question of whether Kissinger would retain the inside track on SALT matters with the new president.[22] However, as indicated among other things by his central role in bringing off the November 1974 Vladivostok agreement, Kissinger's hold on the conduct of SALT remained essentially intact throughout the Ford administration, even after Schlesinger was replaced in November 1975 by a more politically agile Secretary of Defense, Donald H. Rumsfeld, and after Kissinger himself had turned over immediate supervision of the NSC staff to one of his top assistants.[23]

The advent of the Carter administration in January 1977 brought the first substantial changes in about eight years in the U.S. government's organizational arrangements and operating practices for the conduct of SALT. Perhaps the major change lay in moving away from the centralized and tightly controlled NSC system over which Henry Kissinger presided during the Nixon-Ford periods toward a much less structured system, somewhat reminiscent of the looser and more diffuse NSC operation of the Kennedy-Johnson eras.[24] Zbigniew Brzezinski, the new president's national security adviser, had come to Washington reportedly determined to maintain a lower profile than his predecessor, and in keeping with President Carter's emphasis on a "team effort" in the area of national-security decision-making, had overhauled the NSC apparatus by reducing its staff personnel about 20 percent and shearing away some of the tightly centralized mechanisms through which Kissinger kept a grip on policy.[25] Although Brzezinski later apparently grew more interested in making his own weight felt in decisions on major policy issues, in addition to sorting out for the president recommendations from the various agencies concerned with national security, Carter himself seemingly preferred to have no single person in his administration become the kind of dominant figure on matters of national security and foreign policy that Kissinger had been.[26]

In the SALT arena itself, although some of the organizational changes under Carter may have been largely a matter of renaming entities inherited from the previous administration, the concentration of policymaking influence and authority formerly to be found in Kissinger's hands came to be diluted, or perhaps better said, replaced by a broader distribution of policy leverage among the major bureaucratic principals concerned with SALT—Secretary of State Cyrus Vance, Secretary of Defense Harold Brown, ACDA Director and chief SALT negotiator Paul Warnke, CIA Director Stansfield Turner, as well as Brzezinski.

Against this general background, we shall next take up in somewhat more detail the basic U.S. organizational machinery for dealing with SALT as it evolved in SALT I and II. This machinery consists of what might best be termed a central or interagency apparatus through which the management of SALT has been carried out, together with internal arrangements in various departments and agencies for handling their contributions to the interagency process. Here we shall consider in turn the SALT apparatus in the Nixon-Ford and the Carter periods.

## CENTRAL SALT APPARATUS OF THE NIXON-FORD PERIOD

The organizational structure of this apparatus is shown in Figure 2-1. Its several components and their functions were as follows:

*The Verification Panel (VP)* was the key deliberative body dealing with SALT within the National Security Council system. Its deliberations furnished, in effect, the final input to each decision formally taken in the NSC, and usually issued as an NSSM or an NSDM. The Verification Panel, as noted above, originally was formed to conduct a high-level review of the SALT verification problem, but its charter was quickly broadened to make it the key instrument for the control of analytical work and policy guidance relating to all aspects of SALT, functions it never relinquished.

As assistant to the president for national security, Kissinger was the panel's chairman from the start.[27] Its primary participants were the heads (or in some cases senior representatives) of six agencies— NSC, State, ACDA, CIA, OSD (Office of the Secretary of Defense), and JCS. The senior State Department representative, the deputy secretary of state, served as deputy chairman of the Verification Panel. His staff support within the State Department on SALT matters came mainly from the Bureau of Politico-Military Affairs, though during SALT II an increasing role was played by the Bureau of Intelligence and Research (INR), whose 1974-75 director, William G. Hyland, was formerly an NSC staff member and close Kissinger associate.

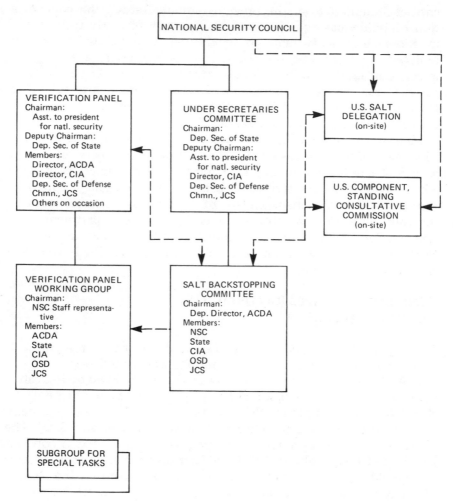

**Figure 2-1.** U.S. Interagency SALT Apparatus of the Nixon-Ford Era

In addition to the agency principals listed in Figure 2-1, the director of the Atomic Energy Commission, the president's science adviser, and the attorney general sometimes attended sessions of the Verification Panel.[28] Meetings of the panel were not held on a regularly scheduled basis, but tended to increase in frequency during periods when the NSC had to take up issues relating to a new stage or a deadlock in the SALT negotiations.

It was largely upon the work of the Verification Panel that Kissinger rested his claim that intramural controversy and a narrow adversary approach to arms control had been "virtually eliminated." Outside observers, assessing the performance of the Verification Panel in the Nixon period, would not necessarily agree that it altogether eliminated familiar habits of intragovernmental bargaining, but many would join in the judgment that it did prove to be an effective instrument for keeping the White House informed on a range of negotiating options while U.S. SALT positions were being forged.[29]

One of the main recurrent questions with regard to the Verification Panel's functioning after Kissinger became secretary of state in 1973 was whether he could continue to give the panel the close personal attention that had made it the hub of the internal SALT process. Without doubt, the demands of diplomacy made increasing inroads upon his time, but as one observer puts it, Kissinger in effect moved the NSC over to State and continued to run it "from his hip pocket."[30] In the process, he retained control over the Verification Panel, while delegating day-to-day responsibility for overseeing its work to Lieutenant General Brent Scowcroft, a close aide who formally took over Kissinger's title as presidential assistant for national security affairs in November 1975, and who was assisted in SALT matters by William Hyland, his deputy.

President Ford's working style brought some change in the Verification Panel's operations after August 1974. Most notably, there was a somewhat greater tendency to thrash out important SALT issues in full meetings of the National Security Council, rather than relying upon final inputs to decision from the Verification Panel to the degree practiced in the Nixon era. An illustrative case was the series of NSC meetings in October 1974 in which, with the President's participation, the SALT decisions relevant to the Vladivostok summit were taken.[31] However, though there was perhaps a slight shift of the center of gravity for SALT decisionmaking from the Verification Panel to the full NSC with the president and other major government officials in attendance, this apparently did not mean a significant reduction of Kissinger's strong influence on SALT decisions.

*The Verification Panel Working Group (VPWG)* was set up at the same time as the panel to provide staff support for it—specifically, to conduct or to oversee the carrying out of appropriate research and studies relating to SALT. Originally headed by Laurence E. Lynn, then one of Kissinger's senior NSC staff aides, the VPWG was chaired in turn by Lynn's several NSC successors, including Jan M. Lodal. Participation in the Working Group was confined to the six primary agencies represented on the Verification Panel, their work program being dictated in the main by the panel and the NSC staff. Both of these groups reflected Kissinger's personal guidance, though the VPWG was also responsive to some extent to other requirements arising out of either on-site SALT delegation proceedings, or what Paul Von Ins has rather delicately described as "various agency persuasions," that is, challenges to a Kissinger-favored position by one agency or another.[32]

As shown in Figure 2-1, subgroups for special-study tasks were formed under the VPWG from time to time. Most of the basic long-term work of the VPWG was carried on during the breaks between negotiating sessions, when some consultation took place with SALT delegation members. During active negotiations, work referred to the VPWG often tended to be linked to current negotiating problems.

*The Under Secretaries Committee for Salt (USC)*, chaired by the deputy secretary of state, was originally a non-SALT senior body set up under the Nixon NSC system to ensure uniform implementation of foreign policy decisions throughout the government. By common account, the Under Secretaries Committee never became very active in discharging this function.[33] During the early part of the SALT I period, this group was given staff support by the SALT Backstopping Committee (see below), with the avowed purpose of making it the focal point for immediately responsive Washington support for the SALT delegation during negotiating sessions only.

However, since agency representation on the Under Secretaries Committee closely duplicated that of the Verification Panel, with most of the same principals simply wearing different hats, this group's SALT role, like its other functions, tended over time not to match its charter. In actual practice, requests from the SALT delegation for backup work that could not be routinely handled by the staff group (SBC) were generally referred, in ascending order, to the VPWG, the VP, or the NSC staff for decision—with Kissinger providing the guidance deemed appropriate at each level.

One SALT-related function to which the Under Secretaries Committee did apparently give some attention after SALT I was that of monitoring observance within the U.S. government of SALT commitments already made. Although this was a function that could become quite important if the number of SALT agreements and issues arising out of their observance by the United States should increase, little activity by the USC in this area had come to light by the end of the Nixon-Ford period.

*The SALT Backstopping Committee (SBC)* was the focal point for SALT support activities in Washington during actual negotiations.

Chaired by the deputy director of ACDA, the committee was composed of representatives of the six primary agencies at the VPWG level. In effect, it directed the traffic to and from the SALT delegation and initiated staffing actions responsive to the proceedings in Geneva. As noted above, problems that were beyond this committee's ability to resolve—for example, decisions on deadlocked issues, general policy guidance, fresh instructions to the delegation, and the determination of new areas for study and analysis—were referred to the Verification Panel.

*The SALT delegation* throughout SALT I was headed by Gerard C. Smith, who was at the same time the director of the Arms Control and Disarmament Agency in Washington. Beginning in March 1973 after the initial session of SALT II, and down to the close of the Ford administration in January 1977, the U.S. delegation was led by Ambassador U. Alexis Johnson, a distinguished career diplomat who, unlike his predecessor, did not also serve as ACDA's director.

The original SALT delegation had five principals, including Ambassador Smith, all of whom were presidential appointees, as well as an executive secretary who, while not a principal delegate, was nevertheless a key member of the delegation.[34] In addition, the delegation originally included nineteen staff members and advisers, plus logistics support personnel for such functions as communications and security. One of the principals on the original delegation and three of the advisers were military men. After the appointment of a new delegation in March 1973 (with two holdover principals from the SALT I delegation), a sixth principal member was added to give ACDA representation.[35] The size of the advisory staff fluctuated from about twenty-five to forty; with administrative support personnel, the delegation sometimes numbered up to one hundred people.

During SALT I, the negotiating sessions were held alternately in Helsinki and Vienna. With the beginning of SALT II in November 1972, however, in order to reduce the administrative burdens of shifting from one site to another, it was agreed to make Geneva the permanent meeting place for the SALT delegations.

Upon several occasions during SALT I and II, suggestions were made that there be congressional participation in the U.S. SALT delegation, an idea that Ambassador Smith is said to have favored,[36] but which was not put into practice until after the Nixon-Ford period.

In addition to the delegation's task of conducting formal negotiations with the Russians, as well as that of carrying on a variety of informal contacts with the Soviet delegation,[37] another responsibility that fell to it was that of keeping the NATO allies of the United States informed on the progress of negotiations. For this purpose, periodic briefing visits were made to NATO headquarters in Brussels by the head of the delegation and other delegates.

Several questions involving the on-site SALT delegation's interface with Washington seem to have arisen recurrently during the Nixon-Ford period. One was the question of how much authority and initiative in negotiations might be exercised by the delegation on its own. In general, the U.S. delegation apparently operated under rather detailed instructions from Washington, although it probably enjoyed somewhat more leeway than its Soviet counterpart. Nonetheless, a touchiness with respect to the U.S. delegation's sphere of responsibility was present at times in SALT I, as indicated by the reminiscences of some delegation participants.[38] Ambassador Smith was said to have resigned as head of both the delegation and ACDA shortly after the start of SALT II because of feeling that he had been "persistently denied the responsibility he thought he should have."[39]

The question of leeway allowed the delegation, as well as the apportionment of credit or blame for negotiation outcomes, was closely related to—and in a sense compounded by—the so-called back-channel phenomenon. The manner in which the delegation's on-site negotiating activities were bypassed by the back channel, and the implications of this way of bringing high-level consideration to bear upon critical issues, will be explored in Chapter 4.[40]

A third area of recurrent ambiguity concerned the extent to which the SALT delegation principals were to be considered more or less autonomous representatives of their parent agencies (State, OSD, JCS, ACDA), or simply members of a negotiating team for which the sole authoritative voice was the head of the delegation. During the latter part of SALT I, and again in SALT II, according to some observers, the biases of major bureaucratic factions were sometimes reflected in the delegation's operations, despite guidance from the White House intended to discourage internal bureaucratic maneuvering and to limit the delegation's negotiating mandate.[41] Paul Nitze has said that differences of approach among individual members of the delegation did arise during his tenure in SALT I and II, but were generally settled satisfactorily, either by arguing them out until a consensus was reached or by decision of the delegation chief.[42]

*The Standing Consultative Commission (SCC)* is a joint U.S.-Soviet body that was set up to implement the provisions of the ABM Treaty and the Interim Agreement of May 1972. Among its functions was to be to "consider questions concerning compliance with the obligations assumed and related situations which may be considered ambiguous."[43] Officially constituted in December 1972 during the initial session of SALT II after the organizational details had been worked out by the two SALT delegations,[44] the SCC began its operations separate from the main SALT negotiations in May 1973. Its first official business was the adoption of a set of joint regulations, which provided among other things for confidentiality of SCC proceedings.[45]

At the outset of the SCC, the American side chose to be represented by a civilian commissioner and a military deputy commissioner, supported by an on-site staff of eight to ten members drawn from various agencies.[46] After Ambassador Johnson served briefly in 1973 as the pro tempore U.S. commissioner, Sidney N. Graybeal of ACDA, formerly a SALT delegation principal, took up the post. The first deputy commissioner was Brigadier General William F. Georgi, USAF, who was also chief of the International Negotiations Branch, J-5 Directorate, Joint Staff, JCS. Colonel Charles G. Fitzgerald, a retired army officer, fluent in Russian, who had been a member of the SALT negotiating team from the beginning of SALT I, became the executive secretary of the U.S. component of the SCC.[47]

The first substantive business of the SCC was to establish agreed procedures for notification, replacement, and dismantling of strategic systems as called for by the ABM Treaty and Interim Agreement of May 1972. Completion of this task was announced during the mid-1974 summit visit of President Nixon to Moscow,[48] where the two protocols on procedures worked out by the SCC were signed, but not made public—at the request of the Russians.

In November 1974, the U.S. component of the SCC for the first time asked for an SCC meeting to air its concern about certain Soviet activities, including installation of possible new missile silos, that might be in violation of the May 1972 accords.[49] The Soviet side apparently countered by raising several questions in the SCC about U.S. compliance, while denying publicly that there had been any Soviet violations.[50]

Although no confirmed details of SCC exchanges on compliance or other matters were officially made public at the time, this joint U.S.-Soviet body obviously continued to deal with a number of compliance questions during the Nixon-Ford period and into the Carter period, as subsequently documented by a public report in February 1978 from the secretary of state to the Senate Committee on Foreign Relations on compliance issues taken up in the SCC.[51] These issues and the considerable volume of critical allegations of

Soviet noncompliance that appeared in the U.S. press after the late fall of 1974 will be discussed in Chapter 10.[52]

Regular sessions of the SCC, averaging four to six weeks in length, have been held twice annually since the SCC began operations in 1973. In addition, a "special" session on compliance matters was held in early 1975, and another in 1977 to carry out the formal review of the ABM Treaty called for at five-year intervals by Article XIV of that treaty.

## CARTER ADMINISTRATION CHANGES IN THE CENTRAL SALT APPARATUS

The organizational structure of the central SALT apparatus as it stood in late 1978, after changes introduced at the outset of the Carter administration, is shown in Figure 2-2 and discussed briefly below. In some instances, organizational entities inherited from the previous administration were allowed to become defunct without being replaced, like the Under Secretaries Committee. In other cases, like that of the Verification Panel, a new replacement body was created.

*The Special Coordinating Committee,* one of two committees into which the National Security Council was divided under the Carter administration, replaced the old Verification Panel of the Nixon-Ford period, although unlike its predecessor, it was meant to deal with non-SALT as well as SALT issues. Chaired by Brzezinski, the Special Coordinating Committee retained essentially the same membership and SALT policy-formulating functions as the Verification Panel,[53] but there were several notable differences in the way the two bodies operated.

Perhaps the chief contrast with Kissinger's Verification Panel was that the principal agencies involved—State, OSD, JCS, ACDA, and CIA—were given a good deal more latitude in advancing their institutional views on SALT issues, with the president's assistant for national security tending to play the role of "referee" among bureaucratic equals, rather than the dominant framer of policy.[54]

Thus, while the Special Coordinating Committee under Brzezinski's working style was wont to task the national security bureaucracy for analytical studies as before, it was said to leave the interested agencies pretty much to their own devices thereafter (except perhaps for occasional telephone inquiries on progress) until the projects were finished.[55] The final products were then critiqued for presidential consideration through an interagency review process, rather than by Brzezinski and his NSC staff alone. In the meetings of

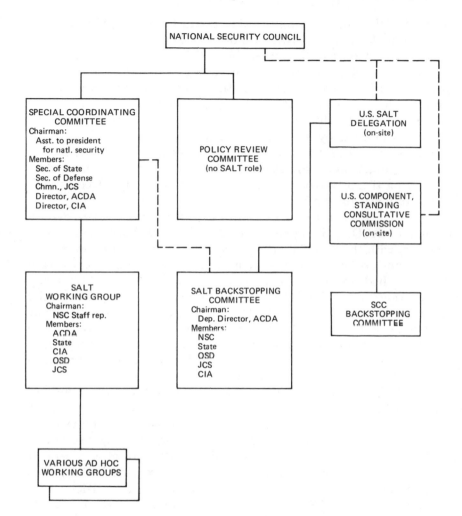

**Figure 2-2.** U.S. Interagency SALT Apparatus of the Carter Period

the Special Coordinating Committee, another change from past practice was that the departmental representatives in attendance usually included the secretary of state (Vance)[56] and the secretary of defense (Brown), rather than the deputy secretaries of their departments, as had generally been the case with the Verification Panel prior to late 1973.

While the membership of the Special Coordinating Committee overlapped to a considerable extent the other NSC committee created by the Carter administration,[57] the Policy Review Committee, SALT issues apparently were confined largely, if not exclusively, to the former in the division of labor between the two.[58]

*The SALT Working Group* established by the Carter administration was charged with basically the same duties and responsibilities for support of the Special Coordinating Committee that were earlier borne by the Verification Panel Working Group that it replaced. Its interagency membership continued to parallel that of the old VPWG, and it was chaired by a senior NSC staff representative. No formal subgroups for SALT tasks were set up under this body, but ad hoc working groups were sometimes assembled to deal with specific issues or particularly troubling problems, and then dissolved as soon as their task was finished.

*The SALT Backstopping Committee* was chaired by the deputy director of ACDA, Spurgeon M. Keeny, Jr., and shared some of its personnel with the SALT Working Group.[59] It was carried over from the previous administration with its functions remaining essentially what they had always been—to transmit guidance on SALT issues and provide other kinds of day-to-day support for the on-site delegation in Geneva. However, these activities of the Backstopping Committee under the Carter administration were apparently carried out in a less-structured fashion and with much less referral of problems up the line to the level of the Special Coordinating Committee than had been the case in Kissinger's day.[60]

*The SALT delegation* changes introduced by the Carter administration affected both the personnel composition of this body and to some extent its manner of operation. The first significant move made was to revert to the earlier SALT I organizational principle of having the director of ACDA also serve as chief SALT negotiator, roles that were allotted to Paul C. Warnke. An alternate SALT delegation chairman in the person of Ralph Earle II, an ACDA official with prior service as a SALT delegate, was appointed to head the on-site delegation when Warnke was absent from Geneva.[61]

Another personnel step taken in June 1977 at the invitation of Warnke was the appointment of twelve House members and twenty-five Senators as congressional advisers to the SALT delegation, a number of whom sat in on negotiating sessions with the Soviet side during 1977 and 1978.[62] As noted earlier, such congressional exposure to the negotiating process had been suggested in the past,[63] but reportedly had been opposed by Kissinger.[64]

Changes of operational style in the Washington SALT apparatus apparently were reflected in the SALT delegation's interface with

Washington. In the "looser" and less-structured NSC system presided over by Brzezinski (who was said to give much less attention to the management of SALT than his predecessor)[65] and with Warnke having assumed a prominent role in both the policy and negotiating aspects of the SALT process, the previous tendency to keep the SALT delegation on a rather short leash apparently diminished a good deal. At the same time there was said to be an increase of informal telephone consultation between the on-site delegation and various Washington agencies—ACDA, State, JCS, and OSD.[66] When an idea that seemed good enough to become a possible negotiating position had emerged from this informal traffic between the delegation and Washington, it was then put through the more formal rigors of the interagency review process supervised by the SALT Coordinating Committee.[67]

The impression of unanimity of view among members of the U.S. delegation that tended to prevail during the first year of the Carter period reportedly had begun to disappear by the end of 1977, after earlier SALT initiatives of the new administration had not met with acceptance from the Soviet side. Matters at issue were said to include the question whether guidance from Washington should permit backing away from positions clearly unacceptable to the Russians, or whether contemplated compromises to accommodate the Soviet viewpoint might harm long-term U.S. security.[68]

*The U.S. component of the Standing Consultative Commission*, at the change of administrations in January 1977, had just been assigned a new commissioner, Robert W. Buchheim of ACDA, who remained in this post under the Carter administration. The post of deputy commissioner, meanwhile, changed hands twice up to mid-1978.[69]

Among the major substantive tasks of the SCC during the first year of the Carter period was a formal review of the 1972 ABM Treaty, conducted in November 1977. In the review session, the two sides concluded that the treaty had operated effectively during its first five years and that it did not need amendment at that time.[70]

Organizationally, no changes were made in the joint SCC itself, but as shown in Figure 2-2, backup arrangements for the U.S. component in Washington underwent some alteration. This was the establishment of an *SCC Backstopping Committee*, an interagency group largely operated by ACDA, and separate from the other SALT backup machinery that had formerly served to support the U.S. SCC component while it was meeting in Geneva.

## THE MILITARY SALT APPARATUS AT THE OSD-JCS LEVEL

Although some internal changes in the SALT machinery within the Department of Defense took place during both the Nixon-Ford and Carter periods, down to the close of 1978, at least, there had been no material alteration of what was doubtless the principal distinguishing feature of the SALT apparatus in the Pentagon—namely, a dual OSD and JCS setup under which the Joint Chiefs, in keeping with their statutory role, retained a relatively independent voice throughout the SALT arena.

This dual organizational structure as it stood at the close of the Ford administration and as it was carried over into the Carter presidency is shown in Figure 2-3. With regard to the JCS side of the structure, there had been a somewhat different arrangement during SALT I and until some organizational changes were made in March 1973. Before then the JCS focal point for SALT matters had been an office directly under the chairman of the JCS, which coordinated JCS SALT interests with the military services and represented the JCS on working-level groups in the interagency SALT arena. The JCS representative on the SALT delegation was the personal selectee of the chairman and was also supported directly by his office.

After March 1973, this SALT office was subordinated to the International Negotiations Branch, J-5 Directorate, under the director of the Joint Staff. Its functions remained much the same as before. The JCS representative on the SALT delegation also was placed under the director of the Joint Staff. When the Standing Consultative Commission began to operate in May 1973, the chief of the International Negotiations Branch was made deputy commissioner of the U.S. SCC component.[71] This dual role continued until mid-1978, when the two posts were divorced after a new deputy commissioner had been appointed.[72]

The OSD side of the structure shown in Figure 2-3 reflects the end result of several successive sets of organizational arrangements for dealing with SALT. The first, which lasted through the SALT I period, had found several OSD offices in a sense competing in the preparation of SALT positions for the deputy secretary of defense (or for the secretary of defense when the latter became involved at the NSC level). Among the offices furnishing major analytical or policy inputs during SALT I were Systems Analysis,[73] especially its Strategic Planning and Arms Limitation Branch, and DDR&E, with ISA making some contributions also, although its influence upon SALT had waned considerably.[74] Under this arrangement, the OSD

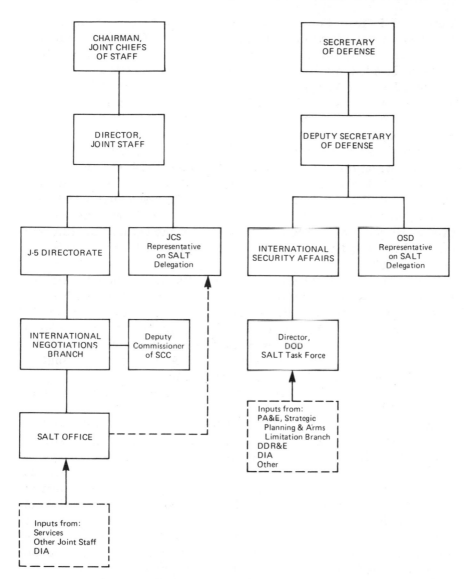

**Figure 2-3.** U.S. Military SALT Apparatus

representative on the SALT delegation, Paul Nitze, also maintained a small office in the Pentagon as assistant to the secretary for SALT.

The second organizational arrangement emerged in the fall of 1973 after SALT II had gotten under way and a new secretary of defense (Schlesinger) had assumed office. A new post, director of the

DOD SALT Task Force, was established at that time under the secretary of defense in order to pull the overall OSD SALT support effort together and to improve coordination with the JCS on SALT matters. Headed by Dr. N.F. Wikner, a senior official previously associated with SALT planning, this task force continued to draw upon the resources of the other OSD offices mentioned above. Nitze continued to serve in the dual capacity of OSD representative on the SALT delegation and as assistant to the secretary for SALT.

Under the third organizational arrangement, which followed Nitze's resignation and Wikner's relief in June 1974, the functions of the DOD Task Force were relocated in ISA under the supervision of Dr. James P. Wade, a former DDR&E official associated with SALT support activities. Some months later he also took over the vacated title of director of the SALT Task Force, indicating that ISA had regained its earlier role as the coordinating center for the OSD SALT support effort.

This arrangement, which is the one depicted on the OSD side of Figure 2-3, was essentially perpetuated when Harold Brown became secretary of defense with the advent of the Carter administration.[75] Leadership of the DOD SALT Task Force, which remained seated in ISA, was taken over by Walter B. Slocombe, who served at the same time as principal deputy to the head of ISA. Slocombe was said to work very closely on SALT with Secretary Brown, who was himself a veteran of the SALT experience and who continued to take a direct hand in SALT matters.[76]

In the past, contrary to popular belief that a solid front could be expected from the Pentagon on SALT issues, the views and positions put forward by the JCS and OSD were evidently not always in agreement. OSD offices, according to some accounts, tended to reflect the attitude of the incumbent secretary of defense, which in the McNamara, Clifford, and Laird periods sometimes differed from the prevailing JCS view. Apparently in SALT I there was also less than unanimity in the OSD and JCS positions advanced in the interagency arena, especially at the working levels of the Verification Panel Working Group and the SALT Backstopping Committee.[77]

The establishment of the DOD SALT Task Force in 1973 near the beginning of SALT II apparently tended to promote a closer coordination of JCS and OSD positions on SALT issues, although there were occasions when the Joint Chiefs were said to have differed notably with Secretary Schlesinger, for example, when they favored Kissinger's proposed approach to the Vladivostok meeting of November 1974 over the proposals advanced in the NSC by Schlesinger.[78]

Some differences on SALT between the JCS and Secretary Brown evidently developed during the first year of the Carter administration, parallel with the president's request for a study to examine the role of the Joint Chiefs in the command structure.[79] Such differences reportedly included Brown's concurrence in proposed limitations on cruise missiles.[80] Neither SALT positions nor command reorganization matters, however, had become major issues between the JCS and OSD, publicly at least, up to the close of 1978, leaving the impression that a more or less united Pentagon front on SALT still existed. But such a front could certainly become quite strained should parts of OSD, and perhaps Secretary Brown himself, come to believe that political imperatives required going along with new SALT agreements that were in serious conflict with what the JCS considered to be prudent strategic options and hedges.

## ACDA'S PLACE IN THE SALT APPARATUS

Created in 1961 to fulfill a campaign pledge by President Kennedy,[81] ACDA acquired less weight in the SALT planning of the Johnson period than its charter—giving it the primary responsibility within the government for advising the president and the Congress on arms control policy—would seem to have warranted. In the organizational apparatus set up to handle SALT I under Nixon, ACDA again failed to acquire a central role in SALT policy formulation, even though its representatives were to be found on all of the panels and committees of the interagency apparatus under the NSC.[82] On the other hand, ACDA's director, Gerard Smith, did become in SALT I the chief U.S. negotiator, as provided for by the Arms Control and Disarmament Act of 1961, although once more, this function was in a sense partly subverted by negotiations carried on by others through the back channel.

Controversy concerning ACDA's role among the U.S. agencies dealing with SALT took on a noticeable edge following SALT I, when Gerard Smith gave up the dual posts of ACDA director and chief of the U.S. SALT delegation, and there was a substantial exodus from ACDA of arms control experts who had been with the agency since its establishment in 1961. The new director, Dr. Fred Iklé, was known as an articulate and well-informed expert on arms control matters in his own right. However, the fact that his post no longer included the responsibility of heading the SALT negotiating team and that ACDA's activities were redirected primarily toward supporting research and staffing functions led to public debate over ACDA's proper place in the SALT arena.

Basically, controversy involving ACDA stemmed from the contention that the balance of policy advocacy within the U.S. government between military and arms control interests had become gradually distorted during the evolution of the SALT apparatus under the Nixon administration. The imbalance led to a situation in which ACDA—the nominal seat of arms control advocacy in the government—was claimed to have suffered an eclipse of its proper role in the SALT policy arena.

Linked with criticism that failure to allot ACDA greater weight in SALT policymaking had led to an "imbalance in the spectrum of informed advice" available to the government was the assertion that this also had left the government's advocacy of "arms control" almost wholly dependent on a single individual—Kissinger. And, it was said, he could not be expected to carry the load "all by himself," despite "his skill and experience."[8 3] Whatever merit such arguments may have had, it is perhaps noteworthy that Kissinger himself seemingly preferred an arrangement whose effect was largely to channel ACDA's SALT contributions into research and support, with policy guidance and control remaining in his own hands.

With the advent of the Carter administration and the confirmation in March 1977 of Paul C. Warnke as both director of ACDA and chief SALT negotiator, ACDA in a sense regained the role, as one observer put it, of a "leading player" in SALT among bureaucratic equals.[8 4] Under Warnke, whose first association with SALT had occurred about a decade earlier when he was a Defense Department official,[8 5] ACDA was reorganized and some of the arms control experts who had left it in 1973 after SALT I now returned, including Spurgeon M. Keeny, Jr., who became deputy director of the agency.[8 6]

Controversy over ACDA's proper weight in the SALT arena did not, however, cease with the advent of a new administration; rather, it shifted to charges from conservative critics of Warnke's appointment that he was an over-zealous arms control advocate under whose leadership in SALT too many concessions might be made to the Russians to the detriment of U.S. security.[8 7] The news coverage given the extended Warnke confirmation hearings did not just expose a wide public to SALT issues and ACDA's role in dealing with them.[8 8] It also tended to place a certain constraint upon ACDA's general approach to SALT, in order to ameliorate criticism in Congress from those whose votes would be needed for approval of any SALT II agreement reached with the Russians. Warnke's subsequent resignation in the fall of 1978, which is discussed in Chapter 11, was apparently in part related to this.

## CONGRESSIONAL INFLUENCE ON THE
## SALT PROCESS

Prior to the conclusion of SALT I in 1972, it seems fair to say that the Congress played a minimal role in the SALT process. It is true that numerous committees and subcommittees in both houses concerned with the armed services, foreign affairs, arms control, and appropriations exhibited an interest in various matters touching on SALT and were in a position to influence the process in some degree. But there was little opportunity for the Congress as a whole to exert direct leverage upon SALT policy while the two and a half years of SALT I negotiations were in progress.

All this began to change after May 1972, when the Congress found itself becoming involved directly in SALT—both through the Senate's formal role in ratifying any treaties produced as a result of negotiations conducted by the executive branch, and through the provisions of the Arms Control and Disarmament Act of 1961 calling for congressional cognizance of arms control understandings. The debate in Congress over the merits of the SALT I accords made it clear that congressional "guidance" would have to be taken into account in the formulation of SALT policy for the future.[89] The immediate vehicle through which such guidance was brought to bear was the joint resolution of September 30, 1972, which incorporated language from the Jackson amendment and amounted in effect to a congressional mandate to adopt a policy of equivalence.[90]

In addition to establishing the principle of numerical equality as one of the basic parameters of a permanent agreement with the Soviet Union, the joint resolution also noted that attainment of more comprehensive agreements would be "dependent upon preservation of the long-standing United States policy that neither the Soviet Union nor the United States should seek unilateral advantage by developing a first strike potential." Further, the joint resolution put the Congress on record in support of the policy of "supreme national interests," the effect of which was to sanction U.S. withdrawal from the ABM Treaty and other SALT obligations if a satisfactory permanent agreement on offensive arms were not reached within five years[91]—an outcome which, in the event, did not transpire.

The outline accord of November 24, 1974, reached at the Ford-Brezhnev meeting in Vladivostok, was responsive to the joint resolution's call for numerical equality, but it provoked a further round of congressional debate as to the kind of follow-up agreement that should be sought.[92] When in May 1976 one of several resolutions that had been proposed after Vladivostok was adopted in the 94th Congress (Senate Resolution 406), it included an amendment reiterating that the only acceptable basis for the strategic force balance and for a permanent SALT agreement remained the principle of equivalence.[93] The resolution also stated that, as an integral part of national security policy, the United States should both keep itself "unchallengeably strong militarily" and seek through negotiations to "reduce and stabilize the military competition" with the Soviet Union—sentiments which, in a sense, put Congress on record as covering all bets.

By the time the Carter administration came to office in early 1977, it had become apparent that congressional interest in SALT policy not only continued to focus upon strategic equivalence, but also increasingly extended to matters of compliance and verification. This interest was stimulated both by recurrent allegations of Soviet violations of SALT I,[94] and by the more troublesome verification problems inherent in such new technologies as cruise missiles.[95] Reflecting the growth of congressional pressure to ensure that SALT verification requirements be given their due was an August 1977 amendment to the Arms Control and Disarmament Act, declaring it the sense of Congress that adequate verification should be an indispensable part of any arms control agreement.[96] Another manifestation of this concern was the specific assurance solicited in February 1978 by the Senate Foreign Relations Committee from the director of ACDA that the proposed SALT II agreement then in the process of negotiation with the Russians be "adequately verifiable."[97]

Besides its increasingly active interest in the formulation of SALT policy, the Congress in 1977-78 began to associate itself in a hitherto unprecedented way with the immediate conduct of negotiations by furnishing some of its members as advisers to the U.S. SALT delegation in Geneva.[98] While in Geneva, the congressional advisers attended both intra-U.S. delegation meetings to discuss policy and tactics and plenary negotiating sessions with the Soviets, as well as meeting privately on occasion with the chiefs and one or two senior members of both delegations.[99] Although this innovation seemed likely to contribute to a better-informed Congress on SALT issues, it was not necessarily endorsed without reservations, either in Congress or by some U.S. negotiators. This was partly because it seemed to violate the principle of separation of powers and to leave room for many complications by involving in negotiations the legislators who would ultimately be required to pass judgment on the end product of the negotiating process itself, for which the executive branch is responsible.[100]

In addition to a congressional presence on the SALT delegation, which had grown out of an invitation from Mr. Warnke, arrangements also were made by the Carter administration to keep key Senate leaders informed about the negotiations through Senator Jackson's Subcommittee on National Security and International Relations. Both moves were generally interpreted as an effort to allay congressional opposition to what was expected to be a controversial SALT II agreement.[101]

When the October 3, 1977, date of expiration of the 1972 Interim Agreement on strategic offensive arms drew near without a follow-on SALT II accord yet having been reached, several questions arose: Could the Interim Agreement with its numerically unequal force levels be "acceptably" extended, and for how long? Would any extension jointly arrived at with the Russians require further congressional authorization?[102] Evidently in order to avoid the kind of heated SALT policy debate in Congress that formal congressional approval of an extension might entail, the administration chose to announce unilaterally in late September that while SALT II negotiations were "being completed," the United States would continue to observe the Interim Agreement, provided the Soviet Union exercised "similar restraint."[103] The Soviet Union in turn issued a unilateral statement in the same terms.[104]

The tactics of avoiding a clash with Congress had been successful in the case of extending the Interim Agreement in the fall of 1977. During the following year, however, Soviet-Cuban "adventurism" in Africa and other tensions in Soviet-American relations produced a deteriorating attitude in Congress toward strategic arms negotiations with Moscow. Thus there was considerable question in late 1978 whether a SALT II treaty, even one embodying more concessions from the Soviet side than the Russians actually were likely to give, would command the two-thirds vote of the Senate necessary for ratification.[105] If such judgments were to prove sound, then it could be said that congressional influence upon the SALT process had indeed greatly narrowed the boundaries within which the U.S. apparatus for the conduct of SALT might for the time being operate.

# Chapter 3

# Soviet Organizational Arrangements for Handling SALT

Decisions on SALT in the Soviet Union have been and are
made in an environment notably different from that in the
United States. Without cataloging all the differences in the
political culture of the two systems, perhaps the most pertinent is
that in the Soviet situation there is no body of informed opinion on
SALT and national security issues independent of, and therefore
capable of criticizing, official government positions. In the public
sphere, neither an inquiring press nor lobbies of defense scientists
and other knowledgeable experts play an active role in the Soviet
Union in fostering public debate on arms control and defense
matters. In the legislative sphere, although the Supreme Soviet is
called upon to give pro forma approval of arms control agreements
like the ABM Treaty, no equivalent is to be found for an independent legislative power like that in the United States, which,
through committee hearings and other congressional actions, can
hold the governing administration accountable on decisions it takes
with regard to SALT.

How the SALT process actually operates in the Soviet Union is
but sketchily known, and the same is true of the internal organizational arrangements for handling it. This paucity of information in
the case of SALT parallels the poor state of knowledge on the inner
workings of the Soviet decisionmaking system in general, and in
particular on the mechanisms for integrating military policy with
political and economic considerations.

One can identify in the Soviet Union several broad institutional
groups that have had interests of one kind or another in SALT, such

as the foreign affairs intelligentsia, the scientific intelligentsia, the military, and that portion of the R&D and industrial establishment best described as the Soviet military-industrial complex.[1] A number of organizational entities with some role in the SALT process also can be identified. But fitting the whole together into a coherent organizational pattern, describing who does what, and above all, determining where the main locus of management and decision-making for SALT lies in the Soviet system—this remains largely a matter of more or less informed guesswork.

In Figure 3-1 an attempt has been made to lay out the various known Soviet organizations within the overall Soviet governing structure that are concerned with SALT, as well as some that can only be postulated on the basis of available information. The overall organizational structure depicted is more or less arbitrarily arranged to show party and governmental entities at four hierarchical levels: (1) the top leadership level; (2) a sublevel at which important "mediating" bodies operate at the interface between the top leadership and the ministerial bureaucracies; (3) the ministries themselves and such other government agencies as State Committees, GOS-PLAN, and the Academy of Sciences; and (4) the SALT negotiating level. The approximate relationships between the organizational entities at these several levels are discussed below in terms of their contribution to SALT policy and its integration with political, military, and other considerations. Needless to say, the tentative nature of much of this discussion should be borne in mind.

## THE TOP LEADERSHIP LEVEL

**The Politburo.**   In the Soviet Union the final power of decision on all matters of policy rests with the Party Politburo. Resolutions of the Central Committee, directives of the Council of Ministers, and decrees of the Supreme Soviet are all essentially decided in advance by the Politburo, among whose members (at this writing, thirteen full and nine candidate members) Secretary General Leonid I. Brezhnev had clearly become primus inter pares by the early 1970s. The bylaws under which the Politburo operates are unknown, but it has been the view of many observers, reinforced by an occasional revelation by Brezhnev himself, that most policy issues are settled by consensus.[2] If consensus cannot be reached, formally equal power to vote on final decisions is apparently shared by the thirteen full members of the Politburo. This prerogative is seldom exercised, however, according to Brezhnev, who has indicated that a small subgroup or committee of Politburo members is usually charged with resolving a disputed issue.[3]

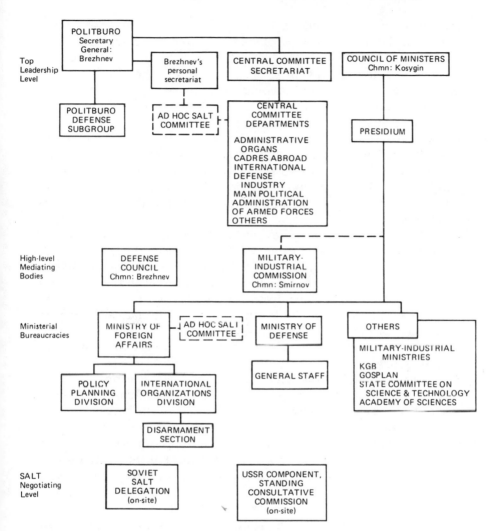

**Figure 3-1.** Soviet Organizations Concerned with SALT

The existence of such subgroups as a working device within the Politburo has long been assumed by expert observers, for the complexity of the modern industrial state and the centralization of the Soviet political system impose such an enormous burden of decisionmaking on the Politburo that it would probably become quickly bogged down without an internal division of labor and appropriate staffing.[4]

Among the Politburo subgroups is believed to be one that concerns itself with defense and national security issues. Headed by

Brezhnev, this group may include A.N. Kosygin, chairman of the Council of Ministers; A.P. Kirilenko, a Party secretary and close supporter of Brezhnev, often considered likely to be the latter's immediate successor; and M.A. Suslov, a senior Party figure in the fields of foreign policy and ideology. Another probable member of this subgroup until his dismissal as head of state in the spring of 1977 was N.V. Podgorny, who also lost his Politburo membership at that time. Marshal Dimitri F. Ustinov, who became minister of defense in April 1976 after the death of Marshal A.A. Grechko, and who is a full member of the Politburo as well, could also be expected to sit with the defense subgroup. So might Foreign Minister A.A. Gromyko, at least when the agenda included items with foreign affairs implications.

Whether SALT policy comes within the routine purview of the defense subgroup is not definitely known, but given the intimate link between national security and SALT issues, it seems reasonable to suppose that this, or a slightly enlarged subgroup, is in fact the body in which final SALT policy decisions are resolved on behalf of the Politburo as a whole. The Politburo retains the ultimate authority to reject recommendations of its subgroups, but it is believed that it generally defers to the judgment of their members on matters in which they have a degree of expertise.

In turn, within the defense subgroup itself Brezhnev's views probably have carried the most weight, partly because of his right as secretary general to nominate the membership of the subgroup.[5] On the other hand, Brezhnev appears to have put emphasis upon a process of consultation and sharing of responsibility for major decisions, including those on SALT, with other Politburo members.[6] This preference for consensus, as some observers have pointed out, may have been not only a bow to collective leadership, but also a matter of elementary precaution on Brezhnev's part.[7]

Given Brezhnev's declining health, the question of what new configuration of decisionmaking power may now be shaping up within the Politburo, or may emerge under his successor, naturally has taken on great interest.[8] Although the answer at this writing remains to be seen, it seems a reasonable supposition that whoever succeeds Brezhnev as Party chief would find himself, at least initially, more dependent on collective assent from his Politburo peers than Brezhnev at the height of his power.[9]

Since no policy is formulated in a vacuum, the staffing through which issues are framed for the Politburo and through which it receives inputs of information is an important part of the organizational picture at the top leadership level. Here again, formal lines of communication and responsibility for SALT matters are not readily discernible. However, there are two partly distinct and partly overlapping staffs of Party functionaries that support Brezhnev and the Politburo and that have some hand in the staff processing of foreign policy and defense matters, including SALT.

**Brezhnev's personal secretariat.** This group represents one of the two staffing bodies in question. Beginning about 1967, but especially after 1971 and coinciding with Brezhnev's rise to preeminence within the collective leadership, this personal staff grew in size and reportedly came to have an increasing role in foreign and national security affairs.[10] Headed by G.E. Tsukanov, a long-time Brezhnev aide, the secretariat includes K.V. Rusakov, A.M. Aleksandrov, and A.I. Blatov, all Party veterans with experience in international affairs, as well as a number of more junior experts such as E.M. Samoteikin. However, no military men of significant stature or specialists in military technology and strategic analysis are known to be members of Brezhnev's secretariat.

The extent to which Brezhnev's personal entourage may make substantive inputs to papers dealing with SALT or other national security issues is not clear, although some analysts have suggested that his staff reviews proposals for both form and substance and that it may call for study of additional options and their consequences.[11] In any event, the secretariat, as a kind of traffic control center, doubtless has a good deal to do with deciding which papers and which officials get through to Brezhnev. Beyond this, according to some accounts, papers and recommendations from the Central Committee Secretariat and its departments—the traditional source of staff support for the Politburo—are now required to be routed through Brezhnev's personal secretariat.[12]

**Central Committee Secretariat and departments.** The second source of staff backup for the Politburo is the Central Committee Secretariat, which in turn is served by some twenty-four departments (*otdeli*), only a few of which are shown in Figure 3-1. The ten secretaries in addition to Brezhnev who constitute the secretariat are powerful political figures in their own right, and six of them are also Politburo members.[13] Presumably those with Politburo status are in a position to bypass Brezhnev's personal secretariat and to raise issues at weekly meetings of the Politburo if they so choose. But the point also has been made that after the heads of the Foreign and Defense Ministries and the KGB acquired full Politburo rank in 1973, this tended to short-circuit oversight of their particular agencies by the Central Committee Secretariat and strengthened Brezhnev's own position in control of these key bureaucracies.[14]

Be that as it may, it is in the Central Committee departments, the heads of which operate under the supervision of members of the secretariat, that the bulk of the staff work immediately supporting the Politburo still appears to be accomplished.[15] Probably no more than five of the departments are involved in matters that touch in one way or another upon SALT. Brief descriptions of these departments and their possible relevance to SALT follow.

- *Administrative Organs.* Headed by I.V. Savinkin, this department's area of responsibility apparently includes matters of personnel selection and administration in the armed forces, as well as security and intelligence agencies.[16] However, it appears to have little to do with general military policy,[17] and except possibly for some connection with the *nomenklatura* system, which earmarks personnel qualified for positions such as members of delegations, it is not likely to be involved in the SALT process.
- *Cadres Abroad.* Formerly headed by A.S. Panyushkin, this department later was reported to have been taken over by N.N. Organov, and possibly placed under the general supervision of P.A. Abrasimov.[18] According to some analysts, it has taken on expanded functions that include developing policy positions for Soviet delegations at conferences on disarmament.[19] If so, it may make inputs to SALT, as well as to negotiations on European security and mutual force reductions. B.N. Ponomarev, a secretariat member, is said to also have supervisory interest over this department.
- *International Affairs.* This is sometimes referred to simply as the International Department. In addition to his role as Central Committee secretary, Ponomarev is also the active head of this department, which deals with foreign policy matters related to capitalist and third-world countries.[20] According to comment by a former member of Ponomarev's staff, the department wields more influence in the making of foreign policy than the Ministry of Foreign Affairs.[21] Although no specific association of the International Department with SALT can be made, in light of Ponomarev's key role in the area of strategy for competing with the U.S.-led capitalist world, it may be surmised that his department may furnish important political inputs to SALT policy.
- *Defense Industry.* Headed by I.D. Serbin, this department is probably the principal staff organ of the Central Committee apparat concerned with the production aspects of weapons policy. Along with other departments that have an interest in industrial

production and research, such as Heavy Industry, Machine Building, and Science and Education, this department was under the general supervision of D.F. Ustinov before the latter's appointment as minister of defense in April 1976. Precisely how this department of the Central Committee apparatus fits into the SALT policymaking process is not clear; however, it may make some inputs to SALT through the Military-Industrial Commission, as discussed further below.

- *The Main Political Administration of the Armed Forces (MPA).*
General of the Army A.A. Yepishev heads this organ, which has a dual locus of activity, serving simultaneously as the overseer of the Party's political apparatus within the Ministry of Defense and as a department of the Central Committee staff. (It is a point of particular interest that neither this agency nor any other department of the Central Committee apparatus appears to have responsibility for general military policy or operational supervision of the military forces.[22]) The MPA's direct involvement in the formulation of SALT policy is probably minimal. However, many of the Soviet military writers who promulgate the Party's line on military affairs do so through journals controlled by the Main Political Administration, such as *Communist of the Armed Forces.* It seems likely, therefore, that the MPA may serve as an indirect channel for venting views on policy issues that bear on SALT.

**Ad hoc committees.** Besides the routine operations of the regular departments of the Central Committee apparatus in support of the Politburo, ad hoc committees are occasionally convened to recommend solutions to knotty issues, including those involving foreign policy and defense.[23] The initiative for setting up such ad hoc committees may come either from the Politburo itself, Brezhnev's personal secretariat, or the Central Committee Secretariat, but in any case the committees are apparently made up of both professional staff from relevant Central Committee departments and of personnel drawn from elsewhere, including a pool of part-time experts described as the "consultative group."[24]

Some analysts have surmised that an ad hoc committee of this kind might have been created to deal with issues arising out of the SALT negotiations.[25] Although there is no specific evidence that this is the case, Figure 3-1 shows a postulated ad hoc SALT committee set up at a level between Brezhnev's personal secretariat and the departments of the Central Committee.

The function of an ad hoc SALT committee at this level might be to frame issues and work up options for the top leadership in the

Politburo, or perhaps for Brezhnev personally.[26] One point that raises some question about this hypothesis, however, is that normally the staffs of the regular Central Committee departments are believed not to include many people with basic military expertise,[27] a province largely monopolized by the professional military establishment. Therefore, unless outside experts co-opted by such an ad hoc committee were to include appropriate high-level military representatives, the body would be somewhat incomplete in terms of its competence to advise the top political leadership on military aspects of SALT policy. Furthermore, as will be discussed below, there are other bodies at the mediating level through which the top political leadership can interact directly with the military high command and in which military considerations bearing on SALT could be ironed out. Although this is not to say that no place remains for an ad hoc committee to serve the top Party leadership on SALT, the grounds for postulating it are certainly a bit spongy.

On the subject of ad hoc committees, it will also be noted that a second postulated ad hoc committee for SALT is shown in Figure 3-1 at the ministerial level, drawn primarily from personnel of the Ministry of Foreign Affairs and the Ministry of Defense. The grounds for positing the existence of this ad hoc body are also less than solid, although Soviet bureaucratic practice would not appear to rule out the duplication of ad hoc SALT groups in both the government and Party. According to Raymond L. Garthoff, direct coordination on SALT between the Ministries of Foreign Affairs and Defense was established as early as 1968; such coordination could have been carried out through the ad hoc group postulated here.[28] The function of an ad hoc group at the ministerial level might be mainly to provide a focal point for response to questions arising in the course of negotiations—somewhat like that of the SALT Backstopping Committee in the U.S. case—as distinct from the policy-recommending function of an ad hoc advisory group at the Politburo-Central Committee level.

**Council of Ministers.** The remaining organization depicted in Figure 3-1 at the top leadership level is the Council of Ministers, headed by Chairman A.N. Kosygin. Although the Council of Ministers is an important institution for executing Politburo decisions and for supervising the day-to-day running of the bureaucratic machinery of the Soviet state, it does not appear to function as a deliberative or decisionmaking body on new issues of policy.[29] To be sure, as government executives in charge of the ministerial bureaucracies, the members of the Council of Ministers can certainly influence both the way in which policy issues reach the deliberative-decisionmaking level in the Politburo and the way in which the policies adopted are carried out.

However, where SALT is concerned, such influence probably makes itself felt more at the ministry level than in the Council of Ministers itself. So far as one can tell, neither the full council, numbering some seventy members, nor its presidium of twelve men is directly engaged institutionally in either the formulation of SALT policy or the conduct of negotiations.

It will be noted that the full Central Committee (of some 426 full and candidate members) has not been shown in Figure 3-1, for although it is used at its twice-annual plenary sessions to sanction decisions already made by the Politburo, it is not itself a decision-making or policy-formulating body.[30] Similarly, the Supreme Soviet, the two-chamber legislative body that gives symbolic sanction to acts of the Council of Ministers on the government side of the house, is not shown.

## HIGH-LEVEL MEDIATING BODIES

Just below the Politburo apex of the Soviet decisionmaking system and above the ministerial level are two bodies that until recently were little publicized, but that apparently play significant roles in the formation of national security policy. Both operate at the interface between the top political leadership and the ministerial bureaucracies, and appear to perform mediating and coordinating functions that other parts of the Party and governmental structure are not fitted to handle expeditiously.

**The Defense Council.** One of these bodies, whose lineage can be traced back to the Council of Labor and Defense of Lenin's day and the Defense Commission that operated under Stalin in the 1930s, has evolved into what today goes by the name of the Defense Council.[31] Evidently, the right to chair this body devolves upon the top Party leader, for Khrushchev took over its chairmanship in his day, as has Brezhnev in his. Precisely when Brezhnev became chairman of the Defense Council (*Sovet Oborony*) is not known, though the first official identification of him in this role came in the same decree that conferred upon him the rank of marshal of the Soviet Union on May 7, 1976.[32]

At the present stage of its evolution, the Defense Council apparently brings together selected members of the Politburo— probably the members of Brezhnev's defense subgroup—together with senior officers of the military high command and representatives of other Party and state agencies, the choice of personnel depending on the subject matter.[33]

Little is known about the mandate of the Defense Council or the procedures under which it operates. In peacetime, it appears to provide a setting in which the political and military leaderships can interact on a broad variety of defense policy issues, rather than to concern itself with day-to-day managerial functions.[34] In wartime, the Defense Council presumably would be transformed into a body similar to the State Committee of Defense, or GKO, of World War II.

Given Brezhnev's reputed proclivity for consensus decisionmaking, one might suppose that he would use the peacetime Defense Council as a forum in which to mediate any differences between the political and military sides of the house, and to rally the latter behind the policy recommendations of his Politburo subgroup before placing them on the agenda of the full Politburo for final decisions.

Precisely what role the Defense Council plays with regard to SALT is not known, although informed observers have credited this body with being "a significant instrument through which the political authorities are involved in the policymaking process on military matters, including SALT."[35] It would seem to be a reasonable conjecture that, in addition to serving as an instrument through which Brezhnev and his Politburo colleagues can line up substantive support on SALT policy from the military high command, the Defense Council also serves in turn as the body in which the military leadership finds its best opportunity to present a unified military position on SALT issues to the political leadership.[36] What happens if a disputed issue goes unresolved here is an intriguing question which, given present knowledge of the inner politics of the Soviet elite, unfortunately cannot be answered.

**Military-Industrial Commission.**   This is the second body shown in Figure 3-1 at the mediating interface between the top political leadership and the ministerial bureaucracies. Like the Defense Council, this body apparently has antecedents that go back many years, but its existence began to receive attention in Western literature on Soviet organization only within the past decade.[37] The Military-Industrial Commission (VPK) is chaired by L.V. Smirnov, a deputy chairman of the Council of Ministers, and is nominally subordinate to that body. In practice, Smirnov appears to have been closely associated with, and probably answered to, D.F. Ustinov when Ustinov served as overlord of Soviet defense production and research in his capacity as the Party Secretariat (and Politburo) member with responsibility for these areas. After Ustinov became minister of defense in April 1976 and acquired the rank of marshal,[38] it was not clear for some time whether he would retain his secretarial role as overseer of defense production, or whether this role would be assumed by someone else. Some analysts believe that Ustinov's role as supervisor of defense research and production has been taken over by another Central Committee secretary, possibly Ya. P. Ryabov.[39]

In any event, the VPK provides a forum for handling matters involving the various ministries that make up what is known as the defense-industry sector of the Soviet economy.[40] The VPK's membership has never been announced, but it is logical to suppose that the principal members are the heads of the eight major industrial ministries of the defense sector, together with participants from such agencies as the State Planning Committee (GOSPLAN), the Ministry of Defense, and the Defense Industry department of the Central Committee apparatus. The latter would give the VPK a joint Party-government composition to facilitate its mediating functions.

The functions of the VPK include the coordination of defense research and production activities that cut across individual ministerial lines,[41] and it may serve as a panel for mediating priorities and planning options for arms production programs, somewhat as did the U.S. Defense Program Review Committee under the NSC system of the Nixon era. In contrast to the policy-oriented, nonmanagerial role ascribed to the Defense Council, the VPK may also have important management responsibilities, perhaps giving closer day-to-day attention to resolving problems that arise out of weapons development and production programs than would be possible for the top political leaders.

An indication that the Military-Industrial Commission's functions touch on SALT-related matters came unexpectedly at the climax of the SALT I negotiations in Moscow in May 1972, when the Soviet side assigned Smirnov to iron out some sticky unresolved issues with Dr. Kissinger. Whether Smirnov's role as the head of the VPK had brought him formally into the SALT picture is not entirely clear, but his familiarity with the issues and the "considerable measure of authority" with which he is said to have negotiated[42] would suggest that Smirnov's duties had in fact given him an important role in the decisionmaking process on SALT matters.

## THE MINISTERIAL BUREAUCRACIES

At this level, the two principal ministries involved in foreign affairs and defense policy matters, including SALT, are the Ministry of

Foreign Affairs, headed by Andrei A. Gromyko, and the Ministry of Defense, now headed by Marshal D.F. Ustinov. Both men, in addition to their ministerial roles, are voting members of the Politburo, a situation that breaks with customary Soviet practice of the past couple of decades,[43] but one which doubtless allows these men to speak with greater authority in the councils of the top leadership than if they merely represented their respective ministerial bureaucracies.

**Ministry of Foreign Affairs.** Although Gromyko's personal stature has grown greatly from the days when Khrushchev could rather crudely joke about ordering him to sit on a cake of ice, most observers agree that this ministry's role continues to lie primarily in the realm of implementing, rather than formulating, Soviet foreign policy. The MFA does have a division charged with foreign policy planning, as well as a Collegium of senior diplomatic officials that is prepared to furnish advice on foreign policy matters. However, recommendations from both of these bodies apparently are rarely sought at the level of the Politburo and Central Committee departments, which tend to task the Foreign Ministry with preparation of reports containing information and analyses, rather than policy recommendations.[44]

In the field of arms control, the International Organizations Division of the Ministry of Foreign Affairs has a disarmament section that deals with SALT and other disarmament activities.[45] There is no Soviet counterpart to the separate Arms Control and Disarmament Agency in the United States, but the disarmament section in the Ministry of Foreign Affairs, staffed by arms control specialists, probably comes closer to approximating ACDA's functions than any other organization on the Soviet side. It is, however, far smaller than ACDA. Some of its personnel have rotated regularly to assignments on the Soviet SALT delegation since the start of SALT, giving it long continuity in the negotiations, somewhat in contrast to the situation on the U.S. side. The Policy Planning Division and the American desk in the Ministry of Foreign Affairs also are said to take some part in preparations for SALT, as well as furnishing personnel for the Soviet SALT delegation.[46]

Although the Ministry of Foreign Affairs has career arms control experts and one of its senior officials—Deputy Foreign Minister V.S. Semenov—has been chief of the Soviet SALT delegation from the start, its role in the formulation of SALT policy appears to be rather circumscribed. The principal SALT inputs of the Ministry of Foreign Affairs in the past are believed to have been largely limited to the diplomatic and political aspects of the negotiations and not to have involved dealing with strategic and technical hardware issues.[4 7] Gromyko's personal role in SALT, however, appears to have grown steadily since SALT I, to the point that next to Brezhnev, he had become by 1978 the most authoritative spokesman for the Soviet SALT position within the top leadership.

In their earlier stages at least, the SALT negotiations reportedly provided evidence of a rather high degree of compartmentalization between foreign affairs and military personnel, with the foreign affairs side (including such senior nonmilitary figures as Semenov himself) often displaying a poor knowledge of basic data on Soviet strategic forces and weapons systems.[4 8] Besides complicating the conduct of negotiations, this lack of relevant information about their own forces on the part of Soviet Foreign Ministry personnel assigned to SALT would suggest that there was rather poor lateral transfer of SALT-related technical and strategic information between the military and foreign affairs bureaucracies in Moscow.

Such compartmentalization, in turn, would certainly have made it awkward for any joint working group drawn from the Ministries of Foreign Affairs and Defense to address effectively SALT issues requiring substantive expertise on strategic and military affairs. The supposition is that position papers and recommendations prepared within the respective ministries were channeled separately upward to higher levels—where lateral coordination presumably was less obstructed. The reported cumbersome response and slow reaction time of the Moscow backup system, at least during the SALT I negotiations,[4 9] would seem to lend credence to the supposition that no prompt mechanism for coordinated lateral action at the ministerial working level was available.

To some degree, compartmentalization between the military and foreign affairs establishments in Moscow may have been alleviated by what some observers believe was the setting up of a jointly staffed ad hoc SALT group at the ministerial level, as shown in Figure 3-1, to provide better coordination and support of negotiations at this level. Furthermore, it would seem likely that the internal process of working out Soviet positions, together with the give-and-take between Soviet negotiators and their American counterparts over the past decade of the SALT experience, may have gradually familiarized Soviet foreign affairs functionaries with a body of strategic lore that earlier had been almost exclusively the province of the military. Presumably, a pool of more strategically literate civilian personnel might thus contribute to diluting the monopoly of the military over strategic thought and planning in the Soviet Union.

**The Ministry of Defense and the General Staff.** Although the military aspects of SALT policy are reconciled with political, economic, and other relevant considerations at the top leadership level and through the mediating bodies that have already been described above, the bulk of the preparation of substantive Soviet SALT positions at the ministry level apparently has been carried out within the military establishment presided over by Marshal A.A. Grechko until his death in 1976, and since then by Marshal Ustinov.[50] Testimony to this effect occasionally has come from Soviet visitors to this country. For example, a department head in one of the Soviet academic research institutes, when asked in 1973 whether his institute made direct contributions to SALT planning, replied: "We do not work on the development of a strategic arms limitation plan: That is Marshal Grechko's province."[51]

Both the Ministry of Defense and the General Staff have made organizational arrangements for dealing with arms control matters, though it is not altogether clear which of them is the main locus of work on SALT. As shown in Figure 3-2, each has offices that are involved in one way or another with SALT-related problems, but which of the two has the chief responsibility for a unified military position on SALT issues remains uncertain.

Traditionally, there has been a muted rivalry between the Ministry of Defense, which represents the interface of the military establishment with political authority, and the General Staff, which regards itself as the real seat of military professionalism and leadership in the USSR and is a somewhat larger organization than the ministry itself.[52] Unlike the U.S. Defense Department, the Soviet Ministry of Defense has no layer of civilian officials with statutory authority over the uniformed military. In the ministry, the top level of authority consists of Marshal Ustinov and twelve uniformed deputy ministers, three of whom are first deputy ministers. One of the latter, Marshal N.V. Ogarkov, is also chief of the General Staff.[53]

Though formally an agency of the Ministry of Defense, the General Staff is institutionally powerful in its own right, and as the central organ of the military high command, it has direct controlling links with the main staffs of the various service branches, military districts, and operational forces. Moreover, one of the enunciated tasks of the General Staff is to ensure "coordinated actions" by all defense entities, including "the main and central administrations of the Ministry of Defense,"[54] which would seem to suggest that the ministry should march to the cadence set by the General Staff.

Where within the internal organization of the General Staff work on SALT is carried out cannot be readily determined. The three

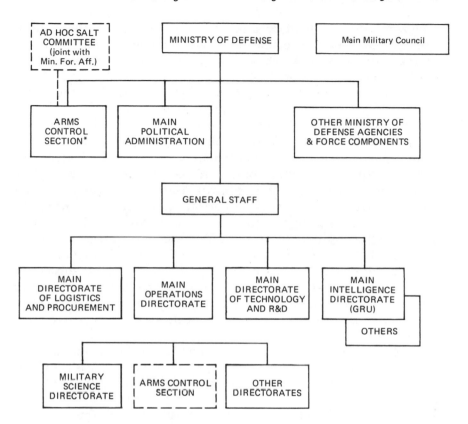

*The Arms Control Section is probably subordinate to some higher echelon in the Ministry of Defense, but that echelon is not known.

**Figure 3-2.** Soviet Military SALT Apparatus

major components of the General Staff—the Main Directorates in charge of operations, logistics and procurement, and technology and R&D—all have interests that bear on the SALT process, as do probably other General Staff components concerned with such activities as intelligence and communications. The Main Operations Directorate, traditionally the hub of the General Staff, directs military operations, develops targeting and war plans, and helps formulate general military policy.[55] It would be logical to suppose that the drafting of substantive parameters for SALT and other arms control proposals might take place somewhere within the Main Operations Directorate; accordingly, an arms control section has been arbitrarily shown in Figure 3-2 under this component of the General Staff. Under the Main Operations Directorate there is also a subdirectorate for military science, which reportedly has studied strategic concepts in connection with the expansion of Soviet strategic forces and which also may make inputs to SALT proposals.[56] Besides its work on SALT proposals, the General Staff also has provided much of the military representation on the Soviet SALT delegation, as will be discussed further below.

With regard to organizational arrangements within the Ministry of Defense for dealing with SALT questions, little is known save that there is an office of some sort—tentatively identified as a "section"[57]—which has arms control responsibilities. At what level within the ministry this arms control section is located, how it is staffed, what kinds of work it performs, whether it provides the Ministry of Defense representation on an ad hoc SALT committee jointly staffed by the Ministries of Defense and Foreign Affairs—all such details are lacking. Also, it is not known whether the Main Political Administration in the Ministry of Defense makes substantive contributions to SALT matters, although, as previously mentioned, it may well have a hand in conveying Party guidance on how SALT issues are to be treated in military publications and troop-indoctrination materials.

As seen by some observers, it is probably in the General Staff that any competing views on SALT among the various services are ironed out and the final attempt made to reach a unified military position.[58] On the other hand, the process may be just the reverse, with the General Staff working up basic positions and reporting any differences for resolution to the minister of defense and his deputy ministers. There is also, however, a third overlapping institution in the military high command that may in effect serve to mediate any differences within the military establishment on recommendations to be carried forward to the Defense Council or Politburo levels. This is a collegial institution called the Main Military Council, probably chaired by Minister of Defense Ustinov, with membership including Chief of the General Staff Ogarkov, the other "first" deputy defense ministers, the head of the Main Political Administration, and the top service commanders.[59] It is not known whether Brezhnev, as a nominal marshal of the Soviet Union and putative supreme commander of the armed forces, has taken part in the deliberations of this body, but if he were to do so, one effect would certainly be to blur the lines between civilian and military authority.[60]

**Other ministries and state agencies** that may contribute in some measure to the making of SALT policy include the eight military-industrial ministries that make up the defense-industry sector of the

Soviet economy,[61] as well as the Committee of State Security (KGB), GOSPLAN, the State Committee on Science and Technology, and the Academy of Sciences, along with some of its subordinate research institutes.

In the case of the military-industrial ministries, the main inputs to SALT policy probably have been funneled through the Military-Industrial Commission under L.V. Smirnov. However, it can be surmised that individual ministries whose research or production activities could be affected by SALT agreements may be consulted in the process of preparing Soviet positions. The defense industry sector has also provided a SALT delegation representative from the start of SALT I in the person of P.S. Pleshakov, an expert in ABM-associated electronics, who rose from Deputy Minister to Minister of the Radio Industry in the course of his SALT service.

The KGB, headed by Politburo member Yu. V. Andropov, who has both a background in foreign affairs and a military rank,[62] can be presumed to have interests of several kinds in SALT. Together with the GRU, the intelligence organ of the General Staff, it has a role in gathering intelligence information pertinent to SALT, although which of the two is charged with preparing finished assessments used by the top leadership in making SALT decisions is not known. The KGB's responsibilities also extend to keeping tabs on the security conduct of Soviet personnel, and in this connection one can assume that KGB operatives are assigned to check up on Soviet SALT delegation members and others in contact with foreigners, as well as to establish such contacts themselves.[63]

The State Planning Committee (GOSPLAN), headed by N.K. Baibakov, makes a substantial contribution to Soviet defense policymaking, especially as a prime source of advice for the top leadership about both requirements for and availability of resources to support civilian and military production programs. The State Committee for Material and Technical Supply under V.E. Dymshits is another source of such advice. Military resource allocation considerations that could arise in connection with SALT agreements, as well as the integration of defense- and SALT-related program planning with the overall five-year economic plan cycle in the Soviet Union,[64] would seem likely to involve GOSPLAN rather extensively in the SALT policymaking network.

The State Committee on Science and Technology, headed by V.A. Kirillin, has a broad charter covering the improvement of the national research effort. The extent to which it may have some institutionalized role in Soviet military policymaking—and by extension, SALT policy—is, however, not clear. It is generally thought that

Kirillin's organization does not have authority over the R&D effort in the fields of defense, space, and atomic energy, but that these areas fall primarily within the purview of the Military-Industrial Commission under Smirnov and the weapons technology management nexus under Deputy Minister of Defense N.N. Alekseyev.[65] The Central Committee's Department on Science and Educational Institutions, headed by S.P. Trapeznikov, also has some oversight role with regard to scientific research institutions, but so far as is known, this does not embrace defense- or SALT-related research matters. Trapeznikov's department, however, does have a committee for systems analysis headed by his deputy, I.M. Makarov.[66] It is possible that for SALT analytical purposes there may be some use of such systems analysis capabilities within the Central Committee apparatus.[67]

Finally in this catalog of organizational contributors to Soviet SALT policy, there is the USSR Academy of Sciences and some of the research institutes that nominally operate under its wing. The academy itself, whose long Russian tradition gives it a certain claim to professional autonomy not enjoyed by most Soviet institutions, apparently plays little direct role in policy matters, but a rather significant impact may be exerted by its members upon both military and SALT policy issues. One channel of influence is through the personal contacts of senior scientists, who have been invited periodically to high policy councils as consultants in their own fields of competence.[68] In the past, scientists given access to the top leadership generally were expected to provide individual professional advice and not to represent the view of a "scientific lobby" or to voice political judgments; more recently, at least some members of the Soviet scientific community may have acquired a broader advisory role. With regard to SALT specifically, one senior scientist, Academician A.N. Shchukin, a prominent electronics expert, has been a member, and apparently one of the more influential figures, of the Soviet negotiating team from the beginning.[69]

A second avenue of scientific influence on the SALT process is through more or less formal study groups, as well as "disarmament sections" set up in institutes operating under the aegis of the Academy of Sciences (see Figure 3-3). In the period before the opening of SALT negotiations, a study group reportedly was formed in the academy to prepare recommendations on possible arms limitation proposals. The group's director was Academician Shchukin.[70] Whether this group has remained in existence is not known. A Commission on Disarmament, headed by Academician V.S. Yemelyanov and said to have the function of coordinating the research of

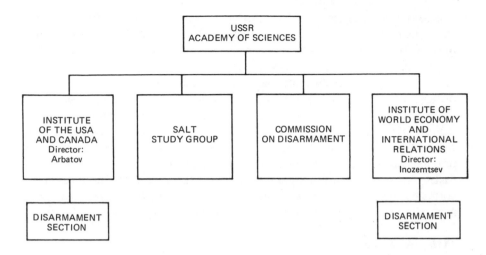

**Figure 3-3.** Soviet Academic Bodies Concerned with SALT

subordinate bodies on scientific aspects of disarmament, is also maintained in the academy.[71] Its functions appear to include some purview over the papers and oral presentations made by Soviet scientists participating in international gatherings on arms control and allied matters.

Among the research institutes under the USSR Academy of Sciences that produce studies in the fields of foreign affairs, defense, and arms control are the Institute of World Economy and International Relations, directed by N.N. Inozemtsev, and the newer Institute of the USA and Canada, directed by G.A. Arbatov. As shown in Figure 3-3, both of these institutes have disarmament sections,[72] as well as divisions to deal with the military-political aspects of international relations, staffed in part by retired or brevetted military officers with academic degrees.[73]

Some of the work of these institutes focusing on arms control questions and strategic, economic, and social trends abroad appears in their monthly journals and other Soviet publications, though the institutes also are presumed to conduct other unpublished studies commissioned by the Ministries of Foreign Affairs and Defense, as well as by Brezhnev's personal secretariat and the Central Committee apparatus, especially its International Department.[74]

The largely unknown factor is how much weight the work of these institutes may have in the actual framing of Soviet foreign and military policy, including SALT policy. Since neither of the institutes ostensibly is authorized or asked to analyze Soviet strategic, economic, and other problems, their inputs to policymaking presumably lie mainly in how they interpret developments abroad—which may differ somewhat from the interpretations provided by the regular Soviet intelligence organizations. Some outside observers feel that institute researchers probably have had a substantial impact on policymaking by providing an alternative transmission belt for information between the United States and the Soviet Union;[75] others have the impression that the interaction between institute researchers and official policymakers has not been very close.[76] It has generally been thought, however, that the directors of the two institutes may have considerably more influence than their research staffs by virtue of their Party standing,[77] and—in the case of Arbatov in particular—reputed access to Brezhnev's ear.

## THE SALT NEGOTIATING LEVEL

Like the United States, the Soviet Union maintains a SALT delegation to conduct negotiations in Geneva, as well as its own representation on the joint U.S.-Soviet Standing Consultative Commission, which also meets periodically in Geneva. These Soviet contingents are approximately the same size as their American counterparts, and their functions are parallel in many respects, though there are obviously important differences in operating style, backup arrangements, and so on.

**The Soviet SALT delegation.** Throughout SALT I and II up to late 1978 the Soviet negotiating team was headed by the same man—Deputy Foreign Minister V.S. Semenov, a seasoned foreign affairs official with more than thirty years of experience in major diplomatic assignments, but apparently not well schooled in strategic matters, at least during the earlier stages of SALT.[78] The original Soviet SALT delegation numbered twenty-four: six principals, of whom two were from the Foreign Ministry, two from the military, and one each from defense industry and the scientific community; plus eighteen advisers, of whom about one-third were identifiable as Foreign Ministry personnel, one-third were military officers, and the remainder, with no announced affiliations, could be presumed to include intelligence personnel.[79] Although the size of the Soviet delegation has more than doubled in the course of the negotiations, owing to a substantial increase in the number of advisers, its ratios of institutional representation appear to have remained about the same.

The two senior military representatives on the original Soviet SALT delegation were Colonel-Generals N.V. Ogarkov (then first deputy chief of the General Staff) and N.N. Alekseyev, also from the General Staff. Both men left the delegation before the completion of SALT I, Ogarkov going on to become chief of the General Staff several years later,[80] and Alekseyev becoming a deputy minister of defense with broad responsibilities for weapons development.[81] Their replacements on the SALT delegation, Lieutenant-General K.A. Trusov and Colonel-General I.I. Beletsky, also were drawn from the General Staff.[82] Another high-ranking General Staff officer who was frequently present in SALT I, though as adviser rather than a principal, was Colonel-General A.A. Gryzlov.

Presumably, one of the functions of the delegation principals and advisers from the General Staff has been to watch over the corporate interests of the Soviet military. Whether the interests of particular components of the Soviet military establishment have been further entrusted to less senior military men on the delegation cannot be ascertained from publicly available information. However, the delegation appears to include officers from most of the military organizations that have institutional stakes in strategic arms, such as the Strategic Rocket Forces, Air Defense (PVO), the SLBM arm of the Navy, and the Air Force, as well as the Ministry of Defense itself.[83]

The civilian principals on the Soviet SALT delegation have had considerably more continuity than their counterparts on the American side. Semenov, the delegation chief; Pleshakov, the defense-industry representative; and Shchukin, the scientific representative, have been aboard throughout SALT I and II. It may be noted, incidentally, that both Pleshakov and Shchukin hold reserve rank as general officers in the Engineering Technical Service.[84] The other civilian delegate's slot, always filled by a Foreign Ministry representative, has been rotated somewhat. Its first occupant was G.M. Korniyenko, then chief of the Foreign Ministry's American Division, followed by Oleg Grinevsky, Roland Timerbaev, and Victor Karpov. The post of executive secretary of the delegation also has been customarily filled by Foreign Ministry personnel, its first occupant being N.S. Kishilov.[85]

There has been some degree of compartmentalization within the Soviet SALT delegation, reflecting in part at least a division of labor under which the political members of the delegation, including Semenov, have tended to defer on strategic and technical matters to their military and technical colleagues, while they in turn have followed Semenov's political cue. However, the available accounts certainly do not suggest that the Soviet delegation has displayed any tendency to present a divided front at the negotiating table. Indeed, its style of operation in formal negotiating sessions apparently has been very disciplined, with all members of the delegation adhering closely to a common line.[86]

On the other hand, in private conversations and other exchanges outside the formal negotiating sessions, one gathers that Soviet representatives have sometimes departed from the official line, even offering hints as to how bureaucratic bottlenecks on their side might be broken if appropriate U.S. moves were taken. Whether such informal approaches should be regarded as breaches of discipline, sincere attempts to narrow differences, or simply a professional technique for influencing the opposite side, is a moot question.

As described in Chapter 1 and above, lack of relevant information on their own strategic forces on the part of civilian members of the Soviet delegation made it necessary in SALT I and at least part of SALT II to conduct negotiations from a data base largely supplied by the U.S. side.[87] Although the attitude of Soviet military delegates to such disclosure of strategic data to their own nonmilitary colleagues was reportedly negative,[88] it would appear that both Soviet civilians and military men actually have been very guarded about even corroborating the information on Soviet forces supplied by the U.S., indicating a common concern for protecting Soviet military secrecy. However, some improvement in the reciprocal exchange of information between the two delegations may have begun in the later stages of SALT II.

On the whole, the amount of initiative allowed the Soviet delegation by Moscow has appeared quite limited in both SALT I and II. Presentations by Soviet personnel in formal sessions customarily have been read from texts prepared and cleared in advance, while positions worked out at the delegation negotiating level almost invariably have been on an ad referendum basis to higher authority in Moscow. Although the Soviet SALT delegation may have found itself operating most of the time on an even shorter leash than that of the U.S., there have been some apparent exceptions to the rule, as when Semenov in SALT I was made privy on occasion to Soviet-American back-channel exchanges at a high level, while the American negotiating team remained in the dark.[89]

**Soviet component of the Standing Consultative Commission.** Unlike the American side, the Soviet Union chose a military officer as the Soviet commissioner of this joint U.S.-Soviet body when it began operations in 1973.[90] He was Major-General G.I. Ustinov, an officer with infantry and General Staff experience, who has remained in his SCC post up to this writing. In 1977, Ustinov—

who apparently is unrelated to the minister of defense with the same name—was also made a member of the Soviet SALT delegation, giving him a dual SALT role not similarly held by his U.S. counterpart, SCC Commissioner Robert Buchheim.

Ustinov's SCC deputy from the start was V.P. Karpov, a Ministry of Foreign Affairs official who also was a member of the Soviet SALT delegation. Karpov's appointment in late 1978 to succeed Semenov as head of the Soviet SALT delegation presumably would call for assigning someone else to his SCC post, but up to this writing no replacement had been named. The first executive secretary of the Soviet SCC component was A.S. Yereskovsky, well known in Washington from his previous service in the Soviet Embassy as an expert on U.S. congressional relations. He has since been replaced on the SCC by another Foreign Ministry representative. The remainder of the Soviet SCC staff of eight to ten people is a mixed group of military and civilian personnel.

As in the case of the Soviet SALT delegation, it is not clear what backup agencies in Moscow directly support the Soviet SCC contingent. It seems a fair surmise, however, that the Ministry of Defense and the General Staff are chiefly responsible for instructing the SCC group and furnishing it analytical support.

The procedures that were worked out within the SCC for implementing the May 1972 SALT agreements have never been made public, at Soviet request.[91] Just why the Soviet Union has wished to keep secret the substantive results of the SCC's endeavors has not been explained by officials on either the Soviet or American sides, although possibly the fact of the SCC's having evolved as a forum in which various strategic arms activities have been dealt with in considerable detail may have something to do with it.

However, it seems plausible, as some observers have speculated, that the Soviet leadership has simply been reluctant to let its own people in on transactions that involve more military details than the Soviet public is customarily exposed to.[92] A previous example of this distaste for public disclosure of military details was the studied omission of the SALT I protocol text—which contained some actual figures on Soviet SLBM forces—from published Soviet material on the 1972 SALT accords.[93] Indeed, to this day the Soviet public has been told neither how many strategic arms each side possessed when the SALT I agreements were signed, nor what numerical levels they would be allowed in the future under the accords. Similarly, the agreed figures of the 1974 understanding at Vladivostok were not revealed to the Soviet public.

## INFLUENCE OF THE SOVIET MILITARY
## ON SALT POLICY

Opinions vary as to what the role of the Soviet military has been
with regard to SALT decisionmaking—a question that can hardly be
separated from broader, but related, questions concerning the nature
of Soviet civil-military relations and the weight of military influence
on Soviet foreign and defense policy as a whole.

With regard to the nature of Soviet civil-military relations, there
have been at least three schools of thought among Western students
of the subject. One school has tended to emphasize a dichotomous
relationship between the Soviet political and military leaderships,
growing out of basic institutional differences and interest-group
politics and making for periodic internal conflict over policy issues.[94] A second school has argued that no meaningful leadership
dichotomy arising out of interest-group politics is to be found, but
rather that Soviet leaders in and out of uniform recognize a common
framework of interests, within which the military leaders traditionally have been and continue to be compliant executors of policies
framed by the Party.[95]

A third school, straddling the other two, has suggested that
institutionally seated interests do appear to alter somewhat the
perspective from which the political and military leaderships view
policy issues. However, instead of a marked cleavage between the
two groups, this perspective contends that there is what amounts to a
division of labor or cooperative partnership between them, with the
political leadership tending to delegate authority for the professional
side of national security planning to the military while reserving to
itself the right of final decision, especially on matters involving large
resources or issues of war and peace.[96] In this view, though policy
conflict in the upper reaches of the Soviet leadership is not to be
ruled out, it is more likely to take place among elite cliques that have
overlapping composition within both the political and military
leaderships than simply between the latter two groups.

But even when the existence of leadership contention over defense
and foreign policy issues is granted, several factors would appear to
restrict both the arena and the extent of internal policy conflict.
These include what Dimitri Simes and others have described as
certain generally observed rules of the game for minimizing elite
conflict—an important one being that support for competing policy
positions is not to be sought outside the elite family itself.[97]
Another factor tending to preserve leadership cohesion despite any
internal differences over particular issues of defense policy is the

sharing of a common outlook by both the political and military leadership elites in a number of broad areas bearing upon Soviet security.[98] Although basic security attitudes of the Soviet leadership are not immune to change, they seem likely to be transformed slowly at best, especially in light of a Soviet political culture that puts a premium on conformity, on minimizing and containing elite conflict—thus tending to discourage any sweeping challenges to the dominant security attitudes by a leadership minority.

Within the Soviet decisionmaking system, two of the mediums through which military influence on policy appears to make itself felt are internal leadership politics and institutional processes.

In terms of elite politics, the situation over the past decade or so might be characterized as one in which Brezhnev carefully cultivated an alliance of convenience with military leaders and defense industrialists,[99] while keeping within the rules of the game by practicing consensus decisionmaking calculated to maintain the stability of collective leadership. In return for backing of his internal power position, Brezhnev presumably lent his support in cases where it might have been needed to win Politburo approval of programs sought by the military. A rough "test" of this presumption—subject, to be sure, to the fallacy of misplaced causality—might be seen in the parallel rise of Brezhnev's personal political fortunes and the Soviet military budget.[100]

Brezhnev's careful dealing with the military also was paralleled by growth of his own public image as an authoritative figure in military affairs, based both on a publicity buildup concerning his past personal contributions in the field of national security[101] and on his being given the rank and prerogatives of a marshal of the Soviet Union in 1976. While such acclaim had the effect of smudging the boundary line between Brezhnev's leadership roles in the civilian and military spheres, it is not clear whether the net effect was to provide a buffer against, or to reinforce the influence of, a "military viewpoint" in Soviet decisionmaking councils.[102]

Viewed in terms of the institutional setting and processes within which Soviet defense policy is forged, another significant, but somewhat different, avenue for the diffusion of military influence also can be postulated. Inputs of information and substantive advice from the major bureaucracies have provided the basis for decisions reached by Brezhnev and the other chief actors at the top level of the policymaking system. Where decisions involved major military programs, these inputs would have to answer at least three broad types of questions: (1) Is the necessary technology for the programs at hand? (2) Are the resources to support it available? (3) How important is it to Soviet security?

As our earlier organizational discussion would indicate, the top political leadership could turn to nonmilitary bureaucracies for answers to the first two questions, or at least for a competent check on answers that might be furnished by the military-industrial bureaucracies. For example, the top leadership could be expected to receive authoritative advice on technology and resource questions from the Central Committee departments, from Smirnov at the Council of Ministers and the VPK, from the science and technology organizations outside the military, and from GOSPLAN.

But for answers to the third question, it would appear that the leadership, in the past at least, has been able to turn for substantive advice only to the bureaucracy whose institutional interests were most at stake in defense policy issues—the military establishment itself. As noted by various observers, this situation has been due to the apparent lack in the policymaking structure of alternative sources of expert advice on the substantive merits of national security proposals.[103] In the absence of overriding objections on technical or economic grounds, therefore, the system has seemed to have a bias in defense policy decisions toward the preferences of the military professionals and their close allies in the defense-industrial ministries.

A salient question now is whether there is emerging, within the Soviet decisionmaking system, an informed and relatively independent source of military-strategic advice and analysis upon which the political leadership could draw. A potential source of such advice has been seen in some of the research institutes under the aegis of the USSR Academy of Sciences—such as the Arbatov and Inozemtsev institutes.[104] Certain knowledgeable scientists with an appreciation of the dynamics of weapons technology and weapons tradeoffs, such as Academician Shchukin, the prominent electronics expert and Soviet SALT delegate, also have been mentioned as alternative sources of expert counsel.[105]

An increasing Soviet interest in various analytical techniques used in Western defense decisionmaking, such as cost-effectiveness and network analyses, also has been cited as likely to widen the expertise available to Soviet decisionmakers.[106] For example, there is some possibility that systems analysis capabilities developed within the Central Committee apparatus may be employed in the study of defense- and SALT-related problems,[107] though most of the use of such techniques for the purpose of defense analysis still appears to be within the military establishment itself. In part, their employment can be attributed to the military's efforts to respond positively to admonitions for more efficient management of defense resources.[108]

Although it is certainly plausible that the Soviet military's virtual monopoly on strategic thought and substantive analysis may be gradually eroding as a result of trends like those mentioned above, the patchy evidence available does not demonstrate that nonmilitary analytical talent has yet become free to encroach upon the traditional turf of the Soviet military by advancing independent judgment on such matters as force requirements, deployments, and basic defense concepts. Thus, more as a consequence of the way the Soviet policymaking mechanism has been structured to give the inside track to professional advice from the military—rather than as a result of what might be called "pressure" upon the Party leadership from the military—the latter can be said to have acquired a substantial amount of leverage both upon national security policy as a whole[109] and upon SALT as an important aspect of it.

With regard to SALT itself, the attitude of the Soviet military was wary from the beginning; indeed, the military had evidently been reluctant to enter the talks at all. This can be judged from, among other things, skeptical articles by military writers in late 1968 and 1969 hinting that it was "illusory" to seek Soviet security through arms agreements and reiterating the familiar theme that Soviet military policy should aim at the attainment of superiority.[110] Once Moscow's delayed decision to enter SALT had been made,[111] the Soviet military leadership found itself in the somewhat ambivalent position of having to support the negotiations while being concerned at the same time lest the talks lead to agreements adversely affecting the Soviet military posture—a dilemma, one might note, not necessarily peculiar to the Soviet side of the negotiating table.

But whatever the Soviet military's reservations toward SALT, the extent of its participation in SALT planning and negotiations, as we have seen, went well beyond that evident in any previous arms control negotiations.[112] During Marshal Grechko's tenure as minister of defense, for example, both his seemingly good personal relations with Brezhnev and his elevation to Politburo membership had given the Soviet military direct access at the highest level to final decisionmaking on SALT.[113] And the presence of Ogarkov, Alekseyev, and subsequently other senior General Staff officers on the SALT delegation gave the Soviet military high-ranking representation at the SALT negotiating level as well.

It is not altogether clear whether the Soviet military's extensive participation in SALT was essentially a matter of giving the soldiers their due as the professional custodians of Soviet security, or whether it came about somewhat more deviously as a calculated stratagem by the political leadership to involve the military deeply in the SALT process in order to counter institutional suspicion and footdragging from that quarter.[114] But in either event, it seems hardly disputable that throughout SALT I and at least much of SALT II, the military leadership has exerted a strong, conservative influence on the negotiations, and that the political leadership—whatever its own bent may have been—has tended to eschew agreements that, in the judgment of the military professionals, might adversely affect the Soviet military posture.[115]

How military influence upon SALT may be affected by the several changes of recent years in the topmost rank of the Soviet political-military leadership remains to be seen. When Ustinov became minister of defense after Grechko's death in 1976, this put at the head of the military establishment a man high in both Party and defense-industry circles, but except for reserve rank as a colonel-general of engineers, without cachet as a military professional. Given his background, Ustinov might on the one hand act to dilute the influence of the professional military viewpoint on SALT issues by interposing independent and not necessarily compatible judgments of his own. However, he might equally well prove to be a powerful amicus curiae for the military, giving the military viewpoint a still more persuasive voice in the highest leadership councils.

The replacement of Kulikov by Ogarkov as chief of the General Staff in 1977 placed in this powerful post a professional military officer with personal experience in the SALT arena. As some analysts have noted, the fact that Defense Minister Ustinov is not a military professional could mean greater influence for Ogarkov and the General Staff on SALT issues where strategic-military considerations were deemed important to decisionmaking.[116] However, Ogarkov's personal familiarity with SALT tells very little about where he might stand on specific issues, or even about his policy preferences in general. Like most other prominent Soviet military figures, Ogarkov has not written for publication on SALT matters. His published writings have instead dealt with the need for strengthening the Soviet defense posture, with particular emphasis on making appropriate use of technology for military purposes.[117]

Finally, Brezhnev's own ascendancy as a figure of multiple authority in the political-military leadership—at once Party secretary general, chairman of the Presidium of the Supreme Soviet, chairman of the Defense Council and marshal of the Soviet Union—has given him a more authoritative voice on SALT policy than any immediate successor could be expected to attain, at least in the short term. In a succession period, therefore, in a time of maneuver at the summit of Soviet politics, a decline of military influence on SALT would hardly seem likely.

It can, indeed, be argued that in the two succession periods since Stalin—those that saw the rise to pre-eminence of Khrushchev and Brezhnev—both of these winning succession contenders went out of their way, initially at least, to court military support. Khrushchev abandoned these tactics after he had been in office awhile, but Brezhnev apparently did not. Whether there is any causal link with the relative political longevity of the two leaders remains an open question.[118]

✳ *Chapter 4*

# Other Aspects of the SALT Institutional Setting: The Back Channel and Summitry

In addition to the organizational arrangements already described through which SALT planning and negotiations have been carried out by the United States and the Soviet Union, there are certain other aspects of the SALT institutional setting that merit some attention here. One of these is the back channel. Representing a form of intervention from outside the formal SALT negotiating forum and involving private and closely held contacts between a few highly placed officials on the two sides, the back channel came into existence during SALT I.

A second form of high-level intervention in the SALT negotiating process has been "summitry"—periodic meetings at which the American president in office at the time and the top Soviet leader, with their respective entourages, have dealt directly with the business of SALT, often on the basis of preparations worked out beforehand through the privacy of the back channel.

There also has been a third level of outside intervention somewhere in between the informal and secret back channel and the more visible and formal summits. This category of intervention has taken the form of occasional exploratory talks on stalled SALT issues, usually carried out between the top leaders of one side and a high-ranking emissary from the other, generally either the American secretary of state or the Soviet foreign minister, or sometimes between the latter two officials alone.

## USE OF THE BACK CHANNEL

Needless to say, what is known as the back channel—that is, secret contacts between individual officials that detour the regular machinery of intercourse either between governments or within them—is hardly a phenomenon peculiar to SALT. In the SALT case, the establishment of back-channel communication between the Soviet and American sides grew out of a stalemate that had developed between the formal negotiating delegations in the latter part of 1970 over various issues, including American refusal to agree upon ABM limitations unless offensive systems were also dealt with, and Soviet insistence on curbing forward-based systems (FBS).[1]

In an effort to keep the negotiations from bogging down, and at U.S. initiative, Presidential Assistant Henry Kissinger and Soviet Ambassador A.F. Dobrynin met at the White House in early January 1971, following which an exchange of personal messages on SALT was opened between President Nixon and Soviet Premier A.N. Kosygin.[2]

This correspondence (to which neither the U.S. SALT delegation nor the majority of senior Washington officials was privy at the time), along with further Kissinger-Dobrynin contacts during the next few months, led to a "compromise" formula for breaking the SALT I stalemate, announced simultaneously in Moscow and Washington on May 20, 1971—an announcement that has sometimes been described as the first major breakthrough in SALT.[3] What is pertinent to the discussion here is that nearly all of the activity that produced the May 20 compromise formula had been carried on through the back channel, thus setting a precedent for tackling tough SALT issues by circumventing the regular SALT machinery.

On the American side, knowledge of what was going on in the back channel during its original use in the period from January to May 1971 had been held to a very small circle by Dr. Kissinger, who, as John Newhouse put it, "kept fully informed only his constituency of one"—the president.[4] Kissinger's back-channel partner, Ambassador Dobrynin, on the other hand, was apparently plugged in to a somewhat wider circle of constituents among the leadership in Moscow. This is suggested by Dobrynin's reported disclosure that his instructions were coming from the whole Politburo rather than from Premier Kosygin alone,[5] together with the fact that some details of the back-channel exchange had filtered down to the head of the Soviet SALT delegation, V.S. Semenov, while his opposite number at the delegation level, Gerard Smith, remained in the dark up to the eve of the May 20 announcement.[6]

During the year of accelerated SALT I negotiations that followed the compromise formula of May 20, 1971, back-channel activity again supplemented the established negotiating machinery. Besides periodic Kissinger-Dobrynin meetings in Washington, there was a continuing exchange of personal messages between President Nixon and the top Soviet leadership, whose spokesman at some point during the Soviet 24th Party Congress in April 1971 had become Leonid Brezhnev in place of Kosygin, reflecting a shift in the locus of authority in the Kremlin.[7]

In April 1972, a new form of back-channel intervention in SALT was introduced when Kissinger flew to Moscow for a four-day session with Brezhnev that was kept in "immaculate" secrecy until after Kissinger's return.[8] On this trip, which reportedly had been taken at Brezhnev's suggestion in order to iron out some unresolved issues and pave the way for the May 1972 summit in Moscow,[9] Kissinger was accompanied by a handful of his top NSC staff aides, including Helmut Sonnenfeldt, his senior deputy for Soviet and East European affairs; Winston Lord, his principal aide on Vietnam; and two other senior NSC advisers, William Hyland and Philip Odeen. Kissinger also was accompanied by Soviet Ambassador A.F. Dobrynin, who was to be his traveling companion on subsequent journeys to confer with the Soviet leadership on SALT.

Although Vietnam was on the agenda at the April 1972 Brezhnev-Kissinger meetings in Moscow, the talks were also devoted to seeking resolution of a number of SALT issues that the delegations had been unable to settle. In addition to problems concerning geographic constraints and radar limitations in connection with ABM, other questions covered the inclusion of SLBMs, to which the Soviets had been opposed, and the duration of an interim agreement on offensive arms. Out of the April talks emerged the general contour of the SALT accords subsequently signed at the May 1972 summit, though several issues—of which Soviet SLBM totals and replacement provisions proved to be the most complicated and controversial— remained up to the last minute to be ironed out at the summit itself.[10]

Just as the back channel had been used in SALT I to supplement and occasionally to supplant the work of the negotiating delegations, so it was also employed during SALT II in attempts to resolve the basic deadlocked issues confronting the front-channel negotiators. Together with continued Kissinger-Dobrynin contacts and further correspondence at the presidential level,[11] there were fourteen additional occasions—apart from summit meetings—when Kissinger met privately with high-level Soviet leaders to deal with SALT and other problems during the Nixon-Ford period. Although most of the substantive details of Kissinger's back-channel exchanges with Soviet representatives on these occasions remained rather closely held, even within the U.S. government, the talks themselves came to be somewhat widely publicized in advance as trouble-shooting interventions into the SALT negotiations.[12]

The first of Kissinger's visits to Moscow following the May 1972 summit at which the SALT I accords were concluded took place September 10 to 13, 1972. Reportedly arranged on two weeks' notice,[13] this visit dealt with questions pertaining to European security negotiations, Vietnam, and Soviet-American trade, as well as SALT. The principal announced accomplishment with respect to SALT was an agreement to begin the second round of negotiations in November 1972.[14]

The next Kissinger-Brezhnev meeting in Moscow consisted of four days of intensive private talks from May 6 to 9, 1973, during which plans were worked out for the June 1973 summit in Washington. Besides arms control questions, trade and Vietnam were again among subjects on the agenda, although at the time nothing was publicly disclosed concerning the substance of the talks.[15] With respect to SALT, Kissinger subsequently revealed that by April 1973—a month before his trip—it had become clear that a comprehensive SALT agreement could not be reached in time for approval at the second summit, and that consequently the private talks with Brezhnev had focused upon working out "principles" to "guide" the two negotiating teams in Geneva.[16] Kissinger also noted that he had provided the "nuances" of his "extensive discussions" with Brezhnev on SALT to the chief American negotiator, U. Alexis Johnson,[17] thus implying that the front channel was now being kept better informed of what was going on in the back channel.

A third Kissinger-Brezhnev private consultation in Moscow dealing directly with SALT came March 26 to 28, 1974, in advance of the third Nixon-Brezhnev summit. The hope that this visit might achieve "a conceptual breakthrough" on the complex SALT issue of controlling MIRV—a hope that reportedly had been fed by Dobrynin's "optimistic" reaction to a U.S. MIRV proposal submitted to him through the back channel several days before the trip—[18] was not fulfilled in Moscow. There, after a special meeting of key Politburo members, including Marshal Grechko (who had been called back from a visit in Iraq to take part), the Soviet leadership took a position that was said to make it unlikely that the MIRV problem and other deadlocked SALT issues could be resolved in time to permit new agreements on strategic arms during the June-July 1974 summit in Moscow. This proved to be the case.[19]

A fourth Kissinger trip to Moscow, during which he discussed with Brezhnev, Gromyko, and others a revised set of U.S. SALT proposals formulated under the new American president, Gerald Ford, took place October 25 to 27, 1974. Kissinger refused at the time to discuss the details of his talks with the Soviet leaders but indicated that he saw a "reasonable chance" for "movement toward an accord" on SALT.[20] This prediction was at least partly borne out a month later when, after an exchange of several back-channel messages between Washington and Moscow to follow up bargaining points raised during Kissinger's October visit,[21] the first Brezhnev-Ford summit convened at Vladivostok.

Following the Vladivostok summit, Kissinger made only one further visit to Moscow. This took place more than a year later, from January 20 to 22, 1976, for the purpose of holding private talks on SALT with Brezhnev and other top Soviet leaders. It was dedicated to working out several problems over which the SALT delegations in Geneva had become deadlocked since Vladivostok, such as the Backfire bomber and cruise missile issues, but although both sides were reported at the time to have made some concessions toward ending the stalemate, Kissinger's bargaining with the Russians on this occasion left the disputed issues essentially unresolved.[22]

Similarly, in five meetings between Kissinger and Soviet Foreign Minister Gromyko that took place in Vienna, Geneva, New York, and Washington in the last year and a half of Kissinger's tenure as secretary of state,[23] attempts to break the post-Vladivostok SALT stalemate and clear the way for a Brezhnev-Ford summit in the United States made what was occasionally described as "marginal progress." In the end, however, neither negotiations carried out through the back channel, the front channel, nor the private meetings in between had managed to resolve the residual hard-core issues.[24]

When the Carter administration came to office in early 1977, it brought with it from the electoral campaign an ethos stressing "open" diplomacy that was ostensibly inhospitable to the kind of secret back-channel dealing associated with Henry Kissinger's management of SALT during the Nixon-Ford era.[25] Initially, at least, there apparently was no inclination on the part of the new president, his assistant for national security affairs, nor his secretary of state to communicate with the Soviets on SALT through the same back-channel arrangements that had come into use in early 1971 under Nixon.

When intervention in the SALT negotiating process from above the SALT delegation level initially took place in March 1977 under

Carter, it was entrusted to Secretary of State Cyrus Vance, whose official party for a three-day meeting on SALT in Moscow (March 28 to 30) with the top Soviet leadership included Paul Warnke in the dual capacity of director of ACDA and chief of the U.S. SALT delegation.[26] So far as is known, no back-channel preparations or other advance notice of a substantive nature had preceded this meeting,[27] at which the unveiling of a new set of U.S. SALT proposals reportedly took the Soviet leadership by surprise and met with a decidedly negative reaction from Brezhnev, Gromyko, and other Soviet leaders.[28]

High-level meetings above the SALT delegation level thereafter continued in much the same pattern as before—seven in eighteen months, or an average of four per year under Carter, compared with fourteen in four years, or an average of about three per year (excluding summits) in the Nixon-Ford period.[29] Of the seven meetings in the first eighteen months of the Carter administration, two saw Gromyko coming to Washington for talks at which the principal American figures were Carter, Vance, Warnke, Brzezinski, Brown; two found Vance going to Moscow to deal with Brezhnev and company; and the other three meetings in New York and Geneva involved no one at a level higher than Vance and Gromyko.[30]

## THE SUMMITS AND SALT

Although summits involving Soviet and American leaders have a history antedating SALT by several decades,[31] and while some of the Nixon-Brezhnev and Ford-Brezhnev meetings at the summit did involve aspects of Soviet-American relations other than SALT alone, nevertheless one can say that since SALT began it has tended to be the dominant subject and centerpiece of Soviet-American summitry.

Prior to the Carter administration, there were five summits involving SALT—three during Nixon's tenure and two during the Ford incumbency, including the 1975 Helsinki meeting at which the primary business was to sign the CSCE accord. Up to the present writing, no summit meeting had taken place during the Carter presidency.

Institutionally, the intended function of the SALT era summit meetings has probably been to give the stamp of approval at the highest political level to agreements already largely worked out in advance—through the back channel, through high-level emissaries, and by arms control experts at the delegation level. In practice, however, the summits have not turned out to be mere symbolic sessions for rubberstamping previously prepared accords. Rather, they appear also to have become in some degree vehicles for direct intervention in the SALT negotiating process, with the top leaders on both sides giving their attention to substantive issues left unresolved through other avenues of negotiation.

At the first Nixon-Brezhnev summit in Moscow in May 1972, for example, though the general outlines and most of the details of the accords reached there had indeed been settled in advance, some substantive issues were still unresolved when the top political leaders began to meet and these had to be negotiated on the spot.[32]

With regard to the second Nixon-Brezhnev summit in Washington in June 1973, it had already been recognized beforehand that there was little prospect of resolving basic substantive differences so as to permit the signing of a new comprehensive SALT agreement on strategic offensive arms there.[33] The agreement that was reached at the summit on "Basic Principles" to guide the negotiators was sufficiently broad and generalized so that it did not appear inconsistent with positions both sides had taken since the start of SALT II.[34] This would suggest that the summit managed to do little more than perpetuate the existing differences. Yet the second summit did have the effect of imposing a political imperative of sorts upon the negotiations by setting a deadline for some form of further agreement on substantive issues before the end of 1974.

As indicated by the third summit of June-July 1974 in Moscow, even an imperative from the top failed to speed up the dynamics of negotiation, or at least, to break the major substantive impasse in which front- and back-channel negotiators alike found themselves stuck. It is true that the third summit ended with several new agreements on the books. These included: a treaty on limiting underground nuclear tests; a protocol to the ABM Treaty permitting only a single deployment area of 100 ABM launchers rather than two; an agreement to explore ways of curbing the dangers of environmental modification techniques for military purposes; and two protocols on dismantling and replacement of missiles, confirming procedures worked out by the SCC in accordance with the May 1972 SALT agreements.[35] These two protocols were kept secret at Russian request.[36]

However, these various agreements, which had been worked out beforehand, were essentially peripheral to such central SALT issues as achieving a permanent accord to replace the Interim Agreement on offensive arms and finding an agreed formula for controlling MIRV deployment. Not only did Nixon's third and final summit meeting with Brezhnev fail to resolve the deadlock on such issues, but it also abandoned the previous objective of a permanent comprehensive agreement in favor of the less exacting one of trying to negotiate another limited interim agreement that would expire in 1985.[37]

On the other hand, the fourth summit at Vladivostok in November 1974, where a new American president entered the picture, helped to bridge the gulf between the two sides, for the time being at least, on a number of basic SALT issues. To a considerable extent the outcome of two days of bargaining at the Ford-Brezhnev summit at Vladivostok rested on prior understandings worked out through the back channel. However, the Vladivostok summit apparently also found the top-level negotiations facing a few new substantive issues, not all of which were resolved without creating certain ambiguities.[38]

The last occasion during the Ford administration for a meeting on SALT matters between the president and Brezhnev came in late July 1975 when the two leaders took time out during the CSCE-signing ceremonies in Helsinki for a private discussion of several sticking points in the post-Vladivostok negotiations. This meeting helped to produce a compromise on the issue of MIRV verification, but left a number of other SALT II differences unresolved, including the cruise missile and Backfire bomber issues.[39]

No further summit meetings materialized during the remainder of Ford's tenure and in the first couple of years after Carter's election. This may have been partly due to continued failure to achieve a full-fledged SALT II agreement whose signing might serve as the centerpiece of a new summit, as well as to the general worsening of U.S.-Soviet relations in 1977-78 over such issues as Soviet "adventurism" in Africa and suppression of dissenters in the USSR, issues that severely strained detente and made a Carter-Brezhnev meeting inexpedient.[40] In a SALT context, it was rather paradoxical that the prospects for a new summit meeting should have receded at a time when intervention from the summit level seemed most needed in order to nail down a SALT II agreement that could not be completed through other avenues of negotiation.

## ORGANIZATIONAL IMPLICATIONS OF THE BACK CHANNEL

There would appear to be nothing inherently objectionable about using back-channel contacts to supplement the interface between the SALT delegations of the two sides, particularly where the practice has succeeded in restoring momentum to bogged-down negotiations by removing obstacles that the front-channel negotiators themselves could not surmount. As a medium for exploratory communications between high officials of the two sides, or for that matter, as a device for helping to break internal policy bottlenecks, the back channel may very well have served a useful purpose in the SALT process. Even from the viewpoint of the negotiating teams, whose instructions from home may occasionally get hung up in the SALT backup machinery, secret intervention by means of the back channel may at times have appeared a not unwelcome way to overcome bureaucratic inertia and to bring top leaders to grips with issues they might otherwise tend to put off for other business.

Nevertheless, despite the arguments that can be made in its defense, the back channel has been the object of considerable criticism, particularly for the way it was employed when Dr. Kissinger kept a tight grip on SALT in the Nixon-Ford era. Not surprisingly, adverse commentary on the back channel was to be heard almost exclusively in the United States, for in the Soviet Union such matters as how SALT policy is formulated and how negotiations are conducted do not lie within the bounds of public discourse.

One line of criticism was that closely held back-channel activity by senior officials implied lack of trust in their subordinates, reluctance to delegate responsibility, unwillingness to let working-level officials in on the reasons for decisions that might run contrary to their advice, and so on. This problem surfaced from time to time with respect to both the functioning of the SALT delegation in the field and internal SALT decisionmaking in Washington[41] and involved some fine judgments on the proper distribution of responsibility for policy and its execution and on conditions of trust necessary to insure an effective working relationship between senior officials and their subordinates. Usually, the resignation of some key figure in the SALT apparatus focused attention on the situation.

For example, as noted in an earlier chapter, Gerard Smith is said to have quit as head of the SALT delegation and ACDA shortly after the start of SALT II because he had been "persistently denied the responsibility he thought he should have."[42] Frequent resort to the back channel when the going got tough in the negotiations may have persuaded Smith that no real role in the settlement of critical issues was left to the U.S. negotiating team or to ACDA, and this in turn may have swayed his decision to bow out.

A later case in point was that of Paul Nitze, a senior member of the SALT delegation from the start of the negotiations, as well as an influential assistant on SALT affairs to the secretary of defense. In a carefully guarded explanation of the reasons behind his resignation from both of these posts in June 1974, Nitze noted that he had been disturbed by what he thought was "excessive suspicion of people down the line," and that where "trust" does not exist, an "effective working relationship tends to break down."[43] Suggesting that the relationship between senior officials and their subordinates "works best" when subordinates are "fully informed on everything which is pertinent to the work they are doing," Nitze on this and subsequent occasions made it clear that in his own view, the nature of the back channel did not lend itself well to such a relationship.[44]

A second line of complaint against negotiating through the back channel and at the summit in SALT I centered on the charge that these circumventions of the regular negotiating machinery adversely affected the quality of the agreements reached. Raymond Garthoff, in particular, has cited some of the ambiguities and confusion arising from the conduct of parallel negotiations, both in the secret back channel preceding the Moscow summit of May 1972[45] and at the summit itself, where the "President and his ad hoc negotiating team" plunged into a "hectic" five-day session with Brezhnev and other top Soviet leaders on the latter's home grounds while the regular U.S. SALT contingent was kept on the sidelines.[46] In Garthoff's view, the May 1972 summit negotiations by the presidential party "represented a model of how *not* to conduct negotiations—against a political deadline, by an ill-prepared political negotiation team," and "without the best technical negotiating advice and assistance."[47]

Another item in the gravamen against the use of the back channel in SALT I was that, though it might have been both feasible and appropriate for Kissinger to be personally active in back-channel SALT dealings so long as he served only as the president's assistant for national security, such immediate personal involvement was no longer compatible with the functions and responsibilities of his subsequent office as secretary of state. Kissinger, in this view, should have delegated more responsibility, rather than continuing to maintain tight personal control over all of the organizational machinery of SALT, including the back channel. Whatever the merits of this argument, the fact remains that Kissinger obviously preferred to set his own style as secretary of state, which appeared to include keeping a large measure of control over SALT in his own hands.

Although use of the back channel may merely have reflected the Kissinger style of diplomacy and his belief in the efficacy of highly confidential methods of operation,[48] it nevertheless led on occasion to charges of "secret deals" with the Russians. Perhaps the chief case in point concerned charges made by Senator Jackson on the eve of the 1974 Moscow summit that a back-channel Kissinger-Dobrynin "interpretive agreement" signed on July 24, 1972, had been withheld from senior U.S. government officials—including the secretary of defense, the JCS, and the head of the SALT delegation—for almost a year, and from Congress for even longer.[49] The agreement dealt with ambiguities about how many modern SLBMs the Soviets would be permitted under the May 1972 SALT Interim Agreement.

According to Senator Jackson's charge, the secret reinterpretation of the 1972 SALT provisions defined "modern missiles" in such a way as to permit the Soviets to modernize missiles on their older, G-class diesel subs, thereby gaining 70 additional missiles that would raise the number of Soviet SLBMs from 950 to 1020. Jackson also claimed that Brezhnev had been privately informed by President Nixon that the United States had "no intention" to exercise its right under the May 1972 accords to deploy up to 710 SLBMs.[50]

In resolving the original ambiguity in favor of the U.S. interpretation that the Soviet Union could have a maximum of 950 SLBMs, rather than 70 more as the Russians had contended, the Kissinger-Dobrynin agreement, according to charges by Senator Jackson and others, opened another loophole that might have supported the Soviet interpretation.[51] Subsequently, this loophole was said to have been closed by an agreement initialed on June 18, 1974, based on negotiations in the Standing Consultative Commission in Geneva.[52]

The controversy in question largely subsided after it became apparent from Kissinger's explanation of the circumstances that no ultimate concessions altering the basic terms of the May 1972 SALT accords had been made to the Russians.[53] However, it can hardly be disputed that the controversy provided further fodder to critics of back-channel diplomacy, who could again argue that "excessive" secrecy with regard to Soviet-American SALT transactions had tended to compound ambiguities and problems that might otherwise have been avoided.[54]

Another fault sometimes ascribed to the back channel was the asymmetry of opportunity for influencing SALT at opposite ends of the back-channel axis. Although both sides evidently valued the advantages of secrecy afforded by the back channel, the effects of secrecy were not necessarily the same for each, owing to differing styles of governmental operations on each side. By playing his back-channel cards close to his chest within the governmental SALT arena on the U.S. side, for example, Kissinger could be charged, as noted above,[55] with having handicapped lesser officials and civil servants whose duties normally would have called for them to be informed about what was going on. In the Soviet case, however, where a rather high degree of internal compartmentalization was standard operating procedure anyway, but where the SALT apparatus was evidently more closely attuned to the results of back-channel dealings,[56] it could be inferred that the Soviets were in a better position to manipulate these dealings for their own ends, as well as to generate an internally less abrasive and more integrated SALT strategy than the American side.

The SALT role of Ambassador Dobrynin, the Soviet diplomat with whom Kissinger's cultivation of the back channel began at the Washington end of the line, also had a bearing on the relative opportunities for influencing SALT at the opposite ends of the back-channel axis. Dobrynin, whose service as Soviet ambassador in Washington went back to March 1962, had come to enjoy regular and unparalleled access to the top echelons of policymaking and decision in the United States by the end of SALT I. His counterpart at the time in Moscow, American Ambassador Jacob D. Beam, enjoyed no comparable access to the inner working of the Soviet establishment, and moreover, unlike Dobrynin, was left out of both back-channel and summit transactions on SALT.

This situation gave Dobrynin both a better window on what was going on in SALT and closer contact with relevant centers of decision than his ambassadorial counterpart on the American side. But it could be argued that these asymmetrical advantages for exerting influence on the SALT process were offset by Kissinger's own periodic forays into the Soviet Union, where he too made his way into the corridors of power in Moscow through his private meetings with Brezhnev and others at the top level of Soviet officialdom. If Kissinger's access to the Kremlin was less frequent and briefer than Dobrynin's almost casual Washington entrée, it perhaps made up for this by its intensity—for virtually all of Brezhnev's time and that of other important Soviet figures was pre-empted during Kissinger's Kremlin visits.

Dobrynin's longevity as an immediate actor in the SALT process proved greater, of course, than Kissinger's. However, after Kissinger left the scene with the change of U.S. administrations in early 1977, Dobrynin's SALT role—though continuing to be important[57]—apparently began to contract somewhat, reflecting in part perhaps the decline of the back-channel mode of dealing with SALT problems.[58] In the meantime, the American ambassadorial post in Moscow had begun to get more involved in the SALT negotiatory process. After Ambassador Walter J. Stoessel took up the post in July 1974, for example, he was given a more active role in SALT-related diplomacy than had been the case in the earlier history of SALT,[59] and at the Vladivostok summit in November 1974 he was made a member of President Ford's delegation. Ambassador

Malcolm Toon, who replaced Stoessel in November 1976 and was retained in the Moscow post by the Carter administration,[60] also continued to be actively involved in the diplomacy of SALT.[61]

To sum up the institutional place of the back channel in the SALT process, it would appear that the kinds of communication on SALT matters that once flowed through the back channel were largely restored to regular diplomatic channels after the Carter administration came to office. Two basic reasons for the decline of the back channel may be surmised.

First, the highly personalized and centralized style of the Nixon-Kissinger team in dealing with the Soviet leadership, which helped to bring the back channel into frequent use, was replaced by a Carter administration style both less congenial to secret back-channel traffic and apparently more difficult for the Soviet leadership to understand and relate to.[62] Hence, there was less disposition on either side to communicate through the back channel.

Second, the secrecy and informal nature of the back channel were perhaps more important in the earlier phases of SALT, when the two sides were feeling each other out and first learning to deal with the complexities of strategic arms limitations. As the handling of SALT problems by the negotiating delegations and in meetings at the summit or foreign ministers level has become more institutionalized, the result may have been a diminishing need for back-channel intervention in the SALT process.

# Chapter 5

# Principal SALT II Issues
# Prior to Vladivostok

When the ABM Treaty and the Interim Agreement on strategic offensive arms were signed in May 1972, there was some reason to believe that SALT I had at least slowed down the quantitative aspects of the strategic competition and that it might even have opened the door, as one observer put it hopefully, to the possibility that the Soviet Union and the United States could find a formula in SALT II that would offer them greater security "at a reduced level of competition in strategic arms."[1]

The pursuit of a SALT II accord in the 1972-1978 period, however, was to prove both longer and more arduous than the SALT I experience. One reason was that some of the tougher issues and areas of disagreement had simply been laid aside in SALT I for later consideration. Another reason was that the SALT I agreements had been essentially a validation of the then existing strategic postures which both sides had already arrived at unilaterally, whereas SALT II faced the basic question of what the future strategic relationship between the two powers was to be.

This would depend in part upon the "legislated" constraints that the two sides might prove willing to adopt jointly in SALT itself, and in part upon the unilateral strategic policies and programs that each might choose to pursue apart from SALT, as hedges against future uncertainty. Specific developments in these two contexts in the course of SALT II have been closely interrelated, but for convenience of discussion it appears best to take them up separately. Thus, in the next several chapters we shall deal alternatively with the SALT II negotiations of the 1972-1978 period, and with the evolution of the strategic policies and postures of the two countries in the SALT era. This chapter will cover the pre-Vladivostok phase of SALT II, which ran from November 1972 until November 1974.

The two years of strategic arms negotiations between the end of SALT I and the Ford-Brezhnev summit at Vladivostok in November 1974 testified to the stubbornness of the SALT issues that remained unresolved. Although a few additional agreements were reached, they were essentially peripheral to the main substantive SALT impasse in which the two sides found themselves.[2]

Among the specific problems over which a deadlock persisted during this period, three sets of major issues seemed to stand out: (1) How to convert the Interim Agreement (IA), which was to expire in October 1977, into a comprehensive permanent agreement that would satisfy both what the Soviet side referred to as "equal security and no unilateral advantage" and what the American side defined as "essential equivalence" in strategic offensive arms; (2) how to apply both qualitative and quantitative controls to MIRV systems on an equitable basis; and (3) what provisions to adopt with regard to nuclear-capable U.S. forward-based systems (FBS), which the United States regarded as tactical forces committed to the defense of NATO allies in Europe, but which the USSR considered to be a strategic threat against the Soviet homeland.

## REPLACEMENT OF THE
## INTERIM AGREEMENT

Although the negotiation of a comprehensive permanent agreement on limitation of strategic offensive arms to replace the Interim Agreement of May 1972 was the principal business originally set before SALT II, and though this goal had been reaffirmed at the June 1973 summit, the differences between the two sides as to what provisions a permanent agreement should contain could not be reconciled, either by the SALT delegations at Geneva or by political authorities at the summit.

Indeed, at the tag end of the July 1974 summit—after the Soviet leaders had turned down the idea that a way out of the impasse over a permanent agreement might be found by extending the Interim Agreement for two or three years, coupled with some MIRV limitations of the same duration[3]—the two sides chose to abandon the objective of a permanent agreement altogether. Instead, in what might have been interpreted either as a tacit admission that SALT was nearing a dead end, or as a constructive move to try to salvage the negotiations,[4] the two sides elected to seek during the remaining life of the Interim Agreement what would amount in effect to a new set of provisional limitations running from 1977 to 1985.[5]

While the goal of a permanent agreement was thus shelved in mid-1974, this did not mean that the issues at stake had thereupon evaporated. Since some of the issues involved and the attitudes of the respective sides toward them could well have a bearing on the prospects for achieving a durable post-Vladivostok SALT accord, it may be useful here to look somewhat more closely at what the available record can tell us about these matters.

To begin with, it appears that both sides had offered several comprehensive proposals for a permanent agreement at various stages in the negotiations prior to the mid-1974 summit. Since the actual texts of these successive proposals have never been made public for comparison, it is rather difficult to judge which side showed the greater willingness over the course of time to accommodate its proposals to the objections of the other, and hence, by inference, which side had the greater interest in seeing the Interim Agreement replaced by a comprehensive permanent accord.

According to some informed American accounts, however, the Soviet side consistently took the more intransigent position, yielding little ground on points in controversy and expressing the conviction that sooner or later the United States would find it necessary to accommodate itself to the Soviet proposals. To quote Paul Nitze: "Soviet officials have indicated the view that what they call the 'correlation of forces,' which in Communist terminology includes the aggregate of forces bearing on the situation, including psychological, political, economic and military factors, is moving in their favor and that, even though we may today believe that their proposals are one-sided and inequitable, eventually realism will bring us to accept at least the substance of them."[6]

With respect to substance, the Soviet proposals evidently sought to preserve the advantages in missile numbers and throwweight incorporated in the Interim Agreement.[7] Under the terms of the Interim Agreement, the Soviets were permitted approximately 40 percent superiority in the number of offensive nuclear-missile launchers, and no limits were set on throwweight.[8] The rationale advanced by Soviet negotiators for carrying over the disparities of the Interim Agreement into a permanent agreement apparently dovetailed with published commentary by various Soviet writers, who argued that true "equality" warranted larger Soviet forces in compensation for geographic, strategic, and technological "asymmetries" alleged to favor the United States.[9]

In addition to the Soviet compensatory claim for a larger number of missile launchers, other substantive aspects of the Soviet proposals for a comprehensive permanent agreement also have been characterized as "heavily one-sided." These included the positions taken on MIRV and FBS (to be discussed separately below), as well as a proposed ban on the deployment of such new U.S. systems as the Trident submarine-based missile system and the B-1 bomber, without a commensurate ban on the Soviet Union's own new family of strategic delivery systems.[10]

For its part, the United States prior to mid-1974 put forward proposals for a comprehensive permanent agreement based on the concept of "essential equivalence," calling for overall equality in the total number of ICBMs, SLBMs, and strategic bombers, but with each side free to determine its own mix of systems under an agreed aggregate ceiling.[11] The systems in the mix were those considered by the United States to be "central" strategic systems upon which limits should first be placed. The Soviets, however, did not agree with the central systems concept, arguing that other forces, such as FBS, must be included. Under the U.S. comprehensive proposals, a formula whose details were not made public was to be applied in order to place equal limitations on the destructive capability of the strategic forces of the two sides, as measured by the throwweight of offensive missiles with an allowance for the equivalent capability of heavy bombers.[12]

What the U.S. side proposed as an aggregate ceiling for strategic forces to meet the criterion of essential equivalence was not disclosed. The alternatives mentioned in some accounts would either have allowed a U.S. buildup to the higher Soviet levels, or required reduction by both sides to an agreed lower common ceiling.[13] Had the figure been keyed to approximately the level of forces existing in mid-1974, it would presumably have fallen somewhere between 2200 and 2375—the figures for the United States and the Soviet Union, respectively, as shown in Table 5-1, giving the comparative levels of strategic forces in 1974 and 1975, and also in 1978. Whatever overall level may have been proposed earlier, however, the figure of 2400 subsequently set at Vladivostok came closer to the Soviet total.

The original SALT II objective of converting the Interim Agreement into a permanent one foundered not only on the failure to agree on a common concept of strategic equality or essential equivalence, but also over a number of complex subissues. Bombers, which are inherently difficult to equate with missiles on the basis of numbers, payload, penetration capability, or any other comparative measurements, were a case in point. The United States had approximately a 3:1 advantage in numbers of intercontinental bombers,

**Table 5-1**

**U.S. and USSR Strategic Force Levels, Mid-1974, Mid-1975, Mid-1978**

| Type of Force | Operational in Mid-1974 | | Operational in Mid-1975 | | Operational in Mid-1978 | |
|---|---|---|---|---|---|---|
| | *U.S.* | *USSR* | *U.S.* | *USSR* | *U.S.* | *USSR* |
| *Offensive* | | | | | | |
| ICBM launchers[a] | 1054 | 1575 | 1054 | 1590 | 1054 | 1400+ |
| SLBM launchers[b] | 656 | 660 | 656 | 700 | 656 | 900+ |
| Intercontinental bombers | 496 | 140 | 498 | 160 | 347 | 140 |
| *Total* | *2206* | *2375* | *2208* | *2450* | *2057* | *2440+* |
| SSBN submarines | 41 | 47-50 | 41 | 52-53 | 41 | 62 |
| Missile throwweight[c] (ICBM & SLBM) in million lbs | 3.8 | 6.5 | 3.8 | 7.0 | 3.8 | 8.5 |
| Force loadings (warheads & bombs) | 7940 | 2600 | 8500 | 2800 | 9000 | 4500 |
| *Defensive* | | | | | | |
| ABM launchers[a] | 0 | 64 | 0 | 64[d] | 0 | 64 |
| SAM launchers | 261 | 9800 | 0 | 10,000 | 0 | 10,000 |
| Air defense interceptors | 532 | 2600 | 405 | 2500 | 330 | 2600 |
| Surveillance radars | 67 | 4000 | 67 | 4000 | 57 | 6500 |

Source: Based on *Report of Secretary of Defense James R. Schlesinger to the Congress on the FY 1975 Budget and FY 1975-1979 Defense Program,* March 4, 1974, p. 50; Admiral Thomas H. Moorer, chairman, JCS, *U.S. Military Posture for FY 1975,* 1974, pp. 20-22; *Report of Secretary of Defense James R. Schlesinger to the Congress on the FY 1976 and Transition Budgets and FY 1976-1980 Defense Program,* February 5, 1975, p. II-19; *Department of Defense Annual Report FY 1979, Harold Brown, Secretary of Defense,* February 2, 1978, p. 47.

[a]Excludes launchers at test sites.

[b]Excludes launchers on diesel submarines.

[c]Approximate figures for 1974, as given in Clarence A. Robinson, Jr., "SALT Extension Trades Pondered," *Aviation Week & Space Technology,* May 27, 1974, p. 14. Figures for 1975 and 1978 estimated on basis of data given in Colin S. Gray, "Soviet Rocket Forces: Military Capability, Political Utility," *Air Force Magazine,* March 1978, p. 52.

[d]Permissible total reduced from 200 to 100 by July 1974 protocol to the ABM Treaty of May 1972.

which were not included in the Interim Agreement. Doubtless, the Soviet side regarded this bomber advantage as one of the asymmetries for which it should be compensated with a greater number of ICBMs and SLBMs. On the other hand, the Soviet Union had a far larger number of air-defense interceptors and surface-to-air-missile launchers (see Table 5-1) for defense against bombers. This asymmetry worked against the United States. However, it could not be taken into account, for the Soviet side apparently insisted that air defenses were not a proper subject for negotiation in SALT.

Another complicated subissue concerned the throwweight or payload advantage of Soviet missiles versus the U.S. advantage in numbers of warheads. As indicated in Table 5-1, the Soviet Union in mid-1974 was estimated to have had about 6.5 million pounds of throwweight, compared to about 3.8 million pounds for the United States, including both ICBMs and SLBMs. Moreover, the new family of missiles then expected to replace the existing Soviet force in the next few years would provide at least a doubling of the Soviet throwweight potential, if not more,[14] whereas that of the United States under existing programs and design philosophy had negligible growth prospects. Partly offsetting the present and future Soviet advantage in missile throwweight was the superior U.S. bomber-payload capacity, approximately three times that of the USSR,[15] but the problem of equating bomber payload with missile throwweight was not easy to unravel.

The situation with regard to numbers of warheads was one in which the United States, thanks largely to its MIRV deployment programs of the early 1970s, enjoyed a wide but perhaps transient lead over the Soviet Union. As shown in Table 5-1, the mid-1974 U.S. combined inventory of some 7900 warheads and bombs (of which missile warheads accounted for more than three-quarters of the total) was to be compared with a Soviet figure of 2600, mostly in missile warheads.

The nub of the issue here was that having attained a deployable MIRV technology, the Soviet Union, with its greater throwweight potential, was in a position that might permit it over a number of years to deploy as many as 15,000 to 17,000 separately targetable warheads,[16] thus wiping out the U.S. lead in numbers of warheads. Finding a formula that would balance the existing U.S. advantage in warhead numbers and the relatively more sophisticated missile and warhead technology of the United States against the greater numbers and size of Soviet missiles (and that would at the same time take into account any future changes) was thus, not surprisingly, a task that defied solution during the first two years of SALT II negotiations.

From the U.S. viewpoint, a SALT agreement that would have equalized the total permissible missile throwweight—after making suitable allowance for bomber payload disparity and the absence of limitations on air defenses—might have represented an equitable solution. But for the Soviet side, this would have entailed acceptance of fewer launchers in order to stay below a given throwweight ceiling, unless it were to alter its missile design philosophy so as to build missiles with less throwweight capacity, comparable to American designs. This was, however, a step that the Soviets appeared unwilling and perhaps technically unprepared to take.[17] The resultant impasse on this issue carried over into the related deadlock on the question of how to achieve equitable MIRV limitations.

## THE MIRV ISSUE

The issue of MIRV limitations was rejoined in SALT II. It had been set aside in the earlier SALT I negotiations, in part because the Soviet Union was then intent on closing the gap in MIRV technology and did not want to entertain agreements that could constrain its development and testing programs. Kissinger had brought out this point in a congressional briefing on June 15, 1972: "We offered a verifiable ban on the development and testing of multiple independent reentry vehicles. The Soviets countered by offering a totally unverifiable production ban, while insisting on the freedom to test, thus placing the control of MIRVs effectively out of reach."[18]

One might recall that in SALT I the Soviets had similarly rejected a proposed U.S. definition of "heavy missile" as any missile exceeding seventy cubic meters in volume, because they were aware at the time that it would have precluded the deployment of the new SS-19 and SS-17 missiles they were in the process of developing as carriers for their future MIRV warheads.[19] In much the same sense, once Soviet development programs began to reach fruition in 1973 in a "true" MIRV technology and in a new family of missiles,[20] the Soviet Union still faced the problem of forestalling agreements that could curb the process of translating this technology into deployed forces of MIRVed missiles. A desire to retain maximum freedom of action during the MIRV deployment phase ahead would seem to account in large part for the evident reluctance of the Soviet side to treat as negotiable the various MIRV limitation proposals offered by the United States in SALT II prior to the Vladivostok summit, although other differences stemming from the terms of the proposals themselves were also probably involved.

The precise history of the exchanges between the two sides on MIRV limitations in SALT II cannot be reconstructed from the available accounts, but apparently the Soviets kept their own views on the subject to themselves until around the fall of 1973, after the initial Soviet testing programs had proved successful. On the American side, how many MIRV limitation proposals had been advanced in SALT II in the period before Kissinger's trip to Moscow in March 1974 also is not known, nor have their specific terms been disclosed. However, beginning with the stepping up of back-channel activity that preceded the Kissinger trip in March,[21] and after the trip itself, more information on the MIRV issue gradually found its way into print.

Reportedly, a new U.S. proposal was laid before the top Soviet leadership in March by Dr. Kissinger, in the hope that it might provide a "conceptual breakthrough" on the complex issue of MIRV limitations. The gist of the proposal was that the United States would be prepared to limit its own further planned MIRV deployment[22] as part of an agreement limiting each side to a roughly equal amount of throwweight in deployed MIRV missiles.[23] At the same time, in order to separate the MIRV case from the overall throwweight problem, there would be no payload limit on missiles without MIRV—a concession calculated to appease Soviet objections to any kind of throwweight restriction. And bomber payload would also not be limited—a provision relatively favorable to the United States.[24]

The Kissinger proposal was turned down, and the Soviets countered with one of their own after Marshal Grechko had been recalled from a trip abroad for consultation.[25] The content of this counterproposal was not disclosed in detail, but what was made known gave the first public indication of the Soviet position on MIRV limitations. The salient point, consistent with the Soviet attitude toward throwweight restrictions, was that MIRVed missiles should be limited by number rather than throwweight.[26] Roughly equal numbers of MIRVed launchers on both sides would be permitted[27]—but how many the Russians had in mind was not publicly revealed on this occasion.

There were hints after Kissinger's return from Moscow that the Soviet side displayed "a little bit of give" on MIRV in their counterproposal,[28] but the nature of this give was not spelled out. Later, it was reported that the Soviets had proposed 1000 MIRVed launchers for themselves and 1100 for the United States, with no throwweight limit.[29] But at the time this offer failed to resolve the MIRV issue, the nub of which remained that a given throwweight limit would permit the United States, with smaller missiles, to maintain a lead in numbers of MIRVed missiles and warheads, whereas a given numerical ceiling on MIRVed launchers would allow the Soviet Union to convert its great throwweight advantage into a large number of warheads with much more explosive power per warhead.

As indicated about three months later by the results of the 1974 Moscow summit, the two sides again were unable to find common ground on the MIRV issue, even though the U.S. side in the course of the talks retreated from its previous stand that MIRV limitations should be based on throwweight rather than numbers of MIRVed launchers.[30] The exact sequence and nuances of the MIRV proposals exchanged at the summit cannot be documented, but according to several informed accounts, the general picture was roughly as follows:

A revised set of American proposals, embodying not only specific numbers but also a supporting rationale, was placed before the Russians. Both sides would limit the number of their MIRVed missile launchers, but since throwweight was no longer to be restricted, the agreed numbers should favor the U.S. side. Reportedly, the proposed figures were: for the United States, its then programmed total of about 1050 ICBM and SLBM launchers; for the Soviet Union, from 550 to 700 MIRVed launchers.[31]

In addition, it was proposed that both sides should begin to phase out some of their land-based missiles with single warheads, as a move toward placing greater reliance on submarine-launched missiles. The reported rationale behind this suggestion was that SLBMs lacked the accuracy to knock out hardened, land-based ICBMs, which were vulnerable mainly to ICBMs of the opposing side; hence, some movement toward the phasing out of land-based missiles would reduce concern on both sides about a first-strike threat. It would also be a step toward reduction in the overall number of missiles on both sides.[32]

As in the case of previous U.S. MIRV proposals, the Soviets again turned down this American approach to solution of the MIRV problem, claiming that it would penalize the Soviet Union, which had chosen to put greater emphasis upon land-based missiles than upon SLBMs, and that it would increase the importance of long-range bombers in which the United States had the lead.[33] Brezhnev and representatives from the Soviet General Staff were said to have presented an assessment of the American strategic arsenal that so overstated U.S. superiority in advanced MIRVed missiles and bombers that it "took the American participants by surprise."[34] The Soviets also criticized the "retargeting program" associated with U.S. Secretary of Defense James Schlesinger as meaning that nuclear war was a possibility, and expressed the view that the United States was seeking a first-strike capability that would disarm the Soviet Union.[35] Apparently on the basis of this "worst case" Soviet analysis of the U.S. posture, Brezhnev also indicated that the Soviet Union was committed to following through on the programs for equipping its newer missiles with MIRV warheads.

On the specific question of a numbers limit on MIRVed missile launchers, Brezhnev reportedly rejected the differential ceilings proposed by President Nixon and set the bottom figure for the Soviet side at "about a thousand missiles."[36] Since this was approximately the number the Soviets could be expected to achieve anyway by 1980 under their own unilateral deployment programs,[37] the implication to be drawn, as expressed by an unnamed American official involved in the Moscow talks, was that the Russians "were not prepared to accept any limits on their planned rate of MIRV deployment."[38]

Although Soviet sources in Moscow were said to have indicated that a deadlock over the permissible number of MIRVed missiles accounted "primarily" for failure to reach a MIRV limitation agreement,[39] other issues, such as the kinds of missiles on which multiple warheads could be installed, may also have been involved. However, if sublimits similar to those applied to large missiles in SALT I[40] had been proposed and rejected during the Moscow talks, no details on this putative area of disagreement were made known.

In a press conference in Moscow, at the close of the mid-1974 summit, Dr. Kissinger dwelt at length on the unresolved MIRV issue, warning that effective controls on MIRV deployment must be achieved "well before 1977," if there were not to be "an explosion of technology and an explosion of numbers at the end of which we will be lucky if we have the present stability, in which it will be impossible to describe what strategic superiority means."[41] Kissinger expressed the hope that the revised overall approach to SALT adopted at the summit might relieve some of the pressure on the Soviets to press rapidly ahead with their deployment of MIRVs and thereby have the effect of allowing negotiating leeway "of about eighteen months to gain control of the multiple warheads . . . by introducing some stability into the rate and nature of their deployment."[42]

On the same occasion, Kissinger offered his much-quoted admonition that "both sides have to convince their military establishments of the benefits of restraint, and this is not a thought that comes naturally to military people on either side." Whether the weight of military influence on SALT decisions was necessarily as symmetrical as implied by this observation, or whether diplomatic tact simply dictated equal treatment,[43] Kissinger seemed to be suggesting that the prospects for resolution of the MIRV issue might be advanced if Brezhnev and his political colleagues were to take the making of Soviet strategic policy more firmly into their own hands.[44] Implicit in such a suggestion, in turn, would seem to have been the assumption that Brezhnev and at least some of his political partners were disposed to entertain a less adamant and inflexible position on MIRV than the Soviet marshals, but had found it expedient for one reason or another to defer to the opinion of the military.

The soundness of such an assumption, however, remained difficult to establish even in light of the subsequent MIRV deal reached at Vladivostok. On the one hand, possibly it was more persuasive assertion of authority by the Kremlin political leaders over the military that had something to do with reaching agreement on numbers of MIRV launchers at Vladivostok. On the other hand, the nature of that agreement may have largely answered to the position espoused by the Soviet military professionals anyway, allowing the MIRVing of a substantial part of their missile force as rapidly as Soviet capacity to do so would permit. But in any event, these are matters to be addressed more fully later in the discussion of the Vladivostok transaction.

## THE FBS ISSUE

The FBS issue involving American forward-based systems represented one of the major unresolved problems of SALT I and re-emerged in SALT II as a critical area of disagreement, though it apparently received comparatively little attention at the 1974 Moscow summit talks, where other issues, especially MIRV, dominated the SALT discussion. To set the FBS issue in perspective, it was first raised early in SALT I when the Soviets insisted that American forward-based tactical aircraft capable of delivering nuclear weapons on Soviet territory from NATO airfields or aircraft carriers must be included in any limitations on strategic forces.[45] The basic Soviet position called for withdrawal of FBS, or short of this, for counting FBS in any agreed aggregate total of U.S. strategic forces.[46] The latter would have had the effect of reducing the permissible total of American ICBMs, SLBMs, and heavy bombers—the central strategic systems that the U.S. side considered the first order of business in SALT. Since the number of U.S. tactical aircraft in the European area alone subject to such an FBS tradeoff might run from around 600 to 1000, the resultant impact on the central strategic balance would have been far from trivial, the more so in view of the fact that the Soviet Union also claimed that its own 650-odd medium-range and intermediate-range missiles (MR/IRBM) targeted against Europe, as well as its force of some 700 medium-range strategic bombers, were exempt from SALT consideration because they could not reach American territory.[47]

The alternative of FBS withdrawal was an even more contentious question because it would involve the credibility of standing American commitments to NATO defense. This withdrawal proposal was in effect the extension of Soviet demands for elimination of foreign military bases around the Soviet periphery that long antedated SALT itself.

Under the joint compromise of May 20, 1971, arranged through the back channel, the FBS issue was temporarily set aside in SALT I while both parties worked toward the initial SALT accords of May 1972.[48] Even though ostensibly shelved, however, the issue was not entirely dormant. In at least a tacit sense, the Soviet Union's claim that it deserved compensation for "geographic and other considerations,"[49] which would seem to include FBS, appears to have been taken partly into account in the differential ceilings of the Interim Agreement favoring the Soviet side of ICBM and SLBM numbers. In a more explicit sense, the U.S. concern to sidetrack the FBS issue in negotiations beyond SALT I was reflected in Article 12 of the "Basic Principles" of relations between the United States and the USSR, signed in Moscow on May 29, 1972, which recognized the point that bilateral agreements between the two countries should not affect obligations "earlier assumed" toward other countries.[50]

Any expectation that a summit declaration on the principle of prior obligations to allies might serve to ward off Soviet pressure upon the United States for FBS withdrawal from Europe was not borne out, however, when SALT II resumed. Despite reaffirmation of this principle at the Washington summit in June 1973,[51] the Soviet SALT negotiators returned to their earlier insistence that no comprehensive agreement on the balance of strategic offensive arms could be reached without taking into account forward-based U.S. systems.[52] The Soviet FBS position was said to have included demands for dismantling U.S. SLBM bases at Holy Loch in Scotland and Rota in Spain, as well as for restricting the number of aircraft carriers permitted to operate in European waters.[53] At the same time, while insisting that the American FBS potential must be factored into the strategic balance, the Soviets continued to argue that neither their own medium-range missile and bomber forces, which could be used against Europe, nor their submarine-launched cruise missile (SLCM) forces, which could attack coastal areas of the United States,[54] were proper matters for negotiation in SALT.

Although the available accounts indicate that the FBS issue remained a major roadblock during the pre-Vladivostok phase of SALT II, there has been a dearth of information about specific FBS proposals advanced by either side. This makes it difficult to judge whether the Soviet Union saw fit in this period to soften its basic position in any way, or whether the U.S. side—which, in the view of some observers, had "little left to bargain with, save FBS," after SALT I[55]—gave ground in the FBS issue. Similarly, not much has been disclosed about any exchanges at the summit on FBS. Among the few indications that the issue may have come up at the 1974 summit in Moscow was a later public statement by Brezhnev that the Soviet Union still favored "the withdrawal from the Mediterranean of all Soviet and U.S. ships carrying nuclear weapons."[56]

Brezhnev's statement came during a July 21, 1974, speech in Warsaw, in a passage assessing the work of the July summit. It was not clear at the time whether he was referring to a proposal made at the summit or earlier, but other Soviet sources subsequently indicated that at the summit Brezhnev had indeed proposed withdrawal of nuclear units from the Mediterranean, a proposal that "unfortunately" was not accepted.[57]

In U.S. press accounts speculating on this point, Washington "observers" were reported to have said that a similar proposal had been part of an earlier Soviet FBS package offered in SALT, and that in a counterproposal the U.S. side had suggested that the whole FBS issue "should be dealt with separately in an overall negotiation on tactical nuclear weapons."[58] This appears to have been the first public hint that transfer of the FBS issue to a third negotiating forum separate from both SALT and mutual balanced force reductions (MBFR) had been broached as a possible way out of the FBS impasse.

Once the SALT II objective of a permanent agreement on strategic offensive arms had been abandoned at the mid-1974 summit, the question of how adamantly the Soviet side might stick to its position on FBS seemed to hinge largely on the nature and strength of the motivations behind Soviet FBS demands.

One set of motivations was clearly political. It had been a long-time aim of Soviet diplomacy in Europe to keep Western unity fragmented—an interest served in several ways by the divisive impact of the FBS issue on U.S.-NATO relations. Through insistence upon FBS withdrawal as the price of bilateral agreement in SALT, the Soviets could hope not only to degrade the U.S. military presence in Europe, but also to play upon the "decoupling" anxieties felt by many Europeans. In Soviet eyes, FBS withdrawal would also deprive the United States of an important part of the leverage it was assumed to rely upon to "enforce" policy unity upon otherwise centrifugal European tendencies. On the other hand, these advantages were somewhat offset by the possibility that FBS withdrawal might stimulate the emergence of a West European nuclear force—a development about which the Soviets had shown some concern.

Another set of Soviet motivations doubtless sprang from military considerations—of which the underlying one appeared to be to try to limit potential damage to the Soviet Union. In the FBS case, what might be called a philosophy of "damage-limitation by negotiation" was to be served by pushing back threats, especially nuclear, as far from Soviet territory as possible. The argument advanced by American negotiators that forward-based U.S. aircraft were tied to the defense of Europe and that they posed no substantial strategic threat to the USSR[59] probably was discounted by Soviet military planners. If so, their professional advice to the Soviet leadership seemed likely to reinforce the latter's apparent belief that the Soviet Union was justified in seeking to eliminate the double standard applying to overseas bases and "encirclement" of homeland territory.

A third motivating purpose behind the Soviet attitude toward FBS appeared to fall in what might be called the instrumental category, in which the issue is used primarily as a negotiating device. This appears to have been the case in the earlier phases of SALT I, when the Soviets were still in the process of building up both the image and the substance of their strategic offensive forces, and FBS was interposed to hold off serious negotiation on these forces. Instrumental use of the FBS issue might also be seen in the negotiating tactics meant to persuade the U.S. side to accept Interim Agreement differentials favoring the Soviet Union as partial "compensation" for U.S. forward systems.

Whether Soviet FBS demands were to be seen as primarily driven by the kinds of political and military considerations noted above, or whether they were regarded as essentially instrumental, the view held by many informed observers of the SALT process was that no Soviet agreement on central strategic systems could be expected so long as the FBS withdrawal issue remained unsettled.[60] It came, therefore, as a considerable surprise that the Soviet side later proved amenable at Vladivostok to dropping its insistence on prior satisfaction of its long-standing FBS claims.

## UNDERLYING CONCEPTUAL DIFFERENCES

In addition to the specific issues noted above, the first two years of fruitless negotiations in SALT II also underscored a number of conceptual differences between the two parties. These differences in what might be called the "strategic culture"[61] of the two sides concerned both their respective approaches to strategic power and their understanding of what kind of strategic relationship SALT might help to bring about. It was by no means self-evident that underlying differences of strategic philosophy were all that stood—or might continue to stand—in the way of a mutually acceptable and durable set of SALT agreements; nevertheless, the conceptual gap could hardly be dismissed as inconsequential.

One aspect of this gap, which had shown up in SALT I and apparently persisted in SALT II, was the lack of a common conception of strategic stability and of what might be required to preserve it.[62] In essence, the SALT II dialogue indicated that the

Soviets had not come to embrace the same functional strategic logic that characterized the American approach to stabilizing the strategic balance.

The U.S. side, for its part, repeatedly sought to establish the importance of offensive force survivability and penetration capability of offensive forces as the cardinal elements contributing to mutual deterrence and a stable strategic relationship, and especially to "crisis stability." Indeed, the U.S. case for replacing the Interim Agreement with a new permanent agreement turned on the argument that perpetuation of the IA differential force levels could, in the course of time, and in combination with technological advance by the Soviet Union, threaten the survivability of U.S. offensive deterrent forces and thus functionally upset strategic stability, no matter what the intentions of the respective parties and their adherence to high-sounding principles might be. For their part, Soviet spokesmen emphasized that strict observance of such principles as "equal security" and "no unilateral advantage" would produce a stable situation, which in turn would automatically assure survivability of deterrent forces.

Although the Soviets could be judged sensitive to the survivability issues as it concerned their own forces, they apparently again, as in SALT I, could not be moved to agree that *mutual* survivability of offensive forces would be good for the security of both parties[63] and hence was a matter that deserved priority in working out the substance of a permanent agreement to replace the Interim Agreement. Rather, the proposals they advanced in the pre-Vladivostok phase of SALT II evidently would have had the practical effect, if adopted, of constraining U.S. ICBMs to a numerical level insufficient to threaten the viability of the Soviet ICBM force; of keeping U.S. SLBMs and carrier aircraft out of range of Soviet territory; and of allowing the USSR to develop and deploy an improved strategic delivery force capable of placing U.S. land-based deterrent forces in jeopardy. In short, rather than serving to enhance the confidence of both sides in the viability of offensive deterrence by showing concern for the mutual survivability of offensive forces, the Soviet approach might be labeled "unilaterally assured survivability,"[64] leaving one to judge that their proposals were still informed by a conception differing from that which underlay the U.S. SALT approach.

Such a judgment, one may note, need not imply that the self-serving character of the Soviet approach made it somehow less worthy than that espoused by the U.S. side. It simply recognizes that in their strategic behavior the Soviets were, and seemingly continue to be, dominated primarily by concern for their own security and how to eliminate perceived or potential threats to it, rather than by a brand of thought congenial to the notion that a stable military-strategic relationship with the adversary might be constructed on the basis of each side's being solicitous of the other's security concerns.[65]

Perhaps the key area of divergence in the strategic philosophies of the two sides that seemed to remain unbridged in SALT II lay in the differing American and Soviet approaches to the nuclear-age dilemma of deterrence versus warfighting and survival strategies. In the United States, the prevailing tendency for some years had been to resolve this dilemma primarily in favor of mutual deterrence—by maintaining a capability to inflict massive retaliatory punishment on the society of an attacking opponent and conceding the other side the ability to do the same. The concept underlying this approach was what came to be known in the American strategic lexicon as mutual assured destruction,[66] a concept further implying that willingness to accept mutual vulnerability would offer the best assurance of strategic stability.

Strongly influenced by the game-theoretic approach of American academic strategists, this concept of deterrence also was rooted in the proposition that nuclear war would be unwinnable in any meaningful political sense. Although amended criteria for strategic force size and design began to be advanced in 1974 after James R. Schlesinger became secretary of defense (as we shall take up later),[67] it seems fair to say that throughout SALT I and at least the first part of SALT II the mutual assured destruction concept formed the central axis of consensus for the making of major strategic posture and arms control decisions in the United States.

The Soviet Union, on the other hand, though no less dedicated than the United States to the desirability of deterring a nuclear attack, had long seemed reluctant to peg its security to a concept akin to mutual assured destruction. Rather, Soviet strategic thought was characterized not only by its antipathy toward a "deterrence-only" strategic posture, but by the persistent doctrine that the Soviet Union should seek "balanced forces," backed by an extensive civil defense system, enabling it to wage war and at the same time limit damage to the Soviet homeland, thus improving the chances of national survival if deterrence should fail.[68]

In essence, the Soviet prescription for deterrence has been that the better the armed forces are prepared to fight and win a nuclear war, and the society to survive its effects, and the more clearly the adversary understands this, the more effectively will he be deterred. This approach has sometimes been labeled "deterrence through denial"—that is, denying the adversary the prospect of a successful military outcome, in contrast to the American conception of deterrence through retributive punishment.[69]

The conceptual gulf between these two approaches runs rather deep. Whatever its shortcomings as an answer to the problem of nuclear-age security, the notion of mutual assured destruction has had the virtue of being functionally compatible with both strategic stability and arms control objectives. This is so, essentially, because it is a much less demanding military task to put the opponent's society in jeopardy than to protect one's own. In effect, the knee of the megatonnage-fatalities curve has suggested itself as a posturally "sufficient" and conceptually convenient point at which two strategic competitors can come to rest,[70] that is, if both accept the idea of living indefinitely with what is often described as "the balance of terror."

By contrast, the Soviet strategic philosophy as promulgated hitherto has appeared functionally incompatible with finding any clear stopping points and striking an equilibrium. Given the woeful "softness" of populations, a nation whose doctrine seeks substantial survival levels for its own society in addition to assured destruction of its opponent places before itself extremely demanding force requirements. So long as this should remain its operational goal, therefore, Soviet doctrine would seem to represent a mandate for endless competition without defined standards of what constitutes enough—short of massive damage-limiting superiority, which would probably be unachievable unless the adversary were to quit trying altogether.

Patently, it would be an exaggeration to say that Soviet strategic policy has been governed simply by this driving doctrinal mandate. Many other considerations and constraints have tempered translation of the doctrine into policy. At the same time, it is worth noting that both the Soviet military and political leaders have had cause for not lightly discarding it. In the military case, the reasons are fairly obvious. Psychologically and institutionally, the military professionals have found congenial a doctrine that justifies generous defense budgets, stresses the traditional goals of defending the country in the event of war, and seems to assign them a meaningful role if such a test should occur.

The outlook of the political leadership, one must assume, has been more ambivalent. Lacking the institutional stakes of the military in the doctrine, Brezhnev and his Politburo colleagues have probably been more free to ponder the benefits, economic or otherwise, of a less-demanding strategic philosophy. But they, too, have had their own investment in a doctrinal consensus calling for more than deterrent sufficiency.[71] The Soviet strategic buildup since Krushchev's day serves as a case in point. Though one may judge that the buildup remains somewhere short of providing an adequate warfighting and survival posture, its political payoff can hardly have failed to impress the Politburo chieftains. The buildup not only gave the Soviet Union greater room for diplomatic maneuver. More specifically, it also "sobered" the American "imperialists," led them to concede that containment of the USSR was a bankrupt strategy, and impelled them to seek adjustment of long-standing issues through negotiation instead of confrontation.[72] Thus, on both the military and political sides of the Soviet establishment, there appears to have been a built-in bias toward perpetuating a doctrine that says in effect that further accretion, or "banking" of strategic power makes policy sense, even though it may seem to offer no logical end point for strategic competition.[73]

## THE ABM TREATY AND THE QUESTION
## OF CONCEPTUAL CONVERGENCE

Despite such underlying conceptual differences as those mentioned above, the view gained ground in the early 1970s that a process of basic convergence in the strategic philosophies of the United States and the Soviet Union was taking place, not only as a parallel to Soviet attainment of strategic parity, but as a result of the SALT experience and other factors.[74]

Chiefly responsible no doubt for the assumption that the Soviet Union was "converging" toward American strategic precepts was the ABM Treaty, which many interpreted as evidence that the Soviet Union had come to realize that ABM systems were destabilizing, and had therefore accepted a concept of mutual deterrence based on holding each other's populations hostage to nuclear retaliation.[75] As others saw it, a Soviet-American strategic relationship based on mutual deterrence had come into being even before SALT began, but both sides had finally agreed to formalize and stabilize this relationship in a treaty barring the building of nationwide defenses against ICBM attack only after deciding that there was no realistic expectation that either country could achieve an effective ABM defense of its territory and population.[76]

In any case, whether or not signing of the ABM Treaty meant that the Soviets had recognized the futility of their traditional search for a viable strategic defense of the Soviet homeland (a point to which we shall return later),[77] the question here is what else the treaty may have signified in the way of change in the Soviet strategic outlook. Did it mean, for example, that the Soviet side had indeed come around to embrace the American concept of mutual assured destruction as an appropriate basis for structuring its own strategic forces and for maintaining mutual deterrence?

Unfortunately, the question is more easily put than answered. One ought first, perhaps, to point out that renunciation of countrywide ABM went only part way toward acceptance of the mutual assured destruction concept. The other key element of that concept is a tender concern for the *mutual* survivability of offensive deterrent forces, without which a contract of shared societal vulnerability would have little meaning. Neither in SALT I nor in subsequent negotiations had the Soviets shown an interest in other than what might be called "unilaterally assured survivability" of offensive forces.[78] Although obviously interested in improving the survivability of its own forces through such steps as hardening on land and mobility at sea, the Soviet Union certainly had not seen fit to eschew measures that would threaten the survivability of the adversary's forces. Unlike the United States, for instance, the Soviets had never gone to a declaratory policy of restricting delivery accuracy in order to avoid posing a counterforce threat to the other side.[79]

On conceptual grounds, another point worth noting is that despite the signing of the ABM Treaty, the Soviets continued to reject the idea of security based on the "balance of terror," a notion inherent in doctrines of shared liability like that of mutual assured destruction. As stated in June 1972 by N.N. Inozemtsev, director of one of the Soviet institutes concerned with studies of strategic and foreign affairs,[80] "the concept that a lasting peace can be ensured by a 'balance of terror' has always been alien to our state."[81] This sentiment was seconded by G.A. Arbatov, director of the parallel Institute of the USA, who wrote in February 1974: "The concept of deterrence itself cannot be defended—it is a concept of 'peace built on terror,' which will always be an unstable and a bad peace."[82]

Neither apparent Soviet indifference to the mutual survivability of retaliatory forces nor disparaging comments on the balance of terror are alone enough to lead one to conclude that the ABM Treaty left the Soviet side unreceptive to the concept of mutual assured destruction, but other evidence of a negative character also seemed to point in this direction. For example, Soviet military literature published after the ABM Treaty came into effect yielded no signs that a new rationale for Soviet strategic forces might be taking shape around a concept like that of mutual assured destruction.

On the contrary, military leaders and theorists continued as before to dwell both upon the importance of strategic defense and upon a prescription for strategic offensive forces stressing their ability to knock out the opponent's strategic delivery means. In Soviet discussions of strategic defense, the ABM Treaty for the most part was simply ignored. When mentioned, no forecast of its impact on strategic defense was offered. The main themes, as prior to the treaty, were that "it is essential to carry out complex measures" to protect the Soviet Union "against enemy strikes" and to ensure "the survivability of the country and the armed forces."[83] In discussions of strategic offense, the dominant themes remained unchanged from those sounded by Marshal Grechko prior to the ABM Treaty, as when he wrote in 1971 that "the Strategic Rocket Forces . . . are intended for destruction of the enemy's means of nuclear attack, his large troop formations and military bases . . . his defense industry, and for disruption of command and control, operations of the rear, and transportation."[84] Thus, Soviet military leaders continued to allude to the specific counterforce role of the SRF as the "chief strike force" to "destroy the enemy's main nuclear-missile weapons and troop formations."[85]

If the ABM Treaty had stirred up a reappraisal of the pretreaty premises of Soviet strategic doctrine, it obviously was not apparent in such expressions as these. Indeed, if any effects of the treaty were to be read into Soviet strategic thinking as reflected in the available military literature, the most likely implication would seem to be that the treaty had given Soviet strategic planners fresh reason for counting upon counterforce systems as the most effective means of carrying out the damage-limitation mission traditionally close to their hearts. That the link between counterforce and damage limitation was an explicit one in Soviet thinking is suggested by the following statement in a Soviet radio broadcast of August 5, 1970, on civil defense activities: "The most effective means of defending the country's population are effective actions aimed at destroying the enemy's offensive weapons both in the air and on the ground at their bases. Missile troops—the new type of armed forces—play a major role in the destruction of the enemy's offensive weapons."[86]

Given such obvious Soviet interest in counterforce, one might even speculate that the ABM Treaty had been seen by at least some Soviet planners as a useful device for enhancing the counterforce potential of Soviet strategic systems, insofar as it placed strict limits on U.S. protection of launch sites and control centers, which would be a good deal easier to defend by ABM than cities.[87]

To sum up, then, the question of strategic convergence, a set of somewhat contrary possibilities emerges. On the one hand, although the doctrinal content of published Soviet military discourse under post-treaty conditions suggested little shift toward such U.S. concepts as mutual assured destruction and functional strategic stability, it did not necessarily follow that Soviet strategic thinking would remain unchangeably set in its traditional groove. The SALT experience itself, for example, may have helped to dilute the military's virtual monopoly on strategic thought,[88] and perhaps sensitized important segments of Soviet officialdom to think in terms of a stabilization of the arms competition along lines hitherto given scant place in Soviet strategic doctrine. In effect, the ABM Treaty could have marked a real watershed in Soviet strategic thinking, even though formal expression of a revised rationale for Soviet strategic forces was yet to appear.

On the other hand, however, the very notion that strategic convergence would be basically a matter of the Soviet side's coming to accept American conceptual tutelage was perhaps way off the mark, reflecting a certain ethnocentric conceit.[89] Aside from the nature of Soviet strategic programs, which themselves were not attuned to concepts like mutual assured destruction,[90] in SALT the Soviets had advanced no proposals, as pointed out by Colin Gray, that would have contributed to the American understanding of strategic stability.[91]

Further, one of the salient effects of the SALT experience on the Soviet leaders might have been to sensitize them—not to the logic of mutual assured destruction—but to the multiplier effect of negotiations on the political value of strategic forces. In an era of power bargaining with one's adversary, these forces tended to become instruments through which gains were to be won at the negotiating table—a point not likely to have escaped a leadership already persuaded that its investment in strategic power should yield returns other than deterrence alone.

But beyond this, perhaps the most discomfiting possibility of all was that convergence might come down in the last analysis, not to emulation of U.S. strategic precepts, but, as remarked by Benjamin Lambeth, to a "growing degree of congruence" between the Soviet Union's own long-held strategic doctrine and the emerging Soviet strategic posture in the mid-1970s.[92] We shall turn in the next chapter to the evolution of this strategic posture in the SALT era.

# Chapter 6

# Evolution of the Soviet Strategic Posture in the SALT Era

By the end of 1978, the Soviet Union had been engaged for a decade and a half in an extraordinarily persistent effort to increase its military power. A goodly share of this effort, and the part of it in which we are most interested here, had gone into strengthening of the Soviet strategic posture through both quantitative expansion and qualitative improvement of Soviet strategic delivery forces and strategic defenses.

If the momentum of Soviet strategic programs before May 1972 might logically have been attributed in large part to an imperative to catch up with the United States, thereafter it became less explicable in terms of catching up than as a drive to forge ahead in various aspects of strategic competition. At any rate, because of the continuing momentum of the Soviet military buildup after SALT I—and under the detente conditions of the mid-1970s—questions obviously arose about what ends it might be intended to serve.[1] Several explanations could be offered.

Were one to take a sanguine view of the situation, for example, it could be said that Soviet military expansion was perhaps meant primarily to buttress the USSR's negotiating posture en route to binding agreements with the United States aimed at stabilizing the overall power relationship between the two. If so, then it was possible that the Soviet military buildup had finally peaked, and that one was merely witnessing a kind of wrap-up process through which the Soviet leadership hoped to establish a durable detente relationship involving among other things a negotiated status of military equality with the United States.

From a less sanguine viewpoint, it could be argued that the Soviet leadership looked upon detente and arms control negotiations merely as tactical modalities intended to earn a "breathing spell" for the Soviet Union. Once the Soviet military posture and the industrial base supporting it had been further strengthened, partly with the help of technological and economic transfusions from the West, the Soviet leadership might then opt for a new phase of systemic struggle in which it would hope to deal with the West from a superior power position.[2]

Or, as a third case somewhere between these two, it might be argued that the Soviet Union was orchestrating its approach in the SALT negotiations with its own unilateral strategic programs in a calculated attempt to checkmate U.S. strategic power and ensure a standoff at the level of strategic nuclear forces, perhaps so as to allow greater freedom of action for pursuit of Soviet advantage in various regional arenas of competition—in Europe, the Middle East, Africa, and elsewhere.

Which of these explanations—or still others that might be proffered—gave the most plausible rationale for the Soviet strategic buildup was a debatable matter that remained unsettled as SALT II proceeded. Whatever the underlying rationale may have been, however, our purpose in this chapter is less to speculate on why the Soviet strategic posture evolved as it did than to describe briefly how it did so.

## STRATEGIC OFFENSIVE PROGRAMS

The growth of Soviet strategic offensive forces for selected years from 1964 to 1978 is shown in Table 6-1 on page 117. Like the United States, the Soviet Union had chosen to develop a triad of intercontinental delivery forces—land-based ICBMs, seaborne SLBMs, and bombers. The mix of these forces in the Soviet strategic arsenal, however, differed considerably from the U.S. case, as may be seen by referring to the comparative force levels in Table 5-1 (p. 97). In the Soviet scheme of priorities, the principal emphasis was given to land-based ICBMs of the Strategic Rocket Forces (SRF).[3]

### Land-based ICBMs

Five different ICBM systems, some of which existed in several variants, were to be found in the deployed inventory of the SRF at the time the SALT I accords were reached.[4] Except possibly for a

Table 6-1

**Growth of Soviet Intercontinental Delivery Forces, 1964-1978**

**(Selected Years)**

| | 1964 | 1970 | 1972 | 1974 | 1975 | 1978 |
|---|---|---|---|---|---|---|
| Intercontinental Ballistic Missiles (ICBM) | | | | | | |
| SS-7, SS-8 | 200 | 220 | 210 | 210 | 210 | 30 |
| SS-9 | 0 | 240 | 290 | 290 | 290 | 220 |
| SS-11 | 0 | 800 | 970 | 1015[a] | 1020 | 730 |
| SS-13 | 0 | 40 | 60 | 60 | 60 | 60 |
| SS-16 | ... | ... | ... | ... | ... | ? |
| SS-17 | ... | ... | ... | ... | ... | 60+ |
| SS-18 | ... | ... | ... | ... | 5 | 100+ |
| SS-19 | ... | ... | ... | ... | 5 | 200+ |
| Total: | 200 | 1300 | 1530 | 1575 | 1590 | 1400+[b] |
| Submarine-launched Ballistic Missiles (SLBM) | | | | | | |
| SS-N-4, SS-N-5 | 120 | 120 | 30[c] | 30 | 30 | 30 |
| SS-N-6 | 0 | 160 | 468[d] | 530 | 540 | 524 |
| SS-N-8 | 0 | 0 | 12 | 100 | 130 | 348 |
| SS-NX-17 | ... | ... | ... | ... | ... | 16 |
| SS-NX-18 | ... | ... | ... | ... | ... | 32 |
| Total: | 120 | 280 | 510 | 660 | 700 | 950 |
| Heavy bombers | | | | | | |
| TU-95 (Bear) | 120 | 100 | 100 | 100 | 100 | 100 |
| MYA-4 (Bison) | 40 | 40 | 40 | 40 | 40 | 40 |
| Backfire | 0 | 0 | 0 | (10)[e] | (20)[e] | (40)[e] |
| Total: | 160 | 140 | 140 | 140 | 140 | 140 |

Source: The numbers in this table, some of which have been rounded off, have been compiled from pertinent issues of *The Military Balance,* published annually by The International Institute for Strategic Studies, London, and from the annual reports and posture statements of U.S. secretaries of defense and the chairman of the Joint Chiefs of Staff.

[a]Increase reflects SS-11 Mod-3s being deployed in new "small silo" types. See Admiral Thomas H. Moorer, chairman, JCS, *U.S. Military Posture for FY 1975,* 1974, p. 18.

[b]Figures for 1978 reflect phasing-in of new ICBMs and phasing-out of old ones. See *Department of Defense Annual Report FY 1979, Harold Brown, Secretary of Defense,* February 2, 1978, pp. 49-50.

[c]Excludes launchers on G- and Z-class diesel submarines, not counted after May 1972 as "strategic missiles." See Moorer, ibid., p. 22.

[d]Does not include launchers "under construction" that were counted in the baseline figure of 740 SLBMs on nuclear submarines allowed the Soviet Union under the Interim Agreement of May 1972.

[e]Role of Backfire uncertain. Numbers shown in parentheses represent about half of estimated Backfire force, which may have intercontinental role. The heavy bomber totals exclude about fifty tankers.

handful of SS-9 and SS-11 missiles that had been modified to carry multiple (MRV), but not separately targetable, warheads, virtually all of the some 1500 ICBMs in this force were equipped with single warheads. Although the SS-11 was the most numerous ICBM in the Soviet arsenal, the SS-9 was about twice its size, and was of most concern to U.S. planners, primarily because of its counterforce potential against Minuteman launchers and control centers.[5]

With the signing of the SALT Interim Agreement of May 1972, the Soviet Union could be said to have brought the quantitative buildup of its land-based ICBM forces to a successful close. It then held a numerical lead of around 50 percent over the United States in ICBM launchers, and this margin was assured for at least the five-year life of the agreement. The sublimit of 313 heavy missiles imposed by the agreement—as well as the curtailment of new silo construction[6] — probably did represent constraints that Soviet planners would not find to their liking, but on the whole it would appear that the quantitative ceilings of the Interim Agreement were probably close to the ICBM levels at which the Soviets would have stopped of their own accord in the absence of a SALT transaction.[7]

In qualitative terms, the Soviet situation was obviously far less comfortable, for the American edge in MIRV technology and headstart in MIRV deployment conferred substantial advantages upon the United States in deliverable warheads.[8] Since the Interim Agreement established no serious impediments to qualitative improvement and modernization of ICBM forces on either side, it was to be expected that Soviet strategic planners would already have turned their attention in this direction.

What proved somewhat unexpected, however, was the scope and tempo of the Soviet follow-on missile programs after SALT I. In the ICBM field, four new missile systems were found to be in an advanced stage of testing by early 1974,[9] leading top U.S. defense officials to state at that time that the USSR had entered a new phase of "unprecedented major commitment" to the modernization of its strategic offensive forces on a scale "far more comprehensive than estimated even a year ago."[10]

The principal fourth-generation follow-on ICBMs were the SS-18, SS-19, and SS-17, each larger than the missile it was to replace, and the SS-16, a solid-fuel missile capable of mobile application in addition to silo emplacement. Some of the estimated characteristics of these missiles are shown in Table 6-2 on page 119. The new missiles were especially notable because they were associated with a true MIRV technology that the Soviet Union finally demonstrated in 1973, after earlier MRV programs had failed to close the qualitative

**Table 6-2**
**Fourth-Generation Soviet ICBM Systems**

| Specifications | SS-18 | SS-19 | SS-17 | SS-16 |
|---|---|---|---|---|
| Predecessor | SS-9 | SS-11 | SS-11 | SS-13 |
| Comparison to predecessor: | | | | |
| Size | larger | larger | larger | approx. the same |
| Throwweight | 1/3 more[a] | 4-5 times more[a] | 3-4 times more[a] | almost double[a] |
| Range (nautical miles) | +5500 | +5500 | +5500 | +5000 |
| Estimated MIRV warheads | 5-8 | 4-6 | 4 | ? |
| Single warhead version also | yes | yes | yes | yes |
| On-board digital computer | yes | yes | yes | yes |
| Accuracy[b] (CEP, n mi) | 0.20-0.25 | 0.20 | 0.3 | 0.25-0.3 |
| Silo type | new large or SS-9 | new small or SS-11 | new small or SS-11 | SS-13 or possibly mobile |
| First year of operational capability | 1974 | 1974 | 1975 | . . . . |

Source: Admiral Thomas H. Moorer, chairman, JCS, *U.S. Military Posture for FY 1975*, pp. 15-17; Testimony by Secretary of Defense James R. Schlesinger on March 4, 1974, in Hearing before the Subcommittee on Arms Control, International Law and Organization, Committee on Foreign Relations, Senate, Ninety-third Congress, Second Session, released April 4, 1974, pp. 5, 33, 43; *Report of Secretary of Defense James R. Schlesinger to the Congress on the FY 1976 and Transition Budgets and FY 1976-1980 Defense Program*, February 5, 1975, pp. II-12-14.

[a]According to unofficial data, the throwweight of the SS-18 is about 15,000 lbs; that of the SS-19 about 7000 lbs; the SS-17 about 6000 lbs; and the SS-16 about 2000 lbs. By comparison, the U.S. Minuteman III and Poseidon each has a throwweight of about 1200 lbs. See "The Deadly Calculus of MIRVing," *Newsweek*, July 8, 1974, p. 24; Colin S. Gray, "Soviet Rocket Forces: Military Capability, Political Utility," *Air Force Magazine*, March 1978, p. 52.

[b]No official figures on the accuracy of these specific missiles have been released. The estimates cited, from unofficial sources, are very approximate. See Gray, in *Air Force Magazine*, March 1978, p. 53; Paul H. Nitze, "Assuring Strategic Stability in an Era of Détente," *Foreign Affairs*, January 1976, p. 231.

gap between the United States and the USSR in the field of multiple reentry vehicles. The new Soviet MIRV, unlike earlier Soviet MRV systems, employed an on-board digital computer and a postboost vehicle (PBV) similar to what was known in the United States as a "bus-type" dispensing system.[11]

Except for the SS-16, the new missiles also proved to be linked with a silo-construction program, first identified in early 1971, involving some ninety silos of new and harder types.[12] Since construction of additional launch silos was ruled out by the May 1972 SALT accords, however, some readjustment of deployment plans evidently became necessary so that the new missiles could be accommodated in old silos housing the SS-9 and SS-11 force. This was done by adopting "cold-launch," or "pop-up," techniques, combined with some silo modification within the dimensional limits allowed by SALT I.[13]

Soviet determination to press ahead with deployment of the new fourth-generation missiles, coupled with insistence that such new U.S. strategic systems as Trident and B-1 should be banned, appears to have contributed to the general deadlock in the pre-Vladivostok phase of SALT II.[14] In late 1974 and early 1975, small numbers of the new Soviet ICBMs began to reach operational status, and by the beginning of 1978 their estimated total came to about 360—including 100 SS-18s, 200 SS-19s, and 60 SS-17s, most of which were MIRVed versions of these missiles.[15] At an observed deployment rate in 1978 of about 125 per year,[16] the ceiling of some 800 MIRVed ICBM launchers, which appeared to be the limit likely to be set in a post-Vladivostok SALT II agreement,[17] would be achievable in about three and a half years.

Parallel with deployment of the fourth-generation ICBMs, the phasing out of older missiles they were to replace commenced around the beginning of 1975.[18] Of the four new ICBM systems, only the solid-fuel SS-16[19] had not been observed in an operational deployment status. However, the land-mobile SS-20 IRBM—consisting of the first two stages of the three-stage SS-16 ICBM—had begun deployment by 1977. Although apparently intended to replace the old medium- and intermediate-range SS-4s and SS-5s in the SRF inventory, the SS-20 deployment became a growing source of concern in the West both because it was exempt from SALT limitations and because it could be converted in a relatively short time without assurance of detection into an SS-16 ICBM capability.[20]

Several other troubling issues had already been posed for U.S. defense officials after the scope and nature of the Soviet fourth-generation ICBM programs first began to become apparent in 1973. One issue, first aired by Secretary of Defense James R. Schlesinger in August 1973, centered around concern that the Soviet Union's new family of ICBMs might enable the USSR to "develop a clear preponderance of counterforce capabilities" that could threaten the prelaunch survivability of U.S. land-based deterrent forces.[21] Particular attention was focused upon the greatly increased throwweight of the new missiles which, according to Schlesinger, could give the Soviet Union within a decade from "10 to 12 million pounds of total ICBM throwweight," compared to about 2 million pounds for the American ICBM force.[22]

In turn, depending on the MIRVing options the Soviet Union

might adopt, this large amount of throwweight could be translated into 15,000 warheads or more,[23] although Schlesinger's view in March 1974 was that the Soviets might not choose to go beyond a MIRVing program that would give them some "7,000 to 8,000 one-to-two megaton reentry vehicles," compared with 2000 to 3000 warheads of smaller explosive yield on board Minuteman ICBMs.[24] But even if the Soviet ICBM force were not to exceed a level on the order of 7000 warheads, the "major one-sided counterforce capability against the United States ICBM force" that would accrue to the Soviet Union was, in Schlesinger's words, "impermissible from our point of view." There must be, he said, "essential equivalence between the strategic forces of the United States and the USSR—an equivalence perceived not only by ourselves, but by the Soviet Union and third audiences as well."[25]

Subsequently, the standard of "essential equivalence" was re-endorsed by both of Schlesinger's successors, Donald H. Rumsfeld and Harold Brown, with Brown stating in February 1978 that it was required of the United States "to insist on essential equivalence with the Soviet Union in strategic nuclear forces. Because of the stakes, no lesser requirement will do."[26]

Another matter of major strategic significance that came to the fore in connection with the fourth-generation Soviet ICBM programs concerned missile accuracy, since accuracy improvements would greatly increase the potential counterforce threat posed by the SRF in the future. Unlike the United States, which had abstained for several years from some programs to improve ICBM and SLBM accuracy in order not to appear to be mounting a threat to the survivability of Soviet land-based deterrent forces, the Soviet Union had never embraced a similar self-denying ordinance.[27] In some measure, this may have been due to a felt need on the part of the Soviets to refine their guidance technology, which had traditionally lagged behind that of the United States, as well as to differing conceptual approaches.

How successful the Soviets might be in developing more accurate guidance systems for their new family of MIRVed ICBMs was at first unclear. Some reports in 1974 suggested that the Soviets had been having difficulty in this area, especially with production techniques—helping to account for their interest in obtaining computers and other pertinent equipment from the United States—and that it might take them as much as eight to ten years to match the then-existing accuracies of U.S. ICBMs.[28]

Were this to be the case, the implications would be by no means trivial. For one thing, the Soviets might feel reluctant to enter agreements that could constrain their effort to catch up with the United States. Another implication would be that the counterforce potential of Soviet ICBM forces might evolve at a somewhat slower rate than their numbers and throwweight would otherwise permit, thus stretching out the period in which a Soviet counterforce threat to the U.S. Minuteman force would have to be seriously taken into account in U.S. strategic planning. In a sense, this would have tended toward repetition of what seemed to be a pattern of past experience, in which Soviet incorporation of advanced technologies into their strategic forces often proceeded more slowly than expected, whereas Soviet numerical deployments of strategic offensive forces usually turned out to be larger than anticipated.[29]

However, as more information on Soviet fourth-generation ICBM programs was acquired, it gradually appeared that accuracy improvements might be running ahead of earlier estimates. Unofficial accounts in 1973, for example, had given the SS-18 an accuracy within 0.5 nautical miles of the target.[30] A year later Secretary Schlesinger testified in closed session that Soviet ICBMs already had, or would soon achieve, accuracies of "about a fourth to a third of a nautical mile,"[31] and in February 1975 he said: "I should stress that the Soviet Union has made more rapid strides in accuracy than is generally appreciated, and has shown an intense interest in various applications of terminal guidance."[32]

Meanwhile, incidentally, it was of some interest that a high-ranking Soviet military officer chose to tell a U.S. military counterpart during the 1974 summit in Moscow that the United States was underestimating the accuracy of Russian missiles.[33] Reportedly, the American was told that Soviet missiles were accurate "to within 500 to 800 meters of the target," or about one-fourth to one-half mile.[34] The lower figure of 0.25-mile accuracy claimed by the Soviet officer represented, of course, a significantly better Soviet missile performance than the upper range of 0.5-miles, for a doubling of accuracy—or what amounts to the same thing, a halving of error—would equate to something like an eight to tenfold increase in target destruction potential.[35]

Precise figures on the accuracy improvements attained by the several fourth-generation Soviet ICBMs as these systems went through further testing and refinement in the 1975-1978 period were not forthcoming from either U.S. or Soviet official sources. Unofficial estimates appearing in the United States credited the SS-18 and the SS-19 with a CEP of from 0.20 to 0.25 nautical miles or even better, and the SS-17 was given a CEP of 0.30 nautical miles.[36] What was emphasized in the annual reports of U.S. secretaries of defense in this period, however, was growth of the threat to Minuteman survivability, partly attributable to improving accuracy along with greater yield of Soviet warheads. As stated by Secretary Brown in February 1978, "It is now clear that . . . with feasible accuracy improvements . . . a relatively small fraction of the current generation Soviet MIRVed ICBMs could, by the early to mid-1980s, reduce the number of surviving Minuteman to low levels."[3 7]

Beyond its fourth-generation family of ICBMs, meanwhile, the Soviet Union also was developing a fifth ICBM generation. As earlier disclosed in 1974, up to ten to twelve new Soviet missile systems, including both land- and sea-based types, were believed to be in the works, in addition to the fourth-generation systems then entering the deployment stage.[3 8] Out of this number, official U.S. estimates by 1978 placed the number of fifth-generation ICBM systems at four, of which at least two were expected to begin flight tests at any time, and which were likely to incorporate accuracy improvements over the fourth-generation systems.[3 9] What the deployment prospects might be for these upcoming fifth-generation ICBMs was yet to be learned, but at any rate there could be little doubt that the Soviet R&D establishment was continuing to operate at its own cyclical rhythm, little affected by SALT.

### Submarine-launched Ballistic Missiles (SLBM)

Although land-based ICBMs of the SRF were given top priority in the Soviet strategic buildup from the beginning, major effort also went into development of an SLBM force under the auspices of the Soviet Navy. This force began its first substantial period of growth following the introduction of a new class of nuclear-powered submarines, the Yankee or Y-class, in 1967.[4 0] Roughly comparable to the early U.S. Polaris-type submarine, the Y-class was fitted with sixteen tubes for submerged launch of the SS-N-6, a liquid-fueled ballistic missile with a range of 1300 nautical miles.

By the time the May 1972 SALT accords were signed, the Soviet Union, according to U.S. estimates, had twenty-nine of these submarines in operation and several more in various stages of assembly.[4 1] It had also begun to build a modified and enlarged version of the Y-class, known as the Delta-I class, the first unit of which was launched in 1972. This submarine, the largest built anywhere up to that time,[4 2] was also notable for carrying twelve SS-N-8 missiles, which were the longest-range SLBMs (4200 nautical miles) in service anywhere.

By U.S. reckoning, the total number of both classes of submarines either operational or under construction in early 1972 was forty-two, a figure disputed by the Soviets during final negotiation of the SALT I agreements in Moscow.[43] In any event, whatever the actual number of submarines and missile launchers in the Soviet SLBM force at that time, the SALT I accords left ample room for further numerical expansion and modernization of the force.[44] On both counts, the Soviet Union continued to move ahead after May 1972.

In quantitative terms, the Soviet Union managed to overtake the United States in numbers of operational launchers by mid-1974, having reached an estimated total of slightly more than 660 SLBMs at that time, compared to 656 for the United States.[45]

Approximately a year later the Soviets crossed another quantitative threshold when a newly launched SSBN, carrying their 741st launcher, began its sea trials. Under the terms of the 1972 SALT Interim Agreement, this was one beyond the baseline figure of 740 SLBMs, after which the Soviet Union was obliged to begin dismantling an equal number of old ICBMs or SLBMs on older submarines, and to notify the United States.[46]

By mid-1978, the Soviet Union had bumped up against the top SALT I ceiling for modern SSBNs, with sixty-two, and was virtually at the launcher limit of 950.[47] The composition of this force now stood at thirty-four Y-class SSBNs and twenty-eight larger units, about evenly divided between Delta-I and Delta-II and -III classes. Deployment of the last two classes had begun in 1973 and 1977, respectively.[48] Since additional Delta units were being constructed, reportedly along with the first of a still newer SSBN class called the Typhoon, believed comparable in size to the U.S. Trident,[49] it was apparent by late 1978 that retirement of some SSBN units, perhaps some of the early Y-class, would be necessary if the Soviet Union were to continue observing the extension of the SALT I Interim Agreement, pending a completed SALT II agreement.

Although the Soviet Union continued to lag behind the United States with regard to some qualitative and operational aspects of its SLBM force, such as having noisier submarines than the United States, longer overhaul periods, and customarily a smaller proportion of its force at sea (about 11 percent compared with 50 percent for the United States),[50] nevertheless the Soviet seaborne strategic missile potential underwent several important improvements after the May 1972 SALT accords. Deployment of the 4200-nautical-mile SS-N-8 on Delta-I and -II classes, for example, not only gave the USSR an operational jump of several years on the United States, which would not have an SLBM of comparable range at sea until 1979-1980;[51] it also gave the Soviet Union the capability of bringing

U.S. targets within firing range from relatively secure operating areas in protected northern waters close to Soviet territory, or even while still in port in Russia.[52]

Other Soviet modernization programs for the SLBM force promised to help close what had been an especially marked quality gap—that concerning MIRVed SLBMs. These had been widely introduced into American SSBNs since mid-1970,[53] whereas the Soviet Union had not demonstrated application of its new MIRV technology to submarine-launched missiles up to 1975.[54] In that year, however, testing of two new SLBM systems with MIRV attributes began. One was the SS-NX-17, the first Soviet solid-fuel SLBM, which employed a postboost vehicle (PBV) and thus appeared to be a candidate for a MIRV role.[55] A program to backfit this missile into Y-class submarines as a replacement for the SS-N-6 was reported to be taking place in 1977, with one Y-class unit so modified by early 1978.[56]

The second new SLBM was the SS-NX-18, a liquid-fuel system with an estimated range in excess of 4000 nautical miles. Equipped with PBV and a more sophisticated guidance system than other Soviet SLBMs, this missile was judged to have a true MIRV capability, probably for delivery of three warheads.[57] It appeared meant for employment in Delta-III ballistic missile submarines, and possibly for retrofitting in other Deltas.[58]

Perhaps one of the major questions facing Soviet planners by the end of 1978 with regard to further evolution of the Soviet SLBM force was whether to move a still greater share of the country's strategic offensive power to sea at the expense of the traditionally favored land-based ICBM forces. Strict observance of the temporarily prolonged May 1972 Interim Agreement would, of course, stand in the way of such a move, toward which a negative Soviet attitude apparently had prevailed up to the time of the mid-1974 summit in Moscow, as indicated by Soviet rejection on that occasion of U.S. suggestions to reduce land-based missiles in favor of greater reliance on SLBM forces.[59]

However, Soviet acceptance some two years later at Vladivostok of "freedom to mix" among sea-based and other strategic delivery systems could have presaged a shift of Soviet thinking on the issue.[60] This, plus the apparent ongoing momentum of the Soviet building programs for new strategic SLBMs and their submarine platforms, might thus suggest that a decision had in fact been made to increase the proportion of Soviet strategic missiles deployable at sea beyond the upper limits set in May 1972.

### Intercontinental Bombers

The third element of the Soviet strategic offensive arsenal is a relatively small force of intercontinental bombers operated by the Long-Range Aviation command (LRA). Unlike the ICBM and SLBM elements discussed above, this force underwent no expansion during most of the post-1964 strategic buildup; rather, after a slight decline from its peak strength,[61] it remained for the next decade at a level of about 140 heavy bombers—TU-95 turboprop Bears and MYA-4 jet-powered Bisons, of the same vintage as the U.S. B-52—plus about 50 Bisons converted to tankers. From the early sixties, following public display in the Moscow air show, air-to-surface missiles also had been fitted to about half of these bombers for standoff weapons delivery.[62]

Although priority was clearly given to the buildup of ICBM and SLBM forces in that order, the Soviet Union did not abandon interest in retaining a manned-aircraft intercontinental strategic delivery capability. Testifying to this were continued training flights to northern coastal areas of the American continent, as well as the disclosure in the fall of 1969 that the Soviet aircraft industry had produced a new supersonic bomber of advanced variable-wing design, the Backfire.[63] This aircraft, about four-fifths the size and roughly similar in configuration to the then-projected, but still to be developed, U.S. B-1 bomber, was to become the subject of continuing controversy.

After several years of testing and modification, the TU-26 Backfire (in its B version) began to enter service in 1974,[64] amid a great deal of uncertainty abroad as to what its operational capabilities and primary mission might be. Much argument centered on the Backfire's unrefueled combat radius—which was variously calculated within the U.S. government and by aircraft industry experts at from about 1750 to 3100 nautical miles.[65] The lower figure would in effect "disqualify" the Backfire as an intercontinental strategic bomber (and thus free it from consideration in SALT), while the higher one would put it in about the same round-trip mission bracket as the Bison, an acknowledged SALT-accountable strategic bomber.

To enliven the Backfire performance issue further, there was also evidence that Backfire B came equipped with a refueling probe, as well as indications that the IL-76 jet transport might be under modification to serve as a tanker.[66] With appropriate air refueling, there was no question that two-way Backfire missions could be flown against the United States.[67] In addition to contention as to whether the Backfire's intended strategic attack mission was peripheral or intercontinental, there also was a basis for ascribing it a major role in support of naval forces, since at least half of the Backfires being produced apparently were being assigned to units of Soviet Naval Aviation.[68]

By 1978, when the estimated number of operational Backfires approached eighty, perhaps about evenly divided between the LRA and Naval Aviation, the question of whether this aircraft was to be considered a SALT-accountable strategic bomber remained a persistent unresolved SALT issue, which we shall take up in its SALT context later in Chapters 10 and 11.[69] Meanwhile, according to U.S. defense officials, the Soviet Union was thought to be readying the prototype of a new modern heavy bomber, which, if so—whatever the outcome of the Backfire issue—would suggest that the Soviet Union remained dedicated to maintaining an intercontinental bomber force.[70]

For Soviet planners, however, there was nevertheless an issue bearing on strategic bomber choices somewhat analogous to that facing them in the SLBM field: Given the likelihood of some sort of SALT ceiling on strategic delivery vehicles, along with freedom to mix, how much of their strategic offensive power should go into bombers at the expense of land-based ICBMs? Judging from the earlier pattern of Soviet strategic priorities, a major move toward much larger intercontinental bomber forces would not seem likely, although the maintenance of advanced development programs to keep other options open might be expected. It is to be noted, incidentally, that if the Backfire were not to be counted as a strategic bomber for SALT purposes, the Soviets might be more tempted than otherwise to acquire substantial numbers of this aircraft, whose characteristics would make it potentially convertible to intercontinental strategic use without a SALT penalty.

## STRATEGIC DEFENSE PROGRAMS

The USSR's dedication to a strategic defense effort substantially greater than that of the United States had long been one of the more pronounced differences in the strategic policies of the two countries, reflecting both the disparate nature of the strategic situation in which the two rival powers found themselves and differing conceptions as to how best to deal with the problems of security in the nuclear age.

Although the ABM Treaty of May 1972 might have marked the beginning of an altered Soviet outlook on the value of strategic defense and its relative importance in the offense-defense equation in the SALT era, no doctrinal revisions that would suggest such a waning of Soviet dedication to strategic defense had been forth-coming.[71] Neither was downgrading of strategic defense apparent in the specific programs pursued by the Soviet Union after the ABM Treaty, particularly those having to do with improving the air defense and civil defense aspects of the USSR's strategic posture.

### Active Air Defense

In the category of active air defenses, the Soviet Union continued to deploy such surface-to-air missile systems as the SA-3 and the SA-5 to complement an already dense network of older SA-2 missiles for defense against bomber attack.[72] Altogether, though some older SA-2 sites were being deactivated, the Soviet Union in 1978 still maintained some 10,000 surface-to-air missile launchers of various types[73] in its strategic air defense organization, the PVO.[74] This was in sharp contrast to the situation in the United States, where the last of the country's then existing 260 "strategic" air defense missiles (down from a peak of about 2400 in the mid-sixties) were phased out of operation by the beginning of 1975.[75]

With regard to the Soviet interceptor force, the other main component of the USSR's strategic air defenses, the overall number of aircraft had declined from about 3600 in the late sixties to 2500 in 1975, but began to rise slightly again in 1977.[76] Concurrently, a process of qualitative updating of the interceptor force was also taking place, with older fighter types having been largely replaced by 1978 by more advanced, all-weather missile-armed aircraft.[77] Again, there was a contrast with the U.S. case, where decisions to cut back on air defense had brought about a reduction in strategic air defense interceptors from 1200 in the late sixties to about 330 in 1978, none of which were of recent vintage,[78] while the newest fighters, such as the F-14 and the F-15, were earmarked mainly for fleet and general purpose use rather than strategic defense roles.[79]

Given the disparity in the weight of the strategic air threat that had traditionally faced the two countries, there had been an understandable logic to the Soviet Union's persistent effort to strengthen its air defenses. And so long as there remained some prospect of combining separate air defense and ABM systems into a fully integrated strategic defense system, there was also a further rationale for a substantial ongoing air defense effort. On the face of it, however, the logic of continuing to sink additional large resources into air defense seemed to have become a bit dubious after SALT I, for even if a 100-percent-effective air defense system were attainable, the yet more formidable problem of strategic defense against missile attack would still remain. Seemingly, further prospects of solving this problem had been barred by the ABM Treaty, which specifically ruled out the deployment of nationwide ABM defenses and thus appeared to leave the USSR irremediably vulnerable to missile attack.[80]

One must note, however, that irrespective of the feasibility of ABM defenses, there were other factors that could have provided a rationale for strong ongoing Soviet air defense programs. For one thing, Soviet planners may have anticipated a growing future requirement to counter unmanned aerodynamic delivery vehicles, such as cruise missiles. They may also have perceived a need for not allowing their air defenses to lapse, in the event that conflicts should arise in Asia or Europe apart from a direct strategic clash with the United States. Another incentive for Soviet air defense planners could have stemmed from SALT itself. Until the issue of future bomber forces and bomber-launched armaments were to be definitely settled in the post-Vladivostok negotiations, the Soviets might have felt loath to slacken their air defense effort appreciably, either out of prudent concern for dealing with a perceived threat, or in order to buttress their negotiating position, or both. And, of course, it was always possible that "bureaucratic momentum" and the entrenched institutional position of the strategic defense military-industrial nexus had something to do with a continuing flow of resources to air defense.[81]

Despite the ample resources devoted to it, the Soviet Union's massive antibomber system was not without weaknesses, of which perhaps the principal one continued to be its vulnerability to low-altitude penetration. However, as pointed out by U.S. defense officials in early 1978, Soviet efforts were being made to improve the situation. These included the placing of radars on elevated platforms to provide better detection and tracking of low-flying objects, as well as deployment of MOSS aircraft for airborne early warning.[82] The development of a "look-down, shoot-down" system that could significantly increase Soviet effectiveness against low-altitude penetration also was believed under way, though not likely to become operational until some time in the 1980s.[83]

### ABM and Strategic Defense

The Soviet Union's persistent effort to improve its air defenses, whatever the motivations involved, naturally stood, and continues to stand, in conspicuous contrast to its decision to enter a treaty in 1972 foreclosing further deployment of defenses against ballistic missiles. How and why the Soviet leadership came to take a step so manifestly at variance with traditional Soviet attitudes toward the value of strategic defense is a question worth addressing at least briefly here.

To begin with, it may be helpful to recall the evolution of the Soviet ABM program up to the time it became an ostensible casualty of the SALT I negotiations. In the period following Khrushchev's removal in 1964, the Soviet Union embarked on a program for deployment of ABM defenses around Moscow—the Galosh system.[84] By 1967 the first launch positions had been installed, and it appeared that the Moscow system, when complete, would have about 100 launch positions. Having taken the historical first step of deploying ABM defenses before any other country, and having laid claim to "solving" the missile defense problem,[85] the Soviet Union was expected to capitalize on its head start by extending the Moscow system to other parts of the country.

At this juncture, however, it became evident that the Soviet ABM program had run into both technical and policy trouble. In late 1968, work on the Galosh system around Moscow slowed to a virtual halt, about two-thirds of the way toward completion, and during the next couple of years there were occasional inklings of an internal policy debate over the pros and cons of further ABM deployment.[86] Although work on the uncompleted Moscow sites was resumed in 1971, the Soviet leadership nevertheless felt impelled to shift from a long-standing policy of seeking viable ABM defense to one that culminated in May 1972 in acceptance of mutual limitations on further ABM deployment. Two years later, these limitations were carried still further in the protocol to the ABM Treaty.[87]

Broadly speaking, there have been two schools of thought about what may have lain behind the Soviet reversal of policy on ABM. One of them tended to regard the ABM Treaty as evidence that the Soviet Union had come to realize that ABM systems were destabilizing and had therefore accepted more or less the American concept of mutual assured destruction and the force posture concomitants that went along with it.[88] Thus, in this view, the policy reversal on ABM, even though prompted in some measure perhaps by expediency, was to be seen as a genuine conceptual retreat from prior Soviet dedication to strategic defense.

According to a second school of thought, the ABM policy shift had been dictated in the main by such expedient considerations as the economic burden of a major ABM program of questionable effectiveness and concern over a superior U.S. ABM technology (Safeguard), which, combined with the U.S. lead in MIRV, could have placed the Soviet Union at a serious disadvantage unless checked.[89] In this view, signing of the ABM Treaty did not necessarily reflect any essential change in Soviet adherence to the goal of strategic defense. On the contrary, it might be argued that the Soviets were simply demonstrating the high value they still placed on ABM, for in order to block further U.S. development in this field, they had been willing to accept constraints on their own.

The final results, of course, are not yet in, but it must be said that the second thesis seems to have held up better than the first. Not only has there been no Soviet rejection of strategic defense on the conceptual plane, but on the practical level a concerted Soviet R&D program involving technologies and components applicable to missile defense has been pursued during the years since the ABM Treaty was signed.[90] This bears out the late Marshal Grechko's September 1972 comment suggesting that the ABM Treaty should not be taken to mean that the search for an effective strategic defense of the country was to be abandoned.[91]

### Strategic ASW

In the planning of its strategic defenses, some share of the Soviet Union's attention since the advent of American SLBMs in the early 1960s had been devoted to the problems of trying to neutralize an adversary's missile-carrying submarines at sea by means of antisubmarine warfare (ASW) operations. This mission, indeed, had been described authoritatively in 1963 as "the most important task of the Soviet Navy."[92] However, the inherent difficulties of this task, plus various geographic and operational handicaps faced by the Soviet Union, had combined to make it appear quite unlikely that the Soviet Navy, employing known methods of acoustic detection and related ASW operations, could threaten the survivability of U.S. SLBM forces—the third and "invulnerable" leg of the American strategic TRIAD.[93]

It came as something of a surprise, therefore, when in May 1975 Admiral S.G. Gorshkov, the well-known head of the Soviet Navy, said with respect to the "threat from the sea" against Soviet territory posed by U.S. SSBNs that "on the basis of the latest achievements of science, technology and production," a Soviet Navy had been created which could successfully "repulse and disarm" such a threat.[94] Gorshkov's implied claim to having developed a new way of dealing with the U.S. submarine threat lacked specifics, and he had been known in the past to express rather sanguine views of the "successes" achieved in Soviet conventional ASW exercises,[95] so he may simply have been bluffing in May 1975. Nevertheless his boast was worrisome enough to stimulate speculation in the West that the Soviet Union might have scored unexpected advances in its extensive nonacoustic ASW program, an area of technology which it apparently had explored more vigorously than the United States since the early sixties.[96]

Some of the nonacoustic techniques discussed in Soviet literature that might have been developed for ASW use included infrared sensors, detection of isotope trails or extremely low frequency electromagnetic currents around a submarine's hull, and radar measurement of surface distortion from internal hydrodynamic waves created by a submarine's movement.[97] Assuming a much better Soviet detection capability than customarily estimated, effective means to localize and attack a submarine target would also be required in order to provide a major Soviet ASW threat to the American SLBM force. In this connection, a catalog of possibilities cited by one prominent Western expert on the Soviet Navy includes—in addition to standard platforms for delivery of ordnance such as ASW ships,[98] aircraft, helicopters, and hunter-killer subs— such innovative means as surface-effect vehicles and ballistic missiles fired from shore or from Y-class submarines, with precision guidance from overhead satellites.[99]

How seriously Soviet ASW developments might threaten the U.S. Polaris and Poseidon force was, understandably, a critical question, especially in view of the long-held belief that this force was likely to remain invulnerable indefinitely, even if Soviet ASW capabilities were to improve.[100] One official U.S. judgment was rendered in early 1976 by Secretary of Defense Donald H. Rumsfeld. Although he noted that Soviet ASW had been undergoing a process of "evolutionary" improvement, and that "the possibility of a technological breakthrough" had to be kept in mind, he did not consider that Soviet ASW capabilities yet posed a serious threat to American SLBM forces.[101] This judgment was repeated two years later by his successor, Harold Brown.[102]

Meanwhile, however, though there was a considerable degree of uncertainty about Soviet ASW trends, legitimate concern about the ultimate impact of these trends persisted.[103] This concern derived not only from the USSR's efforts to improve its ASW capabilities against American submarines and to protect its own strategic missile submarine force from U.S. ASW operations;[104] in a broader sense, it also derived from the cumulative asymmetries of other kinds that had been emerging between the U.S. and Soviet strategic postures.

These included the growing counterforce potential of Soviet delivery forces to threaten the viability of the land-based elements of U.S. strategic deterrent forces, unmatched by a similar U.S. capability against hardened Soviet nuclear forces,[105] as well as the vigorous ongoing Soviet programs of active air defense, compared with a deliberate U.S. choice to minimize activities in this field.[106] Another field in which there was also an asymmetry of priority and effort was that of civil defense.

### Soviet Civil Defense

In the field of civil defense, an asymmetry of emphasis between the United States and the Soviet Union had existed since the early sixties, when a U.S. civil defense program briefly encouraged by President Kennedy began to languish, at the same time that the Soviets were choosing to reorganize their own local civil defense activities into a broad national program in recognition of "the strategic importance of civil defense."[107] However, in the West this asymmetry was generally considered of little consequence until an intensified Soviet civil defense effort began to unfold under new leadership not long after the signing of the May 1972 SALT accords,[108] which had ostensibly put the brakes on at least the ABM element of active strategic defenses.

Thereafter, the effectiveness and significance of Soviet civil defense became a matter of growing debate inside and outside the U.S. government.[109] According to one line of argument, the Soviet Union's measures to protect an essential core of its leadership, population, and industry might in fact enable it to survive and recover from a nuclear war, or at least relevant decisionmakers in the Soviet Union and elsewhere might come to think so, which would mean in either case a "survivability gap" that threatened to upset the strategic balance and weaken mutual deterrence.[110] Those advancing contrary lines of argument either disputed the evidence that actual preparations matched the voluminous manuals and other Soviet literature on civil defense, or held that even if a substantial program were under way, it could not begin to provide effective protection against nuclear retaliation. Hence, they asserted, the notion of a civil defense gap was a spurious issue that should not impair deterrence.[111]

Official judgments in the United States remained ambivalent with regard to the civil defense controversy, reflecting in some measure both of the above lines of argument. In February 1978, for example, Secretary of Defense Harold Brown, generally known to be in the nonalarmist camp on the civil defense issue,[112] noted that Soviet civil defense had turned out to be "more extensive" than estimated a year earlier, and he pointed to the problem that "major active and passive defenses—coupled with the ability to eliminate the bulk of the Minuteman/Titan force—might seriously degrade our retaliatory response in some circumstances."[113] Although expressing the view that neither the Soviet Union's counterforce threat to Minuteman nor its civil defense had yet reached a stage adequate to so degrade U.S. retaliation, Brown cautioned that these factors might be perceived otherwise by the Soviets, leading them to believe they possessed a meaningful advantage.[114]

In another reading of the status of Soviet civil defense by the CIA, a report made public in July 1978 provided considerable detail on Soviet programs estimated to be costing the equivalent of $2 billion a year.[115] The report concluded, however, that even though the Soviet leaders probably believed that their civil defense effort would improve the country's ability to wage war and enhance the USSR's chances for survival following a nuclear exchange, they still could not have sufficient confidence in their existing civil defenses to be emboldened "to expose the USSR to a higher risk of nuclear attack."

The Soviets, for their part, gave no indication of having second thoughts about the wisdom of their civil defense effort. A typical expression of the Soviet viewpoint was furnished in early 1977 by a military spokesman, General of the Army A.I. Radziyevskiy. "Naturally," the general said, "civil defense organization and methods of protecting the population and economy" were "constantly being improved" in the Soviet Union.[116] But, he went on, the Soviets had never questioned the United States' own "big civil defense programs" as a threat to peace or an obstacle to further progress in SALT. Why then the "propagandist ballyhoo" in the United States about a "threatening increase" in Soviet civil defense? The answer, as given by Radziyevskiy, was that a "provocative campaign" about an "imaginary 'Soviet military threat' in general and Soviet civil defense in particular" had been mounted in the United States by circles wishing, among other things, "to wreck detente . . . and to extort new appropriations for the Pentagon and the military-industrial monopolies."

Similarly, in an article written for publication in an American journal in the fall of 1977, Henry Trofimenko, a well-known Soviet commentator on strategic matters, argued among other things that Soviet civil defense measures were but "a belated and very modest reaction" to the "enormous civil defense programs of the United States," and that the U.S. "propaganda campaign" against Soviet civil defense simply illustrated the fact that "every time the American military wants to accelerate one of its programs, it cries wolf and points an accusing finger at the other side."[117]

※    *Chapter 7*

# Shifts in U.S. Strategic Policy

By contrast with the Soviet Union, which had continued to build up its ICBM and SLBM forces during SALT I, the United States emerged from SALT I with virtually the same baseline strategic forces it had at the beginning,[1] with the exception of having begun in 1970 to retrofit part of its Minuteman ICBM and Polaris SLBM forces with MIRVed warheads.[2] If little change in U.S. strategic force levels and structure had occurred, however, this was not altogether the case with regard to strategic nuclear doctrine and planning. The need for amendment in these areas came to be recognized near the outset of the Nixon administration in 1969, when, as one close student of the subject later expressed it, some NSC and Defense Department officials found themselves dissatisfied with the reigning orthodoxy of mutual assured destruction as an adequate basis for deterrence in the 1970s, particularly in light of the continuing Soviet strategic buildup.[3]

What gradually emerged in the next couple of years from a series of studies on American strategic forces that had been commissioned by Dr. Kissinger's NSC apparatus[4] were recommendations for doctrinal change aimed at giving the president a wider and more selective set of nuclear options than those provided by assured destruction alone. Receptiveness to this line of thinking had shown up in President Nixon's foreign policy message to the Congress in 1970, in which the question was first raised publicly whether a president should "be left with the single option of ordering the mass destruction of enemy civilians," knowing that there would be a "mass slaughter of Americans" in return.[5] This issue was broached again in his 1971 and 1972 messages, when it was declared that a "simple 'assured destruction' doctrine does not meet . . . requirements for a flexible range of strategic options."[6]

Actually, expressions of the need for greater flexibility in the application of U.S. strategic forces did not originate with the Nixon administration. Posture statements of several secretaries of defense from 1963 on had noted the desirability of having flexible forces that could be used for limited and controlled response as well as an all-out retaliatory attack.[7] What distinguished the Nixon administration's approach (particularly after Dr. James R. Schlesinger became secretary of defense in July 1973) was a more explicit promulgation of a flexibility doctrine, linked with some revision of actual operational employment planning as embodied in the SIOP (Single Integrated Operational Plan).[8] As Schlesinger once put it, "we are consciously basing our deterrent strategy upon the achievement of flexibility and selectivity in the way that was discussed earlier."[9]

## SCHLESINGER'S 1974 STRATEGIC REVISIONS

It was perhaps somewhat ironic that in the wake of SALT I, when many were of the belief that the ABM Treaty had signaled Soviet embrace of the American concept of mutual assured destruction,[10] the United States had begun to amend its own strategic doctrine and policy in ways that reflected dissatisfaction with the previous dominance of that same concept.

As explained by their chief architect, the doctrinal and planning revisions set forth by Schlesinger in early 1974 involved three separate sets of questions:[11] (1) changes in targeting doctrine, which, according to Schlesinger, were not related to SALT; (2) the quantitative issue of force sizing, directly linked to the kinds of future agreements that might be reached in SALT; and (3) prudential hedges in the R&D field, which would also be conditional to some extent upon the outcome of SALT and would in some cases contribute to an increased counterforce potential.

### Changes in Targeting Doctrine
The rationale advanced by Schlesinger for a more flexible nuclear targeting doctrine was twofold: to "reinforce deterrence" across a wide spectrum of situations by having "sufficient options between massive response and doing nothing" or, if deterrence should fail, to limit the chances of uncontrolled escalation by being able to respond selectively before having to consider the ultimate option of assured destruction strikes against cities.[12]

At bottom, this rationale appeared to hinge on the assessment that the probability of a deliberate, massive nuclear attack was very remote and that the real problem was to deter lower-level attacks and provocations that might escalate into general nuclear conflict.[13] Since deterrence of lower levels of aggression by the threat of massive retaliation against cities had become "less and less credible," a targeting doctrine that would let a potential aggressor know that other usable response options existed was therefore calculated to "shore up deterrence."[14] This shoring up of deterrence, as Schlesinger saw it, would be especially welcome to the U.S. allies in Europe, where there had been a "declining credibility" in the contribution of U.S. strategic forces to European security.[15]

Although some response options short of massive strikes against cities had in fact been incorporated in U.S. contingency plans since the early sixties, these still involved large numbers of nuclear weapons and from the recipient's point of view would have been "virtually indistinguishable from an attack on cities."[16] What the change in targeting would do, according to Schlesinger, was to provide preplanned small strikes against a variety of targets, including military targets, with the option of limiting such strikes "down to a few weapons."[17]

The measures advocated to achieve greater targeting flexibility and a wider range of response options were to include more responsive command and control arrangements, further development of appropriate sensors to determine the nature of an attack, and some improvement in delivery accuracy.[18] The latter, incidentally, marked an official departure from the previous "self-denying ordinance" against accuracy improvements[19] on the American side. Commenting in March 1974 on the inferences the Soviets might draw from programs for greater accuracy, as well as from the establishment of a targeting doctrine that offered a broader range of options for the possible use of U.S. strategic forces, Schlesinger said: "The Soviets would not necessarily draw reassurance from this. It is not our objective to give them reassurance. In order to have deterrence one must have a credible threat."[20]

To the argument that a doctrine of targeting flexibility might tend to make the use of nuclear weapons more acceptable and therefore weaken deterrence and increase the likelihood of nuclear war, Schlesinger also counterposed the view that for deterrence "one has got to have an implementable threat."[21] By this reckoning, deterrence "based upon a nonimplementable threat, such as both sides going after each other's cities," is less sound than "deterrence across the entire spectrum of risk" as a means of reducing the probability of nuclear warfare.[22]

### Force Sizing

Several factors were recognized in the Schlesinger proposals as having a strong influence on planning for the size and composition of U.S. strategic forces. These included arms control objectives and agreements in SALT, the strategic programs being pursued by the Soviet Union, and the effects that perception of the strategic balance might have on the political behavior of potential opponents, allies, and other interested parties.[23] The principal criterion for force sizing that emerged from these composite influences was "essential equivalence" with the Soviet Union: "Preferably by agreement or if necessary by unilateral action, we believe that we must maintain an essential equivalence with them."[24]

The level at which essential equivalence in strategic forces might be pegged was left largely up to the Soviets in the Schlesinger formulation. For its part, the United States was said to be prepared to reduce, maintain, or increase its level of strategic arms, depending on what the Soviet Union would agree to in SALT and on the further evolution of Soviet strategic forces. The United States would prefer "to reduce the present balance in such a way that strategic equivalence can be achieved at the lowest cost and least destabilizing level of forces."[25] If the Soviets were prepared to reduce strategic arsenals "in an equitable fashion," according to Schlesinger, the United States would be "prepared to accommodate them . . . with enthusiasm and alacrity."[26] But if they should insist "on moving ahead with a new set of strategic capabilities, we will be forced to match them."[27] In any case, the level of U.S. strategic arms would be "fixed by the actions of the Soviet Union."[28]

The idea that in sizing its strategic forces the United States would henceforth be obliged to pace itself by the Soviet Union's programs was not one that fit the once-prevalent image of the United States as the pacesetter in strategic competition. In the Schlesinger view, the growth of Soviet strategic power had created a situation in which the issue facing the United States was no longer how to avoid initiatives that might accelerate strategic competition, but how to interpret and respond to a growing range of potential Soviet initiatives.[29] Among potential Soviet steps of great concern to the United States would be their going ahead with deployment of large numbers of MIRVs in an attempt to "exploit the asymmetries" in ICBM-SLBM numbers and payload conceded to them in SALT I.

In the context of force sizing, such a step would further accentuate numerical asymmetries between U.S. and Soviet forces, for its effect would be to cancel out the remaining U.S. advantage in numbers of warheads, leaving the Soviet Union numerically favored in virtually all of the "static" criteria for comparing strategic forces—launchers, throwweight, and megatonnage, as well as warheads. These "apparently favorable asymmetries" might in turn mislead the Soviet leadership into believing that they could be exploited for diplomatic or military leverage.[30] Many "interested observers," as well, might be persuaded that the Soviet side had come to enjoy a pronounced advantage.

Although "exact symmetry" need not exist in order to have essential equivalence, the United States, according to Schlesinger, was not prepared to accept a situation in which "all the visible asymmetries"—as measured by static criteria—appeared "to favor one party." Rather, in the absence of an equitable agreement in which there was "a perceived equality between the offensive forces of both sides," the United States would have "to incorporate 'static' measures and balancing criteria" into its force planning.[31]

Or, in short, what the Schlesinger analysis seemed to suggest was that, regardless of the dynamic military factors that might critically affect the relative strategic capabilities of the two sides, a dominant consideration in the sizing of strategic forces was to ensure against being perceived as Number Two.

### Prudential Hedges and Counterforce

As a hedge against "the unknown outcome of SALT II" and any Soviet attempt to achieve "exploitable superiority,"[32] the Schlesinger proposals included, in addition to continuation of such previously initiated major programs as Trident and the B-1,[33] a number of new strategic R&D projects. Several of these new projects would contribute to improved counterforce capabilities, particularly against hard targets. The most notable among them were for development of a more accurate Minuteman guidance system, a higher-yield Minuteman warhead, and a terminally guided MARV for possible retrofit into both ICBMs and SLBMs, as well as development of advanced technology for a new "MX" ICBM.[34]

The previous U.S. declaratory policy had been to refrain from accuracy improvements that might seem to pose a counterforce threat to hardened Soviet missile silos, and congressional guidance for SALT II had urged that "neither the Soviet Union nor the United States should seek unilateral advantage by developing a first strike potential."[35] In addition, the concept of mutual assured destruction had pivoted upon the absence of counterforce capabilities great enough to threaten the mutual survivability of strategic retaliatory forces. Therefore it was not surprising that the counterforce-related elements of the Schlesinger proposals should constitute their most controversial aspect.

Schlesinger himself took pains to point out that the adjustments being made in U.S. strategic policy did not represent "radical departures from past practice" and that they were by no means meant to imply that the United States was seeking major counterforce capabilities of the kind that would be necessary for a disarming first strike against the Soviet Union.[36] Indeed, as he chose to underscore, there was "just no possibility that a high confidence disarming first strike" would be attainable by either side.[37] While the various accuracy-yield improvements sought for U.S. weapons would make possible their more "efficient" and "discriminating" use against both soft- and hard-target systems, the principal rationale offered for these developments was "to make it clear to a potential enemy that he cannot proceed with impunity to jeopardize our own system of hard targets."[38]

Among other points claimed for the projected weapons improvements were that they would reduce unintended civilian damage, allow greater economy of force against specialized target systems (including some of concern to allies), and help deter another power from exercising any form of nuclear pressure. With regard to increased accuracy, the general proposition was also made that the United States needed it more than the Soviets because of constrained payloads and low-yield MIRVs that had resulted from the disparity in missile throwweight.

Thus, according to Schlesinger, though the United States would prefer that both sides avoid the acquisition of major counterforce capabilities, it was "troubled" by the momentum of Soviet weapons programs and by the prospect that the Soviet Union might exploit its superior throwweight potential to move in that direction. Hence, by putting its own matching counterforce measures into research and development, the United States was in effect serving notice that U.S. policy could not allow the USSR to develop a "marked superiority" in counterforce capabilities.[39]

Besides the hope that a "matching" policy might persuade the Soviets not to develop their full counterforce potential in the first place, the Schlesinger approach also implied that such a policy was best calculated to dissuade the Soviets from exploiting this potential if they should choose to develop it. In effect, the logic ran thus: If the Soviets were to contemplate knocking out the U.S. ICBM force in the first phase of a nuclear conflict, an American president should not be left only with the option of threatened retaliation against Soviet cities; rather, he should have the counterforce option of depriving the Soviets of their ICBM forces also, so that both sides would again be "even." Faced with this prospect, the Soviets would not be tempted to call on their counterforce capability, and would thus remain deterred.

## U.S. STRATEGIC DEBATE OVER THE SCHLESINGER APPROACH

The strategic policy shift espoused by Schlesinger in 1974, which came in the midst of a public debate on strategic issues already under way in the United States, can be said to have met with a decidedly mixed reception in defense and arms control circles. Generally speaking, the lines were drawn between those holding the view that alternatives must be found to a doctrine of mutual assured destruction tied more or less inflexibly to massive retaliation against civilian populations and those persuaded that despite the drawbacks of deterrence based on a mutual hostage relationship, the search for alternative means of deterrence was not only futile but might reduce the chances of preventing nuclear war.

As noted by the authors of a July 1974 article in *Foreign Affairs* on the nuclear debate,[40] these two schools of thought had begun to shape up before the appearance of the Schlesinger proposals, around views advanced respectively by Dr. Fred Iklé and Dr. Wolfgang Panovsky, among others.[41] Although the underlying issue of whether or not a departure from mutual assured destruction was ill advised probably lay at the heart of the debate over U.S. strategic policy, the Schlesinger proposals had the effect of bringing other issues into sharper focus. From the viewpoint of his critics, who were by no means fully agreed among themselves as to what was wrong with the Schlesinger approach, its main faults were said to run along the following lines.

First, with regard to the question of targeting flexibility, some critics appeared to have little quarrel in principle with the idea of giving the president a range of options from which to choose, but argued that the United States already possessed all the flexibility and accuracy needed for lesser options than assured destruction, even assuming that such options were desirable.[42] For the most part, however, opponents of the modified targeting doctrine based their objections on the concern that having a variety of preplanned nuclear options might in one way or another increase the likelihood of nuclear war.[43] Among the dangers cited was that of generating false confidence in one's ability to limit and control the use of nuclear weapons.[44] Another was that the very existence of preplanned nuclear options might during a crisis reduce the inclination to try to defuse the situation by political means and hence increase the chances of touching off a nuclear conflict.[4 5]

The force-sizing considerations set forth in the Schlesinger proposals were probably their least controversial aspect in the eyes of most critics, perhaps because the formula of "essential equivalence" included a declared willingness to hold the size of U.S. strategic forces at whatever level the Soviet Union might agree upon in SALT. Only those critics at one extreme, who felt that U.S. forces should be kept at the minimum level required for assured destruction, regardless of Soviet force levels, and those at the other extreme, who believed that the United States could better afford a numbers race than the Soviet Union and should therefore plan to outbuild them in the absence of lasting SALT constraints, appeared to take serious exception to the Schlesinger approach on force sizing.

However, there were various degrees of dissent from the proposition that perceived images of relative strategic power, as measured by static criteria, can have an important effect on strategic stability and political behavior and therefore must be taken into account in force planning. Some critics, for example, dismissed the political impact of static comparisons of strategic forces as inconsequential.[4 6] Others conceded that the "image projection" role of strategic forces was not to be overlooked but held that perceived changes in the gross strategic balance occur on such a slow time scale that it would be possible for the United States to entertain without undue political risk the short-term unilateral suspension of some programs, in the hope of encouraging the Soviet Union to reciprocate.[4 7]

The most controversial aspect of the Schlesinger proposals doubtless lay in their treatment of counterforce. Critics of accuracy improvements and other measures that were intended to increase U.S. counterforce capabilities against Soviet missile silos argued their case on several grounds. First, it was held that counterforce improvements were not only costly, but unnecessary for strategic purposes. The contention was that they would not significantly reduce the collateral effects of a nuclear attack, that the United States already had enough selective counterforce capability to signal resolution, and that it could not expect in any event to acquire a disarming capability against a large enough fraction of Soviet offensive forces to limit damage to the United States in any meaningful way.[4 8]

A second, and somewhat contradictory, assertion was that U.S. counterforce programs, together with a large antisubmarine warfare program, might be interpreted by the Soviets as pursuit of a disarming first-strike capability against the USSR, despite Schlesinger's denial to the contrary. Strategically, it was argued, this could be very destabilizing, giving the Soviet Union an incentive to adopt a launch-on-warning doctrine and to take pre-emptive action in a crisis in an attempt to limit damage to itself.[49]

A third set of objections to the development of U.S. counterforce capabilities included the claim that the Soviet military leadership would probably be stimulated to respond in kind, and that this would speed up the arms race and jeopardize the chances of further progress in SALT.[50] Accuracy improvements in particular were singled out as being difficult to control and verify and therefore likely to work against any arms limitation agreements. Beyond this, the argument was also made that if the Soviet leaders should see a growing threat to survivability of their missile silos, they could replace them with mobile ICBMs, thus not only rendering U.S. countersilo accuracy improvements useless, but complicating the task of reaching verifiable limitation agreements.[51] The notion that prudential U.S. counterforce programs might have a useful function as "bargaining chips" in negotiations with the Soviet Union was questioned on the grounds that such programs are likely to acquire a momentum of their own and prove difficult to turn off, and so might result in deployment of weapons systems that could otherwise have been avoided.[52]

With regard to what some critics described as "Schlesinger's main justification for the new counterforce programs"—the need to "match any Soviet buildup of a hard-target counterforce capability[53]—commentary drew upon at least three quite different opposing arguments. One was that the Soviets were lagging in accuracy improvements and therefore would have a long way to go before they could mount an effective counterforce strategy. A second argument was that even if the Soviets should acquire an effective hard-target capability, this was insufficient justification for comparable U.S. programs, since the overall strategic balance was likely to remain such that the Soviets could derive little value from possession of a counterforce margin.[54] A third rebuttal was that the proper response to any Soviet counterforce threat to the U.S. Minuteman force was not a matching U.S. counterforce effort, but rather R&D programs to insure the survivability of U.S. deterrents such as mobile ICBMs, air-launched cruise missiles, or special missile defense of ICBM sites.[55]

Somewhat short of blanket condemnation of the Schlesinger counterforce approach, there were to be found in the nuclear strategy debate various shades of opinion that might be described as moderately critical of, but not dead set against, prudential measures.

Thus, for example, there were some who contended that the United States should refrain from deploying counterforce systems that might arouse "anxiety" in the Soviet Union about a possible disarming first-strike threat, but who endorsed continued R&D and intelligence gathering as a hedge against unforeseeable changes in the situation.[56]

On the other side of the strategic debate in defense and arms control circles were to be found those hospitable to the Schlesinger approach in one degree or another. In some cases, his supporters appeared to go beyond what Schlesinger himself had advocated, in their urging that the United States move promptly to acquire a strong counterforce posture. Welcoming "Schlesinger's proposal to restore counterforce targeting as an essential option in U.S. strategic planning," the editors of the *Strategic Review* asserted that in view of "U.S. relinquishment of nuclear superiority . . . and with ABM active defense foreclosed by SALT I, there is no time to lose in achieving [a] counterforce capability to implement the new targeting strategy."[57] The key to achieving such a capability, in turn, was seen to lie in "increased accuracy of warhead guidance," by means of which it was said that the United States could quickly and at low cost "redress" the advantages in megatonnage and launcher numbers enjoyed by the Soviet Union.[58]

Another school of hospitable opinion saw in the Schlesinger shift to counterforce a long overdue challenge to the "reigning ortho-doxy" of mutual assured destruction, which was charged with having not only reduced deterrence to "its most extreme, genocidal form," but also with having ignored the political consequences of a gross numerical imbalance in strategic forces.[59] Recognition of the need for a credible deterrent against limited nuclear attacks on the United States or its allies—another problem said to have been ignored by proponents of the MAD concept—was also claimed to be one of the core virtues of the new Schlesinger strategy.[60]

As for the criticism that the new U.S. strategic measures would simply provoke the Soviet Union to respond in kind and thus stimulate a fresh round in the arms race, it was pointed out by Schlesinger's supporters that development of the latest family of Soviet ICBMs had actually begun in the latter half of the sixties, at a time when the United States had leveled off its own strategic programs and canceled guidance improvement.[61] If U.S. restraint in that period encouraged no reciprocal slowing down of the Soviet strategic effort, the argument ran, why should it be supposed that the Soviets would now reciprocate if only the United States were again to hold back?

Rather, Schlesinger was held to be on the right track in signaling to the Soviet Union that any effort to achieve a counterforce advantage would be matched. Such an approach, it was averred, would not only help to bolster deterrence but offered the best promise of inducing the Soviet Union to exercise strategic self-restraint.[62] However, some skepticism was also voiced as to whether the declaratory signals conveyed by the Schlesinger shift would alone suffice to persuade the Soviet Union to curtail its own development of counterforce weapons. As expressed by one commentator: "The Soviet Union may regard Schlesinger's program as a bluff that will not be backed up by any action, if only because of congressional opposition."[63]

The possibility that congressional opposition might undercut the credibility of Schlesinger's position was not borne out, however, during the remainder of his tenure as secretary of defense. Although some opposition to the counterforce-related items in the FY 1975 military procurement bill arose in the Congress, both houses eventually approved most of what had been requested. The climax came when an effort led by Senator Thomas J. McIntyre in early June 1974 to bar the expenditure of funds on development of counterforce weapons was voted down a few days later by the Senate.[64] As noted in the press, the "effect of the Senate's vote was to put the Congress squarely on record in favor of one of the most basic and controversial changes in strategic doctrine in the last 20 years."[65]

Congressional support of the Schlesinger shift was again manifested during the 1975 appropriations cycle, both following the July 1974 summit in Moscow, where no substantive progress had been achieved in limiting strategic offensive arms,[66] and after the November 1974 Vladivostok summit, where a commitment to set a common ceiling on strategic forces had been reached. Thus, the Senate again in June 1975 said no to another effort by Senator McIntyre's Subcommittee on Research and Development to deny funds for counterforce R&D programs on the grounds that, as the senator put it: "Secretary Schlesinger is trying to move our basic strategic doctrine from our traditional emphasis on mutual assured destruction to a reliance on U.S. nuclear war fighting capability."[67]

## LITTLE STRATEGIC POLICY CHANGE IN FORD/RUMSFELD PERIOD

Just as the overall strategic package associated with Schlesinger's tenure as secretary of defense survived essentially intact up to the time he left the Ford administration in November 1975,[68] so its basic elements were perpetuated with very little in the way of doctrinal or program changes under his successor, Donald H. Rumsfeld.[69] Rumsfeld, like Schlesinger, emphasized the desirability of selective nuclear options and the maintenance of "essential equivalence" with the Soviet Union. He also appeared to line up essentially on the same side as Schlesinger in the national strategic debate over the impact of U.S. strategic policy upon SALT and Soviet behavior.

One thing that had been made evident during the 1974-75 debate was that it involved more than differing analytical judgments about the strategic force characteristics and targeting doctrines most appropriate to U.S. security needs. At bottom, it also involved differing assumptions as to how Soviet behavior might best be influenced. The critics had been saying, in effect, that the Schlesinger approach would make the Soviets uneasy and prompt them to expand their strategic programs still further. But Schlesinger appeared to believe that the best way to nudge the Soviets toward an equitable agreement and "to help" those in the Soviet leadership who might want to halt the arms race would be to make clear that the United States was prepared to put more resources into its own strategic programs if Soviet restraint were not forthcoming.[70] Similarly, Rumsfeld gave it as his view that "to have any prospect" of getting Soviet agreement leading to "durable" equivalence at lower levels of offensive forces, "we must recognize that the Soviets negotiate seriously in SALT only when they face real (not paper) programs, with significant military capabilities and congressional support."[71]

Among the prime problems of strategic policy and force planning that Rumsfeld, like his predecessor, identified as a matter of requiring serious attention was the growing vulnerability of missile forces housed in fixed silos.[72] Displaying little interest in either the early phase-out of the U.S. ICBM force or adoption of a "launch-under-attack" policy (among the steps sometimes suggested as the answer to prelaunch ICBM vulnerability), Rumsfeld took the position that for the sake of "longer-term stability . . . both sides should probably adopt some form of survivable basing for their ICBMs."[73]

In the U.S. case, the preferred move in this direction, described by Rumsfeld as the "most significant strategic initiative" proposed in his last budget request, was a marked acceleration of the program for a new MIRVed ICBM, tentatively dubbed the MX, which had grown out of a request by Schlesinger in 1974 for $37 million to develop advanced technology and alternative basing modes for an ICBM to succeed the Minuteman.[74] Under Rumsfeld, the budget request for the MX program in January 1977 at the close of the Ford administration was upped to $1.5 billion, to cover both further engineering development of the MX missile itself—which was to have greater throwweight and accuracy than the Minuteman—and selection of an appropriate mobile basing mode.[75] The basing concept toward which preference pointed in the Ford/Rumsfeld period involved the random movement of mobile missile launchers on flatcars concealed in underground trenches, the objective being to present a potential attacker with more aim points than he could confidently or economically afford to attack.[76]

It can hardly escape notice, incidentally, that the shift toward a land-mobile ICBM system as a means of assuring greater strategic stability reversed the position the United States had taken on this question in SALT I. Although the SALT I accords did not prohibit development of land-mobile systems, the United States had declared in a unilateral statement appended to the Interim Agreement that it would consider the actual deployment of such missiles to be "inconsistent" with the objectives of the agreement.[77] The rationale behind this position had been that land-mobile ICBMs, which would be difficult to keep track of by national means of surveillance, would introduce an undesirable element of instability into the strategic situation.[78]

The Ford/Rumsfeld period saw a gathering consensus on the changed value of mobile ICBM basing as a means of promoting strategic stability in the face of growing hard-target kill capabilities against fixed land-based ICBMs. In addition, priority attention was also given to two other programs intended to ensure the survivability and improve the effectiveness of the SLBM and bomber elements of the strategic TRIAD. These were the Trident I and the B-1 programs, which together would account for close to half of the approximately $11 billion budgeted for strategic force purposes in FY 1978.[79] Although both programs were to slip somewhat behind their original schedules because of development difficulties, the Trident program would be farther along in early 1977, with construction of the first two submarines under way and the initial operational capability (IOC) of the system set for September 1979.[80] In the case of the B-1 bomber, a formal Defense Department decision approving production had been taken in December 1976 after an intensive two-year flight test program, and procurement funding for the first eight production aircraft had been requested by the outgoing Ford administration.[81] However, a production program for the B-1 was to become one of the casualties of the changeover of administrations.

## TURN TOWARD A SLOWDOWN OF
## STRATEGIC PROGRAMS IN 1977

After the advent of the Carter administration in January 1977, it gradually became evident that though the new president and his national security advisers saw a need to increase overall defense spending by about 3 percent a year,[82] the rationale for this was tied not to the strategic nuclear situation, but rather to a requirement to strengthen the posture of conventional forces facing a buildup of Soviet-theater forces in Europe.[83]

With regard to strategic programs, it appeared that the favored line was one of constraints upon the pace, and in some cases the existence, of programs inherited from the previous administrations. At the same time, however, certain programs came to receive increased emphasis, presumably to compensate for constraints applied elsewhere, all of which tended to give the strategic policy approach of the new administration a somewhat ambivalent character.

The first slowing down of strategic programs came early in 1977 with the Carter administration's revision of the last Ford budget for FY 1978, and included deferral of full-scale development of the Air Force's MX ICBM and a cutback of funding for initial B-1 production from eight to five aircraft. Altogether, reductions in the budget for strategic forces amounted to $0.4 billion.[84] As explained by the administration, these were tentative cutbacks; no radical changes in defense programs or strategy were contemplated, pending a major review of U.S. defense policy and programs.[85] Subsequent strategic programs, according to Secretary Brown, would depend both upon how U.S. strategic needs were assessed during the process of review and upon what might happen in SALT.[86]

One of the pivotal reviews in question, later identified as PRM-10, part of a series of Presidential Review Memoranda, was completed in mid-1977.[87] Among other things, it reportedly concluded that despite the Soviet strategic missile buildup, the United States had sufficient forces to deter both large-scale and limited nuclear attacks, but that the outcome of a conventional war in Europe could be unfavorable. These findings were said to have contributed to an emerging policy of placing more emphasis on conventional force improvement, while slowing the modernization of strategic forces.[88]

How directly PRM-10 and other reviews of defense and related foreign policy issues may have influenced strategic program decisions is difficult to say, but at least one fairly radical decision came at about the same time PRM-10 was completed. This was the president's surprise announcement on June 30, 1977, that he had decided to cancel production and deployment plans for the controversial B-1 bomber.[89] Approved in some quarters as a "sensible" step that would avoid a costly and strategically unnecessary program,[90] the decision also met with widespread criticism. Opposition ranged from charges that rejection of the B-1 meant an "inevitable" end to the manned-bomber element of the strategic TRIAD, which could in turn upset the military balance, to censure for not having extracted significant SALT concessions from the Soviet Union in exchange for unilateral "scuttling" of a major strategic arms program.[91]

In announcing his decision to cancel the B-1 (whose demise, incidentally, was to meet lengthy resistance in the Congress),[92] President Carter also revealed that compensatory steps were to be taken in the form of "deployment of cruise missiles, using air-launched platforms, such as our B-52s."[93] This coupling of the new cruise missile strategic technology[94] to the venerable B-52 bomber[95] was said to have been suggested to the president by Secretary of Defense Harold Brown as the best alternative to the B-1 program, of which Brown himself had been an important advocate earlier in his career.

The case for substituting the B-52/cruise missile combination for the B-1 was spelled out in February 1978 by the secretary of defense, who stated that on grounds both of expected cost and of effectiveness in penetrating future Soviet air defenses, a B-52/cruise missile force was much the better choice.[96] Hence, the development program for the air-launched cruise missile (ALCM), aiming at a limited initial operational capability by March 1980, had been given the "highest national priority." A competitive flyoff of ten test flights in 1979 between the Air Force's ALCM-B and the air-launched version of the Navy's Tomahawk cruise missile, would determine which system was to be selected for deployment.[97]

Meanwhile, how many strategic cruise missiles would ultimately be deployed[98] and what their appropriate performance parameters, especially range,[99] might be, were among questions that were closely linked with the negotiations in SALT II. Indeed, as occasional editorial comment had put it, there was a rather "troubling" contradiction in the administration's having extolled the cruise missile as "a viable substitute for the B-1" on the one hand, while holding it out to the Russians as "expendable bargaining material" in SALT on the other.[100] We shall return to these questions and to some of the other implications of the cruise-missile issue for SALT later in Chapters 10 and 11.[101]

### Re-endorsement of the TRIAD

Although abandonment of the B-1 program had been interpreted by some to sound the eventual knell of the bomber leg of the strategic TRIAD, Secretary Brown held otherwise, stating that "we plan to continue distributing our retaliatory capability suitably among the three legs of the TRIAD."[102] As under previous administrations, survivability of the TRIAD in the face of growing Soviet counterforce capabilities was pronounced to be a matter of prime concern.[103] Of the several "hedges" cited by Brown to help cope with the survivability problem—in addition to the B-52/ALCM program and continuing B-1 R&D[104]—the two principal ones were the Trident I SLBM and the MX ICBM programs.

The Trident program was endorsed by Brown as a "highly survivable system" that would, among other things, "decrease Soviet incentives to procure additional counterforce weapons" for "attacks on U.S. soil." The program had encountered shipbuilding snags that would delay the IOC of the system about a year from the September 1979 date set previously under Ford/Rumsfeld, but otherwise it was averred to be in good shape, including the schedule for retrofit of the Trident I missile into the Poseidon SSBNs.[105]

In the case of the MX ICBM, toward which the previous administration had budgeted greatly increased resources, off-again, on-again support characterized the first two years of the Carter administration. After having been blocked in January 1977, full-scale development of the mobile MX system was approved by Secretary Brown in October 1977,[106] only to be rescinded again by the end of the year when questions of cost and basing concept remained unsettled.[107]

Although Brown in February 1978 included mobile ICBMs such as the MX in his list of hedges against Soviet threats to U.S. offensive forces, especially against possible ASW developments that might threaten SLBM survivability,[108] the MX trench-basing concept fared poorly on grounds of cost and vulnerability in studies carried out in the first half of 1978, leading to reports that the MX program faced an uncertain future.[109]

However, another shift of attitude began to manifest itself in July and August 1978 when Brown and other administration officials made known that an MX basing mode to replace the rejected trench concept was receiving favorable consideration as a U.S. option.[110] The alternative concept, called MAP (for multiple aim points), would involve trucking a given missile around under cover of darkness to any one of twenty empty vertical holes in a kind of "shell-game" fashion, so that the Soviets would not know which hole held a missile. Deployment of 200 to 300 missiles in this way would thus present the Soviets with 4000 to 6000 aim points, more than enough, as the backers of this idea argued, to discourage the Soviets from contemplating a disarming counterforce attack.[111] Again, as in the case of cruise missile deployment, the MAP shell-game concept for MX basing raised questions germane to SALT that we shall take up in Chapters 9 and 11.[112]

Apart from the Trident and mobile MX programs, a third hedge against Soviet threats to survivability of U.S. strategic offensive forces that found its way into Secretary Brown's February 1978 posture statement was one that previously had enjoyed no official U.S. support. This was the suggestion that—given unambiguous confirmation by various warning capabilities that a massive attack was on the way—the United States might on the strength of such advance warning launch a retaliatory attack on Soviet cities and industry before Soviet missiles reached their targets.[113] As if anticipating criticism of this departure from what had been long-held U.S. doctrinal eschewal of a launch-on-warning posture, Brown asserted that despite the "alleged 'irrationality' of such a response," Soviet planners would have to take it into account because they would not have "in advance an absolute guarantee that we would not so respond."[114]

### Main Doctrinal Formulations Reiterated

In other doctrinal respects, no conspicuous innovations were introduced under the new administration, which largely reiterated the strategic formulations that had evolved in the Schlesinger-Rumsfeld periods on the necessity of having essential equivalence with the Soviet Union in strategic forces[115] and on the need to maintain assured destruction and controlled response capabilities to ensure credible deterrence. However, there were some shifts of emphasis.

For example, although flexibility to respond to an attack at a variety of levels remained one of the prescribed requirements of credible deterrence, somewhat less emphasis than before was placed on limited nuclear options, along with less confidence that limited nuclear use could be kept from escalating.[116] On the other hand, the definition of flexibility was broadened, if anything, to take in the capability "to launch controlled counterattacks against a wide range of targets, including . . . targets of increasing hardness; from aircraft runways and nuclear storage sites to command bunkers and ICBM silos."[117] This counterforce-targeting orientation was underscored, incidentally, by the continuation of programs for guidance improvement and deployment of the Mk-12A reentry vehicle on part of the Minuteman III force.[118]

Two areas in which strategic asymmetries between the Soviet Union and the United States had become evident for some time before the Carter administration took office were those involving space defense capabilities and civil defense. Although no major new U.S. initiatives were proposed in these areas, increased attention was given to the implications that asymmetrical capabilities might have for U.S. security.

In the space defense case, Secretary Brown pointed out in October 1977 that whereas the United States had not developed an operational capability against spacecraft, the Soviet Union had developed and tested an antisatellite (ASAT) capability that "could be used against . . . some (of our) satellites."[119] The resulting imbalance, he felt, was a cause for concern, since the United States was coming to rely increasingly on space vehicles for early warning, surveillance, communications, intelligence, and other "legitimate" purposes contributing to deterrence. Modest funds were requested by Brown in February 1978 to begin development of ASAT capabilities, short of operational testing.[120]

In the civil defense case, the strategic implications of a growing asymmetry between Soviet and U.S. efforts had become the subject of both public debate and successive interagency studies by the mid-1970s,[121] but without having aroused a surge of new interest in civil defense preparations in the country at large. The proposed funding of $97 million for civil defense in the FY 1979 budget was approximately the same amount funded under the preceding administration and seemingly reflected much the same philosophy as that enunciated then—namely, to keep peacetime civil defense costs low while providing a basis for expansion of measures to relocate and shelter the population in a period of nuclear crisis, assuming time were available.[122]

An increased emphasis on evacuation preparations appeared to be in the offing when it was reported in late 1978 that the president had approved a new five-year, $2 billion Pentagon program to bolster civil defense, after failure to persuade the Russians to consider cutting back their civil defense effort.[123] However, in December President Carter indicated that the level of funding for additional civil defense preparations was still to be decided.[124]

If one can discern a central thread running through assessments of the U.S.-Soviet strategic competition by successive secretaries of defense in the SALT era, it would probably come down to something like this: The United States had perhaps been the pacesetter in the strategic competition in the 1950s and into the 1960s, but by the mid-1970s the dynamics had shifted, and the interaction between the two competitors was being driven by the depth and momentum of Soviet strategic programs.[125]

What the USSR might be hoping to accomplish by these programs was uncertain, but, as Secretary Brown put it in 1978, much of what was being done under the Soviet programs coincided offensively and defensively "with actions that would suggest a damage-limiting strategy," and possibly even with attempts to acquire "what have been called 'war-winning' capabilities."[126] In this situation Brown, like his SALT era predecessors, depicted the United States as basically seeking mutual deterrence stable enough so that nobody would be tempted to upset it.

This objective, in turn, would be sought through some combination of "unilateral force modernization" and "verifiable arms control agreements,"[127] with the relative weight of each left unspecified. In Chapter 8 we shall return to the latter part of this process, picking up the internal give-and-take over SALT II policy in both countries in the period immediately preceding the Vladivostok summit of November 1974.

*Chapter 8*

# SALT Policy Developments in the Period Prior to Vladivostok

In the span of about five months from the mid-1974 summit in Moscow to the Vladivostok summit in November, during which the American presidency changed hands as a result of Richard Nixon's resignation, a revised U.S. SALT approach emerged out of internal give-and-take in which the two principal protagonists were Secretary of State Henry Kissinger and Secretary of Defense James Schlesinger. In the same period, which saw a strong Soviet external reaction to the "Schlesinger doctrine," there were also signs of some internal debate on strategic and related SALT policy matters in the Soviet Union. These developments on the respective sides in the period leading up to the pivotal SALT II transaction at Vladivostok in November 1974 will be discussed in the present chapter.

## THE KISSINGER-SCHLESINGER PHASE OF POLICY DEBATE

A large share of attention in the national debate that arose in the United States in 1974 around the so-called Schlesinger strategic doctrine was given to such questions as whether significant differences existed between Secretaries Kissinger and Schlesinger over the meshing of strategic policy with the SALT negotiations, as well as in their basic philosophies of how best to deal with the Soviet Union. In addition, there was recurrent speculation that the Kissinger-Schlesinger relationship had taken on the character of a power struggle between two strong and intellectually well matched protagonists representing rival constituencies in the realm of national security policy.

To comment on the question of power rivalry first, Schlesinger, who had come more recently to the higher politics of defense as the top man of the Pentagon bureaucracy, was generally depicted as the challenger in a struggle for power, grown restive under the near total domination of national security policy exercised by Kissinger in his dual NSC and State Department roles.[1] One implication of this view of their relationship was that even if no serious substantive or philosophical differences existed between the two men, bureaucratic rivalry alone was likely to put them on a collision course, perhaps forcing Gerald Ford, the new president, to choose between them.[2]

By contrast, some speculation on the Kissinger-Schlesinger relationship occasionally pointed in a quite different direction. For example, since both men were known to be tough-minded intellectuals long engaged in studying the uses of power in international affairs, it has been suggested that, rather than having spent their energies in vying with each other for pre-eminent influence on the shaping of U.S. security policy, the two may in fact have been working together as subtle collaborators in a carrot-and-stick act to influence Soviet policy.[3] Seen in these terms, Kissinger, sounding the softer line, had held out the carrot, and Schlesinger had brandished the stick.

A variation of the view that the two secretaries might have been operating more closely in concert than sometimes assumed was to be found in the suggestion that the real internal split over U.S. strategic and SALT policy vis-à-vis the Soviet Union lay essentially between positions favored respectively by the uniformed Joint Chiefs of Staff and Kissinger, rather than between Kissinger and Schlesinger, described as the two men who in common "understand the ambiguities, dangers and opportunities of the present situation."[4]

Whether they were to be regarded as rivals in an internal power struggle or as a complementary team working effectively in harness, neither man was known to have exhibited anything but respect for the other's abilities. In Schlesinger's case, though he was perhaps a more redoubtable figure than any with whom Kissinger had previously had to deal in the national security apparatus, those who knew him were of the opinion that Schlesinger had never had any hankering to take on Kissinger. Indeed, some commentators made the point that as secretary of defense, Schlesinger was obliged to spend most of his time dealing with generals and admirals in the Pentagon and with congressional guardians of the purse strings,[5] so that little time was left over for taking on anyone as formidable as the secretary of state. For Kissinger's part, though he was reported to have once said that "if Schlesinger and I start fighting, it will blow the town apart,"[6] and though his associates had at times hinted that he was facing an internal challenge of serious dimensions from Schlesinger,[7] Kissinger himself repeatedly discounted rumors of a feud with the secretary of defense. As Kissinger chose to put it in response to questioning before the Senate Foreign Relations Committee in September 1974: "There is no struggle going on. There are occasional differences of emphasis. There is no power struggle."[8]

### Comparison of Substantive Positions

Turning next to the question of substantive differences between Kissinger and Schlesinger on strategic issues, it would appear that their positions on many key issues were often less far apart than the rhetoric of debate in 1974 might have suggested.[9] For example, though there may have been some hidden bones of contention that went unrevealed in public discourse, the catalog of items upon which the two men appeared to be more or less in agreement included the following:

- The overall military budget proposed by the secretary of defense, as well as the share of it devoted to strategic forces, was supported by Kissinger, who said he found it consistent with the policies he was espousing.[10]
- The goal of "essential equivalence in strategic capabilities" with the Soviet Union, as enunciated by Schlesinger, also was endorsed by Kissinger,[11] and neither man was an advocate of re-establishing "strategic superiority." On the second issue, however, the secretary of state had exhibited somewhat stronger feelings, as when he asked, after the frustrating summit session of mid-1974: "What in the name of God is strategic superiority . . . at these levels of numbers? What do you do with it?"[12]
- The general notion that large imbalances in strategic forces can be destabilizing and are therefore not acceptable was embraced by both Schlesinger and Kissinger, with Kissinger agreeing that "the appearance of inferiority—whatever its actual significance—can have serious political consequences."[13] Of the two, however, Kissinger had been more disposed to emphasize the difficulties of translating strategic power into political advantage, noting that "an upper limit exists beyond which additional weapons lose their political significance."[14]
- The assertion that the United States would never accept the "strategic preponderance of another power" was voiced by both

Schlesinger and Kissinger; both also stressed the point, as Kissinger put it, that "we will maintain the nuclear balance by unilateral actions if we must and by negotiations if at all possible."[15]

- The value of conveying to the Soviets that the United States would not draw back from strategic competition if the Soviet Union should seek to alter the strategic balance through "unrestrained competitive programs" was subscribed to by both men. However, though Kissinger had warned that "if we are driven to it, the United States will sustain an arms race,"[16] he had not gone as far as Schlesinger in applying this warning specifically to the case of "matching" any Soviet attempt to acquire substantial counterforce capabilities.

- The proposition that neither the Soviet Union nor the United States could "realistically" expect to develop a "credible disarming capability" against the other was adhered to by both Schlesinger and Kissinger.[17]

- The various strategic weapons development programs espoused by Secretary Schlesinger and the Pentagon, including the major programs for the Trident submarine and the B-1 bomber, were publicly supported by Secretary Kissinger,[18] though he reportedly had some reservations about their utility.[19] It also was said that Schlesinger had privately raised questions about the Trident and B-1, presumably in the context of looking for cheaper alternatives.[20]

- The Schlesinger shift from the doctrine of mutual assured destruction to a more flexible range of nuclear options and to development of a more discriminating targeting capability was also endorsed by Kissinger.[21] However, Kissinger's position on improvement of missile accuracy appeared more ambiguous than Schlesinger's, for he confined his endorsement to the "obligation" of having the ability to use strategic forces "in the most discriminating manner possible."[22] Some observers speculated that Kissinger had refrained from seeking limitations on missile accuracy primarily out of the belief that such curbs would be too difficult to negotiate, not only with the Soviet Union, but with the U.S. military as well.[23]

Beyond the points of full or partial agreement listed here, there appeared to be several strategic issues over which substantive differences between Schlesinger and Kissinger did indeed exist. One of these, already suggested above, was the secretary of state's apparent lesser degree of commitment to a matching counterforce capability, especially in numerical terms. Other differences also appeared to hinge essentially on numbers—on what would constitute a prudent spread in the numerical levels of strategic arms overall, and in MIRVed missiles in particular, that the United States could afford to accept in a negotiated agreement with the Soviet Union.

Apparently, judging from the available sources, these differences peaked in connection with the June-July 1974 summit in Moscow, with Schlesinger reportedly having wanted to concede fewer MIRVed missiles to the Soviets than Kissinger and President Nixon were prepared to grant, as well as favoring a more comprehensive accord on total strategic force levels than Kissinger and the president believed to be negotiable.[24] According to Nixon's own account in his memoirs, Schlesinger and the Joint Chiefs had brought their opposition on proposed MIRV numbers and other issues "to a head" at an NSC meeting on June 20, 1974, where Schlesinger presented a Pentagon proposal that "amounted to an unyielding hard line against any SALT agreement that did not ensure an overwhelming American advantage." Without specifying the contents of the proposal, Nixon's account quotes himself as having said: "Secretary Schlesinger's proposal simply has no chance whatever of being accepted by the Soviets, so we should try to work out something consistent with our interests that will."[25]

Apart from having supposedly compounded the difficulties of establishing a U.S. negotiating position prior to the summit, the Kissinger-Schlesinger differences became an even more controversial matter immediately afterwards, when at a postsummit press conference in Moscow, Kissinger made his much-cited remark that "both sides have to convince their military establishments of the benefits of restraint."[26]

Not surprisingly, Kissinger's statement was promptly interpreted in the press as implying that the Pentagon shared the blame with military leaders on the Soviet side for impeding agreement at the summit. Just as promptly, Schlesinger in a press conference in Washington rejected this suggestion, observing that "we have firm civilian control in this country," and noting further that none of the Soviet proposals acceptable to Kissinger had been vetoed either by himself or the Joint Chiefs of Staff.[27]

The next phase of substantive differences on strategic and SALT issues involving Kissinger and Schlesinger apparently occurred in the interval between the mid-1974 summit and Dr. Kissinger's October 1974 trip to Moscow,[28] while the new Ford administration was in the process of establishing itself in office. Toward the end of this period, after a series of Verification Panel meetings, a debate pitting the two men against each other reportedly came to a head in an

October NSC meeting over which President Ford presided, and which was addressed to the question of what to try next in order to break the SALT deadlock with the Soviet Union.[2][9]

Although the available details of the options under debate are sparse, Schlesinger reportedly contended that "we must face the Soviets down" on their desire to deploy a large number of MIRVed missile launchers. The basic alternatives favored by Schlesinger were said to be either that both sides should agree to substantial mutual force reductions resulting in overall equality, with a MIRV ceiling low enough so that neither side would be tempted to take advantage of the other, or that, if the Russians would not agree, then the United States should "buckle down for a five-year, all-out arms race."[3][0] Kissinger was said to have argued that Moscow was bound to reject the first alternative, and that it was doubtful that support would be forthcoming in the United States to outbuild the Russians in an all-out race. Therefore, he reportedly favored an approach initially providing for force levels, including MIRVed launchers, high enough to be negotiable with the Soviets, leaving reductions and controls on modernization to be negotiated step by step later.[3][1]

In the debate over these contrasting approaches, the Joint Chiefs were said to have sided with Kissinger—a switch from their putative alignment in a solid "Pentagon front" with the secretary of defense. This shift reportedly came about both because the Kissinger plan would allow completion of various modernization programs upon which the Joint Chiefs had set their sights, and because they too doubted that Congress would vote the funds to make an all-out arms race feasible.[3][2] At any rate, it would appear that by the time Kissinger left Washington in October 1974 to talk with Brezhnev, a U.S. position essentially embodying his approach had been adopted, with Schlesinger's concurrence and the president's approval.[3][3]

The revised set of U.S. SALT proposals that Kissinger carried to Moscow in October 1974 reportedly offered the Soviets two broad choices: (1) an equal aggregate number of 2000 "central systems" delivery vehicles for each side, including an equal ceiling of 1000 MIRVed missile launchers, together with sublimits on both the largest Soviet missiles and American bomber-launched missiles; or, if this were rejected, (2) a greater overall total of non-MIRVed delivery vehicles for the Soviet Union, offset by more MIRVed launchers for the United States.[3][4] The developments following Kissinger's October visit that culminated in the SALT transaction at Vladivostok in November 1974 will be taken up presently.

## Differing Views on How to Deal
## with the Soviet Union

Apart from whatever substantive differences may have obtained between Kissinger and Schlesinger in the pre-Vladivostok period of formulating U.S. SALT policy, there was also the broader question of whether a fundamental divergence lay at the core of their respective philosophies for dealing with the Soviet Union. Needless to say, this was an exceedingly complicated question, subject to a wide range of speculation. Perhaps the first point to be made is that though the two men had sometimes been pigeonholed as holding diametrically opposed views on detente with the Soviet Union, Schlesinger's basic philosophy was not indifferent to the merits of the detente relationship that Kissinger was trying to cultivate. At the same time, however, there did appear to be real differences between the two as to how detente itself might relate to the problem of negotiating SALT agreements with the Soviets. Some variations were to be found in the divergent views ascribed to the two men, but in general they ran along the following lines.

Kissinger, for example, was said to fear that detente had become rather brittle in light of events between the May 1972 summit and the last Nixon-Brezhnev summit of mid-1974, that the pressure of technology was threatening to spur an arms race inconsistent with maintaining detente,[35] and that the opportunity for coming to terms with the Brezhnev regime on curbing the nuclear arms race might be lost unless the United States were willing to settle for what it could get in SALT without prolonging the negotiations—or at any rate, that the longer the U.S. side might wait, the poorer its chances of a reasonable agreement.[36]

Schlesinger, on the other hand, was said to believe that Soviet stakes in detente were so great that it was not in the Soviet interest to break off detente lightly and that there was a chance of educating the Soviets to come around to a reasonable SALT agreement by explaining U.S. concerns and posing hard alternatives if the concerns were ignored. Hence, he was said to favor a tougher set of terms for a SALT accord, as well as prudential fallback programs that would exploit U.S. technological advantages, for which the Soviets had a healthy respect, in the event agreement were not reached.[37]

Assuming that the postures described above represented a reasonably accurate picture of the essential underlying differences between the Kissinger and Schlesinger philosophies, it would appear that the positions of both men entailed certain vulnerabilities. In Kissinger's case, the hope of making satisfactory adjustments with the Soviet Union was predicated basically upon the assumption that an accommodating U.S. SALT approach, combined with economic incentives, would be reciprocated by the Brezhnev regime without undue delay. But if the Soviets were to drag their feet, either because of reluctance to constrain their own strategic programs, or because of a belief that Kissinger had lost control over the economic incentives dangled before them, or for whatever combination of reasons, then the logic of the Kissinger position seemed to leave little choice but to offer ever-increasing concessions.

The Schlesinger case rested upon offering a somewhat narrower, but more disagreeable, set of incentives to the Soviet side. As an incentive to persuade them that their best interest lay in a reasonable agreement with the United States, the Soviets were to be let known, in essence, that they would not be permitted to amass a preponderant counterforce advantage. But the problem here was that this message might be misunderstood by the Russians, who might not believe that the United States would stop merely at matching them, and who therefore might choose to redouble their own strategic programs. In short, while the Kissinger philosophy seemed to entail the risk of an unfavorable deal with the Soviet Union in SALT, the Schlesinger philosophy seemed to involve the possibility of no agreement at all.

At bottom, it might be said that the two positions amounted to a very real dilemma—one which only the Soviets themselves might resolve by demonstrating that in fact they were prepared to come to terms on a "reasonable" agreement.

## SOVIET REACTION TO THE "SCHLESINGER DOCTRINE"

As might be expected, the changes in U.S. strategic doctrine and planning advanced by Secretary Schlesinger in early 1974, around which a public debate arose in the United States, did not go unnoticed in the Soviet Union.[38] How the Soviet Union's own strategic and SALT policy might be influenced by these changes, however, was far from clear in the Soviet reaction to the Schlesinger proposals, at least in those aspects of the Soviet response that became visible to outside observers.

Given the guarded nature of public strategic discourse that is customary in the Soviet Union, it was probably not surprising that the Schlesinger proposals elicited neither much in the way of published professional analysis by Soviet strategic authorities, nor any specific indication of the kinds of strategic measures that the Soviet Union might contemplate in return. Rather, Soviet response in the spring and summer of 1974 was confined for the most part to the polemical level, with the Schlesinger strategic approach being treated as one more manifestation of attempts by the U.S. "military-industrial complex" and other "anti-Soviet circles" to block improvement of relations with the Soviet Union and to "discredit the policy of detente." But, even on the polemical level, Soviet reaction, though uniformly negative, did not prove to be exceptionally harsh, and Schlesinger himself was seldom attacked ad hominem.

This moderate treatment of Schlesinger in the Soviet press changed, however, to a campaign of ad hominem denunciations in mid-1975 after statements by Schlesinger declined to rule out possible first use of tactical nuclear weapons in the event Europe were subjected to a conventional Soviet invasion.[39] Even so, during this period Schlesinger probably fared somewhat better than Senator Henry Jackson, who doubtless enjoyed the distinction of being the principal named target of Soviet ire among those accused of trying to discredit detente.

The general burden of complaint in the Soviet press regarding Schlesinger's and the Pentagon's budgetary and strategic policy statements was that they contradicted "the spirit of detente," that they sought to "revive the myth" of a "Soviet threat" in order to create a "psychological atmosphere for adoption of new multibillion dollar military appropriations," and that they represented an attempt to put "pressure" on the Soviet Union.[40] Occasionally, Soviet commentators also noted that "militarist circles" in the United States professed to be alarmed about "a U.S. lag in the military sphere,"[41] and that these circles were hoping to restore "the lost strategic superiority of the United States by qualitative improvement of weapons."[42]

Up to the time of the mid-1974 summit meeting in Moscow, there was no open indication that high-level Soviet officials had found occasion to register objections to the Schlesinger proposals with their opposite numbers on the American side. At the summit, however,[43] Brezhnev reportedly took exception to the Schlesinger "retargeting program" in strong terms, expressing the view, among other things, that it implied the possibility of nuclear war and that the United States was seeking a disarming first-strike capability against the USSR. It has not been reported what the U.S. side in the summit dialogue had to say on the subject in return, but evidently word concerning Brezhnev's remonstrances filtered down through the Soviet establishment, for thereafter fresh criticism began to appear in

Soviet media along much the same lines as that attributed to Brezhnev. There was also a more noticeable tendency, both in the Soviet press and in informal contacts between Soviet and American students of political-military affairs, for Soviet spokesmen to emphasize that the "Schlesinger doctrine" was regarded as a breach of the principles of "equal security" and "no unilateral advantage," and as a resort to "pressure tactics" against the Soviet Union.

An example of this line of argument was to be found in a September 1974 article by A. Karenin, in which it was asserted that "certain circles in the Pentagon and the military-industrial complex" had been insisting upon "very extensive programs in the field of strategic arms" in order "to provide the American side with notorious 'bargaining chips' "—an approach said to be "quite contrary" to the principle of negotiated solution of international problems on "the basis of equality."[44] The Karenin article also alleged that "dreams of nuclear superiority" on the part of U.S. militarists were "ephemeral," and it suggested that one of the virtues of the ABM Treaty was that it punctured any "illusions" in the United States about escaping retaliation if the United States should start a war.[45]

But perhaps the most explicit Soviet criticism of the Schlesinger doctrine came from G.A. Trofimenko, a well-known writer on strategic affairs and a senior member of Arbatov's Institute of the USA and Canada. Writing in the institute's journal for September 1974, Trofimenko said that despite the "unequivocal" repudiation of "use of force or threats of force" in Soviet-American agreements, some representatives of the U.S. military-industrial complex were still resorting to "signaling via threats."[46] An example, he said, was "the excessive publicity given in recent months in the USA to the so-called 'Schlesinger doctrine' on 'retargeting' strategic missiles." Since the "true character" of U.S. targeting is "obviously a highly important" military secret, Trofimenko asserted, the statements of Pentagon officials therefore could not be taken to represent "objective information" for the enlightenment of the general public, but rather were a "deliberate attempt to exert psychological pressure on the other side—an attempt to gain, if not direct military-technical advantages, then, at least, conceptual and psychological advantages."[47]

Such an approach, intended to create a "more comfortable position" for the U.S. in the strategic arms "dialogue" with the USSR by providing "so-called 'bargaining chips,' " could not help but undermine the "basic principle of equal security." Further, according to Trofimenko, the possibility of mutually acceptable arms limitation agreements was undercut when U.S. representatives, "instead of seeking compromises, try to propose to the other side a solution based on a purely American model, which answers to traditional U.S. military-technical policy but is radically at variance with the traditions and principles of the other side's military-technical policy."[48]

One may note here that Trofimenko's remarks on asymmetries of military-technical policy probably related in part to the issue of throwweight and differences in missile-design philosophy mentioned previously.[49] The throwweight issue, indeed, was later underscored by Trofimenko in a condensed and partly revised version of his September 1974 article, which was supplied (in translation) to the American press in November 1974 by the Soviet Embassy in Washington.[50] In the translated version of his article, Trofimenko inveighed against the "double standards" applied by "American theoreticians" to various strategic issues in SALT, citing among other things American attempts to "reduce all aspects" of the qualitative strategic balance to the "arbitrarily chosen parameter" of throwweight, as well as attempts to retain "intact Washington's 'flexible strategic options.'" However, another example of a "double standard" went conveniently unmentioned: namely, the fact that Trofimenko's arguments against the U.S. SALT posture could be presented in the American press, while the Soviet press remained closed to any American arguments against one-sided aspects of the Soviet SALT approach.

Apart from such published criticism of the "Schlesinger doctrine" as that surveyed above, some insight into Soviet reaction was also to be gained from occasional private exchanges between Soviet and American students of strategic affairs. Without identifying those involved, a pertinent conversation in point can be summed up as follows. The American participant made the observation that Marshal Grechko and other Soviet military authorities had consistently stated that the Soviet Strategic Rocket Forces were intended for counterforce strikes against U.S. "nuclear-delivery forces" and, therefore, that one might be justified in interpreting Schlesinger's ideas as "convergence" toward a well-established Soviet position and movement away from the mutual assured destruction concept that had always seemed unacceptable to Soviet spokesmen. The Soviet participant replied that while it was true that Soviet doctrine called for counterforce strikes in the event of "all-out nuclear war," there was no Soviet doctrine for "limited nuclear warfare" in that part of the spectrum between general nuclear warfare and small-scale conventional conflict. What the Schlesinger approach was aimed at, he charged, was to restore "the political leverage" of strategic forces in this part of the spectrum and, thereby, to "intimidate" and "dictate" to the Soviet Union.[51]

Although obviously the Schlesinger doctrine had been found objectionable in the USSR on a number of counts, especially for what was perceived as an attempt to gain political leverage over the Soviet Union, Soviet commentary—whether written or verbal—gave little indication of what impact the Schlesinger approach might have on the Soviet Union's own strategic policy. If, for example, Soviet planners were thinking of taking the kinds of countering steps that Schlesinger's Western critics had warned they might take, such as adoption of a launch-on-warning posture or conversion of their fixed ICBM silos into mobile ICBMs, no hint of this was to be heard. Neither, for that matter, was any explicit admission forthcoming that the Soviets had found persuasive such arguments as the Schlesinger thesis that their best interests would be served by agreeing to forego a competition in development of counterforce capabilities. To be sure, it would have been quite out of keeping with the Soviet style of strategic discourse if policy positions on such matters were opened to frank discussion and scrutiny in public. At the same time, however, the possibility could not be dismissed that the question of how to respond to the strategic measures advanced by Schlesinger—other than in the polemical mode already described—had in fact become a controversial issue within the Soviet policymaking system.

## POSSIBLE INTERNAL SOVIET DEBATE
## OVER STRATEGIC ISSUES

Periodic speculation about rifts within the Soviet leadership over policy issues of one kind or another is so commonplace that it often fails to merit much credibility. Perhaps the case in question falls into this category. But be that as it may, there would seem to be some grounds for supposing that strategic issues had become the subject of an internal policy debate which, though antedating the Schlesinger proposals, may have been given a new edge after they appeared.

Signs suggestive of some sort of internal controversy involving strategic matters came to the surface in late 1973 and early 1974. At that time, it became apparent that a muted argument was being carried on in the pages of various Soviet publications between two camps that did not see altogether eye to eye on questions relating to detente, SALT, nuclear armaments, and security. One group consisted of writers roughly identifiable as expositors of the Brezhnev detente line, many of whom were associated with Arbatov's Institute of the USA and Canada. The other took in a number of military theorists, whose skepticism about detente and the wisdom of relying on SALT as the avenue to Soviet security showed through their published utterances.

Without tracing the details here, the detentist camp could be found arguing that war in the nuclear age was no longer a viable instrument of politics and that security could no longer be automatically ensured through further "accumulation of military hardware."[52] The military spokesmen, however, writing for the most part under the aegis of the Main Political Administration of the Armed Forces, challenged the notion that nuclear war would mean the "death of civilization" and that there could be no victor in such a war. Instead, they stressed the need to provide forces "necessary for reliable defense of the motherland" and warned against slowing down Soviet military preparations in a world in which the danger of war, though reduced by the shift in the correlation of forces in favor of the socialist camp, still existed.[53]

In many respects, the arguments and idiom of this skirmishing in print were reminiscent of an earlier debate in Krushchev's time, one which had centered around the doctrinal issue of whether nuclear weapons had negated the Leninist dictum that war is a rational instrument of politics and which had testified to a growing awareness of the hazards and complexities of trying to translate military power directly into political gain in a nuclear world.[54] But perhaps the point most germane here is that, just as this earlier debate reflected differences over strategic issues at the top of the Soviet policy pyramid in Khrushchev's day, so its counterpart in the SALT era might have been related to contention over alternative security approaches within the upper echelons of the Soviet policymaking system.

In this connection, one doctrinal question with discordant implications for Soviet strategic planning and SALT policy warrants particular mention. As a matter of long habit, the Soviets have displayed a reluctance to part with the idea that they can successfully ensure their own security, along with an equal reluctance to rely on others to help look out for it.[55] Thus, within the Soviet defense community especially, there has doubtless been a built-in suspicion of agreements with the adversary involving any appreciable inroads upon the Soviet Union's own unilateral strategic planning. But there was also at least an outside possibility that as a result of the SALT experience, this attitude had begun to give way in parts of the Soviet establishment to a new outlook more congenial to the idea that Soviet security might be served by strategic agreements based to some extent on each side's being solicitous of the other's security concerns. Although it would hardly seem warranted to suggest that sentiment favoring the substitution of "shared liability" agreements for unilateral planning had come to prevail within Soviet leadership circles,[56] it might be guessed that there was at least some debate over the relative merits of these two approaches.

Beyond helping to support the conjecture that strategic policy alternatives of one sort or another might again be at issue, however, the evidence at hand gave little basis to judge whether the range of debate in 1974 might cover widely different strategic alternatives, or whether it was mainly at the margin of an internal consensus on what was required for Soviet security—with the differences perhaps narrowing down to how much or how little need be conceded for the sake of agreement in SALT with the United States.

### Impact on Soviet Policy Debate
### of the Schlesinger Initiatives

If it might be surmised only on admittedly speculative grounds that an internal strategic debate of some kind was going on within the Soviet leadership, there was even less basis for knowing what impact the Schlesinger strategic initiatives might be having on it. Again as a matter of conjecture, a potentially disputatious issue that might have arisen within the Soviet establishment was one related to the trend in strategic technologies that promised to render silo-based ICBM forces increasingly vulnerable to more accurate counterforce systems.

Up to around early 1974, Soviet planners appear to have felt reasonably confident about the survivability of a substantial portion of their own ICBM forces, thanks both to hardening measures and to the lower numerical ceiling placed on U.S. missile launchers by the Interim Agreement of May 1972. To some extent, U.S. disavowal of accuracy improvements before Schlesinger's removal of this constraint also may have contributed to a Soviet estimate that the United States could not muster sufficient counterforce capability to jeopardize the survival of Soviet forces.

Then, however, came the Schlesinger shift, warning that the United States no longer intended to abstain from counterforce competition in the absence of satisfactory long-term agreements in SALT. This introduced a new factor into the situation, tantamount to advising the Russians that their large and ongoing ICBM investment would face steady depreciation in the event of such competition. Although it remained a moot question whether this advice would have its intended effect of bringing Soviet decisionmakers around to see the virtues of genuine stabilizing agreements in SALT, or whether they would react otherwise, it would seem plausible to suppose that the counterforce aspect of the Schlesinger initiatives had stimulated some internal debate on the other side.

In addition to the above case, for which no direct evidence could be cited, there were a few other instances in which—with some straining—the effects of the Schlesinger doctrine might be detected. For example, in the several months prior to the mid-1974 summit, there were tenuous indications of some differences among the Soviet leadership over the preferred Soviet approach to the MIRV issue in SALT, the evidence for which might be seen in the reversal of Ambassador Dobrynin's optimistic assurances to Dr. Kissinger that the latter's MIRV "breakthrough" proposal would receive a favorable reception when he took it to Moscow in March 1974.[5 7] Conceivably, a negative Soviet reaction to the then newly advanced Schlesinger doctrine might have had something to do with the turning down of Kissinger's proffered MIRV solution.

Again, the mid-1974 summit itself gave perhaps some slight hint that Brezhnev might have been more receptive to concluding a deal there on MIRV had it not been for the Schlesinger strategic initiatives, to which Brezhnev reportedly voiced strenuous objection on that occasion. This supposition rests on the inference that Brezhnev's own stand on MIRV was somewhat softer than that of the Soviet marshals,[5 8] but that he found it expedient to bow to their position in order to avoid the appearance of having yielded to American pressure emanating from Schlesinger's Pentagon.[5 9]

Besides the possibility that the Schlesinger doctrine might have had the effect of strengthening the hand of those opposed to a more reasonable Soviet approach on MIRV and other strategic issues at the mid-1974 summit, there was also the suggestion offered by some observers that the Soviet leadership might have debated the wisdom of entering a deal with President Nixon, whose political misfortunes at home had left him in a questionable status as a negotiating partner who might be unable to marshal congressional approval of any new agreements reached with him.[6 0]

Apart from such tenuous evidence, however, the mid-1974 summit produced few tangible signs one way or the other about possible policy differences within the Soviet leadership. The fact that the summit ended without a manifest shift in previous Soviet positions on MIRV and other major SALT issues could be taken to mean that the whole of the Soviet leadership actually saw eye to eye on these matters. But it might also be argued that the Soviet leadership had stuck to the previously established line simply because no internal consensus on a change of approach could be achieved up to that time.

At any rate, whatever the reasons for the Soviet stance having remained resistant to change at the mid-1974 summit, something happened in the few months between that summit and Vladivostok that prompted the Soviet leadership to adopt a SALT posture seemingly a good deal less intractable than the one they had previously displayed.

One line of conjecture is that an internal debate within the Soviet leadership over various doctrinal and strategic planning issues—including perhaps some of those suggested above—had come to a head in the months after the mid-1974 summit, resulting in a top-level decision to move toward a new agreement with the United States in the SALT arena. In this connection, elements of the debate involving the code issue of "war as an instrument of politics" came to the surface again just before Vladivostok in a way that suggested that some sort of internal tradeoff might have been arranged between contending schools of thought.

In an article in November 1974 reviewing a newly published edition of various writings by B.M. Shaposhnikov, a renowned Soviet military theorist of an earlier day and a prewar chief of the General Staff, the then incumbent head of the General Staff, V.G. Kulikov, noted that many of Shaposhnikov's precepts, based on a "Leninist understanding" of the "organic relationship" between strategy and policy, "have not lost their significance even today." Among the most important of these precepts, Kulikov recalled, was "recognition of armed struggle as one of the instruments of policy." Having reaffirmed the validity of this precept, Kulikov also observed that "strategic nuclear weapons and the constant threat of their use by the imperialist states" had since Shaposhnikov's day "substantially enhanced the role of the General Staff in ensuring the security of the Soviet motherland."[61]

Kulikov went on to make clear, however, that none of this meant in the Soviet case that military strategy stands "above policy." Rather, he stressed that strategy "ensues" from the policy of the Soviet state, as defined by the Communist Party's leadership. One inference that might be drawn from Kulikov's careful balancing between the principle of Party pre-eminence in policy and the essential role of the military in Soviet security (plus a further comment on Shaposhnikov's awareness of "the need for unity of the political and military leadership") was that this was Kulikov's way of signaling that an internal bargain had been struck on SALT that satisfied both the strategic views of the military professionals whom he represented and the requirements of the political side of the house. Or, a somewhat different interpretation might be advanced, namely, that Kulikov was showing his support for Brezhnev's SALT position against demands for a stiffer Soviet position from more extreme factions within both the military and political leadership elites.[62]

## FINAL BARGAINING STEPS LEADING TO VLADIVOSTOK

Whatever the significance of the Kulikov article with regard to what was going on within the Soviet policymaking system in the pre-Vladivostok period, the steps that were taking place in the Soviet-American bargaining process had begun to quicken at the time of Kissinger's October 1974 visit to Moscow.[63] Somewhat unexpectedly, Brezhnev and Gromyko were said to have expressed interest in the first of two proposals put to them by Kissinger—a proposal for an equal aggregate number of 2000 delivery vehicles for each side, with an equal sublimit of 1000 MIRVed missile launchers.[64]

However, according to Kissinger, it was only after two days of "very difficult and very inconclusive meetings," capped by a special session of the Politburo, that the Soviet side finally accepted the principle of an equal aggregate number of delivery vehicles to be reached at some future stage of a ten-year agreement.[65]

How close the respective parties came to ironing out their other basic differences on this occasion is not entirely clear. Kissinger has indicated that when he left Moscow on October 27 the Soviets were still insisting on "some compensation" for U.S. forward-based systems and for British and French nuclear forces, and that they had not yet agreed to early establishment of equal aggregates.[66] However, an exchange of further proposals through the back channel shortly before the Vladivostok meeting is said to have given grounds in Washington for believing that the chances for a new agreement were favorable, although the Soviets reportedly continued to make clear their preference for numerical levels higher than those proposed by the United States.[67]

Meanwhile, according to anonymous Soviet sources in Moscow, a Politburo decision to try for an agreement along the lines subsequently reached at Vladivostok had been finally firmed up sometime after the Kissinger October visit.[68] These sources also indicated that several options on numbers had been approved by the Politburo for Brezhnev's use in bargaining at Vladivostok. On the whole, therefore, it would seem warranted to suppose that an essential core of understanding had been arrived at between the two sides before the subsequent two-day transaction at Vladivostok took place on November 23 and 24, 1974.

We shall take up the specifics of that transaction in Chapter 9, but before doing so, it may be worth speculating for a moment on what may have led to a Soviet decision to move toward agreement at Vladivostok with the United States.[69] On the one hand, the stretch-out of the SALT negotiating schedule agreed upon at the mid-1974 summit might be credited with having eased some of the pressure upon Soviet planning for rapid deployment of new strategic systems, as Kissinger had hoped would be the case,[70] and thus had allowed room to reconcile any differing schools of thought within the Soviet leadership about what could prudently be entertained in a new SALT agreement. On the other hand, it might be held that the hard alternatives posed by the Schlesinger initiatives if negotiations should lead nowhere had prompted second thoughts in Moscow and induced a majority of the leadership to opt for a more reasonable position in SALT.[71]

But in either event, what distinguishes this first body of explanation is that a change of direction in the Soviet case is presumed to have stemmed essentially from factors inherent in the SALT process and that of strategic planning. By contrast, a second line of conjecture would identify the main impetus for change as having come from outside SALT and the strategic domain.

In this second view, the governing consideration was in essence the preservation of detente, with the Soviet decision to adopt a less intractable position turning on the belief that it was worth paying something in SALT coin to salvage the benefits of detente—technology transfer, industrial aid, a clearing of the decks for the next Five-Year Plan, or whatever other Soviet interests might be served by it. In terms of this explanation, the immediate factor in bringing about a changed Soviet position on SALT might be assumed to have been some sort of sobering advice from Kissinger to Brezhnev in October, and perhaps from President Ford in November, to the effect that detente was in deepening trouble and that therefore there had better be some movement in SALT if it were to be saved.[72]

Which set of explanations best fits the facts can only be left to some future investigation. But as far as the present inquiry goes, it would seem likely that patching up detente had more to do with clearing the way for the Vladivostok transaction than any fundamental shift in the Soviet strategic perspective.

✳ *Chapter 9*

# Vladivostok: A Pivotal SALT II Transaction

The joint agreement reached at the Vladivostok summit on November 24, 1974, after two days of negotiation in which the principals were President Ford and Secretary of State Kissinger on the American side and Secretary Brezhnev and Foreign Minister Gromyko on the Soviet side,[1] was essentially a declaration of intent to work out, during the ensuing few months, a new ten-year agreement on the limitation of strategic offensive arms. In effect, the Vladivostok transaction simply gave advance notice about what the intended features of a new accord would be, if and when it were successfully consummated. Or, as President Ford put it several days later when making public some of the understandings reached in the "working" meeting with Brezhnev at Vladivostok: "It will take more detailed negotiations to convert this agreed framework into a comprehensive accord."[2]

As it turned out, not only detailed but also very lengthy negotiations—stretching out over more than the next four years—were to be needed before the outline agreement at Vladivostok could be brought close to completion in a SALT II accord on limiting strategic offensive arms.[3] In this chapter, meanwhile, we shall consider the nature of the Vladivostok transaction and its implications for SALT and the strategic policies of the two sides.

## SPECIFICS AND AMBIGUITIES OF THE
## VLADIVOSTOK TRANSACTION

The main aspects of the proposed accord outlined at Vladivostok, parts of which were to undergo some change in the course of subsequent negotiations, were these:

- An equal overall ceiling of 2400 strategic delivery vehicles for each side, to include ICBMs, SLBMs, and bombers.
- An equal number of 1320 MIRVed missile launchers for each side, with no limit on throwweight.
- The counting of any missile tested with MIRV against the MIRV ceiling, if the missile should be deployed.[4]
- Freedom to mix within the agreed aggregate of 2400 delivery vehicles.
- A sublimit of 313 on heavy missiles and no new silo construction. (These were provisions to be carried over from the Interim Agreement of May 1972.)
- Deployment of land-mobile missiles and some types of bomber-launched missiles permitted, but to be included in the overall ceiling of 2400 delivery vehicles.
- Apparent dropping of the long-standing Soviet demand to account for FBS in any agreed aggregate of central strategic delivery systems.
- No constraints on modernization that would preclude such measures as improvements in accuracy and deployment of new systems still under development, for example, the B-1 bomber and Trident submarine.
- Duration of the new agreement to be from 1975 to 1985, with relevant provisions of the Interim Agreement remaining in force until entry into effect of the new agreement in October 1977.[5]
- Following conclusion of the new agreement, further negotiations to begin "no later than 1980-1981," on "possible reductions of strategic arms in the period after 1985."[6]

Few of the above provisions, it should be noted, were spelled out in the text of the brief joint agreement issued at Vladivostok; indeed, most of them were not even mentioned.[7] Nor were the aide-mémoire exchanged some days later by the two governments to confirm the Vladivostok understandings made public.[8] Such details as became known were largely revealed in later amplifying statements by President Ford, Dr. Kissinger, and other American officials. Soviet spokesmen, though voicing what some observers termed almost "rhapsodic" approval of the political aspects of the Vladivostok meeting,[9] confined their commentary on its military aspects to generalities. There were thus, in addition to some known specifics, a good many ambiguities in the Vladivostok agreement, though it was difficult to distinguish whether these arose merely out of abbreviated disclosure of what had transpired at Vladivostok or out of actual lacunae in the understandings reached between the two sides. Whatever the case, however, let us look further here at some of the specific features, as well as ambiguities, of the Vladivostok transaction.

Although the total of strategic delivery vehicles for each side was understood to include not only ICBMs and SLBMs but also bombers, nowhere were bombers specifically mentioned in the published agreement. Agreement on equality in overall numbers answered to a principle pressed throughout SALT II by the American side, but equality was pegged at a level to accommodate Soviet preference. The agreed figure of 2400 was said to be about 300 higher than that proposed by the U.S. side and about 100 lower than proposed by Brezhnev at the start of the Vladivostok meeting.[10] This would suggest that there had been some bargaining over numbers, though as Kissinger later indicated, he had seen no plausible way to achieve "lower numbers" in the absence of a U.S. buildup to "produce an incentive to reduce numbers on the other side."[11]

The feature of the Vladivostok accord allowing each side an equal number of MIRVed missile launchers had several noteworthy aspects. For one thing, it marked the successful end of a persistent Soviet effort to exclude restrictions on throwweight from any MIRV agreement, though this had been foreshadowed by the dropping of throwweight limitations from the American position at the mid-1974 summit.[12] Which side at Vladivostok had wanted to set the ceiling on MIRVed launchers at 1320, a figure well above the limits proposed by either side at the mid-1974 summit, was left somewhat unclear.[13] According to Kissinger, the proposed MIRV number was "geared" to "a minimum program that we had established as being in the interest of our own security," and therefore, "the MIRV limits resulted substantially from American proposals and not from Soviet proposals."[14] However, this seemed to conflict with other (though less-authoritative) accounts, according to which the Soviets at Vladivostok had proposed a figure over 1300, at least 200 above what was said to have been the American proposal.[15]

A later explanation by Dr. Kissinger furnished a different logic for the large discrepancy between the MIRV ceiling proposed by the U.S. side at the Moscow summit in July 1974 and that which emerged from the Vladivostok bargaining. The July proposal, he said, "called for a five-year agreement. If you double the number that we proposed for the five-year agreement, you would have a higher number than the one we settled on for ten years."[16]

Meanwhile another comment on the MIRV numbers issue by an unidentified U.S. official gave a still different slant on the bargaining that may have been involved. He said that if the U.S. side had held out for less than the 1320 MIRV limit, it would also have been obliged to agree on an overall total of more than 2400 delivery vehicles for the Soviet side.[17]

Another cloudy aspect of the MIRV question was related to the problems of verifying compliance with a limitation agreement. It was not altogether clear, for example, whether the Soviets had subscribed to the proposition that any missile tested with MIRV would, when deployed, be counted against the agreed ceiling, or whether this was simply an American view still subject to negotiation.[18] Since some of the new Soviet ICBMs had been tested both with and without MIRV, this point—if a genuine ambiguity in the agreement—could become a contentious issue in subsequent negotiations, as in fact proved to be the case.[19]

Other criteria to facilitate the task of MIRV verification, such as restriction of MIRV deployment to specified bases or geographic areas, were also reported to be on the list of collateral constraints that the United States felt were necessary but was uncertain the Russians would accept.[20] One of the side effects of the verification problem became evident in late January 1975, when it was reported that installation of the final fifty MIRVed launchers in the Minuteman III program at Malmstrom Air Force Base, Montana, had been temporarily suspended in order not to prejudice the chances of getting the Russians to agree that all missiles at particular locations should be considered as MIRVed if any of them were actual MIRV types.[21]

The green light given at Vladivostok to deployment of mobile land-based strategic missiles represented acquiescence to a position long favored by the Soviet Union, though in fact earlier U.S. opposition to such deployment had gradually diminished prior to Vladivostok. This feature of the agreement would, so to speak, legitimize any Soviet plans for deployment of a mobile version of the SS-16 ICBM, but it also left the United States with the option of developing and deploying land-mobile systems if it should so choose at a time when a mobile basing mode for the MX ICBM was beginning to be explored.[22] How much attention had been devoted in the Vladivostok meeting to the verification problems connected with mobile missile deployment was not known. Although these problems might perhaps be less severe than in the case of MIRV,[23] it remained uncertain what agreed measures might be found in the next round of negotiations to account for mobile systems within an overall ceiling on delivery vehicles.[24]

Freedom for each side to determine the composition of its overall total of delivery systems was not mentioned in the published agreement but was among the provisions accepted at Vladivostok by the Soviet Union.[25] Answering to a requirement consistently advocated in SALT by the United States, freedom to mix among ICBM and bomber systems within an overall ceiling had at one time also been considered acceptable by the Soviets, but throughout most of SALT II their attitude toward this principle apparently had been lukewarm at best. On the whole, it would appear that this provision posed fewer problems of interpretation than some of the other matters dealt with at Vladivostok.

The provisions relating to bombers, on the other hand, were among the least-clarified aspects of the Vladivostok transaction, leaving a number of rather significant loose ends to be resolved. Although bombers went unmentioned in the published agreement, they were said by the U.S. side to be included in the overall ceiling of delivery vehicles. However, the kinds of aircraft to be counted against the aggregate ceiling had not been defined, other than that they would be aircraft of "international range,"[26] nor was it indicated whether such aircraft as mothballed bombers or bombers converted to tanker use were to be charged against the ceiling.

The particular bomber case that was later to become the center of extended controversy in SALT II concerned the Soviet Backfire bomber, whose potential intercontinental role had previously been under debate in the United States. Some accounts had it that the Backfire issue had been largely ignored in the Vladivostok meeting, though others indicated that at least a tentative understanding had been reached to count neither the Backfire nor the U.S. FB-111 in the permissible total of delivery vehicles.[27]

Another bomber-related question that was left unclear at Vladivostok, and which was later to emerge in a controversial context as the cruise missile issue, concerned missiles launched from aircraft. Agreement reportedly had been reached to consider one bomber as a single delivery vehicle,[28] but in the case of missiles carried as part of a bomber payload, what to count against the overall ceiling of 2400 vehicles apparently had not been fully clarified. For example, there was agreement that missiles launched from aircraft and having ranges in excess of 600 kilometers (372 miles) would be included in the overall ceiling.[29] However, according to a subsequent interpretation by Dr. Kissinger, this provision referred only to air-launched *ballistic* missiles and not to strategic cruise missiles, whereas the Soviets retrospectively insisted that limitations were meant to apply to both ballistic and cruise missiles of more than 600-kilometer range launched from aircraft.[30]

One of the more interesting features of the Vladivostok transaction, without doubt, was the Soviet Union's apparent abandonment of its long-standing insistence that nuclear-capable U.S. forward-based systems be accounted for in any agreed aggregate of strategic delivery systems. No reference to this change in Soviet position was made in the published agreement, nor did the amplifying remarks of American officials indicate whether the FBS issue might merely be transferred to another negotiating forum outside SALT, or whether it had been dropped for good. Some editorial comment indicated that FBS was henceforth to be "dealt with in a *European* negotiating context."[31] On the other hand, a statement by Kissinger to reporters at Vladivostok seemed to suggest that it had been relinquished, for he said that the Soviets had ceased to press for inclusion of FBS because they no longer believed that these weapons were "suitable for a significant attack on the Soviet Union."[32] However, as we shall have occasion to note later, the Soviets would be found at least partially retracting this waiver of their FBS claims within six months after Vladivostok.[33]

Finally, a provision of the Vladivostok agreement that did not long survive its initial unveiling was the point dealing with possible future reductions to take place "in the period after 1985." In the wake of a barrage of criticism in the United States directed at failure to provide for earlier negotiations on reduction of strategic arms levels, this portion of the agreement was modified in the aide-mémoire on the Vladivostok accord.

## MIXED REACTION TO THE VLADIVOSTOK PACT IN THE UNITED STATES

In the United States, the Vladivostok agreement received a mixed reception, marked by initial surprise that the first brief meeting of Ford and Brezhnev had managed to bring the two sides together on even a tentative SALT outline agreement, whatever its substantive merits might be. Perhaps the prevailing sentiment was that though the Vladivostok agreement had given detente a much-needed lift,[34] and was probably better than no agreement at all, there was still considerable room for skepticism as to whether it warranted some of the claims made for it,[35] including Dr. Kissinger's prediction that it would "mean that a cap has been put on the arms race for a period of ten years."[36]

Much of the commentary on the agreement combined praise for its positive features with criticism of what were considered its shortcomings. Cited among its merits were that it established quantitative limits on strategic arms and that it symbolized further U.S.-Soviet commitment to detente. Most frequently mentioned among its deficiencies were that the agreement not only failed to reduce strategic arms levels, but set the overall and MIRV ceilings too high; that it would tend to speed up rather than slow down some aspects of the arms race, especially qualitative competition; that it promised to boost rather than lower arms expenditures; and that by leaving the Soviet throwweight advantage intact, it might stimulate a counterforce buildup that could lead to acquisition of a first-strike capability by one side or both, with a consequent threat to strategic stability.[37]

Doubtless the sharpest critic of the Vladivostok transaction was Senator Jackson, who assailed the agreement for leaving strategic levels "astonishingly high" and suggested that the Ford administration should "go back" and bargain with the Russians for lower levels.[38] Jackson also let it be known in early December 1974 that he would lead a move in the 94th Congress for renegotiation of the Vladivostok accord. A less-demanding resolution somewhat along the same lines was proposed in the 93rd Congress a few days later by Senators Edward M. Kennedy, Walter F. Mondale, and Charles McC. Mathias, expressing support for "the broad purposes" of the Vladivostok agreement, but also urging the president to "make every possible effort to negotiate further nuclear arms limitation and reduction measures" as part of a final accord.[39]

The pressure upon the Ford administration with regard to negotiating lower ceilings evidently was a factor contributing to revision of that portion of the Vladivostok agreement dealing with future reductions, as mentioned earlier. Dr. Kissinger, who reportedly found himself "dismayed" by criticism of what he considered to be a "breakthrough" achievement at Vladivostok, rose to defend the agreement publicly,[40] but at the same time he also dealt privately with Soviet Ambassador Dobrynin to amend the language of the aide-mémoire on Vladivostok. The result, as first disclosed by Kissinger in a *Newsweek* interview in late December, was to drop the dates in the aide-mémoire referring to negotiations on reductions. According to Kissinger, this meant that such negotiations could "start as soon as possible and take effect as soon as there is an agreement."[41] Although the amendment in question did not commit the Russians to renegotiate the Vladivostok agreement itself, as called for by Senator Jackson, it could be interpreted as a canny move by Secretary Kissinger to gain allies in the debate on the Vladivostok agreement in the new Congress.[42]

Support for the agreement that would be helpful in such a debate also was forthcoming from others. Senator John C. Stennis, chairman of the Senate Armed Services Committee, and General George S. Brown, chairman of the Joint Chiefs of Staff, both endorsed the agreement as a first step toward the eventual goal of mutual force reductions,[43] as did Schlesinger. The secretary of defense cautioned that the Vladivostok accord did not mean "the achievement of utopia," but called it "a major step forward," and noted that it satisfied the congressional guidance, laid down at Senator Jackson's behest after SALT I, that any new agreement be based on equal force levels.[44] At the same time, Schlesinger foresaw a need for "some upward adjustment" from the then-current U.S. strategic budget of about $8 billion a year unless reductions were achieved in further negotiations. With regard to specific measures, he indicated that there were no plans to phase down the existing U.S. Minuteman force, but that if the United States should find it necessary to move toward the agreed ceilings, it might add more bombers and Trident submarines than previously planned, and possibly mobile missiles as well.[45]

In arms control circles in the United States, the Vladivostok pact proved to be unusually controversial, with the leadership of such organizations as the Arms Control Association and the Federation of American Scientists divided over the merits of the accord. Generally speaking, sentiment was split between those giving the agreement qualified approval and those condemning it as a backward step in an arms control sense.[46] Supporters held that despite such serious drawbacks as high ceilings, the agreement did mark the first time that MIRV and bomber limits had been set in SALT, and that it deserved support, provided that the United States would seek prompt reductions and refrain from increasing its own forces merely to reach the permissible ceilings.[47] Opponents argued that the agreement simply gave a green light for costly new programs that might otherwise never have been approved, that its high MIRV ceilings would "destabilize the strategic balance,"[48] and that since it would stimulate the arms race, it was "unacceptable as a basis for further negotiations on strategic arms."[49]

For perhaps some of the same reasons that earned the Vladivostok accord an uneasy reception in certain arms control circles, there were others outside the arms control community who found something to applaud in the agreement. For example, one editorialist asserted that although the agreement had not put a "cap" on the arms race, it had laid new ground rules for that competition for the next ten years. Noting that the agreement would allow both sides "to do pretty much what they already contemplated" in modernizing their strategic forces and that this would require heavy U.S. investment in new strategic systems, the editorial suggested that the chief virtue of Vladivostok was that it had extricated the United States from the "bear trap" in which it had been left by its concessions in SALT I. As a further plus at Vladivostok, the editorial cited the concessions obtained from the Soviet side on numerical equality and FBS, which demonstrated, it said, that the Soviets "will move when they are pressed hard and logically."[50]

## SOVIET COMMENTARY ON THE VLADIVOSTOK ACCORD

By contrast with the diverse reaction that greeted the Vladivostok pact in the United States, it was hailed with seemingly unanimous approval in the Soviet Union, where more favorable coverage was given to the summit at Vladivostok than to any of the three previous U.S.-Soviet summits of the SALT era.[51] Setting the tone for the Soviet response was an official announcement that the Party Politburo and the top organs of the government had "examined" and "given their full approval to the activities of Leonid Ilich Brezhnev and the important political results" of the Vladivostok meeting.[52]

Although the flood of Soviet commentary following this announcement contained no discussion of specific features of the Vladivostok SALT agreement beyond those mentioned in the brief U.S.-Soviet joint statement itself, it did repeatedly make several well-orchestrated points on the merits of the Vladivostok summit:

- The summit contributed significantly to "further strengthening of Soviet-U.S. relations" and to helping make this process "irreversible."[53]
- It marked important progress toward "creating a guarantee against the outbreak of a nuclear conflict and against war in general."[54]
- It established a "long-term basis" for a limit on the strategic arms of the two countries, in accordance with "the principles of equality and equal security."[55]
- It proved "the viability of the principles of peaceful coexistence" and would help to head off the development, after October 1977,

of a new "spiral in the strategic arms race" that could have "devastating consequences for the course of detente."[56]

- It was "the most fruitful" of all the summits, and "confirmed the practical value" of "regular Soviet-American summit meetings" for favorable development of relations between the two countries.[57]

In addition to these major themes, there was a counterpoint of complaint now and then about the arguments of those in the West who were critical of the Vladivostok agreement for not going far enough in limiting strategic arms.[58] Such arguments, one commentator wrote, were "false and frivolous," since it should be "clear to everyone that the maximum possible under present conditions was achieved at the Vladivostok talks."[59] Another Soviet spokesman was quoted as saying that "high ceilings are better than no ceilings at all."[60]

Finally, amidst the general chorus of approval for Vladivostok, there was a slight hint of dissonance in the Soviet military press that might indicate some dissatisfaction with at least one aspect of the agreement. In an article in early December dealing with the military threat of "imperialist" forces against oil-producing countries, it was stressed that "foreign military bases constitute a source of war danger" and play "a very important role in the plans of Atlantic strategists."[61] Although the article was not written in a SALT context and made no direct reference to U.S. forward-based nuclear forces in Europe, its timing might be taken—with a bit of straining—to reflect veiled discontent with that portion of the Vladivostok agreement that involved backing away from the previous Soviet FBS position.[62]

## SOME POTENTIAL IMPLICATIONS OF THE VLADIVOSTOK ACCORD

When the post-Vladivostok round of SALT II negotiations began in early 1975, it was generally assumed that a formal agreement following more or less closely the framework of understanding reached at Vladivostok between Ford and Brezhnev would be ready for signing by June or July 1975 at another summit meeting between the two leaders in the United States.

At the same time, however, as the preceding account of the known features of the Vladivostok transaction and the reaction to it in various quarters would suggest, there was also a rather wide range of opinion about what the implications of a ten-year accord on the Vladivostok model might be for the arms race, for strategic stability, for the future strategic policies of the two sides, and for other related matters bearing on their detente relationship. Here we shall address some of these implications, beginning with the issue of the so-called cap on the arms race.

### The Issue of a Cap on the Numbers Race

One of the early claims made for the Vladivostok accord was that it had averted a stepped-up strategic numbers race. Obviously, given the impenetrability of the future, no one really knew what would have happened without the agreed aggregate and MIRV ceilings, but nevertheless governments must try to peer into the future. As Kissinger put it: "All our intelligence estimates indicate that in the absence of an agreement, Soviet MIRV levels would have been substantially higher than they will be under the agreement, as well as Soviet total levels, which in turn would have triggered another series of moves by us."[63]

Thus, the proposition that a numbers race will have been averted rests on whether it can *reasonably* be judged that Soviet planning actually had been aimed at much higher levels than those agreed upon, and that a buildup to such levels would be met by a matching U.S. response.

On the first point, the most persuasive affirmative argument would seem to be that by the time of Vladivostok the overall Soviet force level had already reached the agreed future ceiling,[64] and new missile programs in which large R&D and production resources had been invested were just entering the deployment stage. Programs in motion are hard to stop, in the Soviet bureaucratic system or any other, so it would not appear unreasonable to expect that deployment of the new systems might push Soviet strategic force levels still higher.

Another argument pointing in this direction also could be made on the basis of two pronounced traits exhibited in the past by the Soviet military: a tendency to seek security in big numbers, and a great reluctance to throw anything away.[65] Thus, less perhaps as an expression of purposive policy aims than as the cumulative by-product of ingrained habits and military bureaucratism, the process of modernizing Soviet strategic forces might simply have tended to end up in the adding of new equipment to existing inventories.[66]

It might therefore have been reasonable to anticipate a further upward trend in the size of Soviet strategic forces after the expiration of the Interim Agreement and in the absence of the Vladivostok ceilings. However, there were also several contrary considerations to be taken into account. For example, the economic burden of substantially larger strategic forces, though not necessarily an over-riding factor in Soviet security decisionmaking, could hardly be ignored. Even should generous military budgets continue to be the rule, the claims of other services for a larger slice of resources, including a growing navy, could also cut into the share available for strategic forces. A new philosophy of modernization, less resistant to weeding out old systems that had outlived their day, might also take hold as the higher cost of the new strategic technologies became felt.

Still another factor to be mentioned was the already existing numerical margin in strategic forces favoring the Soviet Union. Although perhaps not so large as Soviet strategic force planners might prefer, it apparently reflected the internal consensus on Soviet ICBM and SLBM force size at the time the Interim Agreement levels were set in May 1972, and hence might then have been considered satisfactory so long as the United States made no attempt to close the numerical gap.[67] To add a somewhat related point, had Soviet planners unilaterally calculated that a much higher level of strategic forces was required by the Soviet Union, it seems not unlikely that Brezhnev at Vladivostok would at least have begun his numbers bargaining with a correspondingly high bid, well in excess of the figure agreed upon; but apparently he did not do so.[68] This is not an exhaustive list of counterconsiderations, but it goes far enough to suggest that the Soviets just might have been satisfied to maintain their strategic forces at approximately the levels sanctioned by the Interim Agreement of May 1972, rather than to boost them substantially.

In addition to these various factors bearing on the future size of Soviet forces affected by the Vladivostok accord, Soviet capabilities for deployment of MIRVed launchers represented an especially important, but somewhat equivocal, consideration. If deployment rates estimated by U.S. defense officials in 1974 had been consistently borne out (100 MIRVed launchers the first year and 200 per year thereafter),[69] the Soviets could by 1985 deploy 1900 MIRVed launchers, and they would reach the permissible Vladivostok level of 1320 in 1981. By this arithmetic, the cap constraint on unilateral Soviet MIRV deployment potential during a ten-year treaty period would amount to almost 600 launchers—a constraint of some significance.

However, by 1978 the Soviets had deployed only 360 fourth-generation ICBMs, and the deployment rate at that point was estimated to be no more than 125 per year.[70] Were it to continue at this rate, and assuming that virtually all new deployments were MIRVed launchers, the Vladivostok ceiling of 1320 MIRVed launchers would not be reached until 1984. Thus, no constraint of consequence as a result of Vladivostok would seem to apply in this case. Moreover, as we shall come to see later, the post-Vladivostok negotiations seemed likely to produce a MIRV ceiling somewhat lower than the Vladivostok figure,[71] and therefore not one that would greatly tax Soviet MIRV deployment capabilities.

On the second point essential to the cap thesis—that a big Soviet buildup would in turn trigger matching U.S. moves and so produce a fresh numbers race—the grounds for judgment are by no means unequivocal either. It takes two to tango—and to engage in a numbers race. Although responsible American officials had declared that the United States could not allow a marked numerical imbalance to arise, the actual U.S. toleration threshold was susceptible to many factors difficult to weigh in advance. Dr. Kissinger himself had suggested, for example, that a matching response might not automatically follow a buildup of Soviet forces, noting that in such a case there would be "the problem of whether we were to match these forces or whether we would permit a growing numerical gap against us to arise."[72]

In sum, a reasonable case might be made that the Vladivostok agreement had reduced the chances of a numbers race, but it hardly seems a foregone conclusion that such a race would have become a certainty in the absence of the agreement. Whatever the merit of claims that the agreement headed off yet more competition, these claims have served as a rationale to blunt criticism of the high Vladivostok ceilings. In turn, however, the high ceilings were probably one of the reasons why an agreement was possible—high enough to accommodate unilateral programs that the Russians in particular were of no mind to suspend and, in the U.S. case, not quite high enough to place on the agenda of future decisions the troubling problem that Kissinger had seen coming up if the United States should have to decide between closing a large numerical gap or living with it.

### The Image of Numerical Equality

In some sense, it can be said that the essence of the transaction at Vladivostok was to forge an agreement that would leave neither party looking like Number Two—an agreement conveying the *appearance* of rough equality in rather simplified numerical terms that public opinion, politicians, and third-party governments could readily grasp. In these terms of perceived relative strategic power, the two sides doubtless came out of Vladivostok looking about even.

From the American viewpoint, despite the high ceilings with

which few professed to be pleased, the agreement met one of the main concerns expressed by Secretary of Defense Schlesinger and others—that a marked asymmetry in the future strategic forces of the two, as measured by static criteria, might have a seriously adverse political and psychological impact. A second prime U.S. concern centering on superior Soviet throwweight potential was left essentially unassuaged by the agreement, as we shall come to presently, but at least one element of this concern seemed to have been put to rest by the Vladivostok ceilings. This was the possibility that the Soviets might exploit their throwweight advantage to gain a commanding lead over the United States in numbers of MIRVed warheads.

Some illustrative figures showing how the two forces might compare in the early 1980s in overall levels of delivery vehicles, throwweight, and warhead numbers under the Vladivostok guidelines may be found in Table 9-1. Although the figures are for the most part only approximations, which could vary somewhat if different assumptions had been used,[73] they nevertheless serve to illustrate the general point that the agreement would leave the two sides in a *perceived* position of rough numerical equality, with each side enjoying advantages in some categories offset by disadvantages in others.

With regard to missile warhead numbers, the Soviets, with about 8500, would draw closer to the United States, but would come out well below the maximum unconstrained potential attributed to them by Secretary Schlesinger prior to Vladivostok.[74] They would, however, surpass the United States in numbers of ICBM warheads about 3 to 1, though the United States would retain a substantial margin in both SLBM warheads and bomber-delivered weapons. With regard to missile throwweight, the Soviets would have widened their already large margin somewhat,[75] but on the other hand a marked American advantage in bomber payload would remain.

Besides the effect that perceived equality in overall strategic levels and MIRV numbers might have on interested third parties, there is another aspect of the equality image that merits mention. This is the proposition that the strategic competition itself has been fed by a perceived imbalance between the two sides and that only on the rare occasions when the relative forces happen to come into approximate balance is there any real chance that the competitors may be willing to agree on lasting arms control constraints upon their unilateral freedom of action.

Seen in these terms, one of the more important functions of the SALT process would be to try to get both competitors to pause on

Table 9-1

Comparative Forces within Vladivostok Ceilings (Early 1980s)

| | U.S. | | USSR |
|---|---|---|---|
| | *Programmed Forces* | *Full Vladivostok Allowance* | *Full Vladivostok Allowance* |
| Heavy ICBM[a] | 54 | 54 | 310 (280 MIRV) |
| Other ICBM[b] | 1000 (550 MIRV) | 1000 (550 (MIRV) | 1000 (740 MIRV) |
| SLBM | 736 (736 MIRV)[c] | 896[d] (736 MIRV) | 950 (300 MIRV)[c] |
| Intercontinental bombers | 350 | 450[e] (34 MIRV) | 140 |
| Total | 2140 (1286 MIRV) | 2400 (1320 MIRV) | 2400 (1320 MIRV) |
| Warheads | | | |
| ICBM | 2154 | 2154 | 6970 |
| SLBM | 7360 | 7520 | 1550 |
| | 9514 | 9674 | 8520 |
| Bombs | 1400 | 1660 | 500 |
| ALCM | . . . . | 680 | . . . . |
| Total | 10,914 | 12,014 | 9020 |
| Missile throwweight (mil lbs) | | | |
| ICBM | 2.6 | 2.6 | 9.5 |
| SLBM | 1.2 | 1.4 | 1.5 |
| Total | 3.8 | 4.0 | 11.0 |
| Bomber payload | 21.0 | 27.0 | 4.2 |

*Assumptions:*

[a]For U.S.: Titan II. For USSR: SS-18 with 8 RVs.

[b]For U.S.: Minuteman II; Minuteman III with 3 RVs. For USSR: SS-11, SS-17, -19, with 6 RVs.

[c]For U.S.: Includes 496 MIRVed Poseidon and 240 MIRVed Trident, 10 RVs each. For USSR, includes SS-N-6, SS-N-8; and assumes arbitrary figure of 300 MIRVed SS-N-17 and -18, with 3 RVs each.

[d]160 notional SLBMs added to reach full Vladivostok ceiling.

[e]100 notional bombers added to reach full Vladivostok ceiling. Arbitrarily assumes that 34 bombers carrying 20 ALCMs each are counted as MIRV.

the same step of the ladder. In this sense, it might therefore be argued that the Vladivostok guidelines provided an opportunity for a long enough pause on the same quantitative rung of the competitive ladder to permit a useful attempt at controlling other aspects of the competition. Indeed, something along this line may have inspired Dr. Kissinger's expressed hope that with the Vladivostok agreement on numerical equality, even at high levels, further "negotiations on reductions will be easier."[76]

If, however, it was the high ceilings that made agreement at Vladivostok possible in the first place,[77] a view that Kissinger himself appeared to hold,[78] then getting the Russians to reduce their forces might not be easy. This would seem particularly the case, if it were assumed that the Vladivostok levels answered to what the Soviet military command considered to be a prudent minimum force level vis-à-vis not only the United States, but China as well. Indeed, one might hazard a guess that the bottom line on any reduction agreement to which the Soviets might be willing to put their signature would reflect a claim for insurance against the "China problem," whether so specified or not.[79]

### The Question of Qualitative Competition

One of the derivative effects sometimes expected of a halt, or pause, at quantitative equivalence is that it might create more favorable conditions for attempting to constrain qualitative competition. However, this hardly seemed to be an immediate prospect in the case of the Vladivostok agreement, which on the face of it had been clearly designed to give both sides plenty of room to proceed with modernization programs that earlier SALT negotiations had left largely undisturbed. In fact, it was hard to escape the conclusion that a major result of the agreement was likely to be a rechanneling of strategic competition into a still more intensive qualitative race within the agreed numerical limits.

The difficulty of controlling technological change and competition has, of course, long been recognized, so that it would scarcely be fair to fault the Vladivostok negotiators for what others also have signally failed to accomplish. In answering criticism of the agreement on this account, Dr. Kissinger took the tack that qualitative change could be tolerated as an inescapable fact of life, so long as its "linkage" with quantity did not threaten to "produce strategic superiority." This, he averred, could be avoided under provisions of the agreement if each side were to act "with a moderate, with even a modicum of circumspection."[80] Whether the respective parties would find it possible to heed this advice, however, was another matter, particularly if the Soviet Union should continue to regard U.S. technological assets as a one-sided advantage that it must strive to overcome. For that matter, to be evenhanded about it, the temptation for the United States to employ its technology to redress some of the advantages left to the Soviets by the agreement, such as throwweight, could also stimulate further qualitative competition.

There was one aspect of the Vladivostok transaction—related to the question of past Soviet attitudes toward U.S. technological resources—that might have broad implications for future Soviet-American strategic competition. In a sense, the core issue in SALT throughout most of its pre-Vladivostok history had been where to draw the line at which Soviet insistence upon safe margins of force levels would cease to represent "legitimate compensation" for technological and other asymmetries favoring the United States and would become a demand for unilateral advantage threatening to tip the strategic balance perceptibly in Soviet favor. From the U.S. viewpoint, the kind of transaction sought in SALT by the Soviet Union had priced U.S. technological and other strategic assets far too low, and therefore was tantamount to pressing for an unprecedented "security discount" much beyond what any great power could be expected to grant voluntarily to another, especially to a declared adversary.

But with Vladivostok, the Soviet Union seemingly dropped its pursuit of compensatory numerical margins and FBS withdrawal, while also apparently giving up, or at least for the time being setting aside, its previous efforts to constrain the application of U.S. technology to new strategic systems. This might suggest a basic shift of Soviet sights in SALT, with the implication that one of the factors facilitating agreement at Vladivostok had been a Soviet change of mind about the demand that U.S. technological advantages be written off below market value for the sake of cementing a long-term accord.

If so, then it might be asked: why? Had the Soviets suddenly become so confident of their ability to keep pace with the United States technologically that they were prepared to take their chances in a stepped-up qualitative race during the next ten years? At the time of Vladivostok the Soviets still presumably lagged behind the United States in such critical strategic technologies as guidance accuracy and MIRVed SLBMs, but they might have felt that their technological position was improving sufficiently to permit them to hold up their end of an unconstrained qualitative competition, especially if they had calculated that American difficulties at home and abroad would keep the United States from holding up its end. An appreciation of the growing gap in the United States between technology and its translation into deployed weapons systems—a gap that the Soviets themselves had experienced in Khrushchev's day— could also have contributed to a somewhat optimistic Soviet stance.

Another equally plausible possibility might have been that the Soviets had begun to worry that their previous SALT approach would not hold back a new surge of U.S. weapons technology. Recession and unemployment in the United States, rather than impeding such a surge, might, as classical Marxist-Leninist theory would counsel, tend instead to trigger it. The strategic R&D tooling up for which Schlesinger had begun to call in early 1974 as preparation for a matching competition might also have had its intended sobering effect in Moscow.

Whatever the reasons, the Soviets seem to have been persuaded that an agreement embodying essential equivalence ought no longer to be delayed. Whether this meant that the Soviets looked upon the Vladivostok agreement as the starting point for a serious mutual effort to dampen qualitative competition, or merely as a better way to constrain U.S. technology while attempting to catch up, remained, however, a salient but unanswered question.

### The Throwweight Issue

In one sense it might be said that apart from the force ceilings set at Vladivostok, strategic planning was little touched by the agreement, for both sides were left virtually free—notwithstanding certain ambiguities in the agreement—to carry on most of the strategic R&D and force-modernization programs already under way or contemplated. Seen from another perspective, however, the agreement pointed up a number of strategic problems and issues that, though not necessarily symmetrical for both parties, nevertheless had important planning implications. One of these concerned throwweight, the "sanctity" of which was confirmed by the agreement.

From the viewpoint of the Soviet side, the benefits of leaving its greater throwweight potential untouched were not inconsiderable. During the life of the agreement, the Soviet Union could end up with far more ICBM throwweight than the United States—as suggested by the illustrative figures in Table 9-1. Although this might not be translatable into Soviet superiority in warhead numbers within the life of the agreement, it would allow warheads of substantially greater yield than those of the United States[81] and make easier the improvement of Soviet guidance technology, thus helping to compensate for U.S. accuracy advantages. A further point to which attention was called by Secretary Schlesinger in February 1975 was that high yields permitted by Soviet missile throwweight would also "compensate to an important degree" for accuracy uncertainties of all-inertial guidance systems under operational conditions.[82]

On the Soviet side, that part of the Vladivostok agreement excluding throwweight limits could have been regarded as a fair trade for numbers equality, as well as for soft-pedaling the FBS issue. At the same time, Soviet insistence on exclusion of throwweight would suggest that there had been continuing strong resistance within the Soviet establishment to altering Soviet missile design philosophy for the sake of structuring a SALT agreement more in line with U.S. preferences and practices.[83]

The extent to which strategic-planning objectives on the one hand, or internal institutional factors on the other, might have driven the Soviet position on throwweight is an interesting question, which unfortunately is not clarified by the data available. However, the possibility ought not to be overlooked that the persistent Soviet refusal in SALT to retreat on the throwweight issue, up to and including the Vladivostok summit, might have been less the result of a calculated intent to maximize their future counterforce potential than of an institutional need to avoid the turmoil into which the Soviet missile design and manufacturing establishment might be thrown if missile parameters were altered to accommodate a U.S. approach calling for a throwweight ceiling. In addition, refusal to back down on this question may have been due to real technical difficulties involved for the Soviets in producing satisfactory missiles with less throwweight.

From the U.S. viewpoint, the throwweight issue looked somewhat different, in part depending on who was looking at it. Kissinger's reported view that it was a "phony" issue was not, needless to say, universally shared. Some observers felt that the throwweight loophole in the Vladivostok accord was in fact a serious deficiency that promised to create future strategic instability and meant that the accord had in no "meaningful way" reduced the "U.S. strategic defense problem posed by the new and technically improved family of Soviet missiles."[84]

In rebutting criticism of the agreement's failure to deal with throwweight, Kissinger pointed out that the accord would not preclude the United States from increasing its own throwweight substantially, "if it is judged in our interests to do so."[85] Whether the United States would choose to alter its own missile design philosophy to match Soviet throwweight—a step comparable, in effect, to what the Soviets had declined to do with respect to their missile design—was not, however, indicated by Kissinger.

Secretary of Defense Schlesinger, who prior to Vladivostok had put heavy emphasis on the throwweight issue, appeared to shift ground somewhat afterward, suggesting in December 1974 that the United States could "live with" some differences in throwweight, partly by restructuring its strategic forces to reduce their vulnerability to Soviet missiles.[86] However, in his annual defense report in February 1975, Schlesinger also indicated that accuracy uncertainties alone would constitute a reason for some increases in U.S. missile throwweight and weapons yields, no matter what future basing changes might be made.[87]

### Vulnerability of Silo-based Systems
Whatever judgments might be reached as to what the United States should do about missile throwweight, this question promised to be

but one facet of a broader strategic issue that was reilluminated, so to speak, by the Vladivostok accord. Specifically, if the quantitative force levels permitted by the accord were to be linked with qualitative improvements in accuracy and yield within reach of both sides, the likely result would be to make fixed and targetable land-based missiles increasingly vulnerable to a counterforce threat during the next decade.

On the basis of purely theoretical calculations, for example, using the standard counterforce formula[88] and assumptions available in the open literature about yield, accuracy, and hardness, it could be shown that the Soviet Union, employing only about three-quarters of the 7000 ICBM warheads expected to be at its disposal in the early 1980s, would be able to wipe out virtually all of the silo-based U.S. ICBM force.[89] A comparable U.S. missile threat to Soviet silo-based systems would depend on counterforce improvements well beyond any hitherto planned,[90] but given U.S. technological resources, there seemed little doubt that such a capability could be attained if the United States should decide to seek it.[91]

In actuality, to be sure, it was a good deal less clear when and under what conditions a significant threat to the survivability of fixed forces might materialize, and which side might first find itself the more vulnerable in this regard. In the U.S. case, various measures, such as silo upgrading, had been initiated well before Vladivostok, giving Air Force spokesmen grounds for confidence that most of the Minuteman force could survive an attack by "any existing enemy force."[92] Similarly, according to Secretary Schlesinger, silo upgrading and other such factors as the "fratricide" phenomenon held promise of extending the period in which the United States could feel confident of the survivability of its ICBM force—provided that the Soviets were to "exercise restraint" in their own counterforce programs.[93] However, should the Soviets make a determined effort to improve their counterforce capabilities, then, as noted both by Schlesinger and his successors, the Soviets by the early 1980s "could come to jeopardize the survival of our fixed-based ICBM silos."[94]

### Measures to Enhance Survivability of Agreed Forces

Among the implications of the vulnerability issue for strategic planning, perhaps the most obvious was to put a high premium on measures to preserve the survivability of the agreed aggregate force levels. Such measures could take a variety of forms, with those emphasizing mobile and recallable systems probably enjoying an edge. However, the various potential survivability procedures would not necessarily prove equally suitable from the standpoint of strategic stability, verification, cost, service interest, and so on—all of which could complicate planners' choices. Nor would the United States and the Soviet Union necessarily find themselves moving in the same direction in dealing with the problem of survivability. Several of the more obvious possibilities are noted below.

**Development of land-mobile forces.** This choice would help survivability, but could raise problems for stability and for reaching verification agreements. The Vladivostok accord left this route open to both sides, though the Soviet Union was in a position to embark upon it first, thanks to its SS-16 program. The United States reversed its earlier objection to land-mobile ICBMs and began to explore such a basing system for the proposed MX ICBM, but by the end of 1978 had not yet fully committed itself to a land-mobile deployment program.[9 5] A common problem for both sides would be deciding how much of their delivery quota to put into land-mobile forces. From the viewpoint of geography, internal secrecy, and population attitudes, the Soviet Union would doubtless be favored in taking this step.

**Moving a larger proportion of strategic forces to sea.** This option, permissible under the freedom-to-mix provision of the Vladivostok accord, would enhance survivability, with less strain on verification than land-mobile systems. It would also seem to make a solid contribution to strategic stability by reducing the possibility of a disarming strike against all elements of strategic forces. However, it might in turn lead to concentration on qualitative-operational improvement in antisubmarine warfare (ASW) capabilities—improvement that eventually could threaten the survivability of SLBM forces also and, if the other TRIAD elements had been greatly reduced, could produce an unstable situation that would weaken deterrence. It is worth noting that the Soviets could find themselves at a disadvantage if disarming capabilities on both sides against targetable land-based systems should tend to shift the critical arena to SLBM forces. Here the United States has had, and for some time will doubtless continue to have, a considerable lead, if not in numbers of nuclear-powered ballistic missile submarines (SSBNs), at least in technological, geographic, and operational advantages, and in numbers of MIRV warheads. In terms of "image," the Soviets could thus begin to look second-best, though in terms of actual wartime capability, they would have sufficient residual capability in their SLBM forces for a continuing retaliatory threat.

**An increase in mobile air-launched missiles.**  One of the effects of
Vladivostok was to increase the attractiveness of mobile aircraft
platforms for air-launched armaments, since recallable mobile systems in this category would have many of the same advantages for
offensive force survivability and strategic stability as sea-based
strategic forces and would add diversity to the forces allowed under
the Vladivostok ceilings. They would also be less targetable than
silo-based forces, although more dependent on warning for survivability at base than land-mobile systems. Although ambiguities in the
Vladivostok guidelines concerning bombers and their permissible
payloads created some planning uncertainties, the Carter administration's subsequent decision to emphasize a B-52/ALCM combination
to compensate for dropping the B-1 program[96] gave this option a
major boost in the U.S. case. In comparative Soviet-U.S. terms,
because the United States enjoys a substantial advantage both in
bomber numbers and strategic-air-launched-missile technology, it
may have grounds for devoting a larger share of its delivery-vehicle
quota to these systems than has the Soviet Union.

**Hard-site defense of offensive missile bases.**  This alternative for
reducing the vulnerability of silo-based missile forces would appear
to be virtually ruled out so long as the ABM Treaty remains in force.
However, the large investments made in hardened missile forces,
together with vested institutional interests in them, especially in the
Soviet Union, might lead to pressure for revision of the ABM Treaty
to permit this form of survivability insurance.

### Strategic Planning Asymmetries

As the preceding comments might suggest, some of the problems
and challenges for strategic planning under a Vladivostok SALT
regime seemed to hold diverse implications for the two sides, owing
in part to strategic asymmetries of one kind or another, not all of
which necessarily tended to favor the same party.

A noteworthy case in point grew out of the differing way in which
the two countries had chosen to structure their strategic forces. The
Soviet choice led to strategic delivery forces consisting largely of
silo-based ICBMs; similarly, most of the Soviet throwweight potential
was concentrated in these fixed, and hence targetable, forces. By
contrast, U.S. force loadings—warheads and bomber payloads—were
spread more widely among diverse systems, leaving only about 25
percent of the U.S. capability in fixed systems, compared with from
60 to 80 percent in the Soviet case.[97] Given this situation, Soviet
planners not only might have to ponder the wisdom of helping to

create a counterforce environment in which a preponderant share of their delivery forces could be placed in growing jeopardy, but they would also face some weighty decisions on how much of their permissible total of delivery forces should be shifted to less-targetable SLBM and aircraft systems, or to land-mobile missiles, in order to alleviate the survivability problem.

The United States, of course, would also face some restructuring problems of its own, including the problem resulting from the fact that its most accurate delivery systems were fixed ICBMs,[98] and hence cutting them back in favor of SLBM and aircraft systems might buy more survivability at the expense of accurate counterforce capability, at least in the short run. However, the magnitude of force restructuring needed to reduce vulnerability would appear to be considerably greater in the Soviet than in the U.S. case.

Which side might encounter more "institutional drag" in restructuring its forces is difficult to judge. The Soviet Strategic Rocket Forces are strongly entrenched and would seem likely to offer stiff institutional resistance to a major downgrading of their silo-based systems. However, the United States is by no means immune to institutional problems, either. For example, one effect of Vladivostok's fixed overall ceilings, combined with freedom to mix, might be to revive internal rivalry among service proponents of different strategic systems, with each vying to establish its share of any new overall mix.

The Vladivostok outline itself incorporated no mutually agreed impediments to the kind of quantity-quality marriage of strategic weaponry that could jeopardize the survivability of fixed ICBM forces, but unilateral strategic restraint might help to head off such a union. In a sense, such restraint would seem to stand as the alternative to what might be called an implied imperative to do whatever might be permitted by a SALT II settlement stemming from the Vladivostok guidelines. At the same time, deciding precisely what criteria should be used to measure strategic restraint would appear to pose a complicated issue for planners on both sides, since some measures entirely permissible within the letter of a SALT II agreement might at the same time contravene the spirit of an exercise in mutual moderation.

Although verification problems of a SALT II agreement on the Vladivostok model would not necessarily fall exclusively on the U.S. side, they appeared likely to put a new premium on improvement of technologies and techniques for surveillance and intelligence collection. At a time when an intensive, though perhaps passing, campaign of exposure of U.S. intelligence activities was being waged in the

United States, there was a question of asymmetrical handicaps, for the Soviet intelligence system hardly seemed likely to be placed under a similar spotlight. Moreover, the unexpected curtailment and possible permanent loss of U.S. surveillance facilities in Turkey in mid-1975 could, as pointed out by the then director of ACDA, Fred C. Iklé, have a crucial effect on "U.S. ability to monitor compliance" with SALT agreements.[99]

Another set of internal constraints, possibly less operative in the Soviet Union than in the United States, could be foreseen in the problems posed for weapons-system planning and development (especially in a period of tight budgets) by some of the ambiguities in the Vladivostok agreement. For example, how much effort should go into particular systems, or what changes in their specifications should be made, if there were a chance—as with some cruise missile systems—that they might be curtailed? Further, when a full-fledged agreement on the basis of the Vladivostok outline might finally be reached, the internal stresses arising within the U.S. establishment between managers and sponsors of affected programs and their allies in Congress on the one hand, and those charged with monitoring and enforcing a shutoff on the other, though difficult to measure in advance, would seem likely to create a less than happy climate for strategic planners.

### The FBS Aspect of the Vladivostok Accord

As we have seen, the explicit nature of the commitment by the Soviet side to drop its demands for satisfaction on the FBS issue was one of the ambiguities left over after the Vladivostok transaction. Assuming that the Soviet side did in fact agree to shelve FBS, the implications of this concession are worthy of speculation.

On the face of it, a retreat from the long-entrenched Soviet position on FBS would suggest at least one of two things. First, that the miltiary and political considerations behind the Soviet FBS stand had been of less moment all along than the deliberate use of the issue as an instrumental negotiating device, or, second, that the urgency of striking a bargain at Vladivostok was felt strongly enough to justify the sacrifice of a highly valued Soviet position.[100] There are, of course, other explanations, such as Kissinger's suggestion that the Soviet Union had reassessed and downgraded its previous estimate of an FBS threat against its territory.

Which of the several possible explanations best fits the case, it is difficult to say. But if the first holds, the implication might be that the Soviets had decided that they could expect only diminishing mileage out of the FBS issue and might as well cash in on it for the last time by getting the U.S. side to yield for good on a "real" strategic issue—such as, perhaps, future throwweight disparity. On the other hand, if the second interpretation holds, then it would seem likely that the concession on FBS did not come easily, that it might generate internal misgivings about Brezhnev's conduct of the Vladivostok negotiations,[101] and that Soviet attempts to hedge on the FBS "give-away" might be expected to reappear as the post-Vladivostok negotiations got down to the business of trying to prepare a full-fledged ten-year accord on strategic arms.

*Chapter 10*

# Stalemate in the Post-Vladivostok Negotiations

When the post-Vladivostok SALT negotiations got under way in Geneva in January 1975, the salient question was whether the outline formula endorsed at the summit the previous November would hold up when the two sides began the more complicated task of translating it into a binding ten-year agreement. As matters turned out, the business of converting the Vladivostok guidelines into a full-fledged SALT II accord was to prove a great deal more difficult than many had expected.

The lack of progress in the Geneva negotiations between the two SALT delegations was said to be one of the reasons for repeatedly delaying until the fall of 1975 and eventually dropping a Ford-Brezhnev meeting in Washington that had originally been planned for June or July, by which time it had been thought that an agreement would be ready for summit signing.[1] It was also no doubt the stalemate into which the Geneva negotiations had again fallen that prompted Dr. Kissinger to announce once more, on the eve of a trip in late May to Vienna to confer with Gromyko, that SALT II had come to "a point where a political decision will have to be made by both sides to move the negotiations forward and to break some of the deadlocks."[2]

## ISSUES IMPEDING A SALT II AGREEMENT ON THE VLADIVOSTOK MODEL

The problems of reconciling the draft treaties proposed by the two sides in the early months of 1975[3] centered around both some

199

familiar issues and some new ones. Among issues in the first category were verification procedures, including an acceptable formula for counting MIRVed missiles, and where to draw the borderline between "heavy" missiles and new Soviet ICBMs like the SS-19 and -17, which substantially exceeded the volumetric threshold for a heavy missile previously defined by the U.S. side.[4] The new issues were whether the Soviet Backfire was an intercontinental bomber and should therefore be included in the USSR's aggregate total of 2400 delivery vehicles, and what limitations should be placed on strategic cruise missiles—a class of weapons that had acquired a new potential, thanks to recent technological advances, and in which U.S. interest had begun to grow since 1972.[5]

In addition to these various obstacles to the prompt wrapping up of a SALT II agreement, the Soviet side also had reportedly reintroduced in its draft treaty text language that would have the effect of honoring previous Soviet claims for compensation for FBS and third-country nuclear forces—issues supposedly buried at Vladivostok.[6]

Initially, the renewed negotiations apparently had snagged mainly on the sticky problem of how to count and verify MIRVed missiles, which Kissinger was said to have described then as the "most critical single issue" in the negotiations.[7] The U.S. verification formula calling for any missile tested with MIRV to be counted in the MIRV quota when deployed was at first rejected by the Soviets, even though Kissinger had declared that "if they reject the verification formula . . . it will be very hard to conceive how there can be a deal."[8] For their part, the Soviets indicated that they intended to deploy both single-warhead and MIRVed versions of their heavy SS-18 ICBM and that it was up to the United States to verify unilaterally which was which.[9]

At Kissinger's May meeting with Soviet Foreign Minister Gromyko in Vienna, a compromise to resolve the MIRV impasse reportedly was discussed. This involved recognition of the Soviet position on the SS-18, in return for which the Soviet Union would be expected to confine its MIRV deployments to specific missile complexes and to display certain specialized MIRV-handling equipment alongside those missile sites where MIRVed launchers were being installed—as an aid to verification by U.S. reconnaissance satellites.[10] Subsequently, when President Ford and Secretary Brezhnev met in late July 1975 in Helsinki during the CSCE-signing ceremonies, the MIRV verification issue was again taken up, leading apparently to Soviet acceptance during the next month or two of most of the basic U.S. position on verification, whereby all missiles tested with MIRV, including the SS-18, would be counted as MIRVed types.[11] Final ironing out of jointly agreed provisions on MIRV verification, however, was to take at least a couple of more years.[12]

If encouraging progress had been made toward resolving the MIRV verification issue following the Ford-Brezhnev meeting in Helsinki in July and early August 1975, the same could not be said for two other matters that had been left in an ambiguous status at Vladivostok—the Backfire and cruise missile cases.[13] Rather, it had become apparent by that time, as underscored a month later when Gromyko conferred in Washington with Ford and Kissinger, that these two issues had emerged as the "principal barriers" to a new SALT accord.[14]

Although the Backfire and cruise missile issues had separate antecedents, in the post-Vladivostok negotiations from early 1975 on they became rather closely linked when proposed solutions, particularly those coming from the American side, tended to involve tradeoffs between the two types of delivery vehicles. With regard to Backfire, the swing-wing bomber that the USSR had begun to deploy operationally in 1974,[15] the U.S. negotiators at Geneva contended that the aircraft could under a variety of conditions carry out strategic attacks against the United States, and therefore it should be counted in the bomber portion of the delivery-vehicle aggregate, along with U.S. B-52s and Soviet Bears (TU-95) and Bisons (MYA-4). The Soviet side resisted inclusion of any Backfires in the SALT quota, essentially on the grounds that the aircraft was only a "medium-range" bomber not intended for intercontinental missions.[16] Since Brezhnev had apparently been personally emphatic on this score in his conversations with Ford at Helsinki, the engagement of his prestige in the issue tended to ensure that the Backfire would be a sticky problem.[17]

This proved to be the case during the remainder of 1975, as Kissinger reportedly sought to find a compromise formula on Backfire that would satisfy both the Pentagon's position that it be included and Soviet insistence that it be excluded from a SALT II agreement.[18] One such proposal made to the Soviets in September 1975 definitely linked a Backfire tradeoff with cruise missile deployment. It called for allowing a certain number of Backfires above the Vladivostok SALT ceiling (reportedly from 200 to 400), in return for excluding a corresponding number of U.S. cruise missile carriers from the ceiling.[19] In early November, the Soviets rejected this proposal, without apparently countering with one of their own, which led Kissinger to announce that it was up to the Soviet Union to put forward a compromise proposal to break the deadlock.[20]

Before the cruise missile issue got tied to the Backfire in Kissinger's September 1975 proposal, the initial American position on cruise missiles had been that the Vladivostok guidelines called for counting *only* ballistic missiles with ranges of more than 600 kilometers (372 miles) and not cruise missiles.[21] Air-launched cruise missiles, in particular, were held to be simply bomber armament not subject to inclusion in the SALT aggregate of 2400 vehicles. But the Soviets argued that cruise missiles exceeding this range standard and launched from any platform—land, sea, or air—had to be included in the SALT II ceilings; if the United States were not prepared to count them against its quota of strategic vehicles, then cruise missiles with more than 372 miles' range must be banned entirely.[22] Among other things, this posed the question of whether the Soviet Union's own operational cruise missiles (launchable from air, surface ship, and submarine platforms) would become SALT-eligible, although interestingly enough, none of the Soviet cruise missile systems then deployed apparently fell within the range category of more than 372 miles.[23]

Since neither counting individual cruise missiles within the SALT II launcher ceilings nor imposing a ban of the type proposed by the Soviet Union was acceptable to the United States for a variety of reasons,[24] the post-Vladivostok negotiations soon came to an impasse over the cruise missile problem, which Kissinger sought unsuccessfully to resolve with his compromise proposal of September linking the cruise missile and Backfire issues. The next major effort to find a compromise formula to break the SALT II deadlock centering on these two issues was to come in January 1976.

The January 1976 exchange of proposals probably represented the closest the Soviet and American sides would come to wrapping up a SALT II agreement during the remainder of the Ford administration. Before taking up these proposals, however, it may be useful to review briefly the state of detente and other aspects of the U.S.-Soviet relationship, including charges of Soviet SALT I violations, that helped to condition the political climate in which the post-Vladivostok search for a SALT II accord was conducted.

## INTERACTING FACTORS BEARING ON
## DETENTE AND SALT

When the post-Vladivostok SALT II negotiations resumed in early 1975, both the United States and the Soviet Union appeared to share a continuing commitment to detente, with each side, for whatever reasons, apparently considering that the expeditious conclusion of a

SALT II accord answered to its respective interests. Which side may have been more strongly committed to detente was much less clear, for strength of commitment is difficult to measure. In the U.S. case, and with the reader's indulgence, we would simply assert that official policy was still firmly set on a detente course as long as the Soviet Union reciprocated, although negative attitudes toward the viability and value of detente had certainly grown in many quarters since the highwater mark of Soviet-U.S. amity in the spring of 1972.[25]

### Soviet Attitude toward Detente

The Soviet attitude toward detente midway through the 1970s could be said to have been a rather complicated one, embracing several disparate elements.[26] It contained, for example, what might be called a visionary ideological element, implicit in assertions that detente is a historical process involving a "fundamental restructuring of international relations" on the basis of the "principles of peaceful coexistence."[27] Seen from this viewpoint, the capitalist system had already lost the historical initiative, and detente was a vehicle that, if properly managed, could facilitate a further "transition to socialism" and to a "genuine collective security system," replacing an international order based on "the balance of forces and mutual intimidation."

A second and somewhat more pragmatic element in the Soviet attitude toward detente was the view[28] that Soviet military might, especially the growth of Soviet strategic power, had "sobered the imperialists" and helped to shift the "correlation of forces" in the world in favor of the socialist camp, thus making detente possible in the first place.[29] Underlying this view was the implication that unremitting effort to maintain a "correlation of forces" favorable to the Soviet Union would be needed in order to keep detente on the track and to ensure continued detente behavior by the USSR's political adversaries.

Several specific detente- and SALT-related incentives for maintaining a relatively unabrasive relationship with the United States were perhaps evident to the leaders of the Soviet Union in the period after the Vladivostok summit. These might have included the following:

- The contribution of detente to crisis management and to reducing the risk of nuclear confrontation with the United States—perhaps the most compelling of all the incentives favoring detente.
- A Soviet need for economic and technological transfusions from the West, together with a requirement to nail down the terms of

such transactions for purposes of orderly long-range economic planning in the USSR.

- The unresolved status of the "China problem," which still counseled a policy of trying to keep China politically and militarily isolated, and in the context of which SALT might be seen as a kind of compact with the United States to help ensure against Chinese-American "collusion" at Soviet expense.
- The usefulness of SALT to "validate" Soviet strategic equality with the United States and its potential contribution to slowing down a new U.S. technological "surge," especially with regard to missile accuracy and new delivery systems such as long-range and highly accurate cruise missiles.
- The interplay of Soviet elite politics, especially Brezhnev's considerable investment of prestige in continued improvement of U.S.-Soviet relations, which in some sense may have made him hostage to finding further avenues of agreement in SALT.
- A Soviet desire to pin down as many detente and SALT commitments as possible while the U.S. negotiating and policy approach remained in the hands of the Ford-Kissinger team, lest the 1976 elections in the United States produce a successor administration more difficult to deal with.
- An apparent consensus among the Soviet leadership that the first stage of Soviet-U.S. detente (roughly 1969 to 1975) had yielded generally "positive" results, though by late 1974 Soviet spokesmen were beginning to warn that "antidetente circles" in the United States had managed to slow detente, requiring that "new momentum" be imparted to it.

If such positive incentives as these might plausibly have been evident to the Soviet leaders, a corresponding catalog of negative factors bearing on detente and SALT could also have called for their consideration. These "disincentives" to cultivation of a smoother U.S.-Soviet working relationship might have included the following:

- Growing Soviet disillusionment about receiving economic and technological benefits from detente on the scale and under the conditions originally contemplated, together with possible misgivings in some Soviet quarters about the internal organizational complications of tying Soviet planning too closely to economic-technical inputs from abroad.
- Some reduction of earlier Soviet concern about the potential extent of U.S.-Chinese collaboration against the USSR, in the light of internal Chinese developments and a cooling of rapprochement between Washington and Peking.

- A probable suspicion on the part of some influential groups in the USSR that the "Schlesinger doctrine" had been basically aimed at regaining U.S. strategic superiority and restoring the political leverage of nuclear weapons, thus fortifying the views of those within the Soviet leadership who held that the "imperialists" had not "changed their spots."
- Difficulty in getting the Conference on Security and Cooperation in Europe (CSCE) to ratify finally the territorial division of Europe without having had to make some commitment to freer East-West movement of ideas and people, coupled with some concern about the internal effects of detente in Eastern Europe and perhaps the USSR itself.
- Apparent Soviet pique against the United States for pre-empting the main diplomatic role in efforts to arrange an Arab-Israeli settlement, which, if successful, could lead to some loss of Soviet influence in the Middle East, even though (ambivalently) a settlement could also yield benefits by reducing the chances of a new outbreak of conflict that might lead to a Soviet-American confrontation.
- Signs of growing political disintegration in the West and the rising strength of left-oriented movements in a number of NATO countries, creating the kind of situation that might tempt the Soviet leadership to return to disruptive diplomacy. Combined with this, a possible temptation to exploit the post-1973 oil situation and associated economic problems in the West, accompanied by some rekindling of ideological expectations that "internal contradictions" were bringing closer a real "crisis of capitalism."

In addition to the factors listed on both sides of this ledger, some of which could obviously have cut in more than one direction, there was another that doubtless had an important bearing upon how the Soviet leaders may have assessed the USSR's relationship with the United States, and in particular, upon their perception of the net value of seeking to nail down a SALT II accord promptly in the post-Vladivostok negotiations. This was the downturn in U.S. fortunes in world politics that seemed to have set in during the spring of 1975.

### "Delicate Moment in World Politics"
### for the United States
The particular developments to which we owe brief attention here were those connected with the Indochina debacle and other setbacks to U.S. interests on the international scene in the bleak first half of

1975. Besides the trauma of seeing a ten-year investment of U.S. prestige and effort go down the drain in Southeast Asia, other reverses to U.S. interests at that juncture included the increasingly shaky state of NATO's southern flank from Portugal across to Greece and Turkey, the rebuffs to U.S. mediation diplomacy in the Middle East, and the growing inclination of peripheral countries in Asia to reassess their security alignments. And all of these manifestations of rapid change and potential instability on the world scene were compounded by problems of dealing with recession and unemployment at home.

One of the key considerations for American policymakers arising out of this period of travail for the United States was uncertainty about how the Soviet Union might assess and act upon the opportunities that the trend of events seemed to have unexpectedly placed before it. At a time when U.S. global commitments and defense policies had come under intense scrutiny by both friends and adversaries in what one commentator described as "a delicate moment in world politics,"[30] American leaders were patently concerned by the possibility that the Soviet Union might interpret U.S. difficulties and debates to mean that a slackening of American strength and resolve had set in. This situation might in turn encourage the Soviet Union to believe that it could safely fish in troubled waters and otherwise exploit detente to its advantage. Something of this sort seemed to have been very much on the mind of President Ford when he said in his April 1975 State-of-the-World message: "We cannot expect the Soviet Union to show restraint in the face of the United States' weakness and irresolution."[31]

Whatever image of the United States might eventually emerge in the eyes of its own people and others, the immediate one proved to be rather mixed. On the one hand, U.S. officials sought to project an image of strength and responsible international involvement, so as to reassure allies and to counsel continued restraint by the Soviet Union. Thus, the president, the secretary of state, and the secretary of defense all played variations on the theme that the United States would find strength through adversity—keeping U.S. defense measures and alliances in good repair, looking hopefully toward a SALT agreement with the Soviet Union, but not permitting "detente to become a license to fish in troubled waters."[32] Secretary Kissinger warned that "if detente turns into a formula for more selective exploitation of opportunities, the new trends in U.S.-Soviet relations will be in jeopardy,"[33] and a point stressed by Secretary Schlesinger was that "valid hopes for detente" would directly depend upon "the retention of an underlying equilibrium of force in areas of vital importance to the free nations of the world."[34]

On the other hand, the utility of fresh U.S. defense endeavors intended to maintain a balance of forces in order to insure Soviet restraint and to reassure U.S. allies did not go unchallenged. Rather, a debate appeared to be shaping up in the United States around arguments that the takeover in Southeast Asia by communist regimes merely capped a process at work throughout the world in which military power as an instrument of policy was being largely superseded by political, economic, and other nonmilitary forms of power.[35] Notwithstanding the rather contradictory fact that communist political successes in Indochina grew out of long and persistent application of force that finally turned the local military balance around in their favor,[36] such arguments were not without appeal to many segments of an American public and a Congress weary after years of global exertion. At the least they suggested that U.S. defense policy moves intended to offset loss of prestige and credibility from the Indochina setback might encounter increasing domestic opposition.

Contributing to the domestic debate on foreign and defense policy in the United States was still another set of opinions reflecting the belief in some parts of the U.S. defense community that it would be the wrong time, in the aftermath of U.S. overseas reverses, to begin retrenching militarily because of the "crossover" problem with regard to the overall military balance between the Soviet Union and the United States. In this view, the United States was seen as having passed from a long period of military dominance into a short-lived era of parity, which in turn could be transformed into inferiority if growing Soviet military power were to be simultaneously linked with declining U.S. force levels and to precipitate retrenchment from commitments abroad. Since the United States had never been obliged to deal with the Soviet Union under conditions in which the latter enjoyed clear-cut military superiority, one of the cardinal uncertainties troubling this school of thought was: What kind of Soviet behavior might be encountered if the crossover situation were to become a reality?[37]

This brings us then to the question of how Soviet attitudes toward detente and SALT might have been affected, if at all, by the adverse trend of events affecting the United States. Was the Soviet leadership in fact inclined to perceive the U.S. predicament as pointing toward an unraveling of American national will and confidence, toward an erosion of alliances, and a return to isolationism—all of which in turn could produce a changed Soviet assessment of political opportunities and the relative risks of pursuing them?

Needless to say, no outside observer could hope to ascertain with confidence what was going on in the minds of the men in the

Kremlin. But even though Soviet officials were plainly buoyed by the new situation and were reported to have told visitors to Moscow that the Western crisis was "indeed the greatest the capitalist world has known,"[38] the bulk of the available evidence would indicate that Brezhnev and his colleagues thought it best to maintain a relatively low profile with regard to trying to profit from American adversities.[39]

Various reasons might account for this circumspect Soviet approach. Perhaps the most compelling may have been to avoid rubbing the United States the wrong way at a touchy moment in world politics, either out of a healthy respect for the resiliency and staying power of the United States, or out of a belief that the United States might react dangerously, or both. As one writer put it, even though the Russians doubtless recognized opportunities to expand their influence and prestige, their immediate concern seemed to be that "in entering the areas where United States diplomacy [was] conspicuously unsuccessful, they avoid bumping into the Americans on their way out."[40]

Another consideration bearing on the Soviet response to developments in the spring of 1975 was the somewhat murky situation taking shape in Southeast Asia following the American withdrawal. Though there were reports that the Soviets had asked for naval and air base privileges at Cam Ranh Bay in return for their support of North Vietnam,[41] such factors as rivalry with China for influence in Vietnam and the coolness toward the USSR of the peasant-oriented Khmer Rouge victors in Cambodia implied that the field had not been left clear for unimpeded Soviet influence in that region.[42] Elsewhere, though perhaps persuaded that long-term "objective conditions" were running in their favor, the Soviets seemed concerned lest counterrevolutionary "forces of reaction" be set in motion if immediate gains were pressed too hard, as suggested by M.A. Suslov.[43] Portugal appeared to represent a particular case in point, where a promising swing toward the left might be jeopardized by a too open and abrupt attempt at communist takeover.

The extent to which internal leadership politics may have conditioned the initial Soviet response to the 1975 "crisis" in the capitalist world was difficult to judge. However, the dismissal from the Politburo in mid-April of A.N. Shelepin was widely interpreted to have had some connection with an internal debate over the appropriate Soviet line to be followed. Shelepin's "release" from his Politburo duties was noted in an "Informational Announcement" on the April 16, 1975, plenum of the Central Committee, at which Brezhnev's detente policies were given "approval and complete support."[44] According to one hypothesis, the fifty-six-year-old Shelepin, a dynamic opportunist, may have wanted to press a more activist line than Brezhnev thought prudent or necessary.[45] An alternative theory was that Shelepin had emerged as the putative organizer of a faction intending to seize power and switch to a harder line after Brezhnev's retirement (rumored to be upcoming at the 25th Party Congress in February 1976), and that in the interest of an orderly succession as well as policy continuity, Brezhnev had acted to shunt Shelepin aside.[46]

But for whatever combination of reasons, it would appear that Brezhnev and a majority of his colleagues had decided that Soviet interests would be best served, at least for the time being, by displaying their solicitude for detente, if only to keep the United States from "overreacting" and adopting a sterner set of defense and foreign policy priorities than might otherwise be the case.[47] At the same time, however, the Soviet leadership apparently also decided not to abstain from taking advantage of opportunities opening up for Soviet political gains in areas where the risk of vigorous American reaction seemed remote, such as Angola, where stepped-up and successful support for the Soviet Union's client faction was rendered, with Cuban cooperation, in the latter part of 1975. As for SALT, the balance of decision within the Kremlin by the end of 1975 appears to have tilted toward the view that there was no compelling reason to make substantial changes in the Soviet bargaining position for the sake of an early SALT II accord and a new summit.

### Allegations of Soviet SALT I Violations

The post-Vladivostok climate for working out compromises to resolve deadlocks in SALT and to relieve growing strains in the U.S.-Soviet relationship was rendered notably more sticky, not only by Soviet disinclination to give ground on disputed SALT issues, but also, it must be said, by a resurgence in the United States in midsummer 1975 of charges that the Soviet Union was not living up to its SALT I obligations. Critics alleged that some of Dr. Kissinger's earlier compromises for the sake of agreement in SALT I and at Vladivostok had been systematically exploited by the Soviets to serve their own unilateral interests, to the point of violating not only the spirit, but in some cases the letter, of past understandings. Some six or seven areas of suspected Soviet transgressions were singled out.[48]

One was alleged flouting of the distinction drawn by the United States between "heavy" and "light" missiles. By deploying as a replacement for the SS-11 their new SS-19, a missile with a volume reportedly close to 100 cubic meters, the Soviets were said to have circumvented the assumed dividing line of 70 cubic meters between light and heavy missiles, thus in effect assuring themselves of many more heavy missiles than the sublimit of 313 specified in the Interim Agreement and carried over to the Vladivostok formula.[4 9] A second alleged Soviet infraction concerned the placing of camouflage covers over mobile missile launchers and other concealment practices; a third was said to be the introduction of new measures to impede U.S. monitoring of telemetry data on Soviet MIRV testing, all putative violations of Article V of the Interim Agreement stating that "each party undertakes not to interfere with the national technical means of verification of the other party and . . . not to use deliberate concealment measures which impede verification."[5 0]

A fourth case of suspect Soviet activity was the construction of 100 to 150 new silo-like installations, claimed by the Soviets to be "command and control" capsules for missile launching, but which skeptics felt might be readily convertible into additional missile silos, in violation of Article I of the Interim Agreement. A fifth area of alleged Soviet transgressions concerned testing of modified SA-5 air defense missiles and associated mobile radars in "an ABM mode," presumably ruled out by the ABM Treaty,[5 1] and another infraction was the installation of an ABM radar on the Kamchatka peninsula.

Precisely where the truth lay with regard to such allegations was not at the time easy to establish, especially since the question of Soviet violations had become a politically charged issue in the United States. In May, unnamed administration officials said that the Soviets had offered private explanations that served to ease at least some suspicions of either outright violations or of their having taken undue advantage of SALT ambiguities.[5 2] Dr. Kissinger himself, when asked in a mid-June interview about violations, stated that the "Soviets have worried us in several areas . . . we have received answers which—while not fully satisfactory—are moving in the right direction."[5 3]

A couple of weeks later, however, at a press conference on foreign and domestic matters at which a reporter asked whether the president was concerned about published charges by former Secretary of Defense Melvin Laird of repeated Soviet SALT infractions, President Ford said that he had "investigated" such allegations and found that the Soviets "have not violated the SALT agreements. They have not used any loopholes."[5 4] This statement, in turn, was promptly challenged by Senator Jackson, who said it did not "reconcile" with testimony given in March by administration officials before his Senate Armed Services subcommittee.[5 5] A further commentary was offered in early July by Secretary Schlesinger, who said that though some "ambiguities" had arisen about Soviet activities, "as yet there is no demonstrated proof of Soviet violations of the agreement."[56]

Subsequently, a report to the Senate in February 1978 by the secretary of state covered each of the alleged Soviet violations mentioned above, along with several other instances dating after 1975.[57] The general thrust of the report was that a satisfactory resolution of the various Soviet activities of concern to the United States had been achieved through the medium of the Standing Consultative Commission, though the report carefully skirted an outright assurance that no violations, inadvertent or otherwise, had ever occurred.[58] The report also covered five complaints raised by the Soviet side in the SCC concerning U.S. observance of SALT I, including the placing of environmental shelters over Minuteman silos, construction of an alleged ABM radar on Shemya Island in the Aleutians, improper dismantling of old Atlas launchers and of ABM radars at Malmstrom, and failure to maintain the confidentiality of SCC proceedings. These issues too were said to have been satisfactorily resolved.

However, the clarifying documentation of the February 1978 report came several years after the matter of SALT I violations had become a controversial question in midsummer 1975, and therefore contributed nothing to improvement of the climate at that time for negotiating a SALT II accord.

## THE "NEAR MISS" ATTEMPT OF JANUARY 1976 TO WRAP UP A SALT II ACCORD

Despite the seemingly unpropitious prospects at the outset of 1976 for breaking the stalemate that had settled over the SALT II scene, Dr. Kissinger in January 1976 gave it another try on what was to be his last meeting as secretary of state with Brezhnev and company in Moscow. And although the outcome was again failure to bridge the remaining differences between the two sides, one may venture to say that Kissinger probably came very close on this occasion to sewing up a SALT II agreement with the Russians.

In November 1975 Kissinger had said the next move was up to the Russians,[59] but within a month, apparently after resuming back-channel exchanges with Moscow, he was again reportedly looking for "something to offer" that might stimulate a compromise.[60] Plans for another Moscow trip had in fact been set for early December, only a few days after Kissinger would be returning with President Ford from a journey to Peking. Internal bargaining in Washington over what new SALT proposals to offer the Russians, especially on the eve of the 1976 presidential election campaign, seems to have held things up.

In the meantime, however, some advance understanding with Moscow on the nature of a possible compromise solution to the Backfire and cruise missile problems apparently had been reached by early January 1976, when it was reported from the Soviet capital by journalist Robert Toth that the "core of a compromise" for breaking the SALT stalemate had already been struck.[61] Beyond suggesting that the United States had modified its prior position by acquiescing to inclusion of cruise missile limitations in SALT in return for Soviet assurances that Backfire deployment would be restricted so as not to pose a strategic threat against the United States, this account provided no details of the compromise formula under consideration.

The details were to emerge gradually later, some time after Kissinger's three-day meeting with Brezhnev in the latter part of January had taken place. As pieced together from various accounts, proposals along the following lines were put forward by each side at the talks in Moscow.[62]

The U.S. proposal was said to have several provisions regarding Backfire. The USSR would be permitted to deploy at least 250 Backfire bombers, not charged against the 2400 aggregate, during the period 1977-1982. From 1982 until the end of the treaty in 1985, no limits would apply to Backfire numbers. Operational restrictions on Backfire were to include: no use in exercises simulating nuclear attack on the United States; no deployment in areas from which unrefueled Backfires could reach the United States; and tankers for servicing Backfire were to be restricted.

The cruise missile provisions in the American proposal dealt separately with air-launched and sea-launched missiles. In the former case, each bomber carrying twelve to twenty ALCMs with a range of more than 372 statute miles would be counted within the Vladivostok subceiling of 1320 MIRVed launchers, but not the individual ALCMs.[63] The maximum permissible range of an ALCM would be 1500 statute miles (approximately the design range of the U.S. ALCM-B). With regard to SLCMs, there would be no numerical limits on the submarine-launched version, but its range would be restricted to 372 miles—far below the Tomahawk design range of 2000 nautical miles, which would mean essentially that the system could not be effectively employed for strategic attack against the Soviet Union. On the other hand, SLCMs launched from surface ships would be allowed to have a range of 2000 miles or more, but they would be limited numerically to 250 missiles that could be deployed on no more than twenty-five surface ships. In effect, these 250 long-range cruise missiles were to represent a tradeoff against the 250 Backfires allowed the Soviet Union, although critics would charge that this was an asymmetrical tradeoff favoring the Russians.[64]

The January 1976 Soviet proposal with which Brezhnev responded to Kissinger's compromise package reportedly included—in addition to Backfire and cruise missile provisions—a suggested reduction in the overall SALT ceiling from 2400 to about 2200 delivery vehicles, which was a move clearly in the direction of American preferences at Vladivostok. According to some sources, however, this reduction would be conditional upon satisfactory prior resolution of the Backfire and cruise missile issues.[65]

With respect to Backfire, the Soviet position, as before, was that it should not be counted in the aggregate for strategic delivery systems, but Brezhnev was said to have indicated that the Soviet Union would be prepared to restrict Backfire deployment to areas from which it could not strike targets in the United States.[66] Whether he also acceded to the other collateral restrictions on Backfire operations proposed by the United States is not made clear in the available accounts.

The cruise missile provisions proposed by Brezhnev were to count each bomber carrying ten or more ALCMs against the 1320 MIRV ceiling, but ALCM range would be limited to 1000 miles.[67] Cruise missiles on all other platforms—submarines, surface ships or land-based—would be restricted to a maximum range of 372 miles. Certain restrictions on short-range cruise missile R&D also were reportedly proposed, but details of these are lacking.

On the face of it, the two sets of proposals exchanged at Moscow in January 1976 were fairly close together on most points—so close, indeed, that it might be inferred that such "remarkable similarity," as some commentators put it,[68] had been rehearsed in advance. Although critics would find fault with the substance of the January proposals on various grounds,[69] there seemed on the surface to be no differences between the negotiating parties of a magnitude that could not have been ironed out if an accommodation were equally desired by both sides.

In fact, Kissinger's earlier comments in October and November 1975 that "90 percent" of a SALT II accord had been "substantially completed"[70]—though having appeared somewhat oversanguine at that time in view of the hard 10 percent of differences remaining over the Backfire and cruise missile issues—could now be considered close to the mark, to the extent that such scorekeeping might be meaningful at all.

Precisely what then kept the January 1976 exchange of proposals from culminating in due course in a 100 percent complete SALT II agreement? Unfortunately, this does not come through very clearly in any of the available accounts.

Substantively, the single most likely hang-up could have occurred in connection with the Soviet side's declining to accept a proffered allowance of 250 Backfires for 250 long-range SLCMs, and proposing instead that Backfire remain cost-free in SALT coin, while a 372-mile range limit be imposed on all cruise missiles except a finite number of bomber-launched ALCMs.

In a sense this was a pivotal issue that could greatly affect the future of what might be called the "reborn" cruise missile that had emerged from U.S. development of new technology. From the U.S. viewpoint, the cruise missile development programs reinstituted in the early 1970s—at least partly to improve the U.S. negotiating position in SALT[71]—had by 1976 yielded what amounted to a new class of weapons with a variety of promising strategic and tactical functions that many felt could prove essential to future defense requirements. Although not threatening to supplant existing strategic systems, the long-range cruise missile had complementary attributes that recommended it to many defense planners—an accurate, relatively inexpensive system that in its ALCM version could help prolong the life of the bomber force, and which at the same time, because of its slow transit, was essentially a second-strike weapon that should not upset strategic stability.[72]

Despite dissenting views from some parts of the arms control community in particular,[73] there was a strong disposition in the Department of Defense and elsewhere to avoid the kinds of SALT constraints that might prematurely forfeit U.S. technological assets and the promising military potential seen in the new cruise missile systems. The Soviet proposal to ban all non-aircraft-launched cruise missiles of more than 372-mile range would impose such a constraint. It was not unlikely, therefore, that Kissinger would have come under strong pressure from some quarters not to concede to the Russians on this issue.

From the Soviet viewpoint, the same issue could have had pivotal aspects also. In the early 1970s the Soviets apparently had taken little note of the revived U.S. cruise missile development effort, but by 1975 they had awakened to its implications and had begun both to brand cruise missiles publicly as an example of the "Pentagon's desire to step up the arms race"[74] and to seek broad constraints on them in SALT.

The situation of the Soviet Union was one in which it probably could over the course of time acquire a cruise missile technology to match the United States if this were felt necessary,[75] but in the meantime the Soviets would also have to face the problem of defense against cruise missiles in Western hands.

The provision in the Soviet January 1976 proposal most likely to curtail the deployment and proliferation of large numbers of sea- and land-based cruise missiles capable of attacks from many azimuths against the Soviet Union was the 372-mile limit on all except bomber-launched ALCMs. The numbers of such ALCMs deployable against the USSR, meanwhile, could be held down to manageable proportions by the MIRV quota applied to their carriers. Without changes in programmed U.S. forces, for example, only thirty-four bombers would be eligible as ALCM platforms.[76] Even if this number were to be increased somewhat at the expense of MIRVed ICBMs and SLBMs, institutional and other pressures within the U.S. establishment might be expected to keep fairly tight limits on the bomber element of the U.S. strategic TRIAD.

Other substantive questions may also to some extent have prevented elimination of the remaining "10 percent" of differences between the two sides in the January 1976 exchanges. One concerned the Backfire. Even though the American proposal on Backfire alone could hardly have been more generous, when the Russians declined to accept the linkage with 250 long-range SLCMs they assured in effect a surge of resistance within the U.S. establishment to allowing Backfire a completely free ride—whatever professed Soviet intentions for it might be.

Another likely troublesome area was cruise missile verification. Among criticisms directed from the outside at both the U.S. and Soviet proposals of January 1976 was that they had failed to resolve the enormously complicated problem of verification,[77] without which some critics claimed that SALT limitations on cruise missiles would be meaningless.[78] This was not, however, a universally shared view, for there was also a body of opinion arguing that the counting of cruise missile carriers, whose maximum missile capacity could be ascertained, would obviate the need for more precise and intensive verification procedures.[79] But in any event, the apparent failure of the January proposals to come to grips with verification problems may have left another area of unresolved substantive difference between the negotiating parties.

Richard Burt has described factors like those discussed above as the complexities of trying to mesh the defense planning and arms control considerations attending the introduction of a new class of weapons like the "reborn" cruise missile.[80] But along with those factors, a further impediment to resolving the SALT II impasse by means of the January proposals was doubtless a bit of diplomatic intransigence on both sides. This was related in the American case to the president's need to maintain the domestic allegiance of conservative supporters important to his 1976 candidacy, or for that matter, to ratification of any SALT II accord he might bring to the Congress.

The operation of these latter considerations evidently became more significant in the few weeks after Kissinger's return from Moscow in late January. Kissinger had come home reportedly optimistic that the remaining differences in the two sets of proposals could be reconciled,[81] which would probably have required moving at least part way toward the Soviet position. However, with criticism to be expected from potent figures in American politics like Ronald Reagan and Senator Henry Jackson if he were to offer the Russians further concessions,[82] President Ford instead reportedly proposed in February to Brezhnev, through Ambassador Dobrynin, that they sign a SALT II agreement covering only the noncontroversial items, putting aside the Backfire and cruise missile issues for SALT III.[83]

In March 1976, for whatever the reasons that may have also prompted them not to offer any concessions helpful in closing the "10 percent disagreement gap," the Russians replied that Ford's proposal was unacceptable.[84] With that, the attempt of January 1976 to sew up a SALT II accord that could be solemnized at another Ford-Brezhnev summit meeting had become, at best, a near miss.

After March no new SALT proposals were advanced by the Ford administration, though it was reported in midsummer that some consideration was being given to one last try at an agreement before the November elections.[85] For its part, the Soviet side also expressed an interest in getting negotiations back on the track. In late June, for example, at a conference of European communist parties in East Berlin, Brezhnev declared publicly that the Soviet Union felt it to be of "paramount importance" to improvement of U.S.-Soviet relations to conclude an agreement in the strategic arms talks that had been "dragging on" for several months through "no fault of ours whatsoever."[86] Neither publicly nor privately, however, did the Soviets offer any new proposals of their own, evidently preferring to wait for the U.S. side to make the next substantive move.

Meanwhile, as both the exigencies of the presidential election campaign and U.S.-Soviet tension over the Angolan situation continued, a more or less tacit decision was made within the Ford administration to put the strategic arms negotiations on the shelf until after the election,[8 7] leaving it to November's victor to resume the initiative in SALT. Although the SALT delegations did resume their Geneva talks in late September on a rather low-key basis,[8 8] when the American election in November produced a new president, it was formally agreed between Washington and Moscow to suspend further SALT II negotiations sine die until after the administration of Jimmy Carter had assumed office.[8 9]

# Chapter 11

# Renewed Search for a
# SALT II Accord

At his first formal press conference on February 8, 1977, President Carter emphasized his interest in reaching a SALT II agreement along the lines of the Vladivostok formula, offering to put aside the disputed Backfire and cruise missile issues until SALT III in order to "conclude a quick agreement."[1] Although earlier, in his inaugural address and in interviews, Carter had also alluded to goals of nuclear disarmament more far-reaching than anything ever proposed in SALT,[2] it appeared that at least for the time being—while SALT policy was under initial review within his administration[3]—the new president was essentially picking up where Ford and Kissinger had left off with a similar proposal about a year earlier to detour the unresolved SALT issues.[4]

As later noted by its chief SALT negotiator, the Carter administration, in addition to unresolved issues, had also inherited some fifty pages of draft treaty text already jointly agreed with the Russians.[5] It was this that made up the frequently cited "90 percent complete" SALT accord passed along by the Ford administration.

As for the Soviet side, Brezhnev, too, speaking in Tula on January 18, two days before Carter's inauguration, had given high priority to a strategic arms limitation agreement, saying that it must not be put off, but adding that what had to be done first was "to consolidate" and "implement" the accord already reached in Vladivostok.[6] The fact that the 1972 Interim Agreement on limitation of strategic offensive arms was due to expire in October 1977—only about eight months away—gave further reason for both sides to think about resuming the negotiations that had been dormant since November 1976.

Steps toward this end had been discussed by Secretary of State Vance and Ambassador Dobrynin in Washington while the new administration was getting its SALT negotiating and backup personnel in place, and at the end of January it was announced that the opening step in resumption of negotiations would be a visit to Moscow in March or early April by Vance.[7]

Meanwhile, however, the atmosphere for resuming the search for a SALT II accord was becoming somewhat disturbed. On the one hand, in the United States a debate over Soviet military capabilities and intentions that had been inherited by the Carter administration,[8] but brought into sharper focus by the controversy over confirmation of Paul Warnke as head of ACDA and chief SALT negotiator,[9] helped stimulate questioning of the SALT process and its contributions to U.S. security.

Within the Soviet Union, on the other hand, it was apparent that the Soviet leadership had been at first confused and then angered by the new moral tone struck by the Carter administration in foreign affairs and especially its focus on the "human rights issue" in public pronouncements having to do with Eastern Europe and the Soviet Union. Reporting in late January that Ambassador Dobrynin had already begun to complain privately to Washington officials about this trend, Hedrick Smith of the *New York Times* predicted that it was likely to complicate the resumption of negotiations on a SALT II agreement.[10]

Confirmation of this prediction was not long in coming, as the brief postelection honeymoon between the new American president and the Kremlin leadership gave way to a spate of critical commentary from Moscow and warnings that if Carter's human rights policy were carried too far it could damage the atmosphere for reaching a SALT agreement.[11] A particularly harsh excoriation of the new U.S. leadership's policy approach was delivered by Brezhnev himself in a major speech before a congress of Soviet trade unions on March 22, in which Brezhnev attacked "Washington's claims to teach others how to live," and singled out this "interference in our internal affairs," along with a "slanderous campaign about a fictitious 'military threat' on the part of the USSR," as circumstances "directly opposing" further improvement of Soviet-American relations.[12]

Despite this and subsequent expressions of irritation in Soviet media,[13] seen by some as meant to put the U.S. side on the defensive in the first testing round of negotiations on SALT and other issues in Moscow,[14] President Carter himself said he was not discouraged by Brezhnev's speech, unlike some people who seemed concerned "every time Brezhnev sneezes," and that in fact parts of the Soviet leader's speech dealing with the need for progress in arms limitations were encouraging.[15]

On the eve of Vance's departure for Moscow, the president in a March 24th news conference outlined "two alternative packages" of SALT proposals that would be presented to the Russians. One was described as a comprehensive proposal seeking substantial reductions in the Vladivostok ceilings for strategic missiles and bombers, and the other a "fallback position" (later labeled the "deferral option") amounting essentially to adoption of the Vladivostok formula to replace the expiring Interim Agreement in October, but deferring for subsequent negotiations the disputed issues over what weapons were to be included.[16]

Against this background, the Vance negotiating party[17] arrived in Moscow in late March for what was hoped to be a session with the Soviet leadership that would help break the deadlock in SALT II, but which turned out to be what many at the time regarded as a debacle.

## THE MARCH 1977 AMERICAN PROPOSALS AND THEIR FATE

Of the two alternative U.S. SALT proposals which were presented to the Soviet side in March, the first or "comprehensive" package was the one that broke new ground, and which Secretary Vance referred to upon his arrival in Moscow as the preferred alternative intended to be "the central piece" of discussion, so far as the United States was concerned.[18] As later reconstructed, the comprehensive proposal contained some eleven provisions along the following lines:[19]

- Reduction of the Vladivostok aggregate of 2400 delivery vehicles to 2000 or 1800.
- Reduction of the Vladivostok MIRVed launcher limit of 1320 to 1200 or 1100.
- Sublimit of 550 on MIRVed ICBM launchers, to include all Soviet SS-17, -18, -19 ICBMs, and U.S. Minuteman III.
- Within the 550 MIRV subceiling, still another sublimit of 150 on the number of MLBMs (Modern Large Ballistic Missile Launchers) to be allowed the Soviet Union, that is, SS-9s, and SS-18s. The United States to be permitted no MLBMs.
- A freeze on the existing ICBM deployments of both sides, together with a ban on modification of existing ICBMs, and a ban on development, testing, and deployment of new ICBMs.
- No development, testing, or deployment of mobile ICBMs,

together with working out of a method to assure that mobile SS-20 IRBM launchers could not be used to launch ICBMs.

- A limit of six per year on flight tests for all ICBMs, and a similar limit for all SLBMs.

- Continuation of the 1972 Interim Agreement's prohibition on building new ICBM launchers at new locations.

- A ban on armed cruise missiles with a range greater than 2500 kilometers (1550 statute miles).

- An understanding that cruise missiles with ranges between 600 and 2500 kilometers would be carried only by heavy bombers, subject to inclusion in the MIRVed launcher limit, but that other types of aircraft would be permitted without SALT penalty to carry cruise missiles of less than 600-kilometer range.[20]

- A requirement that the Soviet Union provide assurances that the Backfire bomber would not be used as a strategic vehicle, in order to exclude it from the aggregate total of ICBMs, SLBMs, and bombers.[21]

Without question, this comprehensive package amounted to a radically innovative proposal.[22] For the first time in the history of SALT it would mean making a real cut into the strategic "muscle" of both sides. It also would severely restrict the "modernization" process, which hitherto in the SALT experience had been treated as relatively sacrosanct by both sides. Whether the measures proposed would make a significant contribution to greater strategic stability, as its sponsors evidently hoped, was less clear. For, unlike the Vladivostok formula, which left each side considerable "elbowroom" for adjustments to meet its own strategic concerns, the comprehensive proposal would narrow such latitude in favor of a complicated scheme of constraints whose questionable verifiability in some cases could promote instability rather than reducing it.[23]

From the American viewpoint, a salient purpose of the comprehensive proposal's several levels of numerical limits on ICBMs and its curbs on ICBM modernization obviously was to bring further growth of Soviet counterforce capabilities to a halt at a stage in their development, it was hoped, where they would still fall short of posing a credible disarming strike against U.S. ICBM forces. The United States, too, of course, would be foregoing the possibility of measures to improve the counterforce capabilities and survivability of its ICBM forces. Moreover, it would find itself locked in by the freeze on further ICBM development to a position of substantial disadvantage in ICBM throwweight—a disparity on the order of 4 to 1.[24] On the other hand, little change in planned U.S. ICBM programs, other than cancelling of accuracy improvements and research on the MX missile, would be required by the terms of the proposal, whereas in the Soviet case major cuts in deployed ICBMs, as well as cessation of several active modernization programs, would be required.[25]

From the viewpoint of the Russian leaders, the substantive content of the comprehensive proposal doubtless came across as an effort to spike their guns in the field of ICBM competition—where they had the strongest position and the biggest investment in ongoing programs—while also trying to keep the rest of the strategic competition channeled in directions where the United States enjoyed technological and operational advantages, such as strategic systems employing seaborne and airborne launch platforms.

Even with regard to Backfire, which the comprehensive U.S. proposal would allow to go free outside the new aggregate total of 1800 to 2000 delivery vehicles, except for unspecified collateral assurances, there was an item that may have looked loaded to the Soviet side. This was the provision that ALCMs of strategic range (600-2500 kms) could be carried only by heavy bombers, which would rule out Backfire as a potential ALCM platform, since by Soviet claim it was *not* a heavy bomber. Other substantive aspects of the U.S. package that probably piqued the Russians were its backtracking with regard to the Vladivostok accord's approval of land-mobile ICBM systems and the requirement for special procedures by the Soviet side to prevent conversion of the SS-20 IRBM into the SS-16 ICBM.

Apart from substantive content, there were other aspects of the U.S. comprehensive package that the Soviets found objectionable, and to which we shall come in a moment. But in any event, as widely reported at the time, when the new U.S. proposal was presented in Moscow on March 28—without Brezhnev's being present—[26] it was brusquely rejected. So, too, was the alternate "deferral option." As for the only Soviet proposal put forth, a reiteration by Gromyko of the last Russian proposal made to Kissinger more than a year earlier in January 1976,[27] it was turned down by the U.S. side. Thus, on March 30 the three-day Kremlin talks broke off amidst speculation that the impasse arising from the Carter administration's first major venture into the SALT arena would cloud the chances of a new accord before the Interim Agreement expired in October, and might even portend collapse of the SALT II negotiations.[28]

This prospect seemed hardly diminished by a caustic statement delivered by Gromyko at a hastily convened press conference on March 31. In it, Gromyko charged that the American proposals were "aimed at obtaining unilateral advantages for the USA, to the detriment of the Soviet Union,"[29] and he spelled out Soviet grievances on a long list of points, including the complaint that the provision to ban modernization of missiles was a "cheap" and "dubious device" that "would be advantageous to the United States and disadvantageous to the Soviet Union."[30] He also warned that resurrection of the FBS issue was being considered, saying that "in light of the latest U.S. proposals ... we are entitled to raise the question of elimination of American forward-based nuclear means."[31]

Various reasons, apart from substantive objections, might account for why the Soviet leadership had flatly turned down the U.S. proposals as "unacceptable" and had felt it necessary for Gromyko to denounce them publicly on the final day of the Vance visit—the first such departure ever from the studied etiquette of high-level meetings on SALT. One of them probably was Soviet displeasure with the Carter administration's public style of diplomacy.[32] Another, the president's advance revelation of the comprehensive package in a way that implicitly challenged Soviet pretensions as the foremost champion of peace and sweeping disarmament initiatives. Some scent of sour grapes at being outflanked on this score was certainly evident in Gromyko's remark about which country was to be regarded as the real champion of disarmament.[33] Perhaps a third Soviet motivation was to send a signal that progress on SALT and other issues would require some backing off by the United States on human rights criticism and related transgressions against the "principle of non-intervention in internal affairs."

Soviet rejection of the March 1977 proposals found President Carter saying that he intended to "hang tough" in trying to negotiate an agreement that would not be merely "a superficial ratification of rules by which we can continue the arms race," and that if the Soviets failed to negotiate in good faith toward such an agreement, he would be "forced to consider" development and deployment of additional U.S. weapons.[34] The next test of the Carter administration's approach to getting the strategic arms negotiations back on the track would come in May 1977, when another American initiative was to be put forward.

## THE NEW "THREE-TIER" FRAMEWORK FOR A SALT II ACCORD

The formal communiqué issued at the close of the March talks had made no reference to the new impasse at which SALT II had arrived,

stating merely that the two sides had agreed to "continue consideration" of the issues at a meeting between Vance and Gromyko in
May 1977 in Geneva, where "an exchange of views on the Middle
East problem" would head the agenda.[35] However, the May meeting
in Geneva, preceded by some exploratory talks between President
Carter, Secretary Vance, and Ambassador Dobrynin in Washington,[36] proved to be an important turning point, producing what was
described at the time as a "new blueprint" for negotiations,[37] which
later came to be called the "three-tier framework" for a SALT II
agreement.

Essentially, the three-tier approach submitted to the Soviets in
May was a compromise arrangement that might be viewed as an
amalgam of the Vladivostok formula and the two U.S. alternative
proposals of March 1977, intended by its American sponsors to
accommodate both the Soviet desire to retain the Vladivostok
guidelines for an agreement and the U.S. preference for more
comprehensive limitations in SALT II.[38] The arrangement envisaged
a SALT II accord in three parts, which were to be interdependent.

First, there would be a Treaty that would run through 1985, based
on the Vladivostok accord. Precisely what the aggregate ceilings
might be remained open to negotiation, with the American preference pointing to lower ceilings.

Second, there would be attached to the Treaty a Protocol of about
three years' duration. Its function would be to allow time to find
mutually satisfactory solutions to such controversial issues as cruise
missile constraints, the Backfire, mobile ICBM limitations, and
qualitative constraints on ICBMs. Any of the limits contained in the
Protocol would be of a temporary character, and would be subject to
further negotiation in SALT III.

Third, there would be a joint Statement of Principles, to provide
an agreed set of guidelines for follow-on negotiations for substantial
reductions and other constraints on strategic arms.

Despite having taken a strong position publicly that the previously
rejected American proposals of March 1977 could not serve even as a
basis for further discussion,[39] the Soviet leadership evidently recon-
sidered to the extent of accepting the idea of the three-tier approach
at Geneva in May.[40] However, as both Secretary Vance and
Gromyko indicated at the time, some important disagreements
concerning this approach remained unresolved.[41] Among them were
whether given items should be dealt with in the Treaty or the
Protocol, or left out entirely, as well as differences over the nature of

a set of principles for future negotiations. It was not until September 1977, when Gromyko visited Washington for talks with President Carter and Vance, that some of these disagreements were sufficiently ironed out so that the SALT delegations, which had reconvened in Geneva in May, could go forward with negotiations on the details of a SALT II accord based on the three-tier approach. Even so, the September meeting—which took place after previously scheduled Vance-Gromyko talks in Vienna and Geneva had been scrubbed—[42] came too late to offer any prospect of a SALT II agreement in time to replace the expiring Interim Agreement in October.

Sometimes referred to as the "September breakthrough,"[43] the Washington meeting with Gromyko elicited from the Russians assent to several key propositions, according to Paul Warnke: (1) that a SALT II agreement could go beyond the Vladivostok parameters; (2) that it could contain sublimits on the "more dangerous systems"; (3) that it could cover some reductions; and (4) that it could lay down some prohibitions on new strategic systems.[44]

For all practical purposes, therefore, the three-tier framework as agreed in September 1977 effectively replaced Vladivostok as the basis for subsequent intensive negotiations over the next year or so, during which differences were gradually narrowed, bringing a SALT II accord close to the final stages of completion by the fall of 1978.

## THE NARROWING OF DIFFERENCES BETWEEN THE TWO SIDES AFTER SEPTEMBER 1977

This process was by no means an uninterrupted march toward agreement, as a brief review here of some of the vicissitudes encountered in the negotiations following the September "breakthrough" in Washington may indicate. Perhaps one of the first problems that it was necessary to tackle was what to do about the expiration of the five-year-old Interim Agreement on October 3, 1977. Studies of various options had been carried out within the U.S. government,[45] and possibly within the Soviet bureaucracy as well, but the problem was eventually disposed of by a unilateral American announcement on September 23 that the United States would continue to honor the Interim Agreement while SALT II was still being negotiated, provided the Soviet Union would do the same. Two days later Moscow offered a similar pledge.[46]

With regard to negotiations toward a SALT II agreement of the three-tier type, "significant progress" was achieved during the last quarter of 1977, according to Paul Warnke.[47] Although no official details of the negotiations in this period were furnished, accounts that found their way into the press indicated that both sides had made substantial concessions in the hope of reaching an agreement by the end of the year, but that a number of difficult questions remained to be resolved.[48]

The central compromise reportedly involved U.S. assent to modernization of the Soviet force of some 300 "heavy" missiles, in effect, allowing the USSR to complete its SS-18 deployment program. This represented a retreat from the ceiling of 150 heavy missiles sought by the United States in the March comprehensive proposal. In return, the Russians were said to have relaxed some of their previous demands for cruise missile restrictions. Specifically, the United States would be left free during the SALT II Protocol period of three years to continue to develop—though not deploy—long-range cruise missiles other than the air-launched variety, with the deployment issue being deferred into the SALT III negotiating period; while in the case of ALCMs, to be carried by heavy bombers, the Soviets acceded to the U.S.-proposed range limit of 2500 kilometers.[49]

Other reciprocal concessions were said to have been made in connection with three separate sets of sublimits on MIRVed delivery systems. In the first instance, the U.S. side agreed to an aggregate MIRV ceiling of 1320, to include ALCM-equipped heavy bombers as well as MIRVed ICBMs and SLBMs, a provision deemed to be in the direction of Soviet preference, since it would bring air-launched cruise missiles under a SALT regime. For its part, the Soviet side agreed to the idea of two further MIRV sublimits: one of 1200 to 1250 on the combined number of land- and sea-based MIRVed missile launchers, and within this sublimit, a separate ceiling of 800 to 850 on the number of MIRVed land-based ICBMs—with the latter provision in particular seen as a concession in the direction of U.S. concern about the survivability of the Minuteman force.[50]

In addition to these central areas of agreement, the negotiations in the last quarter of 1977 also appear to have brought the parties close together on several other items. Among them were provisions for a common data base hitherto lacking in SALT, marking a precedent-setting if somewhat limited departure from customary Soviet practice,[51] as well as Soviet agreement not to deploy the SS-16 ICBM in a mobile mode because of its similarity to the SS-20.[52] An agreed ban on construction of additional fixed ICBM launchers, and a final wrapping up of rules for MIRV verification also apparently came about during this period.[53]

If the foregoing achievements reflected the "progress" registered in the last quarter of 1977, the negotiations of that period also left unresolved a large number of issues that were to persist in some degree during subsequent rounds of negotiation in 1978. One of these, perhaps among the least critical, was disagreement on the size of the reduction from the Vladivostok aggregate of 2400 delivery vehicles, with the United States favoring a cutback to 2160, and the Soviets holding out for a reduction only to 2250, the figure finally agreed on.[54]

But a more persistent disagreement apparently arose around the question of when steps to reduce Soviet forces (the only ones affected by the lower ceiling) should begin and end, with the U.S. side proposing that the process should be completed by the end of 1980, and the Soviets arguing for a later date. The duration of the Protocol period also remained a disputed issue, with the United States proposing that it terminate in December 1980, and the USSR that it should expire three years after entering into force, which could run into 1981 or beyond.[55]

The modernization issue, as it bore on testing and deployment of "new types" of ballistic missiles, proved to be a particularly vexed question. Although both sides professed an interest in prohibiting deployment of new missiles during the life of the Protocol as an important qualitative constraint, each side wished to make exceptions. The Soviet Union wanted to exempt a new single-warhead ICBM it had under development, presumably to replace some of its SS-11 force, but did not favor exempting any MIRVed missiles. The United States, on the other hand, in order to preserve its option to develop and deploy a land-mobile MIRVed ICBM (the MX) to relieve the problem of Minuteman vulnerability, and also because it would have been symbolically undesirable to allow Russian but not U.S. deployment of a new missile, suggested that each side be permitted to deploy one new ICBM, either MIRVed or non-MIRVed.[56]

Other missile-related items over which disagreement was to be found included the maximum number of reentry vehicles (RVs) to be permitted on a MIRVed missile; the precise definition of constrained systems, especially what constituted a "new type" of system and the volume threshold for a "heavy missile"; and the question of setting an upper limit on missile throwweight, or payload.[57]

Two of the most familiar issues under dispute since Vladivostok, Backfire and cruise missiles, also continued to present problems, even though differences were narrowed somewhat in the negotiations after September 1977. In the Backfire case, the U.S. side had assented to not counting the bomber in SALT, and the Soviets agreed not to raise its production rate, refusing, however, to disclose what the rate was. Other questions remained, not only about a quid pro quo for exempting Backfire from SALT, but also with regard to basing, refueling, and other restrictions on Backfire's "strategic" use, and how to incorporate them in a treaty.[58] In the cruise missile case, one fundamental difference—potential deployment of nonbomber launched and conventional cruise missiles after the Protocol period—had simply been postponed, as already noted. Other differences that persisted included how to measure the range of ALCMs in maneuvering flight, how many ALCMs to allow per bomber, and whether ALCMs could be carried by aircraft other than heavy bombers, such as wide-body transports suitably modified to distinguish them from civilian transports.[59]

Another contentious issue not unrelated to the cruise missile case was the noncircumvention provision sought by the Soviets to prevent transfer of strategic technology, especially the new cruise missile technology, to third parties. Because of the sensitivity of this issue to America's alliance relationships, particularly in NATO, the U.S. side found itself in the position of seeking to minimize transfer restrictions that could damage cooperative alliance arrangements without appearing to oppose a noncircumvention provision in SALT.[60]

And finally, in connection with working out the Statement of Principles for future negotiations, the question of what matters were to be taken up in SALT III found the United States trying to place priority on large reductions and further qualitative restrictions, while the Soviets, reportedly somewhat cool to these suggestions, sought to bring the FBS issue back into the picture, pressing to make U.S. forward-based systems subject to limitation in the next round of SALT.[61]

Despite the attainment of a rather significant core of agreement, each side by early 1978 evidently began to grow impatient at what was perceived to be the intractability of the other with regard to clearing away the various SALT II issues that remained unresolved. The Soviet side was perhaps the first to give vent to its impatience, particularly through a bold-headlined *Pravda* editorial article on February 11, 1978, which chided the United States for dragging its feet in SALT, and went to unusually detailed lengths to draw a contrast between the "constructive" Soviet position and the "one-sided" American position on each of the major SALT issues in dispute.[62] The article bore down particularly hard on the U.S. positions regarding cruise missiles and banning of "new types" of ICBMs. It also branded as "futile" any attempts "to intimidate the Soviet Union" by saying that unless the SALT agreement is tilted in American favor, the "U.S. Senate will not ratify it."

The following month, another prominently displayed *Pravda* article, this one signed by Georgi Arbatov, head of the Institute of the USA and Canada, also lectured the United States on its having come to a "halt in the settlement of important questions in Soviet-American relations," including SALT, where, according to Arbatov, there were "only a few items on the agenda still to be decided."[63] Heading Arbatov's roll call of those in the United States responsible for the deteriorating state of affairs were, as might be expected, the various "opponents of detente," whose attacks upon SALT had become "the more bitter" as prospects for an agreement became "the more real."

But also high on the list was "President J. Carter," whose administration was accused of "vacillation" toward concluding a SALT agreement,[64] and whose Wake Forest speech of March 16, 1978, was criticized for the contradiction between its assurances that "America would strive to bring the SALT negotiations to a successful end" without "seeking unilateral advantage" and the "main emphasis" placed on "strident promises to strengthen the military might of the United States" in view of "the 'Soviet threat' and the USSR's 'sinister intentions.' "

Dismissing as "groundless" the "old argument about a 'Soviet threat,' " Arbatov asserted that it was really the "stubborn aspiration of U.S. imperialist circles to achieve military supremacy" that gave rise to "dissatisfaction with the future [SALT] agreement, and to heightened concern that it could cement the correlation of strategic forces to the disadvantage of the United States." At the same time, Arbatov noted, it was understandable that it might be "particularly difficult for the Americans," long accustomed to "living beyond two oceans with a feeling of complete security," to "reconcile" themselves to the idea that they "would be vulnerable—in the event of war—to a nuclear strike." In any event, the bottom line of Arbatov's essay was that the time had come for the United States to decide whether it wanted a SALT agreement and peaceful cooperation on the one hand, or rejection of an agreement with accompanying "marked deterioration" in U.S.-USSR relations on the other.

Interestingly enough, a group of twenty-one congressmen, mostly members of the House Armed Services Committee, who happened to be visiting Moscow in March, got much the same message as that delivered by Arbatov, but from a different source: Marshal Nikolai V. Ogarkov, chief of the Soviet General Staff. Ogarkov, himself a veteran of earlier SALT negotiations,[65] spent four hours on March 29 with the congressional group, reportedly giving an informative but tough recital of the Soviet position on SALT issues, and echoing

Arbatov's counsel that Americans would have to reconcile themselves to no longer enjoying the complete security of the past.[66]

Still another powerful voice joined the dialogue on SALT a few days later when Brezhnev, speaking, symbolically, from the deck of a Soviet cruiser in Vladivostok, noted that three and a half years had passed since the Vladivostok accord without a follow-up agreement's having been reached. Assailing the United States for stalling in the strategic arms negotiations, the Soviet leader warned that "time was running out for SALT."[67]

Meanwhile, in the United States, the other side of a growing chorus of dissatisfaction with SALT was also being heard. The assurance given Congress by ACDA in February 1978 that the proposed SALT II accord would be "adequately verifiable"[68] had begun to come under challenge by various critics, including, according to some reports that were themselves unverifiable, the Joint Chiefs of Staff.[69] There was also reported to be considerable concern in the Pentagon, supposedly shared by Senator Henry Jackson, that the Protocol portion of the agreement—described in some quarters as "the dumping ground of unresolved problems"[70] — might prove to have a stifling effect upon programs believed necessary in the future to ensure strategic deterrence, such as the survivable ICBM basing system for the MX and cruise missiles.[71]

At the same time, the rise of tensions in U.S.-Soviet relations over Soviet-Cuban "adventurism" in Africa and other issues outside SALT, such as Soviet treatment of dissidents and harassment of American news correspondents and business representatives in Moscow, also began to have spillover effects upon the SALT negotiating environment, leading to increasing speculation about the possibility that the Senate might reject a SALT agreement, with opposition likely to focus on the Protocol portion of the three-tier arrangement.[72]

A further factor bearing on the SALT negotiating environment was the putative adoption of "freeze" tactics by the Carter administration. In early June, an article in the *Washington Post*, which immediately drew an indignant denial from the president himself, reported on the basis of "inside" information that Carter had decided to go through the motions of negotiating with the Russians, but to avoid serious efforts to sew up an agreement—in order both to await a more favorable domestic political climate for an accord, and to send a signal to the Russians indicating American displeasure with Soviet actions in Africa.[73] Whatever the accuracy of this story, which in a sense paralleled what the Russians themselves had been claiming, its effect—as a *Post* editorial the following day observed—

had seemingly been to pressure the president into a public commitment to "proceed aggressively with SALT discussions."[74]

By early June there had already been two high-level U.S.-Soviet
meetings in 1978 on SALT issues—one in April when Vance went to
Moscow for another session with Brezhnev and Gromyko,[75] and a
return visit to Washington by Gromyko late in May. On the first
occasion it was announced that there had been "a narrowing of the
parties' positions on some of the remaining unresolved issues," which
apparently included working out a noncircumvention provision with
language sufficiently ambiguous to avoid alarming NATO.[76] On the
second occasion, only "limited gains" toward a new agreement were
claimed, and some accounts suggested that a new Soviet proposal on
banning ICBMs had even served to slow down the negotiations.[77]

It is difficult to say how much the pace of negotiations may have
picked up again as a result of such factors as a presidential resolve in
early June to "proceed aggressively" or a growing Soviet concern
about China's improving ties with the West,[78] but in any event the
next few months found American and Soviet SALT negotiators at
several levels actively engaged in trying to narrow further the range
of differences. In July, Vance and Warnke met in Geneva with
Gromyko,[79] while during the first week in September, Warnke
headed a U.S. negotiating team dispatched to Moscow "to obtain
Soviet reactions" to some U.S. ideas in advance of a scheduled trip
by Gromyko to the United States later in the month.[80]

It was during Gromyko's exchanges with the president and Vance
in the last few days of September, at a point where the president's
domestic and international prestige had risen dramatically after his
mediator's role in the Camp David Arab-Israeli conference, that
optimistic statements from SALT negotiators on both sides began to
suggest that the final round in six years of SALT II negotiations
might be at hand.[81]

The actual outcome of Gromyko's Washington visit fell short of
making it the final round,[82] though the remaining differences
apparently had been whittled down enough to prompt an estimate
from Paul Warnke that "95 percent" of a SALT II agreement—a new
highwater mark for such estimates—had been completed.[83] Within a
few days of Gromyko's return to Moscow, it was reported that
further adjustment of differences had "brought the two superpowers
to the verge of final agreement" on a new SALT accord, and that
administration officials were hopeful that the last differences could
be worked out during a scheduled visit to Moscow by Vance and
Warnke in the second half of October.[84] Events were not to bear out
these expectations.

## THE PERSISTENT "FINAL FIVE-PERCENT GAP"

Perhaps because of some indication through diplomatic channels in the week or so before Vance's October 22 to 24 trip to Moscow that new difficulties had arisen, or perhaps simply to hedge against high public expectations' not being met, there was a distinct dip in the barometer of official optimism in Washington on the eve of Vance's trip regarding his chances of returning with an agreed SALT II document.[85] It proved to be warranted.

Although guarded statements to the press suggested that a little progress had been made in inching toward an agreement,[86] the two days of talks in Moscow failed to close the final "five-percent gap," leaving the last few sticking points still unresolved. Precisely what the details of the remaining differences were nobody was saying officially, but according to more or less informed speculation, they ran along the following lines.

### Cruise Missile Differences

In all probability, the most vexed area of differences had to do with cruise missiles. In Washington in September, Gromyko had said the Soviets would drop their previous insistence on a 2500-km limit for ALCMs, provided the United States would agree to strict enforcement of the 600-km limit on GLCMs and SLCMs, and application of the limit throughout the life of the Treaty to 1985, rather than the three-year Protocol period as previously proposed.[87] This switch of limitations on ground- and sea-launched cruise missiles from the Protocol to the Treaty period exacerbated the already touchy problem for the United States of persuading its European allies that it would not jeopardize in SALT a cruise missile option to counter the Soviet SS-20/Backfire threat against Europe.

Given the political and military implications of this issue, it was not surprising that the U.S. side balked at the tradeoff proposed by the Soviets, apparently insisting at Moscow that it would accept the 600-km limit only during the Protocol period.[88] This would keep open the option to build and deploy cruise missiles suitable for European defense purposes in the early 1980s. It would also spike a rather obvious Soviet attempt to drive a wedge between the United States and its other NATO allies.

Another unsettled cruise missile question involved establishing the number of aircraft-borne ALCMs that would count in the SALT quota as one MIRVed vehicle. Apparently, the Soviets argued that multiples of twenty should be treated as MIRV equivalents, so that if a large aircraft had sixty ALCMs aboard, for example, it would be counted as three MIRVed vehicles. The United States opposed this approach, favoring a figure of around thirty-five ALCMs.[89]

### Limits on Number of RVs per MIRVed Missile

Described also as establishing "fractionation" limits, this issue concerned both existing types of MIRVed ballistic missiles and any "new types" to be permitted by the SALT II accords. With regard to existing types, the United States was pressing either for a freeze on the number of RVs at the highest number tested per given missile, or failing that, an upper limit of ten.[90] The effect of this would be to prevent the Soviet Union from equipping its large fourth-generation ICBMs, especially the SS-18, with as many as thirty to forty smaller RVs,[91] and thus preclude the Soviets from fully exploiting their superior throwweight potential. Naturally it can be supposed that the Soviets did not warm to this American proposal.

The shoe was on the other foot, apparently, with regard to "new types." Here the Soviets were pressing to set a limit of no more than six RVs, while the U.S. figure was again ten.[92] Since the one Soviet "new type" ICBM to be allowable under the accords was understood to be a non-MIRV type, the Soviet aim was obviously to restrict the number of warheads on the MIRVed MX missile, should the United States go ahead with it. From the U.S. standpoint, MX considerations were also involved in trying to set RV limits on existing Soviet ICBMs like the SS-18, since the multiple aim point (MAP) basing option for the MX would work better, the fewer the number of Soviet warheads available. In the case of SLBMs, however, the Soviet side pressed no objection to an American proposal for a limit of fourteen RVs per missile.

### Backfire Bomber Restrictions

Although some of the differences that had made the Backfire issue a continuing obstacle to a SALT II accord since Vladivostok in 1974 had been narrowed by the time of the October 1978 Moscow meeting, it was not possible to dispose of the remaining differences there, in part because the Soviets apparently were not willing to put in writing the "assurances" the U.S. side considered necessary to keep the Backfire issue from becoming politically damaging to the ratification of a SALT II agreement.[93] The formula designed by the U.S. side prior to Moscow, under which the Soviets would offer various assurances against the strategic use of Backfire while the United States would "reserve the right" to deploy a future bomber similar to Backfire,[94] may have encountered other difficulties also; but if so, no details were made known.

One other apparent problem from the American side was that though Gromyko had earlier agreed that the Soviets would not increase the current production rate of the Backfire, the Soviet side subsequently declined to confirm what the rate was, leaving an obvious loophole.[95] For their part, the Soviets were said to have accused the United States of making a big issue of the Backfire in order to gain points with Germany and China for protecting their interests against this Soviet "medium-range" bomber.[96]

### Timing of Reductions

Two issues concerning timing—one with respect to when the Protocol period was to start and end, the other, what the deadlines for force level reductions were to be—had been under contention from the time the two sides agreed upon a "three-tier" approach for a SALT II accord. In general, the U.S. position aimed at getting the Protocol period over sooner, as well as completing reductions sooner, than the Russians preferred.[97]

Apparently, the question of Protocol duration was one of those on which some progress had been made during the Vance party's discussions with Brezhnev, Gromyko, Marshal Ogarkov, and others in October, but the timing of reductions—which only the Russians would be obliged to carry out—remained a sticking point. The United States argued for reductions from the 2400 "Vladivostok level" to begin January 1980, and to be completed by December 31, 1981. The Soviet side on the other hand, asserting that more time would be needed for dismantling and other procedures involved in reducing their forces, wished to begin the reduction process no sooner than January 1981, with up to eighteen months to complete it. According to one report, the Russians wanted to put off the reductions even longer, to after expiration of the Protocol period.[98]

In the case of some of the issues noted above, resolution of one was tied to concessions on another, which, as Gromyko had put it shortly before the October Moscow meeting, made the reaching of a final agreement "very complicated."[99] There also were a few other matters on which the two sides did not yet see eye to eye. These reportedly included some remaining disagreements on the content of the Joint Statement, with the Soviets opposing the U.S. desire to specify that restrictions on air and civil defenses be taken up in SALT III. Also said to be still unclarified were certain verification problems and the question of whether the Soviets would accept the U.S. assertion that a MAP basing mode for ICBMs was compatible with SALT undertakings.[100]

## PRO AND CON ARGUMENTS FORESHADOWING
## A RATIFICATION DEBATE

Although the October Moscow meeting had left some differences unresolved and thus failed to produce the long-awaited SALT II accords, the general shape of the fifty-page, three-part agreement and most of its provisions had become fairly well known by then,* and the lines had already been drawn in the "SALT debate" getting under way in the United States between those supporting the accords and those critical of them. To give here the general flavor of this debate, which could be expected to foreshadow the eventual ratification debate, the proponents of the agreement stressed the following points:

- Even though the SALT II agreement was by no means ideal, it was better for the United States and the Soviet Union than no agreement at all. Failure to reach an accord after six years of SALT II would precipitate a new and costly round of strategic arms competition that would mean superiority for neither side and diminished security for both. It could also bring about a dangerous deterioration in U.S.-Soviet relations.[101]
- From the U.S. viewpoint, the equal aggregates for strategic delivery vehicles carried over from Vladivostok, along with reductions in the SALT II Treaty, were a significant improvement over SALT I, answering to the guidelines expressed by Congress, and holding the Soviet Union below the levels it could have been expected to achieve in the absence of an agreement.[102]
- In particular, the missile subceilings would place a limit on the expansion of the most threatening element of Soviet strategic power—the MIRVed counterforce-capable, land-based ICBM force,[103] and restrictions on new types of ballistic missiles would have the effect of halting, or at least delaying, introduction into the Soviet operational inventory of most of the USSR's fifth generation of ICBMs, already well along in development. Although these provisions of the accord might not solve the long-term problem of Minuteman vulnerability, they should at least alleviate it, and in any event, U.S. deterrent capability was not dependent only on Minuteman.[104]
- Because of the reductions required to reach the agreed SALT II ceilings, the Soviet Union would have to dismantle about 300

---

*The main features of the three-part SALT II accords, as the nearly completed agreement was reported to stand in January 1979, are given in Appendix E, along with brief comment on the evolution of its various provisions.

nuclear delivery systems. In the absence of an agreement, intelligence estimates had indicated the Soviets "would increase their present total by more than 600 nuclear delivery systems," which meant that under the SALT II accord there would be "some 1000 fewer strategic nuclear weapons directed against the territory of the United States."[105]

- On the other hand, because of being below the ceilings, the United States could, if it wished, add about 250 missile launchers or heavy bombers to its strategic forces. In other words, there was nothing in the agreement to prevent the United States from building the B-1 or some other penetrating bomber if this were considered necessary.[106]

- With regard to cruise missiles, the formula allowing deployment of 120 ALCM-armed bombers would mean, at 20 to 30 ALCMs per bomber, from 2400 to 3600 of these new weapons. These numbers would be adequate to "fully accommodate" the ALCM program the Pentagon had in mind.[107]

- In the case of long-range GLCMs and SLCMs, the ban on deployment during the Protocol period[108] would not be a serious constraint on the United States, since these missiles would probably not be ready for deployment in that period anyway, and at the expiration of the Protocol, the United States would be free to decide whether to deploy the new systems or use them as a "tradeoff" for further limitations on Soviet forces.[109] Inasmuch as the USSR probably would not yet have comparable cruise missile systems of its own ready at that time, the situation would give the United States significant negotiating leverage.

- Difficult as some of the verification problems posed by the three-tier SALT II accord might be, the agreed procedures employing NTM would be adequate to determine that quantitative and qualitative limits were being met.[110] In any case, the Soviet Union and not the United States faced the more difficult verification problems, such as verifying how many B-52s might be armed with ALCMs of what range.[111]

- There was no valid basis for claiming that a SALT II Treaty should be judged inadequate for failing to force concessions from the Russians in other areas, such as their policy in Africa or treatment of dissidents. This would mean making SALT hostage to the ups and downs of U.S.-Soviet relations.[112]

- Similarly, a SALT II accord should stand on its own merits as another step in the process of limiting strategic arms, rather than being made contingent upon "approving new weapons systems" that might otherwise not be warranted to meet "actual defense needs."[113]

By contrast with the points marshalled in its favor, the SALT II agreement was found wanting by its critics for a variety of reasons. Among the major criticisms were the following:

- The equal aggregates of the accord, though improving on SALT I and apparently satisfying the principle of numerical parity, actually disguised some disturbing asymmetries. These included increasing Soviet advantage in throwweight, deliverable megatonnage, and other indices of strategic potential, which could swing the strategic balance in Soviet favor during the life of the Treaty.[114]
- The missile sublimits portion of the Treaty, in particular the ceiling of 820 MIRVed ICBM launchers, would leave more than enough room for the Soviets to develop a serious threat to Minuteman survivability, and thus the accord would have failed to achieve some of the primary U.S. objectives in SALT—not only to preserve U.S. deterrent capability, but to enhance strategic stability.[115]
- The reductions required of the Soviets to reach the aggregate ceilings were all to the good, but nevertheless the Soviets in effect would be trading surplus numbers of old systems for advanced systems with greater net capability than those replaced. Moreover, any concessions on reduction deadlines and Protocol duration made to the USSR for the sake of wrapping up the accord would ease the reduction process for the Soviets and might even allow them to achieve a force level "bulge" near the end of the permissible period that could have destabilizing effects.
- Rather than providing a period for unencumbered development of exploitable U.S. technologies like cruise missiles and a mobile MX, the Protocol could well operate to dampen U.S. technological initiative and to limit U.S. unilateral options for responding to problems like the threat to Minuteman survivability.[116] The risk of this would grow were Protocol restrictions to be accepted as precedent upon expiration of the period, as in the case of the 1972-1977 Interim Agreement, or should strong pressures upon U.S. strategic planning decisions not to prejudice the chances of a SALT III agreement be felt during the Protocol period itself. Furthermore, the United States would be better off in general by subjecting itself in SALT to the fewest restraints on technology.[117]
- The noncircumvention provision of the SALT II accord, though having at least the tacit approval of America's NATO allies, could operate to constrain the development in Europe of cruise missile

capabilities, which essentially would serve as a replacement for FBS—a likely Soviet target in SALT III. The problem would be exacerbated by the fact that Soviet systems posing a threat to NATO, such as the SS-20 and Backfire, had not been constrained by the bilateral U.S.-Soviet agreement in SALT II.[118]

- The verification means adequate for monitoring compliance with the relatively simple 1972 Interim Agreement might not in fact be adequate for the SALT II accord, with its comprehensive provisions and qualitative constraints.[119] Even though the verification ambiguities growing out of implementation of the accord might not prove serious in a strategic sense to U.S. security, they would doubtless give rise to debate more acerbic than that linked with alleged Soviet noncompliance in SALT I.

Which set of the above arguments about the SALT II accords may eventually merit the best marks must be left to the passage of time. Meanwhile, one may agree with Richard Burt that while supporters of the SALT II agreement perhaps erred by overemphasizing its virtues and the dire consequence of failure to achieve it, critics on the other hand may have fallen into the opposite fallacy of holding SALT primarily responsible for the emergence of U.S. strategic problems as well as for failure to remedy them.[120]

## PROSPECTS FOR BREAKING THE U.S.-SOVIET DEADLOCK

Efforts following the October Moscow meeting to break the Soviet-U.S. deadlock over the remaining unresolved issues in SALT II came at a time when the Carter administration was heavily engaged in what had come to be known as a "SALT-selling" campaign,[121] aimed at ensuring ratification of the anticipated SALT II agreement, and also when several important personnel changes in the government's SALT apparatus took place.

The principal personnel change was Paul Warnke's resignation October 31, 1978, as both chief SALT negotiator and head of the Arms Control and Disarmament Agency.[122] Although the resignation was widely interpreted as a move to help smooth the way for a SALT II accord through the Senate, the "personal reasons" cited by Warnke for leaving the latest of his several stints in government were also persuasive.[123]

Appointed on an interim basis to be Warnke's successor as head of ACDA was George M. Seignious, a retired Army three-star general, who had been a member of the U.S. SALT delegation since

September 1977.[124] However, controversy over the choice of a career military man to fill the government's top arms control post left it uncertain how long this interim appointment might last.[125] Taking over Warnke's job as chief of the U.S. SALT delegation was Ralph Earle II, an ACDA SALT veteran who had served as the deputy chief of the delegation since May 1977, and who was said to have succeeded Warnke in order to provide "continuity and institutional memory."[126] The return to the practice of separating the ACDA and SALT negotiating posts, incidentally, may have meant that ACDA would to some extent lose the pivotal role in SALT that it had gained earlier in the Carter administration when Warnke wore both hats.[127]

In what was apparently an unrelated move by the Soviet Union, it became known at the time of Warnke's resignation that the USSR also was replacing the head of its SALT delegation, Deputy Foreign Minister Vladimir S. Semenov, who had held the post continuously since the start of SALT I in November 1969.[128] Semenov's successor was to be Victor P. Karpov, a Foreign Ministry official with long SALT delegation experience who had also served as the Soviet deputy commissioner of the Standing Consultative Commission since 1973.[129]

The prospects of resolving the remaining SALT II issues probably were not affected materially one way or the other, however, by the personnel changes in the fall of 1978 on the two sides. By that time, though Gromyko had spoken of additional meetings being needed to work on the SALT impasse,[130] it seemed likely that further meetings in Geneva or elsewhere would amount to little more than probing for the limit of concessions on each side. And in both cases, the room for further concessions appeared to have been narrowed down to the point that, as on a few previous occasions in SALT, the deadlock was likely to be broken only by political decisions at the highest level.[131] Such decisions, in turn, would reflect ultimately how much the leaders on each side—neither wishing to be the first to blink—wanted a SALT II agreement.

In the U.S. case, powerful factors limiting the room left for concession included the potential political effects on allies of certain issues such as cruise missile restrictions, and the effects that yielding on this or other disputed issues might have on the chances of getting congressional approval, especially Treaty ratification by the Senate, where—as some senators cool to the SALT II accords were quoted— "it takes only thirty-four senators to defeat ratification."[132]

In the Soviet case, although there were no comparable constituencies to influence the decisions of Brezhnev and the top Soviet leadership, differences of view among elements of the Soviet bureaucracy could operate to make it difficult to reach decisions on a SALT compromise with the United States.[133] Also, internal leadership politics at a time when succession might not be far off could have an effect on Politburo decisions. However, whether the effect would be to harden the Soviet position or to soften it enough to permit Brezhnev to leave office with a SALT II Treaty to his credit, was essentially unpredictable.

Another possibly telling factor was the extent to which the Soviet leaders might believe what they reportedly had been told by U.S. officials—that "political reality" in the United States left little flexibility to make adjustments in the U.S. position "without jeopardizing" the chances of getting a SALT agreement ratified.[134] On this question, too, no ready answer was available, although it might well be doubted whether the Soviet leaders would in fact understand and find credible the "separation of powers" aspect of the American political system. Indeed, interesting testimony on this point was furnished by a group of U.S. senators after meetings in Moscow in November 1978 with Brezhnev and other high-ranking civilian and military leaders. The group reportedly found the "Russians' understanding" of what goes into the U.S. treaty approval process, and their "grasp of the dynamics of American politics" to be "surprisingly weak."[135]

At the point in the history of SALT where this account leaves off—in late 1978—the question whether the six-year quest for a SALT II agreement would finally be realized was still uncertain. It seemed to this author, however, that by a very thin margin, the odds probably still favored the eventual reaching of an agreement between Washington and Moscow,[136] perhaps through the device of postponing additional areas of disagreement until SALT III. What might happen to SALT either if no agreement proved possible, or in the event a SALT II agreement successfully negotiated by the administration were to be turned down by the Congress, is difficult to say, but one could not rule out either an indefinite suspension of negotiations or a collapse of the SALT process itself.

*Chapter 12*

# Concluding Reflections on the SALT Experience

In offering these closing reflections on SALT, it may be useful to recall that the SALT experience has been more than a lengthy set of arms control negotiations aimed at agreements on the limitation of strategic arms. Now in its tenth year, SALT also has become a pivotal aspect of great-power relations between the United States and the Soviet Union, a medium through which some accommodation of both the disparate political interests and the perceived strategic necessities of the two sides has been sought.

## SALT'S DUAL
## POLITICAL-STRATEGIC CHARACTER

As a political phenomenon, SALT in the early seventies helped to facilitate the passage from cold war to detente. In the process, what might be called a symbiotic relationship developed between SALT and detente, each in a sense seeming to be a necessary condition for the other. While some semblance of progress in SALT has been useful periodically to give detente a boost, it also appears probable that SALT would become increasingly difficult to pursue in the absence of a detente climate. At least, the reaching of agreements would seem likely to become a still more protracted and difficult process, as suggested perhaps by the strung-out history of SALT II, which paralleled a perceptible cooling of detente relations between the United States and the Soviet Union after the high point of the 1972 SALT I accords.

The intimate link between SALT and detente in the political dimension, however, should not obscure the fact that the negotiations in SALT must also address the strategic concerns of each side. Here one finds that the political and strategic functions of SALT have sometimes been out of phase, so to speak. The two answer to somewhat different imperatives and time scales, so that agreements that may have helped to lubricate Soviet-American political relations at a given temporal juncture may not have served to satisfy perceived strategic needs.

SALT I, for example, was politically successful as a benchmark in the warming of Soviet-U.S. relations. But it left important strategic concerns on both sides unassuaged. The U.S. side came away bothered by failure of the accords to relieve the potential Soviet missile threat to the survivability of Minuteman, and by differential quantitative force levels intended to compensate the Soviet Union for a notable, but not necessarily permanent, U.S. technological lead. For its part, the Soviet side's concern to close the qualitative gap in certain strategic technologies, especially MIRV, had not been met, nor had its attempt to defuse the threat of U.S. forward-based systems in Europe been satisfied. SALT I did, of course, bring the two sides into strategic agreement on the ABM issue, although their differences on other issues, such as MIRV, missile throwweight, and FBS, persisted into SALT II.

What was probably the basic strategic deadlock in the pre-Vladivostok phase of SALT II found the Soviet Union determined not to allow significant constraints upon its new fourth-generation missile programs and, above all, its hard-won, but as yet undeployed, MIRV systems. The U.S. side, responsive in part to domestic political pressures, felt that it must rectify the numerical imbalances of the Interim Agreement and, at the same time, maintain some margin of MIRV advantage as insurance against the future linking of superior Soviet throwweight with MIRV technology.

In SALT II, the Vladivostok transaction of November 1974, which came after a two-year negotiating stalemate, probably answered primarily to a need felt on both sides to give detente a political shot in the arm, though it also dealt with the unequal-numbers legacy of SALT I. In its strategic dimension, the Vladivostok tentative accord probably was possible because it set quantitative levels high enough to suit the Soviet side and left enough room to accommodate most of the planned R&D and force modernization programs on both sides. However, though the range of strategic differences was somewhat narrowed, this seeming convergence was in part illusory, as became abundantly clear after Vladivostok when the attempt to draft a follow-up SALT II agreement encountered not only a number of obdurate strategic-technical issues such as those centering on the Soviet Backfire bomber and American cruise missiles, but also a deterioration in Soviet-American political relations.

In the post-Vladivostok SALT II negotiations, stretching out for more than four years, both reductions of strategic offensive arms and qualitative limitations were introduced in SALT as serious propositions for the first time, posing more complex problems than the task of establishing force-level ceilings, upon which in essence the negotiations on strategic offensive arms had previously been concentrated. However, the tolerance of domestic political constituencies in both the United States and the Soviet Union for radical moves in the direction of reductions and qualitative limitations was such that only relatively modest measures dealing with these matters found their way into the "three-tier" SALT II accord—in effect, postponing most of the hardcore problems posed by steep reductions and qualitative restrictions until SALT III.

Throughout SALT I and II, the political-strategic duality of the SALT process has operated to create what might be called a "SALT imperative"—a stake in avoiding actions, strategic or political, that might seriously threaten to derail further negotiations. This imperative certainly has been strained at times, and its durability could become more questionable should the utility of SALT as perceived in the West decline greatly and thus weaken pressure on political leaders to produce SALT "results." How SALT is perceived after about a decade of operation is therefore a matter of some interest.

## SEVERAL WAYS OF LOOKING AT SALT

One way of looking at SALT is to see it as an institutional process that has taken on an important role in the historical readjustment of the global-power and political relationship between the United States and the Soviet Union. In this view of SALT, which is essentially the one underlying the opening remarks of this chapter, its process may contribute something to "solving" strategic and political problems, but it is unlikely to culminate in some climactic end product, such as a permanent agreement that will define and govern the Soviet-American strategic relationship indefinitely. Rather, SALT is seen more as a process for establishing rules of the game pro tempore for strategic competition—rules requiring redrafting from time to time, if only because they are reflective of what is essentially a changing and dynamic political-power relationship.

Obviously, there are also other ways of looking at SALT that merit comment. At the risk of some oversimplification, one can identify at least three other distinct schools of thought in the West about the nature of SALT and what it can be expected to accomplish.

At one end of the spectrum, there is a school that regards SALT as the only realistic alternative to an unbridled nuclear arms race that neither side could win, and which both therefore must be equally interested in avoiding.[1] Given the maintenance of some "reasonable" level of strategic retaliatory forces for nuclear deterrence, mutual limitation agreements negotiated in SALT are seen to be greatly preferable to unilateral strategic programs as a means to preserve deterrent stability and enhance national security. Failure to achieve a major new SALT agreement or series of agreements to replace the SALT I Interim Agreement on strategic offensive arms would, in this view, have a number of very undesirable consequences, including higher defense expenditures, sharp deterioration of Soviet-American relations, and increased danger of nuclear war. Hence, the tendency of this school is to argue that even an agreement with many imperfections is better than no agreement at all.

At the opposite end of the spectrum is a school of thought that sees SALT as an essentially unsatisfactory alternative to unilateral strategic planning, even though ongoing negotiations may be politically necessary.[2] Unilateral planning and programs are seen to be more important foundations of deterrence and national security than the kinds of arms control agreements the Soviets have been, or are likely to be, willing to sign, and therefore SALT bargaining needs should not be allowed to dictate the U.S. strategic posture. Should SALT begin to drive strategic policy and become an end in itself, it could damage rather than enhance U.S. national security and political interests, especially those related to the Western alliance system. Failure to achieve a major new SALT agreement would not fundamentally alter U.S.-Soviet relations, in this view, because the basic adversary relationship between the two has never been affected much one way or the other by arms control agreements. Nor would the absence of a SALT II accord necessarily precipitate a new arms race, since SALT undertakings have been essentially tailored to accommodate unilaterally planned strategic programs in any event.

Somewhere about midway between these opposite ends of the spectrum is another perspective that gives SALT good marks as a kind of continuous diplomatic institution useful for "registering" changes in the strategic balance brought about primarily by unilateral efforts, and for trying to establish broad parameters within which future U.S.-Soviet strategic competition may operate.[3] SALT, in this view, is only marginally relevant, if at all, to "solving" U.S. strategic problems like the survivability of land-based missile forces, but at the same time, it is not to be blamed for past failure to resolve problems that were either essentially unsolvable or clearly in the province of unilateral remedial measures. From this standpoint, perhaps the principal recommendation for SALT agreements has lain in their symbolic-political value as a manifest of superpower ability to both compete and cooperate, but even this attribute could decline in value if the negative effects of a new SALT agreement were to constrain unilateral efforts to remedy U.S. strategic and related political problems.

Which of these several viewpoints most aptly conveys the "real" nature of SALT is certainly moot, but the last no doubt comes closest to capturing what Richard Burt, one of SALT's more astute observers, has described as a mood of diminishing optimism and lowered expectations about SALT in the West.[4] In the past few years this mood has crept over many in the West who had initially greeted the negotiations with enthusiasm, and who believed that the SALT I accords meant that the Soviet leadership had come to share prevailing Western notions of deterrent stability—based essentially on not trying to defend hostage populations, and on avoiding unilateral measures that would threaten the survivability of nuclear retaliatory forces.

The erosion of earlier expectations can be attributed to many factors, among which perhaps two of the more important ones have been discussed at some length in this study of the SALT experience. One—the long and often frustrating track record of negotiations in SALT II itself, testifying to the difficulty and complexity of trying to bring the disparate strategic forces of the two sides under a common SALT regime. The other—the uninterrupted momentum of Soviet strategic force modernization, involving large investment in successive generations of new and improved strategic systems and posing serious questions about what Soviet SALT policy and objectives might be.

## COMPARING SOVIET AND U.S. SALT AIMS

Assumptions widely held during the SALT I period credited the Soviet Union and the United States with much the same set of aims in SALT, which might be summarized as follows: (1) to freeze the strategic balance at the level of parity; (2) to stabilize mutual deterrence; (3) to regulate the strategic competition so as to reduce its resource costs, lower the risks of accidental nuclear war outbreak, and discourage the need for new cycles of improved strategic weapons systems.

It is unlikely, of course, that these ostensible aims ever enjoyed unanimous assent on either side, but the relevant point here is that despite the Soviet Union's continuing public commitment to the success of SALT, there has been growing doubt whether Soviet criteria for "success" in SALT have ever necessarily matched the aims the USSR was once thought to share with the United States. If not, what then can usefully be said about the nature of Soviet SALT policy and objectives, including how and why they may differ from those of the United States?

Soviet SALT policy has had several distinctive characteristics. First, it has been pursued as an integral element of a broader "detente diplomacy," intended among other things to buttress Soviet military power by helping to limit the military-industrial and political response of the United States to the growth of Soviet strategic power. In essence, whereas the primary U.S. SALT aim was to try to stabilize the strategic relationship on the basis of common value assumptions, the Soviet Union's basic strategic aims were to use SALT to protect Soviet strategic gains of the recent past and to improve its future competitive position. In this process, a subsidiary Soviet objective has been to try to contain particular U.S. strategic programs that Moscow has found most disturbing—Safeguard, Trident, the B-1, MX, cruise missiles, among others.

Second, in the service of Soviet aims, the SALT negotiations have had several important political functions, the foremost perhaps having been to "validate" Soviet claims to be a superpower. Another, based on recognition of "strategic equality" between the superpowers, has been to weaken European confidence in the U.S. commitment to the defense of Europe. Helping to ensure against playing of the "Chinese card" at Soviet expense also has been a useful political function from the Soviet viewpoint of the bilateral Soviet-American SALT connection.

Third, Soviet policy probably has not counted upon being consistently able to exercise direct constraints upon U.S. technological and economic capabilities through SALT, but using SALT for indirect influence upon what Vernon Aspaturian has termed the U.S. technological-economic "mobilization potential" appears to have been a considered Soviet aim.[5] Probably the best example was the ABM Treaty, calculated to prevent this potential from being mobilized by the United States to deploy an ABM system that the Soviet Union was not in a position to match. Accepting constraints upon their own ABM effort was a price the Soviets proved willing to pay in order to block the deployment of U.S. technology and resources in this field.[6]

Apart from the major exception of the ABM case, and acceptance of a number of less-consequential contraints upon Soviet strategic forces as a necessary sacrifice to keep the SALT process alive, a fourth salient characteristic of Soviet SALT policy has been its stout resistance to SALT proposals involving alterations of Soviet military-industrial practices or force plans and doctrine. It has been this latter aspect of Soviet SALT policy that has contributed most to the impression that the SALT process has in no significant way diverted Soviet strategic thinking from its focus upon warfighting and survival capabilities as inseparable from effective deterrence.

The salient prescription for deterrence in Soviet strategic thinking has been that the better the armed forces are prepared to fight and win a nuclear war, and the society to survive its effects, the more effectively a potential adversary will be deterred.[7] The fact that most of the Soviet political and military leaders have tended to equate effective deterrence with superior warfighting capability does not mean that they have been planning to start a nuclear war, as sometimes claimed or inferred, but this outlook has left them unreceptive to such doctrines as mutual assured destruction—the basic strategic rationale that has tended to inform American SALT policy.[8]

The strategic, political, and conceptual differences between the two sides that in the last analysis probably underlie their differing aims in SALT grow essentially out of the continuing rivalry of the two global powers as exemplars of opposing sociopolitical systems. Without trying to elaborate here on all these differences, one may note a few crucial asymmetries that appear to lie at the heart of the matter.

Apart from disparate strategic conceptions such as those mentioned above regarding what it takes to create effective nuclear deterrence, the most troublesome asymmetries are to be found in the underlying political premises upon which the two parties in SALT have been operating. Throughout most of SALT I and II, the American attitude toward SALT has been mainly informed by the general belief that mutual agreement to regulate strategic competition would promote better U.S.-Soviet relations and contribute to a more stable world environment within which the two global powers could mediate their conflicting interests with less strain upon the existing international order and its established institutions.

Although the Soviet Union also undoubtedly has had an interest in improving U.S.-Soviet relations for a variety of reasons, including the avoidance of dangerous confrontations that might lead to nuclear war and gains to be had from such detente dividends as technology transfer, Soviet interest has stopped well short of cherishing SALT as a means of shoring up the established international order. Rather, the Soviet Union has sought to persuade the United States to accede gracefully to a "fundamental restructuring" of the old international order, or failing this, at least to discourage its "imperialist" adversary from blatantly obstructing the process. In short, SALT and detente, as well as Soviet military power itself, are all seen as instruments of policy useful in one way or another to keep the United States from trying to arrest what, from the Soviet viewpoint, constitutes an inevitable, though admittedly uneven, process of transition to a new "correlation of forces" in the world favorable to the Soviet Union and other "fraternal" countries.

The pragmatic U.S. conception of SALT as part of an ongoing, interactive process involving both competition and accommodation, but essentially aimed at optimizing mutual gains and implying observance by both parties of the same basic set of political ground rules, thus stands in sharp contrast to the teleological Soviet view of history in which SALT is seen as one element in a broad strategy for helping to bring about a preordained shift in the structure of world politics to the advantage of the Soviet Union.

## CAN SALT PRODUCE
## USEFUL AGREEMENTS?

Whether such fundamentally dissimilar conceptions can ever be bridged by agreements in SALT seems unlikely. But the relevant question is whether useful SALT agreements can be reached despite such divergent views of its purpose.

For those persuaded that agreements already reached in SALT have indeed been useful on balance for one reason or another, such as curbing the ABM dimension of the arms race, strengthening strategic stability, establishing a precedent for offensive arms restraints, or helping to improve Soviet-U.S. relations, the question tends to answer itself in the affirmative. For those believing that SALT has helped to undermine rather than strengthen strategic stability, to mask the momentum of Soviet weapons programs, and to dampen U.S. unilateral responses needed to repair a deteriorating strategic balance, the answer may well appear negative.

In either case, the point seems to be that judgments as to whether SALT can produce useful agreements depend more on how particular SALT outcomes are perceived in terms of benefits outweighing defects, or vice versa, than upon underlying differences of purpose.

Again, the ABM Treaty serves as a relevant illustration. The two sides had different motives for the treaty—those of the Soviet Union probably being dominated, as noted above, by a desire to foreclose competition in an area where the USSR was technologically lagging. The treaty did prove compatible, however, with U.S. aims of shoring up functional strategic stability, and in that context therefore could be regarded as a useful agreement.[9]

For that matter, it might even be argued that the most antithetical political-ideological motivations could conceivably contribute, under some circumstances, to desirable SALT outcomes. For example, should the Soviet leadership come to feel strongly that detente must be preserved in order to keep the United States sedated, so to speak, during a delicate transitional period of history and that new SALT agreements acceptable to the United States were, in turn, necessary to keep detente alive, this interest might override any preferences on the Soviet side for a strategic planning approach bent on maximizing relative advantages for the Soviet Union. If so, one might find a certain irony in a situation where detente politics aimed at constraining the United States could turn out to have a double edge, acting also to circumscribe the avenues available to the Soviet Union for enhancing its own power position.

## SALT CONSTRAINTS VERSUS
## UNILATERAL ELBOWROOM

Perhaps the essence of the SALT experience that emerges from this study is the inherent strain—internal contradiction might be a more apt term—between the professed SALT goal of seeking mutually acceptable limits upon strategic forces and the deep-seated impulse to preserve as much unilateral strategic elbowroom as possible.

This inner contradiction has shown up at each major juncture in the history of SALT. It was, of course, present at the very beginning, when the United States entered SALT hoping to slow down the momentum of the Soviet strategic buildup and perhaps to freeze the strategic status quo at a then-favorable level, but unwilling to forgo the unilateral insurance of pressing on with a MIRV deployment program. The Soviet Union, for its part, while prepared to entertain selective constraints that might impede the full realization of U.S. technological advantages in ABM and MIRV, could not bring itself to surrender its own unilateral opportunity to acquire MIRV technology, and in general, treated SALT I as a holding device to permit improvement of the Soviet relative strategic position.

Again in the May 1972 Interim Agreement there was mutual acceptance of some constraint—mainly the five-year "stop-in-place" on numbers of strategic missile launchers (which at least the United

States and quite possibly the Soviet Union did not intend to exceed anyway)—along with provisions leaving ample room for unilateral programs of strategic modernization and replacement.

In SALT II, a conspicuous example of the tendency to resist long-term constraints that could compromise unilateral freedom of action was the abandonment in mid-1974 of the once-declared goal of a permanent and comprehensive agreement on the limitation of strategic offensive arms. Such an agreement, even though mutual, would have amounted to a strategic freeze, leaving no room for unilateral adjustment to the dynamics of an evolving power-political relationship.

The Vladivostok transition of November 1974 itself owed a good deal to the fact that at bottom it left both parties largely free to carry on most of their then-contemplated R&D and force modernization programs, and its freedom-to-mix provision was certainly a concession to unilateral choice in the planning of force structures. And as SALT II finally was drawing to an apparent close four years later, a similar tendency to leave a generous amount of unilateral breathing space again manifested itself in the three-tier SALT II arrangement, a central feature of which was its formula for constraints of limited duration during the Protocol period upon various strategic systems still under development.

Let it be said at this point that contrary to the unilaterally oriented tendencies stressed above, the proposition also can be made that SALT is gradually creating a new imperative to design strategic forces increasingly responsive to SALT-sanctioned criteria, rather than to unilateral preferences. With each new agreement, or even in anticipation of forthcoming agreements, the independent scope of each side to plan forces and weapons systems in accordance with its traditional practices and concepts may tend to shrink somewhat. (Witness the progressive extension of constraints from the stop-in-place measures of 1972 to the reductions and qualitative limitations introduced into the SALT II accords six years later.) Over time, the argument runs, the cumulative effect of this process of narrowing the scope for autonomous planning and of substituting for it a degree of "joint" Soviet-American strategic planning within the SALT framework could be to greatly reduce asymmetries in the force characteristics on each side, making it easier, in turn, to find further common ground for equitable strategic constraints.

While the long-term effects of SALT may bear out this proposition, which is not without merit, the SALT experience to date seems to yield little evidence that unilateral preferences and programs are becoming readily expendable under the impact of such a SALT imperative. Many of the most stubborn issues in the negotiations have involved resistance to adoption of common strategic criteria, the throwweight parameter being one example, and most of the agreements concluded or seriously discussed seem to have been aimed as much at minimizing encroachments on unilateral freedom of action as at conformity to mutually agreed restrictions.

It has been observed, incidentally, that the two sides in SALT sometimes have not even been able to agree on what constitutes a problem,[10] so that working out a "mutually-agreed solution" can founder at the start on this awkward reality—leaving recourse to its own unilateral solution the only real choice available within a particular time span to either side.

Why the urge to preserve unilateral elbowroom has remained resistant to SALT-legislated constraints can be explained in a perfectly logical fashion—as a hedge against future contingencies, because neither side has been too keen about entrusting its ultimate security to agreements with a powerful adversary, or out of awareness on both sides that today's arms control contract could be tomorrow's regret in an uncertain world.

The effects of this phenomenon, however, seem not to have borne uniformly upon the SALT and related strategic policies of the two parties, who—as this study has indicated—entered SALT from disparate strategic positions and with differing strategic philosophies, styles of negotiation, and institutional processes.

## IMPLICATIONS OF DIFFERENT U.S. AND SOVIET SALT APPROACHES

If a prime asymmetry in the SALT negotiating approaches of the two sides can be identified, it would appear to be that the Soviet Union has displayed less inclination to alter its own basic positions and to accommodate itself to the concerns and preferences of the other party for the sake of achieving agreements than has the United States. It may be argued that deriving some strategic advantage one way or the other from the negotiations makes little difference so long as the essential interests of each side are safeguarded in the actual agreements made. But the deleterious effects of a process in which the United States has more consistently assumed the burden of accommodation could be to fortify the apparent Soviet conviction that the correlation of forces is shifting in their favor and that "realistic" appreciation of this factor will eventually bring about further U.S. acceptance of the substance of Soviet SALT proposals.

In part the more tenacious approach of the Soviet Union in SALT can be attributed to well-known differences in political culture and negotiating tactics. But in larger measure it probably reflects the fact that the Soviet Union entered SALT as the strategically inferior party and came to regard the negotiations as a means by which it might be compensated for technological and other advantages histori- cally enjoyed by the United States, in lieu of narrowing such advantages by unilateral effort alone.

For its part, the United States tended to concede to the Soviet Union its "right," as the world's other superpower, to shorten through SALT negotiations the time required to do what it otherwise intended doing unilaterally—that is, to catch up with the United States in the strategic fields where it was behind and thus achieve "strategic equality." Hence, U.S. acquiescence to agreements that were structured toward this end. In effect, the United States recognized as "legitimate" the Soviet view that SALT should serve to redress asymmetries favoring the United States—technological, geo- graphic, alliance assets, and so on. At bottom, this meant that the United States was "discounting" its advantages in the strategic power arena at below market value for the sake of finding grounds for agreement.

In the course of time, SALT I receded into the past and the SALT II period grew longer without the big dividend expected by the United States having been realized—namely, an unmistakable deci- sion in Moscow to rest the Soviet strategic catch-up effort at parity. This brought to the fore a question long implicit in the SALT experience, but seldom acknowledged in the formal channels of SALT negotiation: Where should the line be drawn at which meeting Soviet claims and preferences would cease to represent proper redress for past inequities and become pressure to tip the balance of strategic advantage to the Soviet side? Obviously the two sides have had different views about where this line should be drawn, but these differences have represented one of the core issues in SALT, which is "legislating" not today's but *tomorrow's*, strategic relationship and the boundaries of constraints that will apply to the differing military-technical-strategic systems of each side.

The purely military significance of how such boundaries may be drawn in SALT is probably of less moment than the political impact. What a gradual accession of strategic advantage to the Soviet Union could mean thus needs to be measured more in political than in narrowly military terms. Although not quantifiable, the political effect of SALT outcomes suggesting to other countries that U.S. strategic power could be expected to decline relative to that of the Soviet Union in the years ahead would certainly not be to inspire confidence in America's standing in the world, but might well be to damage it badly. In some sense, a phenomenon akin to the 1978 decline of the dollar abroad could set in—an inexplicable flight of confidence despite a basically strong U.S. economy.

## INFLUENCING THE SOVIETS IN SALT

What kinds of approaches by the U.S. side may offer the best prospect of bringing the Soviet Union to subscribe to meaningful SALT agreements? Opinions on this salient question tend to divide along essentially two lines. The first holds that the United States can best persuade the Soviet Union to move in the right direction by the setting of a good example, by the practice of "restraint" in its own strategic programs and by advancing serious SALT proposals that do not "threaten" legitimate Soviet strategic interests. The second view holds that real incentives to bring the Soviets to enter meaningful SALT agreements must pose unpalatable consequences for failure to do so. These would include giving unequivocal evidence of U.S. resolve to carry out whatever unilateral measures might be needed to ensure its security and that of its allies, including programs that could threaten Soviet strategic assets. Or, as expressed by Colin Gray in more picturesque language: "the coin of the SALT negotiations realm is money committed to weapons that speak to Soviet anxieties."[11]

After ten years of the SALT experience, it remains difficult to demonstrate which of these approaches—or any other combination of statecraft, countervailing military power, "bargaining chips," or economic and political "linkages"—may be best calculated to move the Soviet leadership in the direction desired by the United States.[12] One thing that many observers do agree on is that the United States must have a clear conception of how its own strategic policy and its SALT negotiatory positions mesh—which has not always been the case—[13] before it can hope to influence the Soviets effectively.

Several aspects of the SALT record may afford some instruction as to what kinds of U.S. activity have or have not helped to shape Soviet SALT policy decisions. First, to take the formal negotiating process itself, although the bargaining skill and diligence of the U.S. negotiating personnel at the SALT delegation level have been important in working out the substantive details of agreements, it appears doubtful that debate at the delegation level has ever had a real impact on major Soviet policy decisions. Decisions on significant issues seem to have been influenced, when at all, through high-level intervention from outside SALT—the back channel and periodic meetings at the summit or foreign minister level.

The bargaining chip approach affords an obvious means of attempting to influence Soviet decisions, but its efficacy is a contentious matter. Critics assert that it is a devious device upon which military planners have seized as the entering wedge for new programs that otherwise might not receive approval, but which once started usually acquire their own momentum and thus tend to fuel the arms race and jeopardize progress in SALT.[14] Many strategic planners, on the other hand, are themselves less than enthusiastic about the bargaining chip approach on the grounds that it may distort sound planning, and that programs that should receive support on their own merits are subject to being cut back when negotiating exigencies no longer require them. Defenders of the bargaining chip approach, however, see the situation in a different light, asserting, for example, that the bargaining chip function of the U.S. Safeguard ABM system was an important factor in persuading the Soviet side in SALT I to reverse its traditional ABM position and to opt for the ABM Treaty.

In SALT II, the most conspicuous example of a U.S. weapons system that started out as a bargaining chip but became a nonexpendable program was the new class of "reborn" cruise missiles. Although the cruise missile unquestionably had an impact on the Soviet side, which made it a central issue in the post-Vladivostok negotiations, the Soviets have strongly resisted giving up any strategic systems of their own in order to get rid of the cruise missile "threat," thus leaving its efficacy as a means of exerting leverage on Soviet SALT decisions in some doubt.

Another situation with some relevance to how Soviet strategic and SALT policy decisions might be affected by a U.S. "threat" approach is to be seen in the case of the large Soviet land-based ICBM force. It has frequently been remarked that the Soviets have neither displayed much concern about the growing vulnerability of fixed, land-based missiles nor shown a particular interest in moving a larger share of their own strategic arsenal to sea, despite the fact that a preponderance of Soviet delivery forces and throwweight potential is concentrated in targetable, silo-based ICBMs.

Since it is this same land-based Soviet ICBM force whose growing counterforce potential has been the principal source of U.S. concern about the survivability of the Minuteman leg of the U.S. TRIAD, U.S. SALT policy has sought to secure significant reductions in the size of the Soviet ICBM force and to encourage its restructuring so as to put more of the Soviet delivery vehicle quota in sea-based missiles of lesser yield and accuracy. The Soviet Union, however, apparently has had no incentive compelling enough to lead it to consider major alterations of the ICBM force in which it has such a heavy and ongoing investment. Such an incentive might exist if the vulnerability of the force were to begin bothering the Soviets, but the vulnerability problem will only become serious for the Soviet Union if the United States develops a commensurate counterforce threat.

In this connection, one of the complaints lodged against the three-tier SALT II accord was that its limits on heavy and MIRVed ICBMs were too high to do much to reduce the Soviet counterforce threat against Minuteman, while its Protocol restrictions could impede U.S. unilateral options to deal with the Minuteman survivability problem through such systems as MX—which would not only provide a less-vulnerable basing mode, but could also pose a more severe counterforce threat to the Soviet ICBM force.[15]

The question posed by all this, therefore, is whether American, and for that matter, Soviet strategic interests might not be best served by a stepped-up U.S. counterforce program. Such a move, however, is strongly opposed by most of the arms control community, even though its effects might be to provide the missing incentive for the Soviets to move in the direction of more stable strategic forces, long a desideratum of the arms control community. The history of SALT abounds with ironies, and this may well be one of the more poignant ones.

At another juncture in the SALT record, a test of alternative U.S. approaches to dealing with the Soviet Union can be found in the case of the November 1974 Vladivostok transaction. In the several months before that meeting, James Schlesinger and Henry Kissinger had advocated somewhat divergent U.S. SALT proposals.[16] The secretary of defense apparently favored proposals with strict constraints and low ceilings as openers, to be backed up, should the Soviets respond negatively, with a hard-line warning that U.S. strategic programs would be put in high gear to match any unilateral effort the Soviet Union might choose to pursue. Kissinger's alternative would seem to have favored adjusting to Soviet preferences for the sake of consummating an agreement, leaving to subsequent negotiations the business of reducing ceilings and finding constraints to deal with possible future threats to strategic stability.

Which of the two alternatives may have been "best" in terms of helping to bring the Soviet leadership around to the agreement reached at Vladivostok is one of those elusive questions that defy categorical answers. But since the second alternative appears to have been closer to the policy track actually followed, it might be argued that Kissinger's strategy was more responsible for the outcome achieved at Vladivostok. At the same time it is also possible that the harder implications of the Schlesinger alternative—such as the strategic R&D retooling for which he had begun to call in early 1974 as preparation, if need be, for a matching competition—had been borne in on the Russians and served as a persuasive factor in the Soviet decision to sign at Vladivostok. Thus, in a sense, the Vladivostok transaction might be said to have at least partly vindicated both the Kissinger and Schlesinger approaches.

Another potential source of U.S. leverage upon the Soviet Union in SALT has lain in the structural division between the executive and legislative branches of the U.S. government. The fact that there is no guarantee that SALT positions taken by the executive will necessarily be endorsed by Congress has probably given U.S. negotiators at times a good excuse to turn down what might appear to be unreasonable Soviet demands, although it is reported that Brezhnev also has played a similar game by hinting that he could not settle points at issue without ad referendum appraisal by his Politburo colleagues or the military.

With the general increase in U.S. congressional influence upon the SALT process in the course of SALT II,[17] and especially upon the chances of approval of agreements negotiated by the administration, a situation of some delicacy began to confront the Soviet Union. On the one hand, the Soviet leaders presumably considered that failure to conclude a SALT II agreement would aid circles in the United States hostile to the USSR. But at the same time they could not help being aware that an agreement on their preferred terms would face a rough reception in the U.S. Congress. Thus, despite their declarations that they would not let themselves be intimidated by a potential "congressional veto,"[18] the Soviet leaders were placed in a position where they may have felt obliged to adopt a less-intractable SALT stance than their preferences otherwise would have dictated.

## WHAT LIES AHEAD?

Perhaps the best way to conclude these reflections on the SALT I and II experience of the last ten years may be to venture a brief glance ahead at SALT III prospects and at some of the changes that could occur during the next ten years in the SALT process and the kinds of problems with which it will have to deal. Needless to say, the speculative element in these remarks far outweighs their predictive value.

A first presumption is that the SALT process will continue on into a SALT III period and beyond, although—as we saw at the close of the preceding chapter—there was an outside possibility toward the end of 1978 that a failure to attain congressional approval of the three-part SALT II accords, after the intensive negotiating effort expended upon them, might bring about an indefinite suspension or even collapse of the strategic arms negotiations.[19] Should that be the case, the voluntary extension of the 1972 Interim Agreement probably would become a collateral casualty, especially in light of the pressure of cumulative Soviet strategic weapons acquisitions, mainly SLBMs, upon the IA ceilings.

But assuming survival of the SALT II agreement, the follow-on SALT III negotiations would probably face the general problem (likely to be a never-ending one in the SALT process) of redressing asymmetries left by preceding agreements. In a more specific sense, SALT III might be expected to address, among other things:

- Further reductions and modernization constraints
- The unresolved problems of the "gray-area" systems—SS-20, Backfire, cruise missiles, FBS—as seen from the differing perspectives of the two sides
- Concerns about ICBM vulnerability and the crisis instability of strategic offensive forces, probably brought to the agenda by the U.S. side
- Various issues related to strategic defense, including civil defense and air defense systems, mobile basing modes for ICBMs, hard-site defense, and possibly reopening of the ABM Treaty
- New questions arising around military activities in space[20]

With respect to further reductions, several kinds of difficulties might be anticipated. On the Soviet side, resistance to substantial reductions, as in the reaction to the Carter March 1977 proposals,[21] would probably be fed not only by Soviet military conservatism and the China factor, but also by the fact that the Soviet Union's international power and prestige rest largely on its massive military machine. To cut deeply into the Strategic Rocket Forces, the "leading" element of their military power, would thus be especially painful for the Soviet leaders, the more so because their technical-economic assets to compensate for any drastic cutback of Soviet military power do not compare with those at the disposal of the United States. For its part, the U.S. side, though less dedicated to high force levels, would have to take into account the possibility that large reductions would breed the very strategic instability that its arms control policy has traditionally sought to avoid.[22]

Gray-area problems promise to intrude increasingly into the SALT process, making it very difficult for the Soviet Union and the United States to maintain the bilateral character of past strategic negotiations—even if both should wish to keep it that way in SALT III. The core issue could come down to insistence by America's West European allies on cruise missile deployments in Europe to offset a Soviet SS-20/Backfire threat against Europe. To deal with this issue, along with the perennial FBS question, which the Soviets have placed high on their SALT III agenda, will probably make it necessary for the two superpowers to "decompartmentalize" their strategic relationship and find a prescription—possibly a third negotiating forum—that will bring European (NATO and Warsaw Pact) interests into the picture.[23]

The ICBM vulnerability problem and strategic defense considerations could become closely joined in SALT III if what Deborah Shapley has called "technology creep" should begin to make ABM defense look much more practical,[24] thus inviting strategic planners to turn to relatively cheap missile site defense as an alternative to more expensive solutions to the Minuteman vulnerability problem,[25] such as the new MX mobile-based ICBM system. A unilateral planning move in this direction, of course, would run afoul of the ABM Treaty if hard-site defense of more than a single ICBM complex were contemplated, so that the question of changes to the treaty could become a major SALT issue. Whether an attempt to reopen the ABM Treaty would, as one observer has put it, "rattle the foundations of arms control itself,"[26] may perhaps depend to a considerable extent upon the general state of Soviet-American relations at the time—strained or mellow.

Several other factors that might in SALT III or beyond begin to shake the whole previously constructed edifice of SALT agreements can also be discerned upon the horizon. One of these is the dynamism of technology, leading to greatly improved accuracies of both ICBM and SLBM warheads, the appearance of new classes of small, mobile delivery vehicles, and the increasing development of space-based sensor and control systems.[27] Somewhere farther down the line, there may be still more esoteric developments such as high-energy laser and particle beam systems, although their feasibility for strategic purposes remains at present a contentious matter.[28]

These trends in strategic technologies promise to make the tasks of arms control far more complex and difficult than ever before, especially with respect to verification. Essentially, the monitoring of SALT compliance in the past has amounted to identifying and counting rather large items of hardware: missiles, missile silos, submarines, bombers, ABM radars, and the like. But the relatively simple procedures required to verify these readily observable objects by unilateral NTM reconnaissance satellites—which helped to make SALT feasible in the first place[29]—may no longer suffice when the items to be verified include not only the existence of small, mobile, and poorly observable delivery vehicles, but also the qualitative attributes of constrained systems.

Taken together with agreements of increasing scope and complexity like the three-part, fifty-page SALT II accords, the problems of implementation and verification could overburden the SALT process to the point that either a return to simpler and less-ambitious limitation agreements not relying on close counting and scrupulous verification,[30] or else increased tolerance of intrusive inspection, would be needed in order to keep the SALT process viable.

Another alternative, of course, which some observers have considered not unlikely, would be increasingly to seek solutions to some strategic problems, like Minuteman vulnerability and others in the "technical stability" category, outside the formal framework of SALT itself.[31]

But if, for political or whatever other reasons, both sides continue to operate under some kind of imperative to maintain the SALT process and its institutions, and to seek further agreements dedicated to progressively extended limitations and controls over strategic forces, then a pertinent question that arises is whether the Soviet Union would consider the breaching of its traditional secrecy safeguards a fair price to pay for keeping SALT workable.

Some small chinks in the Soviet secrecy tradition have been opened in the course of SALT—such as agreement on exchange of a common data base, which may have appeared to the Russians a more momentous concession than to others from a different political culture.[32] Anecdotally, for example, a Soviet official is said to have remarked after the agreement to a common data base had been reached: "There goes 500 years of Russian history." However, the SALT record on the whole hardly encourages one to expect any significant relaxation of Soviet secrecy attitudes.

By and large, the period ahead can be expected to produce more strains and stresses growing out of SALT implementation and compliance issues than before, not only because of the more complicated verification situation mentioned above, but also because the stakes increase as limitations on strategic forces become more restrictive.

With respect to both internal arrangements on each side for ensuring compliance with obligations entered into and the institutional interface between the U.S. and Soviet sides in such joint bodies as the Standing Consultative Commission (SCC), the whole mechanism for supervising treaty observance and making adjustment to new or unforeseen circumstances will certainly be put to a more severe test in carrying out its functions than has been the case to date.[33] In view of the larger burden likely to fall upon the SCC in the future, it is rather curious that virtually no analytical attention at all has been paid it in the literature of SALT. Indeed, at some point in SALT's future, assuming that a series of basic agreements then exists, the negotiating delegations presumably would fade away— leaving the SALT process, institutionally, largely in the care of the SCC.

Without attempting here to anticipate the specifics of future compliance problems that may arise, one may foresee at least two general problems very much related to institutional asymmetries between the two sides. The first of these concerns what some thoughtful observers have considered to be a requirement for a degree of mutual trust—over and above verification machinery as such—in order to make agreements hold up. A statement made by former Senator James W. Fulbright in connection with the ABM Treaty and the Interim Agreement illustrates this viewpoint: "They depend upon the good faith of the parties to them. If we do anything to arouse suspicion on the part of the other party that may raise the question of deceiving or of not wanting to live up to the terms, of course the distrust will be mutual and destroy respect for the agreements."[34]

Given the asymmetrical nature in the two societies of what might be termed self-policing institutions and practices—involving such phenomena as investigative reporting, fact-finding commissions, and other kinds of private and official inquiry into how the government conducts its business and lives up to its agreements—it would appear that a far more rigorous burden will fall upon the U.S. side to avoid self-policing accusations that might arouse Soviet distrust than vice versa. Indeed, should Senator Fulbright's injunction be widely heeded, one can imagine that in order to demonstrate its own continued good faith and trust, the United States might be prone to lean over backward not to raise embarrassing questions about possible Soviet violations in cases where only ambiguous evidence was available.

The second problem relates to the burden placed upon the national intelligence resources of each side to help monitor the observance of agreements and to detect violations. Here again, the United States would appear to shoulder the greater handicap, if only because its intelligence operations must cope with the problems of peering into a closed society, whereas the Soviet intelligence apparatus operates against a relatively more open one. What effect these particular asymmetries may ultimately have on the durability of

SALT agreements is a moot question, though it would seem that they may contribute to a situation making it easier for the Soviet Union to stretch the spirit and the letter of SALT agreements, if it should so choose, than vice versa.

The future of the SALT process, as one sees it being shaped by the various forces and trends posited above, does not appear all that bright. In a nutshell, more complicated SALT agreements become more difficult to implement and verify; "technology creep" not only slips through the cracks in SALT agreements, but threatens to break into a trot or even a gallop that could produce a dynamic, ever-changing strategic situation with which SALT would be hard-pressed to deal effectively; and the institutions, habits, and practices underlying the competitive relationship between the two super-powers over the past decade will change little during the next one.

But, if SALT cannot be expected to usher in the millenium, neither can it be considered a fruitless endeavor. Politically, so long as a kind of imperative exists to keep SALT alive, the spillover effect will also help to keep Soviet-American relations from breaking down, which could—in turbulent times—prove to be one of SALT's more important contributions. Even in a strategic sense, and with a bit of luck, SALT might do better than the SALT experience to date would suggest in helping to bring about a state of affairs approximating what one might call the arms control vision of the strategic future.

In this conception, the numerical growth phase of modern stra-tegic forces has been brought to a close, roughly at a level of parity, by some combination of unilateral calculation and mutual agreement in SALT. The next major phase, to be marked by reductions and qualitative limitations on strategic forces, has now begun. Thanks to the Protocol period of the SALT II accords, a breathing spell has also been provided in which measures can be worked out to tame the more dangerous and dynamic technologies before their deployment can threaten strategic stability. Despite the difficulties ahead, self-interest can be expected to impel both parties to persevere in SALT, in order to enhance their own security.

It would be fitting if this book on SALT could be brought to a conclusion by predicting which of these futures for SALT will prove to best approximate reality. This question, however, belongs to a chapter of the SALT experience still to be written.

✳ *Appendix A*

# Glossary of Acronyms and Technical Terms

**ABM**  Antiballistic missile.

**ACDA**  Arms Control and Disarmament Agency.

**ALCM**  Air-launched cruise missile. (See also Cruise missile.)

**ASAT**  Antisatellite.

**ASW**  Antisubmarine warfare.

**Back channel**  Secret contacts between individual officials that circumvent the usual channels of communication either between governments or within them.

**Backfire (TU-26)**  NATO code name for a Soviet variable-wing supersonic bomber, which first entered service in 1974. In the context of SALT II, there was much debate as to whether its unrefueled range classified it as intercontinental or intermediate, and SALT-accountable or not.

**Bear**  NATO designation for the TU-95, Soviet turboprop intercontinental bomber.

**Bison**  NATO designation for the MYA-4, Soviet jet-powered intercontinental bomber.

**Bus**  On a MIRVed missile, the postboost vehicle, which carries low-thrust engines and guidance and control equipment for maneuvering after the initial boost and dispensing multiple warheads at a sequence of targets.

**CEP (circular error probable)**  The radius of the circle around a target within which half of the warheads launched at that target are expected to land. It is a measure of the accuracy of missiles attacking point targets.

**CIA**  Central Intelligence Agency.

**Correlation of forces**   A Soviet term describing the factors bearing on the world situation—psychological, political, economic, and military—often used to argue that these factors are shifting in favor of the socialist camp.

**Counterforce**   The policy of targeting attacks against an opponent's nuclear strike force, thus presumably depriving him of the capability to retaliate following a first strike. It is the opposite of countervalue, that is, targeting enemy population centers and industry.

**Cruise missile**   A small pilotless jet aircraft to be used as a delivery vehicle for either conventional or nuclear warheads. Can be launched from various platforms, including submarines, other aircraft (B-52s, 747s), and ground launchers. Its attributes include difficulty of interception because of its very low altitude flight path and high accuracy due to its terrain-matching (TERCOM) guidance system.

**CSCE**   Conference on Security and Cooperation in Europe.

**Damage limitation**   A term denoting measures taken to lessen the effects on a country of enemy nuclear attack. May include such things as counterforce pre-emptive attacks, active defense (ABM systems), and passive defense (civil defense systems).

**DDR&E**   Director of Defense Research and Engineering (U.S. Department of Defense).

**Delta-I, -II, -III**   Modified and enlarged versions of the Soviet Y-class nuclear-powered submarine (SSBN). Deployment of the three versions took place in 1972, 1973, and 1977, respectively.

**Deterrence**   A strategy, usually pertaining to nuclear weapons, intended to persuade an opponent that the costs and risks accompanying nuclear aggression severely outweigh any possible advantage to be gained from that aggression.

**Essential equivalence**   An American concept calling for U.S. and Soviet strategic capabilities to be effectively equal, though not necessarily numerically identical, as measured by static criteria such as launcher numbers, throwweight, megatonnage, and warheads. (See also Parity.)

**FBS**   See Forward-based system.

**Forward-based system (FBS)**   U.S. aircraft and other nuclear delivery systems that could be launched from bases outside the territory of the United States in strikes against the Soviet Union. Primarily, however, these forces were designed for the support of NATO ground forces in Western and Central Europe.

**Freedom to mix**   The concept, in a SALT negotiating context, that each side should be free to determine the composition of its overall total of strategic delivery systems, as set by an agreement.

**GKO** (Soviet) State Committee of Defense.

**GLCM** Ground-launched cruise missile. (See also Cruise missile.)

**GOSPLAN** (Soviet) State Planning Committee.

**GRU** Main Intelligence Directorate of the (Soviet) General Staff.

**Hard target** Generally refers to land-based missile silos and support facilities such as command-and-control centers that have been reinforced against damage from nuclear blasts.

**Headroom issue** The SALT I Interim Agreement allowed the Soviets a numerical advantage in strategic delivery forces because the U.S. was considered to have a great qualitative lead. However, Congress felt that this disparity in numbers would afford the Soviets an opportunity to catch up qualitatively, thus leaving the U.S. in a strategically inferior position.

**Heavy missile** In the SALT context, a missile whose volume is greater than seventy cubic meters; by unilateral U.S. definition in SALT I.

**IA** Interim Agreement of 1972 on the limitation of strategic offensive arms.

**ICBM** Intercontinental ballistic missile.

**INR** Bureau of Intelligence and Research (U.S. Department of State).

**IRBM** Intermediate-range ballistic missile.

**ISA** International Security Affairs (U.S. Department of Defense).

**J-5 Directorate** Group in charge of plans and policy under the director of the Joint Staff, U.S. Department of Defense.

**JCS** Joint Chiefs of Staff.

**KGB** (Soviet) Committee of State Security.

**Launch-on-warning** Policy of launching a retaliatory strike upon receiving intelligence that an enemy first strike is in progress.

**Long Range Aviation (LRA)** The component of the Soviet armed forces responsible for operating the small Soviet strategic force of intercontinental manned bombers.

**"Look down, shoot down"** A term denoting combined radar and air-to-air weapons capability for intercepting low-flying aircraft, intended to alleviate the air defense problems associated with low-level penetration and conventional tracking radars.

**LRA** See Long Range Aviation.

**MAD** See Mutual assured destruction.

**Maneuverable reentry vehicle (MARV)** Ballistic missile warhead or decoy that can be internally or externally steered after reentering the atmosphere, in order to evade defenses, correct targeting, etc.

**MARV** See Maneuverable reentry vehicle.

**MBFR** Mutual Balanced Force Reductions.

**MIRV** See Multiple, independently targeted reentry vehicle.

**MLBM** Modern large ballistic missile launcher.

**MOSS NATO** designation for type of Soviet aircraft used for airborne early warning.

**MR/IRBM** Medium-range and intermediate-range ballistic missiles.

**MRV** See Multiple reentry vehicle.

**Multiple, independently targeted reentry vehicle (MIRV)** A weapon system that comprises a missile carrying several warheads, each of which can be programmed to strike a different target.

**Multiple reentry vehicle (MRV)** A weapon system composed of a single rocket carrying several warheads, not independently targeted but dispersed in a pattern over a target area.

**Mutual assured destruction (MAD)** A concept of strategic stability under which rivals are deterred from nuclear aggression because each maintains the capability to inflict massive retaliatory punishment on the society of the attacking opponent, even after absorbing a surprise first strike.

**MX** A U.S. MIRVed ICBM system under development, designed to be deployed in a land-mobile basing mode.

**MYA-4** See Bison.

**NSC** National Security Council.

**NSDM** National Security Decision Memorandum.

**NSSM** National Security Study Memorandum.

**National technical means (NTM)** Methods of unilaterally verifying compliance with arms limitation agreements through the use of observation satellites and other surveillance instruments.

**Nike-X** Second generation American antiballistic missile system, preliminary to Sentinel.

**NORAD** North American Air Defense Command.

**NTM** See National technical means.

**OSD** Office of the Secretary of Defense.

**PA&E** Program Analysis and Evaluation (U.S. Department of Defense).

**Parity** A standard for force structure requiring that the sum of military forces and weapon systems be effectively equal to those of an enemy counterpart. (See also Essential equivalence.)

**Polaris** A U.S. strategic weapon system comprising a nuclear-powered, missile-launching submarine carrying sixteen SLBMs.

**Policy Review Committee (PRC)** One of two committees created in the National Security Council under the Carter administration. This committee, unlike its companion, seemed to have little or no role in the SALT policymaking process. (See also Special Coordinating Committee.)

**Poseidon** A U.S. MIRVed submarine-launched missile, an advance in payload, range, and accuracy over the Polaris missile.

**PRC** See Policy Review Committee.

**PRM** Presidential Review Memorandum.

**PSI overpressure** Pounds per square inch greater than normal atmospheric pressure. This measure is commonly used to determine whether an object can withstand the added pressure of a nuclear explosion.

**PVO** (Soviet) air defense.

**RV** Reentry vehicle. That part of a ballistic missile designed to reenter the earth's atmosphere.

**SA** Systems Analysis (U.S. Department of Defense).

**SAC** Strategic Air Command.

**Safeguard** U.S. antiballistic missile system, successor to Sentinel. Designed primarily to protect ICBM sites, with only light defense of population centers.

**SALDEL** SALT delegation.

**SALT** Strategic Arms Limitation Talks.

**SALT Backstopping Committee (SBC)** A National Security Council group established by the Nixon administration and retained during the Ford and Carter years. Its functions included transmitting guidance on SALT issues and providing other kinds of day-to-day support for the on-site delegation in Geneva.

**SALT Working Group** Staff supporting the Special Coordinating Committee on SALT-related matters. Located in the National Security Council.

**SBC** See SALT Backstopping Committee.

**SCC** See Standing Consultative Commission.

**SCC Backstopping Committee** An interagency group established during the Carter administration to give staff support to the Standing Consultative Commission. Operated largely by ACDA.

**Sentinel** U.S. antiballistic missile system, successor to Nike-X, predecessor to Safeguard. Intended to protect cities against small-scale attacks, although it could be expanded into a "thick" system to protect against larger attacks.

**Single Integrated Operational Plan (SIOP)** The U.S. contingency plan for strategic retaliatory strikes in the event of a nuclear war. Covers various options in regard to targets, timing, tactics, etc.

**SIOP** See Single Integrated Operational Plan.

**SLBM** Submarine-launched ballistic missile.

**SLCM** Submarine/sea-launched cruise missile. (See also Cruise missile.)

**Special Coordinating Committee** One of two committees created in the National Security Council under the Carter administration, replacing the Verification Panel of the Nixon-Ford years. However, unlike its predecessor, it was meant to deal with non-SALT as well as SALT issues. (See also Policy Review Committee.)

**SRF** (Soviet) Strategic Rocket Forces.

**SS-4, SS-5**   Medium- and intermediate-range Soviet missiles, exempt from SALT limitations.

**SS-9**   A large Soviet ICBM, liquid-fueled.

**SS-11**   Liquid-fueled Soviet ICBM which, at the time of the SALT I Accords, was the most numerous ballistic missile in the Soviet arsenal.

**SS-13**   First Soviet solid-fueled ICBM. Roughly equivalent to U.S. Minuteman I.

**SS-16**   Fourth-generation Soviet ICBM, solid-fueled, capable of being deployed either in the mobile mode or in silos, with or without MIRV. Successor to the SS-13.

**SS-17**   Fourth-generation Soviet ICBM, follow-on to the SS-11, deployable with or without MIRV. First showed operational capability in 1975.

**SS-18**   Fourth-generation Soviet ICBM, follow-on to the SS-9, deployable with or without MIRV. First showed operational capability in 1974.

**SS-19**   Fourth-generation Soviet ICBM, follow-on to the SS-11, but with a throwweight four to five times greater; capable of being deployed with or without MIRV. First operational year was 1974.

**SS-20**   Soviet land-mobile IRBM, made up of the first two stages of the three-stage SS-16 ICBM. First deployed in 1977, it caused concern in the West because, though it was exempt from SALT limitations, it could easily be converted to an intercontinental SS-16.

**SS-N-6**   A Soviet liquid-fueled SLBM with a range of 1300 nautical miles, deployed on Yankee- (Y-) class nuclear submarines.

**SS-N-8**   Soviet SLBM with a range of 4200 nautical miles, deployed on Delta-I-class nuclear submarines.

**SS-NX-17**   First Soviet solid-fueled SLBM, which employs a post-boost vehicle and thus could be modified for a MIRV role. Reported to be replacement for SS-N-6 SLBM.

**SS-NX-18**   Soviet liquid-fueled ICBM with estimated range in excess of 4000 nautical miles. Judged to have MIRV capability because it carries a postboost vehicle and sophisticated guidance system. Probably for use in Delta-III SSBNs.

**SSBN**   Nuclear-powered ballistic missile submarine.

**Standing Consultative Commission (SCC)**   A joint U.S.-Soviet body set up in December 1972 to implement the provisions of the ABM Treaty and the Interim Agreement of May 1972. Its functions include considering questions of compliance and related ambiguities.

**Three-tier framework**   Format for the SALT II accord, composed of three parts: Treaty, Protocol, and Statement of Principles.

**Throwweight** The total payload capacity of the postboost vehicle of a ballistic missile, including all reentry bodies (warheads, decoys, etc.). Larger boosters permit greater throwweight.

**TRIAD** Refers to the three-part U.S. strategic retaliatory force, comprising land-based ICBMs, the bombers of the Strategic Air Command (SAC), and the Polaris/Poseidon submarine fleet.

**Trident** A U.S. nuclear-powered submarine and SLBM system of greater size and range than the present Polaris/Poseidon system. First unit scheduled to become operational in 1979-1980. Originally designated ULMs (Underwater long-range missile system).

**TU-26** See Backfire.

**TU-95** See Bear.

**Typhoon** Soviet nuclear-powered submarine, first of which was under construction in 1978. Said to be similar in size to the U.S. Trident.

**ULMs** Underwater long-range missile system. (See Trident.)

**Under Secretaries Committee (USC) for SALT** Originally a non-SALT senior body, in the early SALT I period its functions were to include providing responsive Washington support for the SALT delegation during negotiating sessions only. However, it never became very active in that role.

**USC** See Under Secretaries Committe for SALT.

**Verification Panel (VP)** A policymaking body located in the National Security Council during the Nixon-Ford years for the interagency study of the strategic implications of SALT and verification problems associated with strategic arms limitation agreements.

**Verification Panel Working Group (VPWG)** Support staff for the Verification Panel within the National Security Council.

**VP** See Verification Panel.

**VPK** (Soviet) Military-Industrial Commission.

**VPWG** See Verification Panel Working Group.

**Yankee or Y-class** NATO designation for a modern Soviet nuclear-powered submarine with sixteen SS-N-6 SLBM launchers.

**Yield** The total effective energy produced by a nuclear explosion, including nuclear radiation, thermal radiation, and blast. Usually expressed in kilotons or megatons of TNT equivalent.

*Appendix B*

# Pros and Cons of the "Headroom" Issue After SALT I

The pros and cons of the headroom question involved many interrelated issues bearing on the merits of the SALT I Interim Agreement. To condense an intricate web of arguments into a somewhat simplified format, the respective cases made in defense of SALT I and in criticism of it around the headroom issue in 1972 can be summarized as below:

| Arguments in Defense of SALT I on the Headroom Issue | Arguments Critical of SALT I on the Headroom Issue |
|---|---|
| a. The Interim Agreement put a quantitative limit on Soviet programs that could otherwise have gone much farther during the five-year span involved, thus serving to check the momentum of the Soviet strategic buildup. According to projected figures cited for the eventuality that Soviet momentum had gone unchecked, the Soviets would have been able to build an additional 1000 ICBMs and to increase their modern SSBN force to 90 submarines or more in the 1972-1977 period. | a. The Interim Agreement's quantitative ceilings were high enough so that they would allow the Soviets by 1977 to build to levels they probably would not have much exceeded without SALT. The projected Soviet increases without SALT also went substantially beyond preagreement estimates by the U.S. The net effect of the differential ceilings therefore could be to constrain future U.S. strategic programs without demonstrably slowing down the Soviet momentum during the period of the agreement. |

## Arguments in Defense of SALT I on the Headroom Issue

b. Some quantitative disparity in permissible force levels was compensated for by U.S. technological superiority. Especially in such fields as MIRV and delivery accuracy potential, the U.S. held a lead which the Soviets could not expect to overcome in five years if the U.S. continued the vigorous qualitative improvement effort open to it under the agreement.

c. The tradeoff provisions of the agreement required the Soviets to reduce their ICBM force more than the U.S. (by 210 compared to 54) to attain the maximum SLBM ceiling. Also, the provisions prevented the Soviets from building more new silos to expand their heavy ICBM force (SS-9 or better) beyond the 313 existing or under construction, which checked a counterforce threat that was of great concern to the United States.

d. Thanks to its MIRV lead, the U.S. had a large advantage in warhead numbers, on the order of 5700 to 2500. This warhead margin helped to balance the greater number of Soviet ICBM launchers and SLBMs permitted by the agreement.

## Arguments Critical of SALT I on the Headroom Issue

b. In five years, the Soviets could do a lot of catching up in MIRV and other technologies, especially since the greater throw-weight of Soviet missiles (in all, about four times the throw-weight available to the U.S.) allowed more ultimate scope for developing MIRV packages than smaller U.S. missiles. There was also no guarantee that the U.S. would continue to maintain a high-cost technological effort in the political climate of further SALT negotiations.

c. The old missile launchers to be traded in (SS-7 and SS-8) represented an obsolete generation that the Soviets may have intended to scrap anyway, especially the soft sites included in the 210. As for the upper ceiling placed on the Soviet heavy ICBM threat, modernization programs permissible under the agreement might result in upgrading older heavy missiles, like the hardened SS-7, into the equivalent of additional modern heavy ICBMs.

d. While the U.S. had a lead in warhead numbers, this was a short-term advantage that could not be expected to last when the Soviets acquired MIRV technology, which—combined with greater numbers and larger payload of their missiles—would permit them eventually to deploy many more warheads than the U.S.

| Arguments in Defense of SALT I on the Headroom Issue | Arguments Critical of SALT I on the Headroom Issue |
|---|---|

**Arguments in Defense of SALT I on the Headroom Issue**

e. The U.S. had an advantage in heavy intercontinental bombers of about 3 to 1, which helped to compensate for the greater number of Soviet ICBMs. The U.S. also had under development a new bomber, the B-1, superior to the Soviet Backfire.

f. The lower U.S. ceiling on SLBMs partly reflected the fact that geographic and operating disparities would reduce the number of SLBMs the Soviets could keep on distant patrol. In addition, the agreement would allow the U.S. to proceed with orderly replacement of its older SLBM force with the much improved Trident system.

g. It remained to be seen whether the Soviets would actually try to exercise all the options open to them under SALT I, for their resources were not unlimited and they had important alternative claims on them.

h. The Soviets had a vested interest in the SALT agreements, which validated Soviet attainment of strategic "equality" with the U.S. Any perceived Soviet attempt to acquire one-sided military advantages over the U.S.

**Arguments Critical of SALT I on the Headroom Issue**

e. The U.S. bomber advantage was precarious because limitations on strategic bombers were still subject to negotiation. In addition, the Backfire was already flying and could lead to a more advanced follow-on bomber if the Soviets chose to keep the bomber competition open, whereas the B-1 was not scheduled to make its first flight for another two years.

f. Geographic disparities did not entirely favor the U.S., since the bulk of prime U.S. targets were more accessible from the sea than those in the continental USSR. Changes in Soviet operating practices, such as adoption of a two-crew system and utilization of forward logistics facilities, as in Cuba, could help to even out the existent patrol asymmetry.

g. The resource argument was previously used to suggest that the Soviets could not stand the economic burden of their strategic buildup. It could prove no more valid in the future.

h. National means of detection might not suffice to keep the U.S. adequately informed of Soviet activity, especially in the critical area of technology. Further, a Soviet attempt to attain clear-cut military advantage

| Arguments in Defense of SALT I on the Headroom Issue | Arguments Critical of SALT I on the Headroom Issue |
|---|---|
| would jeopardize the whole SALT process, allowing the U.S. to invoke "supreme national interest" to abrogate the accords. | might prove less likely than political exploitation of the changed strategic power status of the USSR, as reflected in the differential force ceilings already accepted. |
| i. SALT II would offer an opportunity to resolve ambiguities and to replace any features of the Interim Agreement that might prove clearly disadvantageous to the U.S. with more equitable long-term arrangements. | i. Given the precedent set by SALT I, in which the U.S. found itself in a less than "brilliant" bargaining position because of ongoing Soviet ICBM and SLBM construction programs, it was unrealistic to expect the Soviet Union to give up in SALT II what it managed to gain in SALT I. |

*Appendix C*

# Chronology of SALT Meetings

### SALT I: November 1969-May 1972

| SALT Session | Summit | Other Meeting | Chief Participants | Dates |
|---|---|---|---|---|
| 1. Helsinki | | | Delegations | Nov-Dec 1969 |
| 2. Vienna | | | Delegations | Apr-Aug 1970 |
| 3. Helsinki | | | Delegations | Nov-Dec 1970 |
| | | Washington[1] | Kissinger/Dobrynin | Jan 1971 |
| 4. Vienna | | | Delegations | Mar-May 1971 |
| 5. Helsinki | | | Delegations | Jul-Sep 1971 |
| 6. Vienna | | | Delegations | Nov 71-Feb 72 |
| 7. Helsinki | | | Delegations | Mar-May 1972 |
| | | Moscow | Kissinger/Brezhnev | Apr 1972 |
| | Moscow | | Nixon/Brezhnev | May 1972 |

### SALT II: September 1972-January 1979

| SALT Session | Summit | Other Meeting[2] | Chief Participants | Dates |
|---|---|---|---|---|
| | | Moscow | Kissinger/Brezhnev/Gromyko | Sep 1972 |
| 1. Geneva | | | Delegations | Nov-Dec 1972 |
| 2. Geneva | | | Delegations | Mar-Apr 1973 |
| 3. Geneva | | | Delegations | May-Jun 1973 |
| | | Moscow | Kissinger/Brezhnev/Gromyko | May 1973 |
| | Washington | | Nixon/Brezhnev | Jun 1973 |
| 4. Geneva | | | Delegations | Sep-Nov 1973 |
| 5. Geneva | | | Delegations | Feb-Apr 1974 |
| | | Washington | Nixon/Kissinger/Gromyko | Feb 1974 |
| | | Moscow | Kissinger/Brezhnev/Gromyko | Mar 1974 |
| | | Washington | Nixon/Kissinger/Gromyko | Apr 1974 |
| | | Geneva | Kissinger/Gromyko | Apr 1974 |
| | Moscow | | Nixon/Brezhnev | Jun-Jul 1974 |

[1] This meeting marked the opening of a secret back channel between Moscow and Washington, which comprised numerous meetings between Kissinger and Dobrynin, and personal messages between Nixon and Kosygin, and later, Brezhnev. During the SALT I phase of negotiation, the back channel apparently continued to function straight up until the time of the Moscow summit in May 1972.

[2] Omitted from the tally of Moscow visits is Kissinger's hurried trip in October 1973, which dealt almost exclusively with the problem of arranging a cease-fire in the Arab-Israeli Yom Kippur War.

277

| SALT Session | Summit | Other Meeting | Chief Participants | Dates |
|---|---|---|---|---|
| 6. Geneva | | | Delegations | Sep-Nov 1974 |
| | | Washington | Ford/Kissinger/Gromyko | Sep 1974 |
| | | Moscow | Kissinger/Brezhnev/Gromyko | Oct 1974 |
| | Vladivostok | | Ford/Brezhnev | Nov 1974 |
| 7. Geneva | | | Delegations | Jan-May 1975 |
| | | Geneva | Kissinger/Gromyko | Feb 1975 |
| | | Vienna | Kissinger/Gromyko | May 1975 |
| 8. Geneva | | | Delegations | Jul-Nov 1975 |
| | | Geneva | Kissinger/Gromyko | Jul 1975 |
| | Helsinki[1] | | Ford/Brezhnev | Jul-Aug 1975 |
| | | Washington | Ford/Kissinger/Gromyko | Sep 1975 |
| 9. Geneva | | | Delegations | Dec 1975 |
| 10. Geneva | | | Delegations | Jan-May 1976 |
| | | Moscow | Kissinger/Brezhnev/Gromyko | Jan 1976 |
| 11. Geneva | | | Delegations | Jun-Jul 1976 |
| 12. Geneva | | | Delegations | Sep-Nov 1976 |
| | | New York | Kissinger/Gromyko | Sep 1976 |
| | | Washington | Ford/Gromyko | Oct 1976 |
| | | Moscow | Vance/Brezhnev/Gromyko | Mar 1977 |
| 13. Geneva | | | Delegations | May-Dec 1977 |
| | | Geneva | Vance/Gromyko | May 1977 |
| | | Washington | Carter/Vance/Gromyko | Sep 1977 |
| 14. Geneva | | | Delegations | Jan 1978-Jan 1979 |
| | | Moscow | Vance/Brezhnev/Gromyko | Apr 1978 |
| | | Washington | Carter/Vance/Gromyko | May 1978 |
| | | New York | Vance/Gromyko | June 1978 |
| | | Geneva | Vance/Gromyko | Jul 1978 |
| | | Moscow | Warnke/Gromyko | Sep 1978 |
| | | New York | Vance/Gromyko | Sep 1978 |
| | | Washington | Carter/Vance/Gromyko | Sep-Oct 1978 |
| | | Moscow | Vance/Brezhnev/Gromyko | Oct 1978 |
| | | Geneva | Vance/Gromyko | Dec 1978 |

[1] For signing of CSCE accord. SALT discussed at meetings between Ford and Brezhnev.

*Appendix D*

# Summary: Principal Alleged Soviet SALT I Violations and Subsequent U.S. Compliance Statement

| Allegations | Document #7 Response* |
|---|---|
| 1. Heavy-light missile distinction flouted. | U.S. raised issue in early 1975, though it was not a violation. Since then, after discussion in SCC and SALT delegations, agreement reached on clear demarcation between heavy and light ICBMs. (p. 5) |
| 2. Camouflage covers over mobile missile launchers and other concealment practices. | Soviet concealment activities increased substantially in 1974, but did not prevent verification of SALT compliance. By early 1975, after discussion in the SCC, U.S. monitoring indicated there was no longer an expanding pattern of concealment practices. (p. 5) |
| 3. U.S. monitoring of telemetry data on Soviet MIRV testing impeded. | Soviet encoding of test telemetry has not been considered to have impeded verification of SALT compliance. (p. 10) |

*SALT ONE: Compliance, Selected Documents No. 7, Department of State, February 1978. Several additional items bearing on alleged Soviet noncompliance, as well as the Soviet claims of U.S. noncompliance, have not been included in this summary.

| Allegations | Document #7 Response |
|---|---|
| 4. Launch control facilities convertible into additional missile silos. | These special-purpose silos detected under construction in 1973 were discussed with Soviets for several years, and in early 1977 after review of intelligence, U.S. closed the issue on the basis that the silos are used for launch control purposes, as claimed by the Soviets. (p. 4) |
| 5. Possible testing of SA-5 air defense radar in ABM mode. | U.S. observation in 1973-74 indicated Soviets were using an SA-5 radar to track strategic ballistic missiles. The issue was raised in the SCC, where the Soviets asserted that no violation was involved since range safety use of non-ABM radar was permissible. However, the protested SA-5 radar activity ceased soon afterwards. (pp. 5-6) |
| 6. Installation of a Soviet ABM radar on the Kamchatka peninsula. | An ABM radar was installed in the impact area of the Soviet ICBM test range on Kamchatka in October 1975. After considerable discussion of the ambiguous question whether Kamchatka was an ABM test range at the time of the ABM Treaty (and hence permissible), it was decided to regard it as such, but to insure that establishment of any additional ABM test range is jointly agreed beforehand. (p. 6) |
| 7. Soviet failure to dismantle replaced ICBM launchers on time. | It became apparent to U.S. by early 1976 that the Soviets would not meet on time the requirements for ICBM dismantling worked out in the SCC in connection with putting new SLBMs |

Allegations                    Document #7 Response

to sea. The Soviets acknowledged the discrepancy, and took further deactivation steps that eventually satisfied the essential substantive requirements. (p. 7)

*Appendix E*

# The Shape of the Salt II Agreement

The main features of the SALT II agreement, as it reportedly stood in early 1979 with a few issues still unresolved, are given here, along with brief comment on their evolution. The agreement, numbering by then some sixty pages, followed the "three-tier" concept—Treaty, Protocol, Statement of Principles.

## THE TREATY

**Duration:** From ratification through 1985

The concept for a nonpermanent treaty goes back to the proposed alternative to a permanent offensive arms treaty that was agreed upon at Moscow in July 1974. The idea was then codified in the November 1974 Vladivostok pact. There was no particular contention over the duration of a prospective SALT II accord after mid-1974.

**Aggregate total:** 2250 (ICBM, SLBM, heavy bomber, with partial freedom to mix, as limited by subceilings)*

The aggregate figure represents a cut of 150 from the Vladivostok ceiling of 2400, as proposed by the USSR, rather than the cut of 240

---

*Also possibly included in the aggregate total would be any launchers for air-to-surface ballistic missiles (ASBM) with a range greater than 600 kilometers. This item and a number of other Appendix E details not previously mentioned in the text have been drawn from an analysis of the SALT II accord by Paul H. Nitze, *Current SALT II Negotiating Posture*, Arlington, Va., January 15, 1979. (Mimeograph) The cited item is from page 1 of that document.

proposed by the U.S. The agreed total is substantially higher than the 1800-2000 aggregate in the Carter March 1977 "comprehensive" package. It will require an actual force reduction on the order of 270 for the USSR, but none for the U.S. The figure of 2250 was finally agreed upon some time in spring 1978.

### Reduction deadlines:   (Not resolved)
There was continuing controversy over this issue from the time the three-tier approach was settled upon in the May-September 1977 period. It was one of the several items still in disagreement after the October 1978 Moscow meeting. (For relevant details, see page 235.)

### Total MIRV subceiling: 1320 (MIRVed ICBM, SLBM, and ALCM-carrying bombers)
This figure, essentially stemming from the 1974 Vladivostok transaction, remained higher than the 1000 to 1200 proposed in the March 1977 Carter package, and also higher than the several ceilings proposed by the U.S. side in pre-Vladivostok SALT II negotiations in 1973-74. These varied from 1000 for each side to 1050 for the U.S. and 750 for the USSR. The inclusion of ALCM-equipped bombers in the 1320 MIRV sublimit, agreed in the fall of 1977, was a departure from the original U.S. position of early 1975 that ALCMs should not be subject to a SALT regime.

### MIRVed ICBM subceiling: 820
This was a new limitation category. It remained substantially higher than the 550 of the U.S. March 1977 package, which first proposed an ICBM-only sublimit. The 820 figure was a compromise between 800 proposed by the U.S. and 850 by the USSR. It was agreed in the spring of 1978. Contention was sharp on this issue, because the Soviet counterforce threat to Minuteman was largely concentrated in this category. Soviet acceptance of any sub-limit was considered a concession, although the 820 figure may have been high enough to preserve a Soviet high-confidence counterforce capability.

### "Heavy" ICBM subceiling: 308
This ceiling affected only the USSR, since the U.S. had no missiles in the "Modern Large Ballistic Missile" (MLBM), or "heavy," category. The origin of the ceiling figure for a "heavy" ICBM subcategory goes back to the SALT I Interim Agreement of 1972, at which time a sublimit of 313 reflected the estimated size of the

then-programmed Soviet SS-9 force.* The U.S. attempt in March 1977 to reduce the heavy ICBM ceiling to 150 aroused strong Soviet reaction. U.S. agreement in September 1977 to leave the SALT I "heavy" ceiling intact to cover the Soviet SS-18 program was said to be a major concession facilitating movement toward a SALT II accord.

**Definition of "heavy" ICBM borderline:** ICBMs exceeding the volume of the SS-19 (understood to be 100 cubic meters)—or alternatively, its useful payload—to be counted as "heavy"

Defining the borderline for a "heavy" missile was resisted by the USSR throughout SALT I and most of SALT II. The U.S. finally won out on this issue as a matter of principle in early 1978, but the SS-19 volume of about 100 cubic meters was substantially greater than the 70 cubic meters of the SS-11, which the U.S. had previously defined unilaterally as the borderline.

**Limit on number of RVs per MIRVed missile:** (Not resolved)

The U.S. had introduced this item in order to constrain the number of reentry vehicles the Soviets might install on their much larger missiles. Part of the hang-up, however, came from the counter-maneuver of the Soviet side to restrict the number of RVs the U.S. might install on a "new missile" (meaning the MX) to six, rather than the ten proposed by the U.S., on the grounds that the U.S. did not have any "heavy" missiles, and therefore had no entitlement to ten RVs, the top number proposed for the Soviet SS-18 "heavy" ICBM. Both sides apparently agreed that with regard to SLBMs, the maximum allowance would be fourteen RVs per missile. (For additional detail, see p. 234.)

**"New-type" missile ban:** Test and deployment of "new types" of ICBMs prohibited during Treaty period, with exception of one new missile (single RV or MIRV) per side

The comprehensive March 1977 U.S. proposal had called for a sweeping ban on new missiles and on modification of existing ones, both of which the Soviets rejected. Following agreement on the three-tier SALT II concept in May and September 1977, this question continued to elude resolution for many months. The first solution adopted sometime in the summer of 1978 allowed the U.S.

---

*The SALT II figure of 308 corresponds to the Soviet MLBM force level as it stood in 1977-78. The number would come to 326, according to the Nitze analysis (pp. 1-2) cited above, if 18 MLBM launchers at the Soviet test range also were counted.

to flight test one new type of land-based ballistic missile, the MX, and the Soviets to test one with a single RV during the Protocol period. This arrangement answered essentially to the U.S. position. (See page 228.) Subsequently, one change was made, shifting the time period of the provision from the Protocol to the Treaty.* It is not known at whose initiative this change was made. SLBMs were not brought under the new-type missile ban.

Limited modifications of existing ICBMs were allowed, but some restrictions also were laid down, including no testing of an ICBM with more RVs than previously installed. Also a part of the "new-type" restrictions in the SALT II accord were those on throwweight of new systems, listed below.

**Throwweight limit:** No deployment of a new system with a greater payload than the SS-18

This was a first. What throwweight was specified as that of the SS-18 was not made known, but unofficial estimates had put it at from 15,000-18,000 lbs. The throwweight issue had been contentious throughout SALT I and most of SALT II, with the USSR strenuously resisting any throwweight limits in principle or in actuality. Soviet acceptance of the SS-18 throwweight limit sometime in the first half of 1978 was, therefore, considered a concession, although as a practical matter, the SS-18 payload probably was high enough already to accommodate foreseeable Soviet needs.

**ICBM storage and reload restrictions:** Storage of "excess" missiles at launch sites banned as well as testing and deployment of rapid reload systems for ICBM launchers

The purpose of this provision, desired by the U.S., was to constrain the rapid reloading of ICBM silos, possible when using "cold-launch" techniques. Exactly when this restriction was introduced in the negotiations, and how contentious an issue it may have been, had not been indicated up to late 1978.

**Verification by national technical means (NTM):** Reaffirmation of SALT I undertaking (Article V of Interim Agreement), to use and not interfere with NTM surveillance for monitoring SALT compliance

Agreement on the principle of using unilateral NTM to monitor SALT compliance, and undertaking not to interfere with the other party's NTM, were part of the SALT I accords of 1972, and were perpetuated in the SALT II agreement. However, some aspects of

*Nitze, *Current SALT II Negotiating Posture*, p. 2.

verification, including the obstacle presented by Soviet encryption of missile-test telemetry, remained under contention in late 1978. (See Chapter 11, note 100.) The Soviets also reportedly respected U.S. suggestions that cooperative measures would be needed, in addition to unilateral NTM, to verify some aspects of a SALT II agreement.

**MIRV verification:**  Any type of missile ever tested with MIRV and any type of launcher that has ever contained a MIRV-tested missile to be counted in the MIRV quota when deployed

There was Soviet resistance to this U.S.-proposed concept in the first six months or so after Vladivostok, but at Helsinki in July 1975 during a Ford-Brezhnev discussion Soviet assent was given in principle. Final details, however, apparently were not agreed until the last quarter of 1977.

**Freeze on existing fixed ICBM launchers:** The relocation of such launchers, or the start of additional ones, to be banned

The antecedents of this provision were to be found in the March 1977 American proposals, which the Soviets had rejected. (See p. 221.) It appears that this measure was one of several accepted by the Soviets some time in late 1977.

**ALCM testing and deployment:** Permissible for ALCMs not exceeding 2500-km range, carried by heavy bomber platforms

Issues relating to air-launched cruise missiles, like other types of small and accurate, or "reborn," cruise missiles developed by the U.S., did not arise in SALT until after Vladivostok, but from early 1975 became among the most contentious issues in the negotiations. On the issue of permissible ALCM range, Soviet assent to the 2500-km figure proposed by the U.S. (as compared with a January 1976 Soviet proposal of about 1000 km) supposedly came with the first group of reciprocal concessions marking the September 1977 "breakthrough." (See p. 226.)

Other items of contention over ALCMs included: (1) whether they were to be restricted to heavy bombers, or could also be carried by other aircraft, such as wide-body transports, with the U.S. taking the latter position and offering to differentiate nonbombers for verification purposes;* (2) how to devise a formula compatible with range limitations to allow for maneuver on the way to target; and (3) how

---

*According to the Nitze analysis (p. 3), agreement had been reached by October 1978 that ALCMs could be carried on transport aircraft or non-heavy bombers, but the aircraft would then be counted as heavy bombers within both the aggregate SALT II total and the MIRV subceiling if equipped with armed ALCMs of more than 600-km range.

many ALCMs permitted per aircraft platform, and what counting method to be used to determine a MIRV equivalent. The last item is treated below. Incidentally, if removal of the ALCM range restriction in exchange for tightening GLCM-SLCM curbs (see pp. 233-34) were to be accepted, ALCMs of any range could be utilized under this provision.

**Number of ALCMs per aircraft platform:** (Not resolved)
This issue found the Soviets attempting to minimize the number of ALCMs to be carried by any one bomber and to charge the highest price in terms of MIRV equivalents. The U.S., naturally, argued the other way around. Although existing U.S. bombers were not likely to be configured for more than twenty ALCMs, the U.S. wished to retain the option to deploy up to thirty-five or more, possibly using wide-body transports, and to have the flexibility of varying the loads carried. The Soviets argued for no more than twenty ALCMs per bomber, or if more, that the "cost" of each multiple of twenty ALCMs be one MIRVed vehicle. (See pages 233-34.)

**Common data base:** Agreed by both sides to exchange data on constrained systems and to furnish advance notice of certain launches
Throughout SALT I and most of SALT II the Soviets resisted U.S. efforts to establish an exchange of relevant information on strategic forces in SALT, though apparently the Soviets were slightly more forthcoming in the SCC, which began to operate in 1973. With the prospect of reductions in a SALT II agreement, an agreed data base, from which a determination could be made that reductions had taken place, became essential. The Soviets finally agreed to an exchange of information to establish a common data base for a SALT II treaty sometime in late 1977, although they continued to deny some categories of information that could be considered relevant to SALT.

**Duties of SCC:** Provisions included for the role of the joint Standing Consultative Commission in connection with implementation of the SALT II Treaty
In SALT I, the general functions of the SCC in implementing the agreement and taking up questions concerning its observance were broadly sketched, although the SCC had not yet been set up. In the 1978 accords, against the background of some five years of SCC experience, the provisions outlining the duties of the SCC to implement the considerably more complicated three-tier agreement reportedly have been amplified accordingly.

Definitions of constrained systems

Soviet reluctance in SALT I to adopt precise definitions for some strategic systems, such as "heavy" missiles, led to unilateral declarations by the U.S. side and considerable subsequent argument. The decision to adopt jointly agreed definitions in the SALT II accord for a "heavy" missile, a "new type" missile, and so on, came only after long haggling and was apparently reached sometime in the first half of 1978.

Noncircumvention: Agreement by both parties not to take actions through third countries that could weaken the SALT II accord

A noncircumvention provision was part of the ABM Treaty (Article IX), though not of the Interim Agreement of 1972. Behind the 1972 circumvention provision there was an ongoing difference of approach, with the Soviets trying to impose more specificity upon nontransfer of weapons and know-how to NATO than the U.S. cared to accept. The same pattern continued during the SALT II negotiations, with the cruise missile technology issue exacerbating it further. The formula eventually agreed upon sometime before mid-1978 involved some U.S. concession, but remained ambiguous enough to be acceptable to NATO. It would not be surprising, however, if conflicting Soviet and American interpretations were to arise with regard to the permissible limits of weapons and technology transfer to third parties.

## THE PROTOCOL

Duration: 3 years

What the duration of the Protocol period should be was in dispute from May 1977 until the fall of 1978. The U.S. initially proposed and held out for the Protocol period to expire December 31, 1980, while the Soviets insisted on three years after ratification of the SALT II accord. Whether full agreement had been reached on when the period should start was not known in late 1978.

Cruise missiles (GLCM and SLCM): Ban during Protocol period on deployment of land- or sea-based cruise missiles of more than 600-km range, but testing to be permitted up to 2500 km

When issues concerning cruise missiles arose in the wake of Vladivostok, the Soviets initially argued that all types of cruise missiles of more than 600-km range should be banned (see page 202), but by January 1976 the Soviets began to change their position, acceding to ALCMs of more than 600 km. However, throughout the rest of SALT II, the Soviets held the line on banning deployment of

GLCMs and SLCMs. The compromise provision listed here was reached in late 1977 or early 1978 (see page 227). It was, however, cast into question by Gromyko's proposal in September 1978 (see page 232) to switch the provision to the longer Treaty period in exchange for removal of ALCM range restrictions.* In addition to this problem, another unresolved aspect of the GLCM-SLCM issue reportedly was whether the deployment ban should apply to both conventional and nuclear-armed versions of these missiles (the Soviet position), or only to nuclear-armed ones (the U.S. position).**

**ALCM range restriction:** Test and deployment of ALCM of more than 2500-km range banned during Protocol period

As already indicated, the Treaty provisions on ALCM allowed for testing and deployment of heavy bomber-launched ALCMs up to 2500 km. The restriction listed here on ALCMs of greater range had been sought by the Russians, but placing it in the Protocol also answered to the U.S. contention that the ultimate range of ALCMs, along with some other cruise missile issues, should be left an open question after expiration of the Protocol. Were the Soviet proposal mentioned under the GLCM-SLCM item above to be accepted, this ALCM range restriction would, of course, be dropped.

**Mobile ICBM restrictions:** Deployment, but not testing, banned during Protocol period

American opposition to mobile ICBMs had continued throughout SALT I, but diminished during the first couple of years of SALT II, and at Vladivostok was withdrawn. Although the U.S. March 1977 package again proposed a mobile ICBM ban, this apparently was not pushed in subsequent negotiations as pressure to preserve a mobile basing option for MX made itself felt.

The U.S. side, however, also faced the problem of having deployment restrictions placed upon mobile versions of the Soviet SS-16 ICBM, because of its similarity to the SS-20 IRBM. The Soviets apparently argued that there was nothing to the U.S. concern that an ICBM "breakout" might be achieved by adding a third-stage and converting SS-20s into SS-16s. Nevertheless, under this provision the Soviets apparently undertook not to deploy the SS-16 during the Protocol period.

With regard to permissible testing of mobile ICBM launchers, this

---

*It was not clear at the time of writing whether the original compromise formula or the Soviet revision—to which the U.S. objected—would be incorporated in the final SALT II agreement.

**See Nitze, *Current SALT II Negotiating Posture*, pp. 1, 5.

Protocol item appears to have been accompanied by a proviso that no test firing of missiles from such launchers would be allowed. In addition to its treatment of mobile ICBMs, the Protocol also reportedly dealt with air-to-surface ballistic missiles in somewhat similar terms, prohibiting deployment but permitting a certain amount of testing.

**Backfire bomber restrictions:** (Not resolved)
This issue first emerged as a major obstacle to a SALT II agreement after Vladivostok, when the U.S. took the position that Backfire had intercontinental capabilities and must therefore be counted in the SALT aggregate total, while the Soviets insisted that it was only a medium bomber and should not be counted. Between late 1975 and January 1976, the U.S. dropped its insistence on counting Backfire, provided the USSR would give various assurances that the bomber would not be used strategically against the U.S. The Soviets apparently declined to give such assurances in writing, which became a major sticking point in 1978. Unresolved aspects of the Backfire question also included production-rate constraints. Although the Soviets had agreed in late 1977 to keep Backfire production at the "current" rate, they declined to confirm what that rate was. (For further detail on the Backfire issue,* see pages 201, 212-14, 228-29, 234-35.)

## THE STATEMENT OF PRINCIPLES

**Future negotiations:** SALT III to commence immediately after conclusion of a SALT II agreement

**Subject matter on agenda:** Not resolved, beyond a proposed formula that would permit either side to bring up any pertinent topic it might wish to discuss
The proposed formula in the Statement of Principles for the SALT III agenda would essentially postpone several basic questions that had been at issue until those negotiations commence. Among them were whether priority should go to trying to negotiate further reductions and qualitative restrictions, as urged by the U.S., or to placing limitations on forward-based systems (FBS), as proposed by the USSR; and whether civil and air defense systems should be regarded as proper subjects for strategic arms limitation agreements,

---

*Although the Backfire issue is listed here under the Protocol section of the SALT II agreement, if it were to be settled by some sort of informal Soviet declaration outside the contractual forms of the agreement, the settlement would not necessarily appear under the Protocol.

as argued by the U.S., or not considered germane, as seen by the USSR. Also left at issue was whether cooperative measures to supplement national technical means of verification should be considered in SALT III.

# Notes

NOTES TO CHAPTER 1
THE SALT I PHASE

1. *Documents on Disarmament 1964*, United States Arms Control and Disarmament Agency, Publication 27, October 1965, p. 8.

2. Ibid., pp. 383-84.

3. See, for example, Alton Frye, "U.S. Decision Making for SALT," in Mason Willrich and John B. Rhinelander, eds., *SALT: The Moscow Agreements and Beyond* (New York: The Free Press, 1974), pp. 72-74; and Ted Greenwood, *Making the MIRV: A Study of Defense Decision Making* (Cambridge: Ballinger Publishing Company, 1975), pp. 108-9.

4. For an account of McNamara's role in the 1967 ABM moratorium proposal, see Morton H. Halperin, "The Decision to Deploy the ABM: Bureaucratic and Domestic Politics in the Johnson Administration," *World Politics*, Vol. 25, October 1972, pp. 83-88. See also John Newhouse, *Cold Dawn: The Story of SALT* (New York: Holt, Rinehart and Winston, 1973), pp. 84-89.

5. Chalmers M. Roberts, *The Nuclear Years: The Arms Race and Arms Control, 1945-70* (New York: Praeger Publishers, 1970), pp. 84-87.

6. Lyndon Baines Johnson, *The Vantage Point: Perspectives of the Presidency 1963-1969* (New York: Holt, Rinehart and Winston, 1971), pp. 480-85.

7. Ibid. For a discussion of various signs that the American ABM freeze proposal may have touched off an ABM policy debate within the Soviet leadership, see Thomas W. Wolfe, *Soviet Power and Europe: 1945-1970* (Baltimore: The Johns Hopkins Press, 1970), pp. 269-271.

8. Roberts, *The Nuclear Years*, pp. 84-85.

9. Halperin, in *World Politics*, October 1972, p. 76. See also Newhouse, *Cold Dawn*, p. 84.

10. See McNamara speech in San Francisco, *New York Times*, September

18, 1967. For a subsequent elucidation by McNamara of the rationale behind deployment of the "relatively light" and "Chinese-oriented" Sentinel system, see his interview with *Life* magazine, September 29, 1967, pp. 28a, b, and c. See also Halperin, in *World Politics*, October 1972, pp. 86-88.

11. See Greenwood, *Making the MIRV*, pp. 115,128. See also Newhouse, *Cold Dawn*, p. 101. The first U.S. MIRV tests took place August 16, 1968.

12. Johnson, *The Vantage Point*, p. 485.

13. Ibid.

14. *Pravda*, June 28, 1968. Among indications that the Soviet decision had been arrived at over considerable opposition were references in Gromyko's speech to unnamed internal critics of entering the arms talks, identified by him as "good-for-nothing theoreticians who try to tell us . . . that disarmament is an illusion." For further discussion of evidence suggesting internal Soviet controversy over the strategic arms talk issue, see Testimony of Dr. Thomas W. Wolfe, in *The Limitation of Strategic Arms, Hearings*, before the Subcommittee on Strategic Arms Limitation Talks, Committee on Armed Services, Senate, 91st Cong., 2d session, Part 2, May 20, 1970, pp. 63-64.

15. Johnson, *The Vantage Point*, p. 487.

16. Ibid., pp. 489-90.

17. Newhouse, *Cold Dawn*, p. 141. See also Roberts, *The Nuclear Years*, p. 99.

18. Newhouse, *Cold Dawn*, pp. 3-5.

19. See, for example, the earlier version of the present study: Thomas W. Wolfe, *The SALT Experience: Its Impact on U.S. and Soviet Strategic Policy and Decisionmaking*, The Rand Corporation, R-1686-PR, Santa Monica, September 1975, pp. v-viii, 219-24.

20. One of the first U.S. officials to suggest publicly in October 1967 that the United States might verify a strategic arms agreement by "our own unilateral capability" was Paul Warnke, then an assistant secretary of defense, who a decade later became director of the Arms Control and Disarmament Agency and the chief U.S. SALT negotiator. See Newhouse, *Cold Dawn*, p. 99. See also Frye, in *SALT: The Moscow Agreements and Beyond*, pp. 70-71; Herbert Scoville, Jr., "A Leap Forward in Verification," ibid., pp. 160-67; Greenwood, *Making the MIRV*, p. 111.

21. The round of intensive U.S. planning for SALT in the summer of 1968, when it had appeared that the opening of talks with the Soviet Union was imminent, produced a package of proposals constructed primarily around unilateral verification. Concurrence of the Joint Chiefs of Staff in this package marked the first time that the JCS had assented to a major arms control proposal not embodying on-site inspection. See Frye, in *SALT: The Moscow Agreements and Beyond*, p. 77.

22. For a succinct account of the Soviet strategic force buildup of the 1960s, see Wolfe, *Soviet Power and Europe*, pp. 432-41. See also Chapter 6, pp. 116-27.

23. Greenwood, *Making the MIRV*, p. 59. See also Alain C. Enthoven and K. Wayne Smith, *How Much Is Enough? Shaping the Defense Program, 1961-1969* (New York: Harper & Row, Publishers, 1971), p. 208.

24. Greenwood, *Making the MIRV*, p. 74; Newhouse, *Cold Dawn*, pp. 75-77.

25. William W. Kaufmann, *The McNamara Strategy*, (New York: Harper & Row Publishers, 1964), pp. 50-55, 148-52; Enthoven and Smith, *How Much Is Enough?*, pp. 174-75.

26. McNamara's Ann Arbor speech of June 16, 1962, may be found in *Vital Speeches of the Day*, August 1, 1962, pp. 626-29. See also Kaufman, *The McNamara Strategy*, pp. 114-17.

27. Greenwood, *Making the MIRV*, pp. 68-69.

28. Enthoven and Smith, *How Much Is Enough?*, p. 176; Robert S. McNamara, *The Essence of Security* (New York: Harper & Row Publishers, 1968), pp. 59-67. See also *Statement of Secretary of Defense Robert S. McNamara Before the Senate Armed Services Committee on the FY 1969-73 Defense Program and 1969 Defense Budget*, January 22, 1968, p. 53. Pages 41-76 of this statement, incidentally, constitute a concise summary of the evolution of McNamara's strategic thinking.

29. Enthoven and Smith, *How Much Is Enough?*, pp. 174-78.

30. See Mason Willrich, "SALT I: An Appraisal," in *SALT: The Moscow Agreements and Beyond*, pp. 263-64.

31. See Chapter 5, pp. 108-13.

32. See Chapter 1, pp. 1-2.

33. As noted by Frye (*SALT: The Moscow Agreements and Beyond*, pp. 74-76), Clark Clifford, McNamara's successor as secretary of defense, seems to have felt that American ABM and MIRV programs would heighten Soviet interest in prompt and productive negotiations, a view shared by many other officials in the Johnson administration. Later, some of the American participants in SALT I were to note that their Soviet counterparts showed concern about the U.S. lead in MIRV and ABM technologies, and that this was apparently among the Soviet reasons for wanting an ABM treaty. See Charles J. V. Murphy, "What We Gave Away in the Moscow Arms Agreements," *Fortune*, September 1972, p. 10.

Some published Soviet commentary also suggested that Soviet interest in an ABM treaty may have been heightened by concern that the U.S. might seek to exploit its technological advantage in ABM, as when a Soviet writer warned that Safeguard could give American strategists an "illusion of invulnerability" that would encourage them to place more reliance on force. See M.V. Belousov, "Technical Aspects of the Safeguard System," *SShA: Ekonomika, Politika, Ideologiia*, no. 5, Moscow, 1970, p. 123.

34. Newhouse, *Cold Dawn*, pp. 155-58; Roberts, *The Nuclear Years*, pp. 100-103.

35. For the most detailed account of the way the MIRV program developed, including its relation to SALT, see Greenwood, *Making the MIRV*, especially pp. 108-38. See also Herbert F. York, "Multiple-Warhead Missiles," *Scientific American*, November 1973, pp. 20-27; Newhouse, *Cold Dawn*, pp. 166-82; Frye, in *SALT: The Moscow Agreements and Beyond*, pp. 82-83.

36. On a conjectural note, it is also worth observing that the long Soviet delay in agreeing to start SALT talks might have been related in part to a concern that the United States would propose an immediate ban on further

MIRV tests before the Soviet Union had a chance to initiate its own test program, thus leaving the United States a monopoly in this particular strategic technology. See Roberts, *The Nuclear Years*, p. 105. For an informed discussion of the handling of the MIRV question in the SALT I negotiations, see Joseph Kruzel, "SALT II: The Search for a Follow-On Agreement," *Orbis*, Vol. 17, Summer 1973, pp. 340-43.

37. Raymond L. Garthoff, "Negotiating with the Russians: Some Lessons from SALT," *International Security* 1, no. 4 (Spring 1977):5. Garthoff, at the present writing U.S. ambassador to Bulgaria, was executive secretary of the U.S. SALT delegation throughout SALT I. His is one of the few available accounts by an immediate participant in SALT I negotiations. A book by Ambassador Gerard C. Smith, head of the SALT I delegation, had not yet been published at this writing.

38. Newhouse, *Cold Dawn*, p. 167.

39. In addition to the ABM Treaty, the Interim Agreement and the Basic Principles of Relations signed by President Nixon and Secretary Brezhnev at the May 1972 summit in Moscow, the SALT I negotiations had earlier in September 1971 produced two spin-off accords, the Accident Measures and revised Hotline Agreements. All of these documents except the Basic Principles of Relations may be found in *Arms Control and Disarmament Agreements*, 1977 edition, U.S. Arms Control and Disarmament Agency, Washington, D.C., June 1977. The Basic Principles of Relations may be found in *Department of State Bulletin*, Vol. 66, June 26, 1972, pp. 898-99.

40. Garthoff, in *International Security*, Spring 1977, pp. 5-6. See also Garthoff's "Negotiating SALT," *The Wilson Quarterly*, Vol. 1, Autumn 1977, pp. 81-82, which covers essentially the same ground.

41. Ibid. See also statement of Dr. William R. Van Cleave, in *International Negotiations, Hearings*, before the Subcommittee on National Security and International Operations, Committee on Government Operations, Senate, 92d Cong., 2d session, Part 7, July 25, 1972, pp. 201-3.

42. See Newhouse, *Cold Dawn*, pp. 55-56.

43. Ibid., pp. 174-76. See also Chalmers M. Roberts, "The Road to Moscow," in *SALT: The Moscow Agreements and Beyond*, pp. 27-28. The forward-based systems as defined by the Soviets would take in both nuclear-armed missiles and aircraft whose geographic deployment in either Europe or Asia (and peripheral waters) would enable them to reach Soviet territory. However, in terms of the SALT I dialogue, the issue came to turn mainly on aircraft deployed in the European area, mostly dual-purpose types capable of delivering either conventional or nuclear weapons. The aircraft included F-4s and F-111s based, respectively, on the European continent and in England, and A-4s, A-6s, and A-7s operating from carriers in the Mediterranean. In all, from 600 to 1000 tactical aircraft were involved.

44. See Chapter 5, pp. 103-6.

45. Newhouse, *Cold Dawn*, pp. 177-91; Garthoff, in *International Security*, Spring 1977, pp. 7, 10-11.

46. Roberts, in *SALT: The Moscow Agreements and Beyond*, p. 28; Frye, in ibid., pp. 85-86.

47. The August 4, 1970, U.S. Proposal called for a total of 1900 strategic missiles and bombers for each side, with a sub-limit of 250 on "heavy" missiles. It would have prohibited silo modification, but allowed conversion from land-based to sea-based missiles. The ABM alternatives offered were either defense of the national command authority (NCA), or a full ban on ABM deployment. The August 4 proposal also dropped earlier U.S. alternatives for restrictions on MIRV testing and deployment. See Newhouse, *Cold Dawn*, pp. 186-89; Garthoff, in *International Security*, Spring 1977, p. 7.

48. Newhouse, *Cold Dawn*, p. 195; Roberts, in *SALT: The Moscow Agreements and Beyond*, p. 28.

49. See Frye, in *SALT: The Moscow Agreements and Beyond*, p. 85.

50. During the impasse period, Moscow launched a press campaign defending itself against what it termed a Western propaganda effort to blame Soviet "intractability" for blocking agreement in SALT, and accusing the U.S. in turn of pursuing policies with respect to ABM, MIRV, and FBS that were aimed at "one-sided military advantages" for the United States. See, for example, V. Shestov, "What Is Hidden Behind the Propaganda Screen?" *Pravda*, February 3, 1971; Bernard Gwertzman, "Soviet Assails U.S. Stand Against Limited ABM Pact," *New York Times*, February 7, 1971.

51. Newhouse, *Cold Dawn*, p. 203.

52. President Nixon initiated a private exchange of letters on breaking the SALT impasse with Kosygin, but after the Soviet 24th Party Congress in April 1971, when the locus of authority in the Kremlin apparently shifted to Brezhnev, the exchange was conducted between Nixon and Brezhnev. See Garthoff, in *International Security*, Spring 1977, pp. 8-9. See also Chapter 4, pp. 80-81.

53. Ibid., p. 7.

54. The text of the May 20, 1971, joint announcement may be found in *U.S. Foreign Policy for the 1970s: The Emerging Structure of Peace*, A Report to the Congress by Richard M. Nixon, President of the United States, February 9, 1972, p. 174.

55. Newhouse, *Cold Dawn*, p. 221. One might also observe that the introduction of triangular politics could have sensitized both sides in SALT to China's potential as a future balance between the two superpowers. The effect of this, in turn, could have been to persuade both the USSR and the United States that the eventual outcome of SALT should not result in paring the superpowers down to such an extent that China would automatically gain a great deal of ground on both of them.

56. The ABM deployment differences were eventually narrowed down to whether a country could have two ABM defense complexes to protect ICBM fields, or one ABM defense of an ICBM field and one of the national capital (NCA), and what the necessary distances apart should be to preclude the establishment of an area defense capability. The one-and-one pattern was ultimately chosen. However, a large number of alternative deployment proposals had been broached and discarded along the road to ultimate agreement. They ranged from zero deployment or NCA defense only, to combinations of three or four ICBM field defenses to one NCA defense, with the U.S. side having favored

a higher ratio of ICBM-site defense than the Russians—partly because the United States by early 1972 had two Safeguard ICBM-site defense projects under way, at Grand Forks and Malmstrom, whereas the Russians had only the Galosh deployment around Moscow. See Frye, in *SALT: The Moscow Agreements and Beyond*, pp. 88-90.

57. Garthoff, in *International Security*, Spring 1977, p. 15.

58. Roberts, in *SALT: The Moscow Agreements and Beyond*, pp. 28-29.

59. Acceptance of the principle of an ICBM freeze at the existing differential levels meant giving up the basic U.S. position calling for equal aggregates. The groundwork for this element of the Interim Agreement was initially carried out through the back channel. See Newhouse, *Cold Dawn*, p. 218.

60. The duration of five years for the Interim Agreement was not settled until Kissinger's talks with Brezhnev in Moscow in April 1972. Previously, the Soviets had proposed up to two years, and on the U.S. side there was internal division over the time span. See Newhouse, *Cold Dawn*, p. 242.

61. The U.S. position on including SLBMs evolved only gradually after having been left open in the back-channel understandings that led to the May 20, 1971, joint announcement. See Garthoff, in *International Security*, Spring 1977, p. 9.

62. Ibid., p. 15.

63. Ibid., pp. 9, 15.

64. Newhouse, *Cold Dawn*, pp. 243-45.

65. As noted by Newhouse, ibid., p. 177, all of the options for substantive positions on the U.S. side in SALT I had been shaped to constrain the threat of heavy land-based Soviet missiles; one way of doing so was to encourage the Soviets to substitute smaller and less accurate sea-based missiles for large land-based ICBMs like the SS-9—hence, the inclusion in all of the U.S. options of "one-way freedom to mix"—from land- to sea-based missiles.

66. Ibid., pp. 238, 249-60. See also the account of the summit negotiations in Moscow by Dr. Kissinger in his May 26, 1972, press conference, and a later account of July 18, 1972, by Gerard Smith, head of the U.S. SALT delegation. These may be found in *Military Implications of the Treaty on the Limitation of Anti-Ballistic Missile Systems and the Interim Agreement on Limitation of Strategic Offensive Arms, Hearing*, before the Committee on Armed Services, Senate, 92d Cong., 2d session, 1972, pp. 105-13, and 362-66, respectively. (Hereafter cited as *Military Implications of the ABM Treaty and the Interim Agreement.*)

67. Garthoff, in *International Security*, Spring 1977, pp. 9, 15. In his memoirs, President Nixon gives an account of the May 1972 summit that indicates there was difficult bargaining with the Russians during the five-day Moscow visit, but he does not concede that the United States paid an excessive price for agreement. Rather, the account suggests the opposite, stating that near the end of the summit, after a special Politburo meeting, the Russians "agreed to accept our final position." See *RN: The Memoirs of Richard Nixon* (New York: Grosset & Dunlap, 1978), pp. 609-16.

68. See Newhouse, *Cold Dawn*, p. 201; William Beecher, "Pentagon Says the Soviet May Have Two New ICBMs," *New York Times*, May 27, 1971. The first disclosure that construction of new missile silos had been detected in the Soviet

Union was made by Senator Henry M. Jackson in a television program on March 7, 1971. Construction of the silos, which later turned out to have been designed for some of the new fourth-generation Soviet missiles which had not yet been tested, apparently began toward the end of 1970. Construction of the silos was halted around mid-1971, and later carried to completion after the May 1972 SALT accords, which permitted the completion of missile launchers under construction at the time of signing. See further discussion of the subject in Chapter 6, pp. 119-20.

69. See Newhouse, *Cold Dawn*, p. 238.

70. In the protocol to the Interim Agreement, the interpretative language stating that the permissible increase in silo size was not to exceed "10-15 percent of the present dimensions" left it ambiguous whether this was to apply to the combined effect on volume of depth and diameter, or to one or the other separately. In the first instance, a 15 percent increase would amount to about 50 percent greater volume; in the separate cases volume increase would be from 15 to 30 percent. This ambiguity, together with lack of a mutually agreed definition that would establish a dividing line between future "heavy" missiles and nonheavy ones, left much room for later disputation as to whether such new Soviet ICBMs as the SS-17 and SS-19, with payloads perhaps three to four times greater than the SS-11 they were replacing, represented in fact a circumvention of the supposed sublimit on heavy missiles. For the pertinent protocol passages, see *Arms Control and Disarmament Agreements*, pp. 142-43.

71. According to the unilateral U.S. definition, "the United States would consider any ICBM having a volume significantly greater than that of the largest light ICBM now operational on either side to be a heavy ICBM." In the Soviet case, the "largest light" ICBM indicated was the SS-11. The United States had also proposed that seventy cubic meters be the dividing line, but this like other definitions was rejected by the Soviets as unnecessary. See testimony by Ambassador Gerard Smith, in *Military Implications of the ABM Treaty and the Interim Agreement*, pp. 363-64.

72. No number for the heavy missile sublimit was ever specified, but the language of Articles I and II of the Interim Agreement amounted to saying that the "heavy" missile ceiling for the Soviet Union would be the existing 288 SS-9 launchers, plus approximately 25 new silos under construction in SS-9 fields, for a total of 313. These figures were estimates by the U.S. side, since the Soviets did not furnish figures for their own ICBM forces.

73. See *Arms Control and Disarmament Agreements*, p. 140.

74. Ibid., p. 145.

75. Ibid., pp. 148-50. In the U.S. case, the eventual ABM deployment outcome was a zero-level of ABM, since the Safeguard installations started at the Malmstrom and Grand Forks ICBM complexes were dismantled in the mid-1970s, and no decision was made to provide ABM protection of the national capital. Up to the present writing, the Soviet Union had kept the Galosh ABM system deployed around Moscow. Rather curiously, this "asymmetrical" outcome of the treaty is rarely noted in the literature.

76. Ibid., pp. 132-35, 141-46. For discussion of how constraints on such exotic devices as lasers, charged particles, and electromagnetic waves were introduced into the ABM Treaty, see Newhouse, *Cold Dawn*, pp. 230-32, 237.

77. The pertinent articles were XII and XIII of the ABM Treaty, and V and VI of the Interim Agreement. See *Arms Control and Disarmament Agreements*, pp. 134, 139. See also Scoville, in *SALT: The Moscow Agreements and Beyond*, pp. 167-75.

78. Remarks by Dr. Kissinger, June 15, 1972, *Department of State Bulletin*, Vol. 67, July 10, 1972, p. 42. As another commentator put it later: "Never before in history had major powers agreed to such important limits on weapons so central to their fundamental security." See Burton R. Rosenthal, "Formulating Negotiating Positions for SALT: 1968, 1969-72," in *Report of the Commission on the Organization of the Government for the Conduct of Foreign Policy* ("Murphy Commission Report"), Appendix K: "Adequacy of Current Organization: Defense and Arms Control," appendix vol. 4 (Washington, D.C.: Government Printing Office, 1975), p. 325. (Hereafter cited as *Murphy Commission Report, Appendix K.*)

79. Conversely, one must also acknowledge that the SALT I accords probably provided a certain amount of reciprocal insurance to the United States against a Sino-Soviet rapprochement.

80. Address by Rep. Gerald E. Ford (R-Mich), before the VFW State Convention, Grand Rapids, Michigan, press release, June 17, 1972. For a representative range of other commentary registering various degrees of approval of the May 1972 accords, see, among others: Editorial, "Moscow (II): Limiting Strategic Arms," *Washington Post*, May 28, 1972; Alton H. Quanbeck and Barry M. Blechman, "The Arms Accords: Everyone Gains," ibid., June 4, 1972; Alton Frye, "SALT: The Accord Deserves Our Support," *Sunday Star*, Washington, D.C., June 18, 1972; Statement of Jerome H. Kahan, "SALT and Strategic Policy Issues," in *Strategic Arms Limitation Agreements, Hearings*, before the Committee on Foreign Relations, Senate, 92d Cong., 2d session, June 28, 1972, pp. 201-19; Michael M. May, *Strategic Arms Technology and Doctrine Under Arms Limitation Agreements*, Research Monograph no. 37, Center for International Studies, Princeton University, October 1972.

81. To commemorate the signing of the SALT I agreements, the symbolic clock on the cover of the *Bulletin of the Atomic Scientists* was moved back from ten minutes before, to twelve minutes before, midnight. See Eugene Rabinowitch, "The Moscow Summit," *Bulletin of the Atomic Scientists*, Vol. 28, June 1972, p. 50.

82. For views giving approval of the ABM Treaty, but critical of the Interim Agreement for falling short of limiting the arms race, see: Bernard T. Feld, "Looking to SALT-II," *Bulletin of the Atomic Scientists*, June 1972, pp. 2-3, 54-55; Statement of Stanley Hoffman, in *Strategic Arms Limitation Agreements*, pp. 191-200; Senator William Proxmire, Senate speech, June 5, 1972, *Congressional Record*, 92d Cong., 2d session, June 5, 1972, pp. S19707-S19708.

83. Paul C. Warnke, "The SALT Agreements As Arms Control," June 28, 1972, in *Strategic Arms Limitation Agreements*, pp. 179-85.

84. See, for example, Donald G. Brennan, "When the SALT Hit the Fan," *National Review*, Vol. 24, June 23, 1972.

85. The Joint Congressional Resolution of approval of September 30, 1972 (H.J. Res-1227, which became Public Law 92-448), contained a softened version

of the Jackson amendment urging the president, in the next phase of SALT, to seek a treaty that "would not limit the United States to levels of intercontinental strategic forces inferior to the limits provided for the Soviet Union." By contrast with extended congressional debate on the Interim Agreement, the ABM Treaty portion of the SALT I accords was ratified by the Senate on August 3, 1972, with relatively little prior commotion. For a convenient collection of material from the *Congressional Record* giving the full record of debate from August 3, 1972, to September 25, 1972, in both Senate and House on the ABM Treaty and the Interim Agreement, see *Strategic Arms Limitation Talks (SALT); Legislative History of the Jackson Amendment, 1972*, prepared by the office of Senator Henry M. Jackson (undated).

86. For a representative range of views suggesting that the Interim Agreement had frozen current U.S. disadvantages, but left the door open for the Russians to catch up in fields where the United States was ahead, see: Edward Teller, "Comments on the Moscow Agreement," June 28, 1972, in *Strategic Arms Limitation Agreements*, pp. 220-25; Statement of Donald G. Brennan, ibid., pp. 188-90; Statement of Dr. William R. Van Cleave, in *Military Implications of the ABM Treaty and the Interim Agreement*, pp. 570-92; Francis P. Hoeber, *SALT I: The Morning After*, The Rand Corporation, P-4867, Santa Monica, July 1972; William S. White, "There Are Perils in Moscow Pacts," *Chicago Tribune*, June 4, 1972.

87. Edward N. Luttwak, "The Trouble with SALT," *Washington Post*, October 15, 1972. See also Van Cleave, in *Military Implications of the ABM Treaty and the Interim Agreement*, pp. 578-86.

88. Comment by Kosygin at the banquet given by the American summit delegation in Moscow, May 27, 1972. See Hedrick Smith, "Soviet Says Arms Accords Show U.S. Accepts Parity," *New York Times*, May 28, 1972.

89. Editorial, "For the Benefit of Peace and Security," *Pravda*, May 29, 1972; "Important Results," ibid., May 31, 1972.

90. G.A. (Henry) Trofimenko, "In the Interests of Mankind," *Izvestiia*, September 5, 1972.

91. Ibid. The gist of most Soviet commentary on the significance of SALT I may be found in this Trofimenko article and in an expanded version of it that appeared in September 1972. See G.A. Trofimenko, "Soviet-American Agreements on the Limitation of Strategic Arms," *SShA: Ekonomika, Politika, Ideologiia*, no. 9 (September 1972):3-16.

92. Moscow television talk by G.A. Arbatov, June 8, 1972, as reported in the *New York Times*, June 9, 1972. See also two major articles on SALT and the Moscow summit by Arbatov: "The Power of a Realistic Policy," *Izvestiia*, June 21, 1972; "Events of Important International Significance: Results of the Soviet-American Summit Talks," *SShA: Ekonomika, Politika, Ideologiia*, no. 8 (August 1972):9-11.

93. Trofimenko, in *Izvestiia*, September 5, 1972.

94. Ibid. See also Iu. Chernov, "A Real Force in International Development," *Pravda*, June 15, 1972.

95. A.N. Druzhinin, in a Moscow radio round-table discussion, June 28, 1972.

96. Suslov speech before a Joint Session of the Foreign Affairs Commissions of the Supreme Soviet, August 23, 1972, *Investiia,* August 24, 1972.

97. The Kulish article on SALT appeared in the British publication *Survival,* Vol. 14, September-October 1972, p. 214. Kulish at the time was head of the Department of International Relations, Institute of World Economy and International Relations, Moscow. See also O. Bykov and S. Fedorenko, "The Pentagon's Appetites," *Mirovaia ekonomika i mezhdunarodnye otnosheniia* (World Economy and International Relations), no. 8 (August 1972):21.

98. Trofimenko, in *Izvestiia,* September 5, 1972. See also Yu. Barsukov, "Flanking Maneuver," ibid., August 23, 1972.

99. Transcript of the President's News Conference of June 22, 1972, *New York Times,* June 23, 1972.

100. Iu. Chernov, in *Pravda,* June 15, 1972.

101. See Hedrick Smith, "Soviet Concedes Some Opposition to Summit Talks," *New York Times,* June 16, 1972.

102. See, for example, Vadim Zagladin, "Adherence to Principle and Consistency," *Novoe vremia,* May 26, 1972; N.N. Inozemtsev, "Principled Nature and Effectiveness of Soviet Foreign Policy," *Pravda,* June 9, 1972; and V.I. Mikhailov, in *Pravda,* June 4, 1972.

103. *Izvestiia,* June 21, 1972.

104. "In the Interest of Strengthening Peace: Joint Session of the Foreign Affairs Commissions of the Soviet of the Union and the Soviet of Nationalities of the USSR Supreme Soviet," *Izvestiia,* August 24, 1972.

105. "Important Contribution to Strengthening Peace and Security: Session of the Presidium of the USSR Supreme Soviet," *Pravda,* September 30, 1972.

## NOTES TO CHAPTER 2
## INSTITUTIONAL SETTING OF THE
## SALT PROCESS

1. See Chapter 1, pp. 1-8.

2. The Committee of Principals had furnished high-level policy guidance for the negotiations on the Nuclear Nonproliferation Treaty between 1965-1968. At the time it became formally responsible for coordinating SALT planning in the summer of 1968, the Committee's members included Secretary of State Dean Rusk; Clark M. Clifford, who had succeeded McNamara as secretary of defense earlier in the year; General Earle G. Wheeler, chairman of the JCS; William C. Foster, the director of ACDA; Richard M. Helms, the director of CIA; and Walt W. Rostow, the president's special assistant for national security.

3. See Chapter 1, p. 2.

4. John Newhouse, *Cold Dawn: The Story of SALT* (New York: Holt, Rinehart and Winston, 1973), p. 87. See also Burton R. Rosenthal, "Formulating Negotiating Positions for SALT: 1968, 1969-72," in *Report of the Commission on the Organization of the Government for the Conduct of Foreign Policy* ("Murphy Commission Report"), Appendix K: "Adequacy of Current Organization: Defense and Arms Control," appendix vol. 4 (Washington, D.C.:

Government Printing Office, 1975), p. 327. (Hereafter cited as *Murphy Commission Report, Appendix K.*)

5. Included in the group were Paul Nitze and Paul Warnke from OSD; Raymond Garthoff from the State Department's Bureau of Politico-Military Affairs; Adrian Fisher from ACDA; and a JCS representative. See Rosenthal, in *Murphy Commission Report, Appendix K*, p. 327.

6. Ibid., p. 328.

7. Newhouse, *Cold Dawn*, p. 111.

8. Detailed accounts of this internal bargaining and maneuvering, which rather closely parallel each other, may be found in ibid., pp. 108-30, and Rosenthal, in *Murphy Commission Report, Appendix K*, pp. 328-31. See also Alton Frye, "U.S. Decision Making for SALT," in Mason Willrich and John B. Rhinelander, eds., *SALT: The Moscow Agreements and Beyond* (New York: The Free Press, 1974), pp. 74-78.

9. Newhouse, *Cold Dawn*, p. 127.

10. In speaking of the National Security Council system, one should note the distinction between the NSC itself and the NSC staff. The NSC is a statutory group of top-level officials created by the National Security Act of 1947 to assist the president in formulating military and foreign policy, whereas the staff is made up of professional personnel working under the president's assistant for national security affairs. The NSC professional staff during the Nixon-Ford period numbered about sixty people; it was later reduced in the Carter period to about forty. In addition to these regular staff members, around twenty people were temporarily loaned to the NSC in both periods by other government agencies.

11. See Brooke Nihart, "National Security Council: New Staff System After One Year," *Armed Forces Journal*, Vol. 107, April 4, 1970, pp. 25-29; John P. Leacacos, "Kissinger's Apparat," *Foreign Policy*, no. 5 (Winter 1971-1972), pp. 3-27; I.M. Destler, "The Nixon System: A Further Look," *Foreign Service Journal*, February 1974, pp. 9-29. Among the Nixon administration's first moves in setting up a highly structured NSC system calculated to tighten presidential control over the national security bureaucracy was the establishment of the NSSM (National Security Study Memorandum) and NSDM (National Security Decision Memorandum) series. The NSSMs generally were used to assign studies of particular security problems or policy options to the bureaucracy, while the NSDMs were used to convey instructions to the concerned agencies after a policy decision had been made and approved by the president. Under Carter, these instruments remained essentially unchanged, but were renamed PRM (Presidential Review Memorandum) and PD (Presidential Directive), respectively.

For an excellent summary analysis of changes in the NSC system from the centrally structured committee system of the Eisenhower period, through the much less structured and largely ad hoc group arrangements under Kennedy and Johnson, back to a structured but more secretive NSC operation in the Nixon period, see Andrew J. Goodpaster, "Four Presidents and the Conduct of National Security Affairs—Impressions and Highlights," *Journal of International Relations*, Spring 1977, pp. 26-37.

12. Rosenthal, in *Murphy Commission Report, Appendix K*, pp. 333-34.

13. Ibid. There was a touch of irony in the fact that this recommendation came from Gerard Smith himself, after he had been dismayed by the harsh reaction of the chairman of the JCS to the treatment of verification in the NSSM-28 study. See also Newhouse, *Cold Dawn*, p. 162.

14. *Cold Dawn*, pp. 161-62. According to Newhouse, the opportunity to "relieve ACDA of its burden of initiative" in SALT by taking up Smith's suggestion for a verification panel had been urged on Kissinger by one of his senior aides, Laurence E. Lynn.

15. Ibid., p. 162.

16. See Rosenthal, in *Murphy Commission Report, Appendix K*, p. 338.

17. See Leacacos, in *Foreign Policy*, Winter 1971-1972, p. 15.

18. For a chronology of the various SALT sessions up to this writing, see Appendix C.

19. In addition to Ambassador Smith, who had "retired" as director of ACDA and chairman of the U.S. SALT delegation in January 1973, others who departed ACDA in the next few months included Deputy Director Philip J. Farley, Assistant Directors Spurgeon M. Keeny, Jr. and Vice Admiral John M. Lee, and Counselor Lawrence D. Weiler. Raymond Garthoff of the State Department, executive secretary of the SALT delegation, and Lieutenant General Royal B. Allison, a delegate, were among others who were separated from SALT at this time. This personnel exodus was generally attributed to criticism of the SALT I accords, including the implicitly critical Joint Congressional Resolution of September 30, 1972. See Rosenthal, in *Murphy Commission Report, Appendix K*, p. 338. See also Herbert Scoville, "Arms for What?" *The New Republic*, May 26, 1973, p. 14.

20. When the new SALT delegation was named on March 8, 1973, White House spokesman Ronald L. Ziegler indicated that the intent was to make ACDA primarily a "research and staffing organization," rather than an agency with direct negotiating functions. See Marilyn Berger, "Go-Slow Approach Seen for New SALT Talks," *Washington Post*, March 8, 1973.

21. As Nixon was later to write, on the day before his resignation he had advised Ford that "the only man who would be absolutely indispensable to him was Henry Kissinger." *RN: The Memoirs of Richard Nixon* (New York: Grosset & Dunlap, 1978), p. 1078.

22. See Chapter 8, pp. 155-57.

23. Kissinger's post as presidential assistant for national security was turned over to his deputy, Lieutenant General Brent Scrowcroft, on November 2, 1975, during the so-called "Halloween Massacre" when Schlesinger lost his job as secretary of defense and William E. Colby his as CIA director. Kissinger retained the chairmanship of the Verification Panel through which control over SALT was exercised, although chairmanships of some of the other NSC committees over which he had presided were split up among Scrowcroft, Rumsfeld, and others. See *Newsweek*, November 17, 1975. See also notes 27 and 57, below.

24. Our discussion of changes in the SALT apparatus under the Carter administration draws substantially on a monograph by a colleague, Rose E. Gottemoeller, *Evolution of the U.S. Organizational Setup for Dealing with SALT*, The Rand Corporation, P-6197, Santa Monica, November 1978, especially pp. 20-36.

25. See Bernard Gwertzman, "Brzezinski Revises Staff and Systems at Security Agency," *New York Times*, January 16, 1976; Dom Bonafede, "Brzezinski—Stepping Out of His Backstage Role," *National Journal*, Vol. 9, October 15, 1977, pp. 1599-1601; Jim Hoagland, "Brzezinski: An Eagerness to Show 'Resolve,' " *Washington Post*, March 14, 1978; "Brzezinski, Foreign Policy Advisor, Sees Role as Stiffening U.S. Position," *New York Times*, March 21, 1978; Elizabeth Drew, "Brzezinski," *The New Yorker*, May 1, 1978, pp. 99-101.

26. Bonafede, in *National Journal*, October 15, 1977, pp. 1596, 1598; Drew, in *The New Yorker*, May 1, 1978, pp. 102, 104.

27. In addition to heading the Verification Panel, Kissinger served as chairman of five of the six other senior bodies that were created during the Nixon administration to support the NSC over the range of national security affairs: the Senior Review Group, Defense Program Review Committee, NSC Intelligence Committee, Net Assessment Group, and Washington Special Actions Group. Only the Under Secretaries Committee was not chaired by Kissinger.

28. Except for Attorney General Mitchell's occasional attendance in the earlier years of the Nixon administration, the office of the attorney general was not institutionally involved in Verification Panel matters. The White House post of science adviser was abolished in January 1973, but re-established under President Ford in May 1976, along with an Office of Science and Technology Policy. The former Atomic Energy Commission, under the title of Energy Resources Development Administration, was still occasionally represented at Verification Panel meetings. According to Raymond Garthoff, the Verification Panel met from twelve to fifteen times in 1971 on SALT issues, compared with two to three meetings of the full NSC on SALT.

29. See, for example, Frye, in *SALT: The Moscow Agreements and Beyond*, p. 82, and Rosenthal, in *Murphy Commission Report, Appendix K*, p. 335. For a critical reminder that voluminous studies and analyses of options were not necessarily relevant in some cases to the decisions actually made, but sometimes had the principal purpose of keeping the bureaucracy busy, see Lawrence D. Weiler, *The Arms Race, Secret Negotiations and the Congress*, Occasional Paper 12, The Stanley Foundation, Muscatine, Iowa, 1976, p. 28.

30. Gottemoeller, *Evolution of the U.S. Organizational Setup*, p. 18. See also Bonafede, in *National Journal*, October 15, 1977, p. 1597.

31. Leslie H. Gelb, "How U.S. Made Ready for Talk at Vladivostok," *New York Times*, December 3, 1974. See also "Background Briefing by Henry Kissinger, 3 December 1974," in *Survival*, Vol. 17, July-August 1975, p. 192. As the author was told by one person who had occasion to observe NSC activity at close range under both presidents, Nixon preferred to be briefed and to read relevant papers in privacy and hence rarely met with the full NSC, whereas Ford liked to draw people out in face-to-face discussions and thus more often preferred meetings of the full NSC.

32. The author owes a special debt for insights into the working of the SALT apparatus in the Nixon period to a former Rand colleague, Paul Von Ins, who had spent four years working on SALT problems during his final preretirement tour in the Pentagon with the JCS.

33. See Leacacos, in *Foreign Policy*, Winter 1971-1972, pp. 7, 10.

34. Besides Ambassador Smith, who had been a State Department official in

the Eisenhower years, but was now the institutional representative of ACDA, the original SALT delegation principals were: Llewellyn E. Thompson, the retired Ambassador to the Soviet Union, representing the State Department; Paul H. Nitze, former Secretary of the Navy and Deputy Secretary of Defense in the last years of the Johnson administration, who represented OSD; Lieutenant General Royal B. Allison of the Air Force, representing the JCS; and Dr. Harold Brown, president of Caltech and former Secretary of the Air Force, who was an at-large member understood to "represent" the scientific community. Thompson was replaced in the spring of 1971, because of illness, by Ambassador J. Graham Parsons, another career diplomat. In the initial session of SALT II, Philip J. Farley of ACDA took Parsons' place on the delegation. Throughout SALT I and the opening session of SALT II, Raymond L. Garthoff of the State Department served as executive secretary of the delegation and personal advisor to Ambassador Smith. See Chalmers M. Roberts, *The Nuclear Years* (New York: Praeger Publishers, 1970), p. 115; Newhouse, *Cold Dawn*, p. 212; *12th Annual Report to the Congress*, U.S. Arms Control and Disarmament Agency, January 31, 1973, p. 6; Raymond L. Garthoff, "Negotiating SALT," *The Wilson Quarterly*, Vol. 1, Autumn 1977, pp. 76-77.

35. After March 1973, the SALT II delegation principals, in addition to Ambassador Johnson, were Nitze and Brown, holdovers from SALT I, and three new members: Boris H. Klosson, formerly deputy chief of mission, U.S. Embassy, Moscow, representing the State Department; Lieutenant General Edward L. Rowny of the U.S. Army, representing the JCS; and Sidney N. Graybeal, an ACDA official representing that agency. Graybeal later left the delegation to become commissioner of the Standing Consultative Commission, his place being taken by Ralph Earle of ACDA. Nitze resigned from the delegation on June 14, 1974, and was replaced by Dr. Michael May, an internationally known physicist, of Lawrence Livermore Laboratory. The post of executive secretary in SALT II was occupied for a time by John C. Ausland of the State Department, and later by Colonel Norman Clyne, an Air Force officer serving with ACDA. See also note 61, below.

36. See Weiler, *The Arms Race, Secret Negotiations and the Congress*, p. 10.

37. Newhouse, *Cold Dawn*, pp. 212-14.

38. See, for example, Raymond L. Garthoff, "Negotiating with the Russians: Some Lessons from SALT," *International Security*, Vol. 1, Spring 1977, pp. 17-20; and the same author's article in *The Wilson Quarterly*, Autumn 1977, pp. 76-85. Garthoff notes that the delegation operated in accordance with NSDMs specifying U.S. positions in detail, but leaving to the delegation decisions on tactics and presentation of positions.

39. Newhouse, *Cold Dawn*, p. 44. See also Bernard Gwertzman, "Alexis Johnson Is Expected to Replace Smith As Negotiator on Strategic Arms," *New York Times*, January 5, 1973.

40. See Chapter 4.

41. Newhouse, *Cold Dawn*, p. 213; Garthoff, in *The Wilson Quarterly*, Autumn 1977, pp. 76, 85. According to Gottemoeller, *Evolution of the U.S. Organizational Setup*, pp. 18-19, an attempt was made by Dr. Kissinger after SALT II began to monitor the delegation more closely, partly by reducing

informal contacts with Soviet delegates and returning to formal plenary sessions and drafting meetings of regularly assigned working groups.

42. "Inside SALT 1 and 2: Soviet's Negotiating Style Assayed," *Aviation Week & Space Technology*, February 17, 1975, p. 43.

43. See Article XIII of the ABM Treaty and Article VI of the Interim Agreement, in *Arms Control and Disarmament Agreements*, 1977 edition, U.S. Arms Control and Disarmament Agency, Washington, D.C., June 1977, pp. 134, 139. The SCC's authorized functions also included one that, though apparently not exercised, would make it a negotiating forum parallel to, or as a successor of, the SALT delegations—namely, the right to consider proposals for further strategic arms limitation measures.

44. The SCC was established by a Memorandum of Understanding signed by the two SALT delegation heads at Geneva, December 21, 1972. For text, see "Standing Consultative Commission on Arms Limitation," *Treaties and Other International Acts Series 7545* (Washington, D.C.: Government Printing Office, 1973).

45. See "Standing Consultative Commission on Arms Limitation: Regulations," *Treaties and Other International Acts Series 7637* (Washington, D.C.: Government Printing Office, 1974).

46. The commissioners and staff of the American SCC component customarily returned to their parent agencies and non-SCC duties when the SCC was not in actual session, with caretaker SCC matters left largely in the hands of Lieutenant Colonel Frank P. Desimone, U.S. Army, detailed to ACDA.

47. Subsequent turnover of SCC personnel in the Nixon-Ford period included the following: Graybeal at the close of 1976 was succeeded as commissioner by Robert W. Buchheim, a former Rand Corporation analyst and ACDA official; and General Georgi was replaced in early 1975 as deputy commissioner by Brigadier General Frank E. Serio, U.S. Army, who also took over Georgi's JCS post. Fitzgerald remained with the SCC throughout.

48. *New York Times*, July 4, 1974.

49. Michael Getler, "U.S. Asks Meeting on SALT Accord," *Washington Post*, November 16, 1974. See also: Charles Corddry, "U.S. Plays Down Soviet Cheating Risk," *Baltimore Sun*, December 12, 1974; "Explanations Requested," *Aviation Week & Space Technology*, February 3, 1975, p. 12.

50. The commander of the Strategic Rocket Forces was chosen in November 1974 to deny publicly that the Soviet Union had installed any new missile silos since May 1972, tested mobile systems, or in any other way violated its SALT obligations. See General of the Army V. Tolubko, "Conquerors of Rockets," *Nedelya*, November 11-17, 1974, p. 19.

51. See *SALT ONE: Compliance*, Selected Documents no. 7, The Department of State, February 21, 1978, pp. 4-10. This report apparently went beyond the limits of confidentiality enjoined upon the SCC by paragraph 8 of the Joint Regulations, but Soviet reaction to its release, publicly at least, was by no means disapproving. On the contrary, Soviet media cited the report frequently as proof that charges of Soviet SALT violations by "opponents of detente" were groundless. See Sergei Vishnevskii, "The International Week," *Pravda*, March 4, 1978; S. Kondrashov, "Mr. Laird Is Cheating," *Izvestiia*, March 16, 1978.

52. See Chapter 10, pp. 209-11. See also Appendix D.

53. See *17th Annual Report to Congress*, U.S. Arms Control and Disarmament Agency, Washington, D.C. March 1978, pp. 28-29. (Hereafter referred to as *ACDA 17th Annual Report*); Bonafede, in *National Journal*, October 1977, pp. 1598, 1601. See also Chapter 2, p. 38.

54. Gottemoeller, *Evolution of the U.S. Organizational Setup*, p. 20. See also Drew, in *The New Yorker*, May 1, 1978, pp. 99-102, 107.

55. Gottemoeller, op. cit., p. 20; Bonafede, in *National Journal*, October 1977, pp. 1599, 1601.

56. It should be noted that Secretary Vance placed reliance regularly upon Dr. Marshall Shulman for advice on Soviet-American issue areas, including SALT negotiating positions. This use by the secretary of state of a prominent Soviet affairs expert from the academic community, an organizational innovation of the Carter period, probably served to improve the secretary's hand in interagency bargaining on some SALT issues. Dr. Shulman's assistant in following arms control developments, including SALT, was John M. Joyce, a Foreign Service Officer with Moscow experience. Important direct support to Vance on SALT was also provided by Leslie H. Gelb, chief of the Bureau of Politico-Military Affairs, and his staff.

57. It might be noted that although there were numerous (seven) committees of the NSC in the Nixon-Ford era, they all had virtually the same principals in membership, as did the two committees of the Carter period. In a sense, the more numerous committees in the former case represented a device of working convenience—particularly in terms of knowing which support staff to call upon for background information, to channel papers and instructions to, etc. By contrast, when the whole NSC was divided into only two committees with overlapping membership, the staff support became less differentiated and there was perhaps more ambiguity as to who should receive which problem to staff out, who had the background in a particular area, etc.

58. Under this division of labor, the Special Coordinating Committee was intended to deal with SALT and other issues that cut across the jurisdiction of several agencies, and with problems of short-term character. After January 1978, it also assumed an important intelligence supervisory role. The Policy Review Committee, on the other hand, initially was meant to deal with longer-term problems and issues in which a single department had the principal role. While Brzezinski always acted as chairman of the Special Coordinating Committee, chairing of the Policy Review Committee was shared with other NSC members, according to the issue being addressed. See Gwertzman in the *New York Times*, January 16, 1977; Bonafede, in *National Journal*, October 1977, p. 1601; Drew, in *The New Yorker*, May 1, 1978, p. 101; *ACDA 17th Annual Report*, p. 29; Bonner Day, "The Battle over U.S. Intelligence," *Air Force Magazine*, May 1978, p. 42.

59. *ACDA 17th Annual Report*, p. 29.

60. Gottemoeller, *Evolution of the U.S. Organizational Setup*, p. 22.

61. *ACDA 17th Annual Report*, p. 27. The other principal delegates appointed following the change of administrations were Dr. Gerald W. Johnson of the Department of Defense; Lieutenant General Edward L. Rowny of the

U.S. Army, a holdover from the previous delegation, representing the JCS; Minister Frank H. Perez of the State Department; and retired army General George M. Seignious, president of the Citadel, serving as member-at-large. In mid-1978, the executive secretary of the SALT delegation, Colonel Norman Clyne, was replaced on an interim basis by Major General John E. Ralph, USAF.

62. Ibid., p. 28. See also "Congressmen Debate Own Role As Advisers in SALT Treaty," *Aviation Week & Space Technology*, November 21, 1977, p. 14; and note 100, below.

63. See Chapter 2, p. 33.

64. *Aviation Week & Space Technology*, November 21, 1977, p. 14.

65. Terence Smith, in the *New York Times*, March 21, 1978. The principal members of Brzezinski's original NSC staff who handled SALT questions were his deputy, David L. Aaron, Dr. Victor A. Utgoff, and Roger C. Molander. In September 1978, when Mr. Fritz Ermarth joined the NSC staff, supervision of SALT matters became one of his responsibilities.

66. Gottemoeller, *Evolution of the U.S. Organizational Setup*, p. 22.

67. Ibid.

68. The principals in this internal clash of views within the U.S. delegation were said to be Ambassador Earle, the alternate chairman of the delegation, representing ACDA, and Lieutenant General Rowny, representing the JCS. See Walter Pincus, "Discord Surfacing in U.S. Delegation on SALT Stance," *Washington Post*, December 5, 1977.

69. In August 1977, Rear Admiral Edward F. Welch, Jr., USN, replaced Brigadier General Frank E. Serio as deputy commissioner of the U.S. component of the SCC. He was in turn replaced in April 1978 by Brigadier General Harry Goodall of the USAF.

70. A joint communiqué summing up the results of the ABM Treaty review session may be found in *ACDA 17th Annual Report*, pp. 31-32.

71. See Chapter 2, p. 35.

72. See above, note 69.

73. Subsequently renamed Program Analysis and Evaluation (PA&E).

74. In the Pentagon SALT policy arena, with the advent of Nixon and his first Secretary of Defense, Melvin Laird, ISA lost the dominant influence it had held in 1968 under Warnke and Halperin. For discussion of the internal competition on SALT and related issues in this period, see Newhouse, *Cold Dawn*, pp. 38ff., 150.

75. Under a Defense Department reorganization plan submitted to Congress by Secretary Brown in 1977, the Office of International Security Affairs (ISA) was subordinated to a new undersecretary for policy, rather than reporting upward as shown in Fig. 2-3. However, the SALT functions, along with those pertaining to NSC affairs, remained as before in ISA—the SALT matters under Walter B. Slocombe and other NSC matters the responsibility of Dr. Lynn E. Davis. See the *New York Times*, September 27, 1977. See also *Federal Organization & Personnel Directory* (Washington, D.C.: Carroll Publishing Company, 1977), p. 20.3.

76. See Henry S. Bradsher, "Pentagon 'State Department,' " *Washington Star*, December 5, 1977.

77. See Newhouse, *Cold Dawn*, pp. 37-38. The author also is indebted here to the firsthand experience of Paul Von Ins.

78. See Leslie H. Gelb in the *New York Times*, December 3, 1974, and Victor Zorza, "The SALT Bargain with the Military," *Washington Post*, December 12, 1974. See also Chapter 8, p. 160.

79. The study requested by the president was said to reflect concern about the capability of the JCS "to provide guidance, to review contingency plans and to resolve differences between commands regarding forces." It was interpreted in some quarters as the forerunner of an attempt by the Carter administration to have the once-amended National Security Act of 1947 again amended so as to further reduce the Joint Chiefs' independence of the secretary of defense on various matters. The study was directed by Richard C. Steadman, a New York banker. However, although the study did recommend increased involvement in military planning by the secretary of defense, it also recommended a stronger role for the chairman of the JCS and the Joint Staff in resource decisionmaking, so that its results were not what some had anticipated. See Bernard Weinraub, "Role of Joint Chiefs Under Study: Overhaul of Command Is Possible," *New York Times*, November 8, 1977; "Joint Chiefs Losing Sway under Carter," ibid., July 6, 1978; *Report to the Secretary of Defense on the National Military Command Structure*, Washington, D.C., July 1978, especially, pp. 47-48, 64-70.

80. John W. Finney, "In Many Ways the Joint Chiefs Are an Island Unto Themselves," *New York Times*, November 20, 1977.

81. See Chapter 2, pp. 24-25.

82. See Figure 2-1, p. 30.

83. An expression of this line of argument may be found in the testimony of McGeorge Bundy before the House Subcommittee on National Security Policy, October 1, 1974, "Ford Aid Held Needed by Arms Foes," *Washington Post*, October 2, 1974.

84. Gottemoeller, *Evolution of the U.S. Organizational Setup*, p. 20.

85. See Chapter 2, p. 25.

86. Other ACDA appointees included John Newhouse, Barry M. Blechman, and Thomas D. Davies as assistant directors, and Adam Yarmolinsky as counselor. One of the controversial aspects of the 1977 reorganization of ACDA that critics attacked was the abolishing of the bureau dealing with verification. See *ACDA 17th Annual Report*, pp. 125, 144. See also William Safire, "Mr. Warnke's Hit List," *New York Times*, April 21, 1977.

87. Opposition to Warnke's appointment surfaced in the extended hearings on his confirmation before the Senate Foreign Relations Committee, and especially before the Senate Armed Services Committee, which together resulted in almost 500 pages of testimony. See *Nomination of Paul Warnke*, Report with Individual Views, Senate, Committee on Foreign Relations, 95th Cong., 1st sess., February 25, 1977. See also Eugene Kozicharow, "Opposition to Warnke Mounts in Senate," *Aviation Week & Space Technology*, February 14, 1977, pp. 21-22; Hedrick Smith, "Warnke Rift Reflects Wider Issues," *New York Times*, February 26, 1977; Martin Tolchin, "Byrd Gives Warnke Reluctant Approval As Arms Negotiator," ibid., March 6, 1977.

88. *ACDA 17th Annual Report*, p. 125.

89. See Chapter 1, p. 16.

90. For the relevant language on strategic equivalence from the Jackson amendment, see Chapter 1, note 85.

91. The pertinent language of the resolution read: ". . . were a more complete strategic offensive arms agreement not achieved within the five years of the Interim Agreement, and were the survivability of the strategic deterrent forces of the United States to be threatened as a result of such failure, this could jeopardize the supreme national interests of the United States."

92. For further discussion of this debate, in which Senator Jackson again took a prominent place, see Chapter 9, pp. 179-80.

93. Senate Resolution 406, entitled "The Importance of Sound Relations with the Soviet Union," was proposed on March 16, 1976, by Senator Alan Cranston, and was passed, with amendments, on May 5, 1976. *Congressional Record*, 94th Cong., 2d session, Vol. 122, No. 65, May 5, 1976, pp. S6597-S6600. See also Christopher M. Lehman and Peter C. Hughes, " 'Equivalence' and SALT II," *Orbis*, Vol. 20, Winter 1977, p. 1045.

94. See Chapter 2, pp. 35-36.

95. For discussion of verification problems posed by cruise missiles and various "gray area" strategic systems, see Fred C. Iklé, "What to Hope for, and Worry About, in SALT," *Fortune*, October 1977, pp. 176-86; Alexander R. Vershbow, "The Cruise Missile: The End of Arms Control?" *Foreign Affairs*, Vol. 54, October 1976, pp. 145-46; Paul Doty, Albert Carnesale, and Michael Nacht, "The Race to Control Nuclear Arms," ibid., pp. 119-32; Harold Molineu, "The Impact of Strategic and Technological Innovations on Nuclear Deterrence," *Military Review*, Vol. 58, January 1978, pp. 7-16; Jack H. Harris and William D. Bajusz, "Arms Control and Gray-Area Systems," *Air Force Magazine*, Vol. 61, no. w, February 1978, pp. 36-39. See also Chapter 10, pp. 199-202, 215.

96. *ACDA 17th Annual Report*, p. 127.

97. *SALT TWO: Verification*, Selected Documents no. 7, The Department of State, February 23, 1978, pp. 11-14. This exchange of communications involved a certain amount of cooperation between Senator John J. Sparkman, chairman of the Foreign Relations Committee, and Mr. Warnke, presumably meant to reduce the grounds for criticism of the proposed SALT agreements. See further discussion, Chapter 10, pp. 215-16.

98. See Chapter 2, p. 39.

99. *ACDA 17th Annual Report*, p. 124.

100. See "Congressmen Debate Own Role As Advisers in SALT Treaty," *Aviation Week & Space Technology*, November 21, 1977. Ambassador U. Alexis Johnson, chief U.S. SALT negotiator, 1973-1977, was one of those entertaining reservations about the net value of involving legislators immediately in negotiating activities, primarily because of problems arising out of the separation of powers principle. (In conversation with the author, May 18, 1978.)

101. Bernard Gwertzman, "Senate to Receive Arms Information," *New York Times*, May 28, 1977.

102. Among those studying the question of an extension on behalf of Congress was the Congressional Research Service. See Robert G. Bell, *Implica-*

tions of *Extending the SALT I Interim Agreement,* CRS, Library of Congress, May 16, 1977. See also Eugene Kozicharow, "Options Studied for Expiration of SALT," *Aviation Week & Space Technology,* August 1, 1977, p. 76.

103. See Richard Burt, "U.S. Plans To Keep Arms Pact in Force," *New York Times,* September 23, 1977. For texts of Secretary Vance's announcement of September 23 and Ambassador Warnke's statement of September 26 before the Senate Foreign Relations Committee, see *Department of State Bulletin,* Vol. 77, November 7, 1977, pp. 642-43.

104. The Soviet Union combined its unilateral announcement of intent to avoid "any actions incompatible with the provisions of the Interim Agreement" with a statement anticipating the affirmative findings of the five-year review of the ABM Treaty. (See Chapter 2, p. 39.) See also: Craig R. Whitney, "Soviet Joins the U.S. in Pledging Observance of Lapsing Arms Pact," *New York Times,* September 26, 1977; "Joint Soviet-American Statement on Strategic Arms Limitation Questions," *Pravda,* September 25, 1977.

105. For commentary on the theme that the climactic stage in SALT II negotiations in 1978 tended to coincide with a deteriorating political climate that prejudiced the prospects of congressional approval of a new agreement, see: Murrey Marder, "U.S.-Soviet Tension Seen on the Rise: Political Climate Darkens for Talks on Arms Reductions," *Washington Post,* May 25, 1978; James Reston, "The Senate and the Soviets," *New York Times,* April 26, 1978; editorial, "The SALT Dilemma and the Horn," ibid., March 8, 1978. See also Chapter 11, pp. 240-41.

## NOTES FOR CHAPTER 3
## SOVIET ORGANIZATIONAL ARRANGEMENTS
## FOR HANDLING SALT

1. For an earlier discussion of various Soviet "interest" groups that may have some leverage on the Soviet approach to SALT, see Thomas W. Wolfe, "Soviet Interests in SALT," in William R. Kintner and Robert L. Pfaltzgraff, Jr., eds., *SALT: Implications for Arms Control in the 1970s* (Pittsburgh: University of Pittsburgh Press, 1972), pp. 28-38.

2. Brezhnev's most revealing public comments on Politburo operations were made to a group of Western news correspondents in Moscow in June 1973, on the eve of his initial visit to the United States. See Theodore Shabad, "Brezhnev, Who Ought to Know, Explains Politburo," *New York Times,* June 15, 1973.

3. Ibid.

4. For well-informed accounts of Politburo policymaking procedures by Western observers, see: Vladimir Petrov, "Formation of Soviet Foreign Policy," *Orbis,* Vol. 17, Fall 1973, pp. 827-31; Matthew P. Gallagher and Karl F. Spielmann, Jr., *Soviet Decision-Making for Defense* (New York: Praeger Publishers, 1972), pp. 28-33; Kenneth A. Myers and Dimitri Simes, *Soviet Decision Making, Strategic Policy, and SALT,* Georgetown University Center for Strategic and International Studies, Washington, D.C., December 1974, especially pp. 11-17; Karl F. Spielmann, Jr., *Analyzing Soviet Strategic Arms Decisions,*

Institute for Defense Analyses, Arlington, Va., April 1977, especially pp. 51-73; Dimitri K. Simes, *Detente and Conflict: Soviet Foreign Policy 1972-1977,* Georgetown University Center for Strategic and International Studies, Washington, D.C., 1977, pp. 49-57. For an account by a former Soviet arms control expert who left the Soviet Union in 1976, see Igor S. Glagolev, "The Soviet Decision-Making Process in Arms-Control Negotiations," *Orbis,* Vol. 21, Winter 1978, pp. 769-72.

5. See Myers and Simes, *Soviet Decision Making,* p. 12.

6. Glagolev, in *Orbis,* Winter 1978, p. 771.

7. Marshall D. Shulman, "SALT and the Soviet Union," in Mason Willrich and John B. Rhinelander, eds., *SALT: The Moscow Agreements and Beyond* (New York: The Free Press, 1974), p. 114.

8. See, for example, Walter Laqueur, "Russia—Beyond Brezhnev," *Commentary,* Vol. 64, August 1977, pp. 39-44; David K. Shipler, "Mystery of Succession in the Kremlin Remains Impenetrable," *New York Times,* February 18, 1978; Henry S. Bradsher, "Contest Sharpens for Brezhnev Post," *Washington Star,* July 18, 1978; Hal Piper, "The Brezhnev era is coming to an end," *Baltimore Sun,* November 19, 1978.

9. See Simes, *Detente and Conflict,* p. 57. The man generally considered the most likely immediate successor to Brezhnev, though perhaps only for a short time because of his age, is A.P. Kirilenko. He was seventy-two in 1978, the same age as Brezhnev.

10. See Myers and Simes, *Soviet Decision Making,* pp. 14-17. See also Dimitri Simes and Gordon Rocca, *Soviet Decisionmaking and National Security Affairs,* Memorandum 20-km-11-1, Georgetown University Center for Strategic and International Studies, Washington, D.C., November 1973, p. 15.

11. Petrov, in *Orbis,* Fall 1973, p. 823.

12. Myers and Simes, *Soviet Decision Making,* p. 16.

13. In addition to Brezhnev, the Party secretaries with Politburo status in 1978 were A. P. Kirilenko, M.A. Suslov, B.N. Ponomarev, K.V. Chernenko, and D.F. Ustinov. The latter may no longer hold a secretarial post. Prior to his death in July 1978, F.D. Kulakov also was included in this group.

14. Myers and Simes, *Soviet Decision Making,* p. 17.

15. Glagolev, in *Orbis,* Winter 1978, p. 771.

16. Petrov, in *Orbis,* Fall 1973, p. 825.

17. Simes, *Detente and Conflict,* p. 53.

18. Myers and Simes, *Soviet Decision Making,* p. 13.

19. Petrov, in *Orbis,* Fall 1973, p. 825.

20. Ibid., p. 824. It might be noted that Ponomarev himself, in a separate capacity as a member of the Supreme Soviet, has twice visited the United States at the head of Soviet "parliamentary" delegations.

21. Comment made to the author in Moscow, September 1974.

22. Myers and Simes, *Soviet Decision Making,* p. 13. See also Michael J. Deane, *Political Control of the Soviet Armed Forces* (New York: Crane, Russak and Company, 1977), pp. 81-83.

23. See Wolfe, in *SALT: Implications for Arms Control in the 1970s,* pp. 32, 49.

24. Petrov, in *Orbis*, Fall 1973, p. 830. According to some analysts, most of the experts drawn into the Central Committee apparatus as consultants have been from the social and political sciences, rather than the "hard" sciences. See Myers and Simes, *Soviet Decision Making*, p. 21.

25. Gallagher and Spielmann, *Soviet Decision-Making for Defense*, pp. 29-30; Myers and Simes, *Soviet Decision Making*, p. 51.

26. The functions of such an ad hoc committee might be considered roughly analogous to those of the Verification Panel and its successor, the Special Coordinating Committee, in the U.S. case. See Chapter 2, pp. 29-31 and 36-38.

27. Simes and Rocca, *Soviet Decisionmaking and National Security Affairs*, pp. 13-15; Shulman, in *SALT: The Moscow Agreements and Beyond*, p. 113.

28. Raymond L. Garthoff, "SALT and the Soviet Military," *Problems of Communism*, Vol. 24, January-February 1975, p. 29.

29. Petrov, in *Orbis*, Fall 1973, p. 823.

30. On certain occasions, when tensions within the Politburo have spilled over, as during Khrushchev's repulse of the "anti-Party group" in 1957, Plenums of the Central Committee have in fact taken on the power of final arbiter that they possess in theory.

31. In the Khrushchev period, the body now known as the Defense Council (*Sovet Oborony*), evidently was called the Higher Military Council (*Vysshii Voennyi Sovet*). For references to the evolution of this institution, see, among others: Gallagher and Spielmann, *Soviet Decision-Making for Defense*, p. 18; John Erickson, *Soviet Military Power* (London: Royal United Services Institute for Defence Studies, 1971), p. 14; David Mark, in *The Military Budget and National Economic Priorities*, Part III, Joint Economic Committee, 91st Cong., 1st session, June 1969, p. 956; Malcolm Mackintosh, "The Soviet Military Influence on Foreign Policy," *Problems of Communism*, Vol. 22, September-October 1973, p. 3; Raymond L. Garthoff, in *Problems of Communism*, January-February 1975, p. 29; Harriet Fast Scott, "The Soviet High Command," *Air Force Magazine*, March 1977, pp. 52-53.

32. Decree of the Supreme Soviet USSR, no. 318, in *Vedomosti Verkhovnogo Soveta* (May 12, 1976), p. 343. Official cognizance was also paid to the existence of the Defense Council in Article 121 of the new Soviet Constitution of October 1977. See *Pravda*, October 8, 1977. p. 5.

33. See Harriet Scott, in *Air Force Magazine*, March 1977, p. 53; Edward L. Warner, III, *The Military in Contemporary Soviet Politics: An Institutional Analysis*, (New York: Praeger Publishers, 1977), p. 46.

34. Gallagher and Spielmann, *Soviet Decision-Making for Defense*, p. 19. Some analysts have suggested, however, that the Defense Council may also serve as the formal medium through which the Ministry of Defense receives its directives from the Politburo. See Mackintosh, in *Problems of Communism*, September-October 1973, p. 4.

35. Shulman, in *SALT: The Moscow Agreements and Beyond*, p. 112.

36. See further discussion of the interaction between the top political and military leaders, Chapter 3, pp. 72-77.

37. See, for example: Andrew Sheren, "Structure and Organization of Defense-Related Industries," in *Economic Performance and the Military Burden*

*in the Soviet Union,* Joint Economic Committee, 91st Congress, 1970, p. 124; David Holloway, *Technology Management, and the Soviet Military Establishment,* Adelphi Paper no. 76, Institute for Strategic Studies, London, April 1971, pp. 6, 38; Garthoff, in *Problems of Communism,* January-February 1975, p. 24.

38. Ustinov was given the rank of marshal of the Soviet Union on July 30, 1976, two months after the same rank had been conferred on Brezhnev. See Decree of the Presidium of the Supreme Soviet, no. 448, in *Vedomosti Verkhovnogo Soveta* (August 4, 1976), p. 530.

39. See Spielmann, *Analyzing Soviet Strategic Arms Decisions,* p. 64; Warner, *The Military in Contemporary Soviet Politics,* p. 47.

40. See Sheren, in *Economic Performance and the Military Burden,* p. 123; Karl F. Spielmann, Jr., "Defense Industrialists in the USSR," *Problems of Communism,* Vol. 25, September-October 1976, pp. 58-61.

41. In the Soviet Union, the bulk of defense research is carried out in scientific establishments under the jurisdiction of the defense-related industrial ministries. See William T. Lee, "The 'Politico-Military-Industrial Complex' of the USSR," *Journal of International Affairs,* Vol. 26, no. 1, 1972, pp. 74-76.

42. See Shulman, in *SALT: The Moscow Agreements and Beyond,* p. 113; John Newhouse, *Cold Dawn: The Story of SALT* (New York: Holt, Rinehart and Winston, 1973), p. 251; Transcript of Kissinger's press conference at the Intourist Hotel, Moscow, May 27, 1972, in *Military Implications of the Treaty on the Limitation of Anti-Ballistic Missile Systems and the Interim Agreement on Limitation of Strategic Offensive Arms, Hearing,* before the Committee on Armed Services, Senate, 92d Cong., 2d session, 1972, p. 110. See also Chapter 1, p. 12.

43. In Gromyko's case, he had served as foreign minister for sixteen years before being elevated to the Politburo in the spring of 1973. Ustinov was already a full Politburo member and Central Committee secretary before succeeding the late Marshal Grechko as minister of defense in April 1976. Prior to Grechko's entry into the Politburo at the same time as Gromyko, professional soldiers serving as ministers of defense—with the exception of Marshal G.K. Zhukov's brief tenure in the Politburo in 1956-57—had not enjoyed Politburo status.

44. Myers and Simes, *Soviet Decision Making,* p. 19.

45. Glagolev, in *Orbis,* Winter 1978, p. 771.

46. Shulman, in *SALT: The Moscow Agreements and Beyond,* p. 111; Myers and Simes, *Soviet Decision Making,* p. 24.

47. Glagolev, in *Orbis,* Winter 1978, pp. 771-72. See also Shulman, in *SALT: The Moscow Agreements and Beyond,* p. 111.

48. As noted in Chapter 1, p. 9, the American side in SALT I was often put in the position of having to supply such data itself in order to advance the work of negotiation. Newhouse has recounted the reaction of N.V. Ogarkov, then a Colonel General and the senior Soviet military representative, to the Americans' supplying relevant information to Foreign Ministry personnel on the Soviet delegation: Ogarkov "took aside a U.S. delegate and said there was no reason why the Americans should disclose their knowledge of Russian military matters to civilian members of his delegation. Such information, said Ogarkov, is strictly the affair of the military." See *Cold Dawn,* pp. 55-56, 142. Some observers

attribute the attitude displayed by Ogarkov to the desire of Soviet military leaders to protect and preserve a privileged position in the Soviet decisionmaking process. See Myers and Simes, *Soviet Decision Making*, p. 30.

49. Newhouse, *Cold Dawn*, pp. 191-92.

50. Myers and Simes, *Soviet Decision Making*, p. 24.

51. Lilita I. Dzirkals, Rand Corporation memorandum, "Soviet Views on the Strategic Arms Control Process," Santa Monica, May 31, 1973, p. 10. (Unpublished.)

52. For useful background on the Soviet General Staff, see William J. Spahr, "The Soviet Military Decision-Making Process" (Paper delivered at Fifth National Convention, American Association for the Advancement of Slavic Studies, Dallas, Texas, March 15, 1972), pp. 14-22. See also Edward L. Warner, "The Soviet Military," *Problems of Communism*, Vol. 23, March-April 1974, pp. 78-79, and John M. Collins, *American and Soviet Military Trends Since the Cuban Missile Crisis* (Washington, D.C.: Georgetown University Center for Strategic and International Studies, 1978), pp. 32-34. For a Soviet account of the evolution of the General Staff, see the article on that subject in *Sovetskaia Voennaia Entsiklopediia* (Moscow: Voenizdat, 1976), 2: 511-13.

53. The other two first deputy ministers are Marshal V.G. Kulikov, who was replaced as Chief of the General Staff by Ogarkov in January 1977 and is now Commander-in-Chief of Warsaw Pact Forces, and General S.L. Sokolov, a sixty-eight-year old army officer whose exact responsibilities are not known, even though he has held the post for the last eleven years. The chiefs of each of the five principal Soviet services—Strategic Rocket Forces, Ground Forces, Navy, Air Forces and Air Defense Forces—are among the deputy ministers.

54. Cited by Harriet Scott, in *Air Force Magazine*, March 1977, p. 55. This General Staff responsibility for coordinated action extends also to Civil Defense USSR.

55. Ibid., pp. 54-56. See also Gallagher and Spielmann, *Soviet Decision-Making for Defense*, p. 39.

56. Ibid. This directorate may trace its origins to a special office for the study of modern warfare that was reportedly set up in the General Staff in 1949. See Raymond L. Garthoff, *Soviet Military Doctrine* (Glencoe, Ill.: The Free Press, 1953), p. 61.

57. Shulman, in *SALT: The Moscow Agreements and Beyond*, p. 110.

58. Ibid.

59. See Harriet Scott, in *Air Force Magazine*, March 1977, pp. 53-54.

60. It is possible that Brezhnev might not ordinarily in peacetime take part in the proceedings of the Main Military Council. However, if it is intended that the council in wartime is to become the counterpart of the World War II Stavka—or Headquarters of the Supreme High Command—as some students of the subject think would be the case (ibid., p. 54), then perhaps Brezhnev might participate occasionally on a peacetime training basis, so to speak.

61. See Chapter 3, p. 58. The eight industrial ministries of the defense sector are as follows (the Russian abbreviation of the ministry's name, as well as the name of the minister, are given in parentheses): Defense Industry (MOP, S.A. Zverev); Aviation Industry (MAP, P.V. Dementev); Shipbuilding Industry (MSP,

M.V. Yegorov); Electronics Industry (MEP, A.I. Shokin); Radio Industry (MR, P.S. Pleshakov); General Machine Building (MOM, S.A. Afanasev); Medium Machine Building (MSM, E.P. Slavskii); Machine Building (MM, V.V. Bakhirev). An additional ministry dealing with production of communications equipment may have been added to the defense sector within the last couple of years. Other ministries that contribute to military production include Instrument Making, Automation Equipment, and Control Systems (K.N. Rudnev); Tractor and Agricultural Machine Building (I.F. Sinitsyn); Chemical Industry (L.A. Kostandov); and Automotive Industry (A.M. Tarasov). See Sheren, in *Economic Performance and the Military Burden*, p. 123; Spielmann, in *Problems of Communism*, September-October 1976, pp. 53-57.

62. Andropov, whose post as head of the secret police includes nominal command of KGB security troops, has the rank of General of the Army, as does the man in charge of the Ministry of Internal Affairs (MVD), N.A. Shchelokov. The KGB's "border troops" are estimated to number about 175,000, about the same as the "internal troops" of the MVD. See *The Military Balance: 1976-1977*, International Institute for Strategic Studies, London, September 1976, p. 10.

63. See more on this point in Chapter 3, pp. 68-69, and note 79, below.

64. See David Holloway, "Technology and Political Decision in Soviet Armaments Policy," *Journal of Peace Research*, Vol. 11, no. 4, 1974, p. 260; Thomas W. Wolfe, *The Military Dimension in the Making of Soviet Foreign and Defense Policy*, The Rand Corporation, P-6024, Santa Monica, October 1977, pp. 24-26. The latter paper may also be found in *The Soviet Union: Internal Dynamics of Foreign Policy, Present and Future, Hearings*, before the Subcommittee on Europe and the Middle East, Committee on International Relations, House of Representatives, 95th Cong., September-October 1977 (Washington: Government Printing Office, 1978), pp. 85-128.

65. Cf. Holloway, in *Journal of Peace Research*, no. 4, 1974, pp. 259-60.

66. According to remarks made to the author and other visiting scholars in Moscow in September 1974 by G.M. Gvishiani, deputy chairman of the State Committee for Science and Technology.

67. See Chapter 3, p. 74.

68. Khrushchev's frequent invitations to prominent scientists to discuss the military implications of their work were a case in point. See *Khrushchev Remembers: The Last Testament* (Boston: Little, Brown & Co., 1974), pp. 58-71.

69. Shulman, in *SALT: The Moscow Agreements and Beyond*, pp. 111-12; Newhouse, *Cold Dawn*, pp. 53, 231, 242.

70. Shulman, in *SALT: The Moscow Agreements and Beyond*, p. 111.

71. Ibid., p. 112; Glagolev, in *Orbis*, Winter 1978, p. 770.

72. According to Igor Glagolev, a Soviet émigré who once headed the disarmament section in Inozemtsev's institute, the section was deactivated in 1968. Other accounts indicate that it was later re-established. See Glagolev, in *Orbis*, Winter 1978, p. 770; Shulman, in *SALT: The Moscow Agreements and Beyond*, p. 112.

73. The original chairman of the Division of Military-Political Problems of

International Relations in Inozemtsev's institute was Colonel V.M. Kulish, and the Division on Military Aspects of Foreign Policy at Arbatov's institute has been headed successively by Colonel V.V. Larionov and Lieutenant General M. Milshteyn. All are well known in professional circles outside the USSR by their writings and personal contacts with foreign colleagues.

74. Cf. Myers and Simes, *Soviet Decision Making*, p. 35.

75. Ibid., p. 36. See also Shulman, in *SALT: The Moscow Agreements and Beyond*, p. 112.

76. The author, for example, has discussed with various members of both institutes in the past the question of what policy use had been made of their research. The general impression gained was that though some papers prepared in the institutes did find their way to offices in the Ministries of Foreign Affairs and Defense, and to the Central Committee staff, interaction between institute researchers and official policymakers was not very close.

77. Both Inozemtsev and Arbatov are candidate members of the Central Committee, which gives them positions of moderate but scarcely high prestige in terms of the Party hierarchy. See "Composition of the Central Committee of the CPSU Elected at the 25th Party Congress," *Pravda*, March 6, 1976.

78. See above, note 48. Semenov was replaced in October 1978 by Victor P. Karpov. See Chapter 11, p. 240.

79. See list in the *New York Times*, November 21, 1969. According to Paul Nitze, one-third of the Soviet delegation staff had KGB experience. "Inside SALT 1 and 2: Soviet's Negotiating Style Assayed," *Aviation Week & Space Technology*, February 17, 1975, p. 42. The one-third figure parallels that given by the Church Committee for the proportion of Soviet officials abroad who are affiliated with the KGB and GRU. *Foreign and Military Intelligence, Book I*, Final Report, Senate, Select Committee to Study Governmental Operations with Respect to Intelligence Activities, 94th Cong., 2d session, pp. 557, 561.

80. Ogarkov, who was elected to the Central Committee in 1971, had been mentioned the same year as a likely successor to Marshal M.V. Zakharov, the ill and aging chief of the General Staff. Zakharov, however, was replaced in 1971 by General of the Army V.G. Kulikov, whom Ogarkov in turn replaced in January 1977. See Ruth Worthen, "Ogarkov and the Current Soviet Military," Washington, D.C., May 1977, pp. 8-9. (Unpublished.) Both Ogarkov and Kulikov were promoted to the rank of marshal of the Soviet Union on January 14, 1977. See Decrees of the Presidium of the Supreme Soviet, nos. 42 and 43, in *Vedomosti Verkhovnogo Soveta*, January 19, 1977, p. 27.

81. Alexander O. Gebhardt and William Schneider, Jr., "The Soviet High Command: Recent Changes and Policy Implications," *Military Review*, May 1973, p. 9.

82. Mackintosh, in *Problems of Communism*, September-October 1973, p. 10.

83. Garthoff, in *Problems of Communism*, January-February 1975, p. 28.

84. The same was true of D.F. Ustinov, the present minister of defense, before he was elevated to the rank of marshal.

85. See Chalmers M. Roberts, "The Road to Moscow," in *SALT: The Moscow Agreements and Beyond*, p. 26; Myers and Simes, *Soviet Decision Making*, p. 24.

86. This discussion of Soviet negotiating practices is based, in addition to the author's conversations with various participants, on the following published accounts: Newhouse, *Cold Dawn*, pp. 55-56, 206-16; Garthoff, in *Problems of Communism*, January-February 1975, pp. 28-29, and in *International Security*, Spring 1977, pp. 5-8; Mackintosh, in *Problems of Communism*, September-October 1973, p. 10; Nitze, in *Aviation Week & Space Technology*, February 17, 1975, pp. 41-43.

87. See Chapter 1, p. 9, and Chapter 3, p. 61, and note 47, above.

88. See note 48, above.

89. See Chapter 1, p. 10, and Chapter 2, p. 34. See also the further back-channel discussion in Chapter 4, pp. 79-84 and 86-91.

90. For previous discussion of the setting up of the Standing Consultative Commission, see Chapter 2, pp. 34-36.

91. Ibid.

92. See Flora Lewis, "Strategic Debate and Secrecy," *New York Times*, July 9, 1974. For a list of the kinds of information considered to be government secrets in the Soviet Union, see William F. Scott, "All Their (Red) Cards Are in the Hole," *Air Force Magazine*, October 1974, p. 33.

93. Another explanation for suppressing the protocol text has been offered by Igor Glagolev, the former Soviet arms control expert. According to him, the "Politburo forbids Soviet specialists to make any mention of the protocol to the 1972 interim agreement precisely because the Soviet Union's superiority in SLBMs is acknowledged therein." To cite the comparative figures would undermine the basis "on which to demand more and more of new weapons for the USSR." See *Orbis*, Winter 1978, p. 775.

94. One of the more widely known studies reflecting this viewpoint is Roman Kolkowicz's *The Soviet Military and the Communist Party*, (Princeton: At the University Press, 1967).

95. An articulate expositor of this view is William E. Odom. See his "The Party Connection," *Problems of Communism*, Vol. 22, September-October 1973, pp. 12-26; "The Militarization of Soviet Society," ibid., Vol. 25, September-October 1976, pp. 34-51; and "Who Controls Whom in Moscow," *Foreign Policy*, Summer 1975, pp. 109-22.

96. This view may be found in a paper by Timothy J. Colton, "The Party-Military Connection: An Overview" (Delivered at an Airlie House conference, March 3, 1977). See also Thomas W. Wolfe, "Military Power and Soviet Policy," in William E. Griffith, ed., *The Soviet Empire: Expansion & Détente* (Lexington, Mass.: Lexington Books, 1976), p. 156.

97. Simes, *Detente and Conflict*, p. 49. The point that rules of the game put a premium on minimizing elite conflict and maintaining the leadership coalition is also made by Dennis Ross in *Rethinking Soviet Strategic Policy: Inputs and Implications*, Center for Arms Control and International Security, University of California, Los Angeles, June 1977, p. 21.

98. See Wolfe, *The Military Dimension in the Making of Soviet Foreign and Defense Policy*, pp. 35-42, for a description of some of the dominant security attitudes of the Soviet political and military elite.

99. See Mackintosh, in *Problems of Communism*, September-October 1973, p. 4.

100. According to revised estimates published by the CIA covering the period 1970-1975, Soviet defense spending increased at an annual average rate of 4 to 5 percent. (In constant 1970 rubles, from approximately 40 billion to 60 billion rubles.) Other analyses have placed the annual rate of increase for the same period at 8 percent or more. See *Estimated Soviet Defense Spending in Rubles, 1970-1975*, SR 76-10121U, Central Intelligence Agency, May 1976, p. 1; William T. Lee, *The Estimation of Soviet Defense Expenditures, 1955-1975: An Unconventional Approach* (New York: Praeger Publishers, 1977), p. 26. For an instructive discussion of the revisions of earlier estimates, see Andrew W. Marshall, "Estimating Soviet Defense Spending," *Survival*, Vol. 18, March-April 1976, pp. 73-79.

101. These included his services at the front as an army political commissar in World War II and postwar assignments giving him important responsibilities for political-military affairs in the Navy, and for supervision of major defense-industry undertakings, among other things.

102. It should be noted that there is not necessarily a single unified "military viewpoint" in the Soviet Union, although interservice rivalry is a good deal more muted there than in the United States. Among matters testifying to some interservice differences of view in the Soviet Union was the creation of the Strategic Rocket Forces, which gave rise to various budgetary and conceptual conflicts with the older services. For relevant commentary, see: *Khrushchev Remembers: The Last Testament*, pp. 52-53; Graham T. Allison, *Essence of Decision: Explaining the Cuban Missile Crisis* (Boston: Little, Brown and Company, 1971), pp. 114-16. See also the discussion concerning internal Soviet military debate in Thomas W. Wolfe, *Soviet Strategy at the Crossroads* (Cambridge: Harvard University Press, 1965), pp. 26-37.

103. See Wolfe, in *The Soviet Empire: Expansion and Détente*, p. 157; Ross, *Rethinking Soviet Strategic Policy*, pp. 5, 19; Holloway, in *Journal of Peace Research*, no. 4, 1974, p. 269; Myers and Simes, *Soviet Decision Making*, p. 35.

104. See Chapter 3, p. 67. Cf. also Myers and Simes, *Soviet Decision Making*, pp. 35-37. These authors take the view that the institutes have in fact gone a considerable way toward providing the political leadership with qualified expertise on strategic issues, other than that furnished by the military-industrial complex.

105. Cf. Spielmann, *Analyzing Soviet Strategic Arms Decisions*, p. 26; Shulman, in *SALT: The Moscow Agreements and Beyond*, p. 112.

106. See Holloway, in *Journal of Peace Research*, no. 4, 1974, pp. 268-69.

107. See Chapter 3, p. 67.

108. The late Marshal Grechko, for example, admonished military planners and defense-industry workers to heed the Party's demands that decisions regarding armaments and combat equipment be "justifiable, effective and economical," since "any miscalculations in this sphere could lead to unjustified expenditure of funds, and of the economic and manpower resources of the country." A.A. Grechko, "The Leading Role of the CPSU in Building the Army of a Developed Socialist Society," *Voprosy Istorii KPSS*, no. 5, 1974, p. 41. See also Holloway, in *Journal of Peace Research*, no. 4, 1974, pp. 268-69.

109. One of the formal indices sometimes used in attempts to gauge the power-standing and policy influence of the Soviet military is the proportion of military men admitted to the Central Committee at successive Party Congresses. By this symbolic yardstick, the influence of the military has declined slightly over the decade covered by the past three Party Congresses, as shown below in a table adapted from Ruth Worthen, "Ogarkov and the Current Soviet Military," p. 15:

### Military Membership on Central Committee

|           | *1966*     | *1971*     | *1976*     |
|-----------|------------|------------|------------|
| Candidate | *18* of 165 | *13* of 155 | *10* of 139 |
| Full      | *14* of 195 | *20* of 241 | *20* of 287 |

110. For a sampling of such articles, see: Colonel E. Rybkin, "Critique of Bourgeois Conceptions of War and Peace," *Kommunist vooruzhennykh sil*, September 1968, pp. 89-90; Lieutenant Colonel V. Bondarenko, "The Contemporary Revolution in Military Affairs and the Combat Readiness of the Armed Forces," ibid., December 1968, pp. 24-29; Major General K.S. Bochkarev, "V.I. Lenin and the Building of the Armed Forces of the USSR," *Morskoi Sbornik*, February 1969, pp. 4-5; A. Galitsan, "For a Leninist Line," *Voenno-istoricheskii zhurnal*, March 1969, pp. 12-13.

111. See Chapter 1, pp. 2-3.

112. Garthoff, in *Problems of Communism*, January-February 1975, p. 27.

113. Douglas F. Garthoff, "The Soviet Military and Arms Control," *Survival*, November-December 1977, pp. 244-45.

114. Which of these explanations seems to ring more true depends in part on whether one applies the "partnership" or the "conflict" model of Soviet civil-military relations.

115. See Raymond L. Garthoff, in *Problems of Communism*, January-February 1975, pp. 29, 37; Douglas F. Garthoff, in *Survival*, November-December 1977, p. 249; Wolfe, in *SALT: Implications for Arms Control in the 1970s*, p. 36.

116. Douglas Garthoff, in *Survival*, November-December 1977, p. 249.

117. Published articles by Ogarkov include the following: "Development of the Theory of Soviet Operational Art in the 30s," *Voenno-istoricheskii zhurnal*, March 1965; "We Stand on Guard," *Izvestiia*, July 20, 1967; "Service Is Honorable and Responsible," *Krasnaia zvezda*, September 3, 1971; "Deep Operations," *Sovetskaia Voennaia Entsiklopediia* (Moscow: Voenizdat, 1976), 2: 574-78; "The Theoretical Arsenal of Military Leadership," *Sovetskaia Rossiia*, February 23, 1977.

118. The point that decisions producing notable buildups of Soviet military forces tended to be clustered in the periods when Khrushchev and Brezhnev were consolidating their domestic political power has been made by Helmut Sonnenfeldt, in "Russia, America and Detente," *Foreign Affairs*, January 1978, pp. 277-78.

NOTES TO CHAPTER 4
OTHER ASPECTS OF THE SALT INSTITUTIONAL
SETTING: THE BACK CHANNEL AND SUMMITRY

1. See previous discussion of this SALT I impasse, Chapter 1, pp. 10-11.

2. The fullest account of the genesis and subsequent cultivation of the back channel in SALT I is to be found in John Newhouse, *Cold Dawn: The Story of SALT* (New York: Holt, Rinehart and Winston, 1973), pp. 203-6, 214-43. A critical account of the parallel back-channel negotiations by a SALT delegation member is given by Raymond L. Garthoff, "Negotiating with the Russians: Some Lessons from SALT," *International Security*, Spring 1977, pp. 8-10, 15-16.

3. See Chapter 1, p. 10.

4. Newhouse, *Cold Dawn*, p. 203.

5. Ibid., p. 204. With regard to the channels of communication employed by Dobrynin for back-channel traffic, according to one study he communicated both with the Ministry of Foreign Affairs and (after Brezhnev supplanted Kosygin as the key link at the Moscow end) with Brezhnev's personal secretariat through A.M. Aleksandrov, who in turn kept the Central Committee and Politburo informed. According to the same study, Dobrynin was assisted at the Washington end of the back-channel operation by Minister-Counselor Y.M. Vorontsov. See Kenneth A. Myers and Dimitri Simes, *Soviet Decision Making, Strategic Policy, and SALT*, Georgetown University Center for Strategic and International Studies, Washington, D.C., December 1974, p. 25.

6. Newhouse, *Cold Dawn*, pp. 206, 214-17, 231. See also Garthoff, in *International Security*, Spring 1977, p. 8.

7. Garthoff, in *International Security*, Spring 1977, pp. 8-9. The personal correspondence on SALT that passed first between President Nixon and Kosygin, and later between Nixon and Brezhnev, has not been made public. In his memoirs, it may be noted, Nixon states that the first of his personal messages opening the back channel on January 9, 1971, was to Brezhnev, and he says nothing about any messages to Kosygin. Whether Nixon's account or the others cited in note 2, above, are more accurate on this point will not be known until the actual correspondence is published. See *RN: The Memoirs of Richard Nixon* (New York: Grosset and Dunlap, 1978), p. 523.

8. Newhouse, *Cold Dawn*, p. 243. Even the American ambassador in Moscow at the time had not been apprised of Kissinger's trip.

9. Bernard Gwertzman, "Brezhnev Linked to Kissinger Trip," *New York Times*, April 27, 1972.

10. For previous discussion of the various issues involved in the April 1972 back-channel talks and at the summit a month later, see Chapter 1, pp. 11-13. See also Garthoff, in *International Security*, Spring 1977, pp. 9-17.

11. The personal messages between Nixon and Brezhnev did not deal exclusively with SALT, of course, as indicated by President Nixon in his memoirs. See *RN: The Memoirs of Richard Nixon*, pp. 875-76.

12. It should be noted that, although Kissinger's trips to Moscow perhaps received more attention in the media, Soviet Foreign Minister Andrei Gromyko

traveled to the United States several times during the Nixon-Ford period to attend UN sessions, in the course of which he also discussed SALT-related business in Washington. For a chronological listing of all the meetings, as well as of the summits and the regular sessions of the SALT delegations, see Appendix C.

13. Carroll Kilpatrick, "Kissinger to Go to Munich, Moscow," *Washington Post*, September 6, 1972.

14. Murrey Marder, "Kissinger Finds Talks Productive," ibid., September 17, 1972.

15. Hedrick Smith, "Kissinger Leaves Soviet after Four Days of Talks," *New York Times*, May 10, 1973.

16. See: "Excerpts from Kissinger's News Briefing on the Forthcoming Visit by Brezhnev," *New York Times*, June 15, 1973; "Excerpts from Kissinger's Briefing on Arms Accord," ibid., June 22, 1973.

17. Bernard Gwertzman, "Brezhnev's Summit Visit to U.S. Scheduled June 18," *New York Times*, May 13, 1973.

18. Murrey Marder, "U.S. Seen Misjudging Soviets: Moscow Found Unready for Early Nuclear Pact," *Washington Post*, March 31, 1974.

19. Bernard Gwertzman, "Kissinger Fails to Sway Moscow on Nuclear Arms," *New York Times*, March 29, 1974. The substance of these stalemated SALT issues will be taken up later. See Chapter 5, pp. 93-106.

20. Bernard Gwertzman, "Kissinger Leaves Moscow Hopeful on Arms Accord," *New York Times*, October 28, 1974.

21. Leslie H. Gelb, "How U.S. Made Ready for Talk at Vladivostok," *New York Times*, December 3, 1974. A detailed discussion of the Vladivostok understanding and the events leading up to it will be found in Chapters 8, pp. 171-72, and Chapter 9.

22. Christopher S. Wren, "U.S.-Soviet Talks Said to Progress," *New York Times*, January 22, 1976; Murrey Marder, "New SALT Proposals Face Tests" and "Arms Pact: A Cap for Kissinger Era," *Washington Post*, January 24 and February 8, 1976. The substantive aspects of the Backfire, cruise missile, and other disputed SALT II issues in the post-Vladivostok period are taken up in Chapter 10, pp. 199-202, 211-17.

23. For a list of these meetings, consult Appendix C. The substantive matters addressed at these Kissinger-Gromyko meetings are taken up at appropriate points in the text. See Chapter 10.

24. See: "Kissinger Meets Gromyko to Talk About Relations," *New York Times*, February 17, 1975; Murrey Marder, "Gains Cited by Kissinger in Vienna," *Washington Post*, May 21, 1975; Flora Lewis, "U.S.-Soviet Talks on Nuclear Arms Reported in Peril" and "U.S.-Soviet Inspection Gain Confirmed," *New York Times*, July 11, 12, 1975; Bernard Gwertzman, "U.S. and Soviet Union Resume Arms Talks: Gromyko Meets Kissinger Here, but Officials See Little Hope of Early Breakthrough," ibid., September 30, 1976.

25. See Dom Bonafede, "Brezezinski—Stepping out of His Backstage Role," *National Journal*, October 15, 1977, p. 1598; Rose E. Gottemoeller, *Evolution of the U.S. Organizational Setup for Dealing with SALT*, The Rand Corporation, P-6197, Santa Monica, November 1978, p. 23.

26. Others in the official party included Marshall D. Shulman, Mr. Vance's adviser on Soviet affairs; Lieutenant General Edward L. Rowny, representing the JCS; Leslie H. Gelb, Director of the Bureau of Politico-Military Affairs; and Arthur A. Hartman, Assistant Secretary for European Affairs. Bernard Gwertzman, "Vance Is in Moscow to Affirm Detente and Seek Arms Cuts," *New York Times*, March 27, 1977.

27. However, according to a brief comment to reporters by Secretary of State Vance, the Soviets had received at least a week of advance notice of the new U.S. proposals. See "Soviet Had Advance Notice," *New York Times*, April 7, 1977. Under previous administrations, it had been the customary, though not invariable, practice to give the Soviets a one- or two-week preview of new proposals in order to permit them to have a response in hand when senior officials met.

28. Bernard Gwertzman, "Arms Talks Break Off As Soviet Rejects 2 Key Proposals by U.S.; Carter Says He Isn't Discouraged," *New York Times*, March 31, 1977; Murrey Marder and Peter Osnos, "Brezhnev Grim; Talks Resume in May," *Washington Post*, March 31, 1977. Further details on this first set of Carter administration proposals will be found in Chapter 11, pp. 221-24.

29. If the summits of the Nixon-Ford period are included, the average of high-level meetings on SALT would go up to four per year.

30. See list of meetings, Appendix C. In addition to those mentioned, American participants in the talks in Washington on September 27, 1977, included Vice President Walter F. Mondale and Ambassador Malcolm Toon.

31. Summitry began with meetings of Roosevelt, Churchill, Stalin, and other allied leaders in World War II, and continued with at least one Soviet-American summit during the incumbency of each American president thereafter.

32. See Chapter 1, pp. 11-13. It was Nixon's style at some summit sessions, according to one of his top aides, to introduce one or two major topics and sketch out the general guidelines of U.S. policy, after which he would withdraw and leave it to Kissinger and other aides to discuss the details with the Russians. See article on William Hyland, "Dealing with the Russian Leaders," *Time*, November 21, 1977, p. 28.

33. See Chapter 4, p. 82.

34. This agreement, entitled "Basic Principles of Negotiations on the Further Limitation of Strategic Offensive Arms," together with a companion agreement on the "Prevention of Nuclear War" that was not a direct product of the SALT negotiations, may be found in *The Washington Summit: General Secretary Brezhnev's Visit to the United States, June 18-25, 1973*, Department of State pamphlet, pp. 17, 30.

35. See "Texts of Nuclear Accords and of Joint Statement," *New York Times*, July 4, 1974.

36. See Chapter 2, p. 35. It may be noted that though most of Nixon's third summit meeting with Brezhnev was held in Moscow, some of the talks took place during a side trip to Oreanda, near Yalta, in the Crimea.

37. John Herbers, "Nixon, Brezhnev Delay Key Curbs on Arms Till '85," *New York Times*, July 4, 1974; Hedrick Smith, "Wait-and-See Summit," ibid.; Leslie Gelb, "Summit Talk Foundered over MIRVs," ibid., July 9, 1974. See also Chapter 5, pp. 94-98.

38. Further discussion of the Vladivostok accord of November 1974 will be found in Chapter 9.

39. Henry S. Bradsher, "Problems Haunt SALT despite Official Optimism," *Washington Star*, August 4, 1975; Statement by Senator James L. Buckley, "The Score on SALT," in *Aviation Week & Space Technology*, September 8, 1975, p. 11. A fuller treatment of the post-Vladivostok issues will be found in Chapter 10, pp. 199-217.

40. For further discussion of trends in the U.S.-Soviet relationship and their bearing on SALT, see Chapters 10 and 11, pp. 202-11, 219-21, 231.

41. See Ray S. Cline, "Policy Without Intelligence," *Foreign Policy*, no. 17 (Winter 1974-1975), pp. 123-24ff.

42. See Chapter 2, p. 34.

43. Marilyn Berger, "Nitze Notes Lack of Trust by Top Aides," *Washington Post*, June 25, 1974.

44. Ibid. See also Nitze's account in *Aviation Week & Space Technology*, February 17, 1975, p. 43, giving the following commentary on secrecy between the delegation level and the top negotiating level: "Nixon had such a passion for secrecy and such a lack of confidence in the reliability and judgment of . . . the bureaucracy that not even the head of the U.S. delegation was kept precisely informed of what was happening at the higher level. This went to such lengths that . . . Nixon would rely on the Soviet interpreters rather than the . . . American interpreters whose notes might be made available to others on the U.S. side. As a result, there is no precise U.S. record of what was said. Even the less precise memoranda of discussion, subsequently dictated by a member of Kissinger's staff, were not made available outside of the White House. . . . A further consequence of these procedures was that the President and his immediate advisers were deprived of available expertise and of the ability to fine comb the relevant detail. This resulted in unnecessary difficulties, some of significant consequence, in parrying Soviet strategy and tactics."

One should note that Nixon himself has given a quite different explanation for using only a Soviet interpreter, Victor Sukhodrev, in meetings with Brezhnev. "I knew that Sukhodrev was a superb linguist who spoke English as well as he did Russian, and I felt that Brezhnev would speak more freely if only one other person was present." *RN: The Memoirs of Richard Nixon*, p. 610.

45. See Chapter 1, pp. 11-13.

46. Garthoff, in *International Security*, Spring 1977, pp. 14-17.

47. Ibid., p. 17.

48. The underlying rationale for managing SALT in a way which involved keeping certain central decisions and back-channel transactions confined to a very small circle was conveyed by Dr. Kissinger in the following words (as reported in the *Washington Post*, January 30, 1972):

"Because management of the bureaucracy takes so much energy and precisely because changing course is so difficult, many of the most important decisions are kept to a very small circle while the bureaucracy continue working away in ignorance of the fact that decisions are being made, or of the fact that a decision is being made in a particular area. One reason for keeping the decisions to small groups is that when bureaucracies are so unwieldy and when their internal morale becomes a serious problem, an unpopular decision may be fought by brutal means, such as leaks to the press or congressional committees. Thus, the only way secrecy can be kept is to exclude from the making of the decision those who are theoretically charged with carrying it out."

49. Murrey Marder, "Jackson Claims Alteration in U.S.-Soviet Missile Pact," *Washington Post*, June 22, 1974.

50. Ibid. See also Murrey Marder and Dan Morgan, "No Loophole in A-Accord—Kissinger," *Washington Post*, June 25, 1974.

51. Marilyn Berger, " 'Secret Deal' over SALT Seen Routine," *Washington Post*, June 28, 1974.

52. Details of this second loophole, said to have been pointed out to Kissinger in a memorandum of March 11, 1974, from the Joint Chiefs of Staff, have not been made public. Instructions to the U.S. component of the Standing Consultative Commission to plug this loophole were reportedly contained in National Security Memorandum no. 252, signed on April 18, 1974. Ibid. See also, Thomas B. Ross, "Kissinger Plugged SALT Loophole," *Washington Post*, June 27, 1974.

53. Editorial, "Secretary Kissinger's Response," *Washington Post*, June 25, 1974. Leslie H. Gelb, "Missile Misunderstanding Clarifies a Power Struggle," *New York Times*, June 26, 1974.

54. For a thoughtful general argument against excessive secrecy in the SALT negotiating process, see Lawrence D. Weiler, *The Arms Race, Secret Negotiations and the Congress*, Occasional Paper 12, The Stanley Foundation, Muscatine, Iowa, 1976, especially pp. 4-12.

55. See Chapter 4, p. 87.

56. See Garthoff, in *International Security*, Spring 1977, p. 9. See also Chapter 4, p. 80.

57. Dobrynin, for example, was apparently intimately involved in mending the damage following the unsuccessful Vance trip to Moscow in March 1977. See Bernard Gwertzman, "Dobrynin Consults with Vance to Seek a New Arms Parley," *New York Times*, April 8, 1977; Bernard Gwertzman, "Carter and Dobrynin Meet on Arms Issue," *New York Times*, April 13, 1977; Hedrick Smith, "Deadlock on Arms Talks Persists As Dobrynin and Brzezinski Meet," *New York Times*, April 14, 1977.

58. See Rowland Evans and Robert Novak, "Signaling Moscow: A Change in Channels," *Washington Post*, December 10, 1977.

59. See Christopher S. Wren, "U.S. Ambassador in Moscow off to Auspicious Start," *New York Times*, November 6, 1974.

60. The appointment of Toon, a Foreign Service veteran with considerable prior Moscow experience and a "hard line" reputation, was at first resisted by the Russians and later reconfirmed only after some delay by the Carter administration. "Soviet, Yielding, Accepts Toon As Ambassador," *New York Times*, November 25, 1976; "Carter Retains Envoy in Moscow and Picks Career Man for Paris," ibid., April 26, 1977.

61. Evans and Novak, in *Washington Post*, December 10, 1977. According to

this article, President Carter had acted to reduce the disparity between the influence of Soviet Ambassador Dobrynin in Washington and that of the U.S. ambassador in Moscow by making much heavier use of Ambassador Toon.

62. See Hedrick Smith, "Carter's Quest: Line on Soviet," *New York Times*, July 14, 1978.

## NOTES TO CHAPTER 5
## PRINCIPAL SALT II ISSUES PRIOR
## TO VLADIVOSTOK

1. Marshall D. Shulman, "SALT and the Soviet Union," in Mason Willrich and John B. Rhinelander, eds., *SALT: The Moscow Agreements and Beyond* (New York: The Free Press, 1974), p. 121.

2. See Chapter 4, p. 85.

3. The idea of "a brief extension of the Interim Agreement tied to an equally brief MIRV agreement" is said to have originated with a back-channel proposal by Dr. Kissinger prior to the 1974 Moscow summit. This proposal reportedly got a cool reception in Moscow during the Brezhnev-Kissinger advance talks in March 1974 (see p. 82). At the summit itself, further discussion between the top leaders confirmed that the proposal was still unacceptable to the Russians. See Clarence A. Robinson, Jr., "Soviets Demand B-1, Trident End," *Aviation Week & Space Technology*, April 15, 1974, p. 14, and Kissinger's July 3, 1974, press conference in Moscow. Text of the latter may be found in the *Department of State Bulletin*, July 29, 1974, pp. 205-14 (hereafter cited as *Kissinger Press Conference in Moscow, July 3, 1974*).

4. See Murrey Marder, "A-Pact Product of Stalemate," *Washington Post*, July 5, 1974; Robert Keatley, "Moscow Summit Failure to Get Arms Pact Spurs a New Approach for Geneva Talks," *Wall Street Journal*, July 5, 1974; Paul Nitze, "Assessing the Strategic-Arms Negotiations in Moscow," *New York Times*, July 26, 1974.

5. The pertinent language of the joint U.S.-Soviet communiqué of July 3, 1974, on the subject was as follows: "They [the two sides] concluded that the Interim Agreement on offensive strategic weapons should be followed by a new agreement . . . that such an agreement should cover the period until 1985 and deal with both quantitative and qualitative limitations . . . that such an agreement should be completed at the earliest possible date, before the expiration of the Interim Agreement."

6. Statement by Paul H. Nitze before the House Armed Services Special Subcommittee on Arms Control and Disarmament, July 2, 1974. See: "Nitze: 'Essential Equivalence' Should Be Arms Talk Goal," *Aviation Week & Space Technology*, July 22, 1974, p. 43 (hereafter cited as *Nitze Statement, July 2, 1974*). Full statement may be found in House Armed Services Committee Document no. 93-69, Hearings held before the Special Subcommittee on Arms Control and Disarmament, 93rd Congress, 2d session, May 8, 13, 15, 21, and July 2, 1974, pp. 57-70. See also Nitze's subsequent commentary, *Aviation Week & Space Technology*, February 17, 1975, p. 43.

7. *Nitze Statement, July 2, 1974*, p. 42.

8. For details of the differential numbers stipulated in the Interim Agreement, see above, Chapter 1, p. 13.

9. See, for example: M.A. Milshteyn and L.S. Semeiko, "Strategic Arms Limitation: Problems and Prospects," *SShA: Ekonomika, Politika, Ideologiia*, no. 12 (December 1973), p. 7; G.A. Trofimenko, "USSR-USA: Peaceful Coexistence As a Norm of Mutual Relations," ibid., no. 2 (February 1974), p. 13; V.V. Larionov, "Arms Limitation and Its Enemies," *Pravda*, April 7, 1974. A. Karenin, "On Restraining Strategic Arms," *Mezhdunarodnye Otnosheniia*, no. 9 (September 1974), p. 15.

10. Paul H. Nitze, "Assuring Strategic Stability in an Era of Détente," *Foreign Affairs*, January 1976, p. 218. See also *Nitze Statement, July 2, 1974*, p. 42.

11. Leslie H. Gelb, "U.S. Urges New Arms Talk Approach," *New York Times*, March 3, 1974; "Questions and Answers on the Talks on Nuclear Arms," ibid., April 12, 1974.

12. *Nitze Statement, July 2, 1974*, p. 42.

13. Ibid., p. 43.

14. See discussion of Soviet missile programs in Chapter 6, pp. 116-25.

15. Official figures were not published, but estimates in the press gave a figure of about 16.7 million pounds of "weapon-delivery weight" or payload for the U.S. bomber force. That of the Soviet Union would amount to a third of that or less. See Clarence A. Robinson, Jr., "SALT Extension Trades Pondered," *Aviation Week & Space Technology*, May 27, 1974. p. 14.

16. These figures were attributed to unnamed American officials after the July 1974 summit. See Leslie Gelb, "Summit Talk Foundered over MIRV's," *New York Times*, July 9, 1974. See also further discussion in Chapter 6, p. 120f.

17. See Chapter 9, pp. 190-91.

18. See transcript in *Military Implications of the Treaty on the Limitation of Anti-Ballistic Missile Systems and the Interim Agreement on Limitation of Strategic Offensive Arms, Hearing*, before the Committee on Armed Services, Senate, 92d Cong., 2d session, 1972, p. 119.

19. As discussed in Chapter 1, the U.S. side had noted in a May 1972 unilateral statement that it "would consider any ICBM having a volume significantly greater than that of the largest light ICBM now operational on either side to be a heavy ICBM." The largest "light" ICBM at the time was the Soviet SS-11, with a volume of about seventy cubic meters. Subsequent Soviet replacement of the SS-11 by the SS-19, a missile of "significantly greater" volume, though not technically a violation since the Soviets did not adhere to the U.S. unilateral statement, was nevertheless taken by critics to represent an evasion of the spirit of the May 1972 accords. See: Protocol to the Interim Agreement, in *Arms Control and Disarmament Agreements: Texts and History of Negotiations*, U.S. Arms Control and Disarmament Agency, Washington, D.C., February 1974, p. 147; Raymond L. Garthoff, "SALT and the Soviet Military," *Problems of Communism*, January-February 1975, p. 32. See also Chapters 1, p. 12, and 10, p. 209f.

20. For further discussion of the MIRV technology demonstrated by the Soviet Union, see Chapter 6, pp. 118-20.

21. See Chapter 4, p. 82f.

22. At that time the United States had already MIRVed about 450 ICBM launchers and slightly more than 300 SLBM launchers. The planned U.S. ceilings under existing programs were 550 MIRVed ICBMs (Minuteman III) and about 500 MIRVed SLBMs (Poseidon), hence the Kissinger offer would entail a cutback of about 300 MIRVings.

23. Leslie H. Gelb, "Kissinger Said to Offer Halt on New Missiles," *New York Times*, March 31, 1974; ibid., April 12, 1974. What specific throwweight figure may have been offered, if any, was not disclosed.

24. It has been questioned, however, whether a bomber payload advantage for the United States would in the long run offset the Soviet Union's unMIRVed missile throwweight, especially if U.S. bombers were to be countered by unlimited Soviet air defenses. See *Nitze Statement, July 2, 1974*, p. 43. See also Michael Nacht, "The Vladivostok Accord and American Technological Options," *Survival*, May-June 1975, p. 108.

25. See Chapter 4, p. 82f. See also Murrey Marder, "U.S., Soviet Fail to Progress on Arms Limitation," *Washington Post*, March 29, 1974.

26. Murrey Marder, "U.S. Seen Misjudging Soviets," *Washington Post*, March 31, 1974.

27. *Nitze Statement, July 2, 1974*, p. 43.

28. See, for example, Joseph Alsop, "Watergate's Impact on Detente," *Washington Post*, April 5, 1974.

29. Editorial, "New Chance for SALT," *New York Times*, December 26, 1974.

30. Hedrick Smith, "Summit Talks at Delicate Stage," *New York Times*, July 2, 1974. See also Paul H. Nitze, "The Vladivostok Accord and SALT II," *Review of Politics*, April 1975, p. 152.

31. Hedrick Smith, "Moscow Sought Parity," *New York Times*, July 9, 1974; Leslie Gelb, ibid. A slightly higher upper limit of 750 was offered to the Soviets, according to Joseph Kraft, who said this was more than the number favored by Secretary of Defense Schlesinger. According to Kraft's arithmetic, Schlesinger had proposed a ceiling of about 600. See Kraft's "Letter From Moscow," *The New Yorker*, July 29, 1974, p. 70.

32. Gelb, in the *New York Times*, July 9, 1974.

33. Ibid.

34. See Garthoff, in *Problems of Communism*, January-February 1975, p. 36.

35. Kraft, in *The New Yorker*, July 29, 1974, p. 70.

36. Ibid. Kraft's article on the mid-1974 summit gave the first public disclosure of the figure of 1000 MIRVed launchers as the proposed Soviet quota. In his memoirs, former President Nixon discussed the inability of the two sides at the mid-1974 summit to agree on MIRV numbers, but his rather elliptical account failed to mention what the respective numbers in dispute actually were. The only figure mentioned came in a statement attributed to Kissinger, in which he remarked that the United States was capable of equipping an additional 500 Minuteman with MIRV over a two-year period. See *RN: The Memoirs of Richard Nixon* (New York: Grosset & Dunlap, 1978), pp. 1031-32.

37. According to information attributed to high American officials, the estimated Soviet deployment rate for MIRVed launchers could run as high as, or higher than, 200 per year, which would bring the level to about 1000 in 1980 for a deployment program beginning in 1975. According to the same sources, the U.S. side in the Moscow talks was aiming at agreement with the Soviets to hold their deployment rate at no more than 70 to 80 MIRVed launchers per year. See Rowland Evans and Robert Novak, "The Dangers in Deadlock," *Washington Post*, June 29, 1974. See also Chapters 6, p. 118, and 9, p. 184.

38. Quoted by Gelb, in the *New York Times*, July 9, 1974.

39. Ibid.

40. See Chapter 1, pp. 12-13.

41. *Kissinger Press Conference in Moscow, July 3, 1974*, p. 215.

42. Ibid., p. 210.

43. With respect to the American military, Kissinger apparently did not feel that they were invariably difficult to deal with. For example, he was once quoted as saying: "In my experience with the military, they are more likely to accept decisions they do not like than any other group." See John P. Leacacos, "Kissinger's Apparat," *Foreign Policy*, Winter 1971-72, p. 4.

44. See Victor Zorza, "Kissinger's Strategic Challenges," *Washington Post*, July 9, 1974.

45. See Chapter 1, p. 9f.

46. John Newhouse, *Cold Dawn: The Story of SALT* (New York: Holt, Rinehart and Winston, 1973), pp. 174-76.

47. Ibid., p. 175.

48. See Chapter 1, p. 10f. See also Alton Frye, "U.S. Decision Making in SALT," in *SALT: The Moscow Agreements and Beyond*, p. 87.

49. See *Nitze Statement, July 2, 1974*, p. 42. See also Chapter 5, pp. 95-96.

50. *Department of State Bulletin*, June 26, 1972, p. 899.

51. See "Agreement on Prevention of Nuclear War," signed June 22, 1973, in *Department of State Bulletin*, July 23, 1973.

52. Hedrick Smith, "A Return to Rivalry," *New York Times*, March 24, 1974; Gelb, ibid., March 3 and 31, 1974; Robinson, in *Aviation Week & Space Technology*, April 15, 1974, p. 14.

53. *Strategic Survey 1973* (London: Institute for Strategic Studies, 1974), pp. 57, 60.

54. The Soviet Navy in 1974 had some 330 SLCMs, which were not included in the SALT I accords. See Richard T. Ackley, "What's Left of SALT?" *Naval War College Review*, May-June 1974, p. 46.

55. Newhouse, *Cold Dawn*, p. 267.

56. *Pravda*, July 22, 1974.

57. See A. Karenin, in *Mezhdunarodnye Otnosheniia*, no. 9 (September 1974), p. 22.

58. See Peter Osnos, "Soviet Urges Recall of A-Fleets in Med," *Washington Post*, July 22, 1974.

59. Newhouse, *Cold Dawn*, p. 175. See also: J.P. Ruina, "U.S. and Soviet Strategic Arsenals," in *SALT: The Moscow Agreements and Beyond*, p. 65; Garthoff, in *Problems of Communism*, January-February 1975, p. 32.

60. See *Nitze Statement, July 2, 1974*, p. 43.

61. A strategic culture can be defined as the body of ideas and attitudes that shapes and circumscribes thought on strategic questions, influences the formulation of strategic issues, and sets the conceptual parameters of strategic debate. For a useful discussion of Soviet strategic culture and some of its contrasts with American concepts, see Jack L. Synder, *The Soviet Strategic Culture: Implications for Limited Nuclear Operations*, The Rand Corporation, R-2154-AF, Santa Monica, September 1977.

62. See Chapter 1, pp. 8-10, 17; see also Nitze, in *Review of Politics*, April 1975, p. 152.

63. At SALT I, the American negotiators had been unable to persuade the Soviets to go on record that the mutual survivability of offensive forces would benefit both parties. This point emerged in one of the unilateral statements put into the record by the U.S. delegation, which noted that "an objective of the follow-on negotiations should be to constrain and reduce on a long-term basis threats to the survivability of our respective strategic retaliatory forces." See *Arms Control and Disarmament Agreements*, p. 146.

64. The phrase has been coined by Benjamin S. Lambeth, and is cited with his permission from a paper delivered at the Fifth Annual National Security Affairs Conference, Washington, D.C., July 17, 1978, entitled "The Political Potential of Equivalence: The View from Moscow and Europe," p. 8.

65. See Thomas W. Wolfe, "Military Power and Soviet Policy," in William E. Griffith, ed., *The Soviet Empire: Expansion and Détente* (Lexington, Mass: Lexington Books, 1976), p. 158.

66. On the evolution of the mutual assured destruction concept during the tenure of Secretary of Defense Robert S. McNamara in the 1960s, see Chapter 1, pp. 6-7.

67. See Chapter 7, pp. 135-41.

68. For examination of these aspects of Soviet strategic thought, see among others: John Erickson, *Soviet Military Power* (London: Royal United Services Institute for Defence Studies, 1971), pp. 8-11; David Holloway, "Strategic Concepts and Soviet Policy," *Survival*, November 1971, p. 365; Leon Gouré, Foy D. Kohler, and Mose L. Harvey, *The Role of Nuclear Forces in Current Soviet Strategy* (Coral Gables: Center for Advanced International Studies, University of Miami, 1974), pp. 71, 77, 94; Benjamin S. Lambeth, "The Evolving Soviet Strategic Threat," *Current History*, October 1975, especially pp. 123-25; Edward L. Warner, III, *The Military in Contemporary Soviet Politics: An Institutional Analysis* (New York: Praeger Publishers, 1977), especially pp. 146-57.

69. See Dennis Ross, *Rethinking Soviet Strategic Policy: Inputs and Implications*, Center for Arms Control and International Security, University of California, Los Angeles, June 1977, pp. 10-11.

70. The knee of the curve in question graphically depicts the point at which delivery of additional nuclear weapons ceases to result in any substantial increase in fatalities.

71. One may note that the political disadvantages of a deterrence-only strategic philosophy were brought home to the Soviet leadership by Khrushchev's Cuban missile venture of 1962, contributing to the "never again"

syndrome displayed by his successors. Their interest in having at their disposal sufficient strategic power not only to deter nuclear war, but to help create an environment favorable to achieving Soviet political aims, was underscored by the massive strategic buildup they sanctioned after Khrushchev's removal in 1964. The nature of this buildup will be discussed in Chapter 6.

72. There is a copious Soviet literature by both civilian and military writers that credits the "strengthening of the Soviet Union's military might" and, in particular, "the presence of the powerful Strategic Rocket Forces" with having had a "sobering effect" on the "reactionary circles of imperialism" and with having "forced" such circles into "recognition of peaceful coexistence" and the "futility of attempts to talk to the Soviet Union from a position of strength." For examples, see: G.A. Arbatov, "U.S. Foreign Policy and the Scientific-Technical Revolution," *SShA: Ekonomika, Politika, Ideologiia*, no. 10 (October 1973), p. 3; K.M. Georgiev and M.O. Kolosov, "Soviet-U.S. Relations at a New Stage," ibid., no. 3 (March 1973), p. 14; Major General Ye. Sulimov, "The Scientific Nature of the CPSU's Foreign Policy," *Krasnaia Zvezda*, December 20, 1973; General of the Army V.G. Kulikov, "Guarding Peaceful Labor," *Partiinaia Zhizn*, no. 24 (December 1972), p. 40. For fuller discussion of these Soviet attitudes elsewhere by the present author, see "Military Power and Soviet Policy," in *The Soviet Empire: Expansion and Détente*, pp. 153-69.

73. For development of the thesis that the Soviet leadership may look upon the building up of its forces in terms of "banking" strategic power as an investment against unforeseen contingencies, see Herbert Goldhamer, *The Soviet Union in a Period of Strategic Parity*, The Rand Corporation, R-889-PR, Santa Monica, November 1971. See also Lambeth, in *Current History*, October 1975, p. 123.

74. In a sense, the idea of "strategic convergence" could be regarded as a logical offshoot of a broader school of convergence thought, whose central argument was that the processes of industrialization, modernization, and societal change would bring the American and Soviet systems closer together, eroding the deeper sources of past antagonism between them and making it easier to find common ground for accommodation of their conflicting interests. See the author's "The Convergence Issue and Soviet Strategic Policy," in *Rand 25th Anniversary Volume* (Santa Monica: The Rand Corporation, 1973), pp. 137-50.

75. See the comments on this point by, among others, Secretary of State William P. Rogers, Senator J.W. Fulbright, Marshall Shulman, Paul C. Warnke, Stanley Hoffman, Jerome H. Kahan, and Wolfgang K.H. Panovsky, in *Strategic Arms Limitation Agreements, Hearings*, before the Committee on Foreign Relations, Senate, 92d Cong., June-July 1972, pages respectively: 5, 11, 160, 178, 183, 191, 202, 358.

76. See Mason Willrich, "SALT I: An Appraisal," in *SALT: The Moscow Agreements and Beyond*, p. 264.

77. See Chapter 6, pp. 127-34.

78. See Chapter 5, p. 107.

79. From 1969 to 1974, it was U.S. declaratory policy, backed up by budgetary controls, not to develop highly accurate weapons that might seem to threaten hardened Soviet military targets. This policy was not universally applauded on the U.S. side, as indicated by news accounts in August 1972 of

Pentagon plans to accelerate the development of more accurate warheads but not to deploy them. Congress, however, rejected appropriations associated with these programs, illustrating continued congressional adherence to constraints upon improvement of U.S. counterforce capabilities. It was only during Schlesinger's tenure as secretary of defense that the declaratory policy against accuracy improvements was formally dropped with congressional approval. See William Beecher, "Pentagon Confirms Shift in Missile Development," *New York Times*, August 10, 1972; John W. Finney, "Senate Endorses New Nixon Policy on Better ICBMs," ibid., June 11, 1974.

80. Inozemtsev was head of the Institute of World Economy and International Relations (known as IMEMO from its Russian acronym). See Chapter 3, p. 67.

81. *Pravda*, June 9, 1972.

82. "The Impasse of the Policy of Force," *Problemy Mira i Sotsializma*, no. 2, February 1974.

83. See, for example, General of the Army V.G. Kulikov, "Air Defense in the System for Protecting the Soviet State," *Vestnik Protivovozdushnoi Oborony*, no. 4 (April 1973), p. 4. See also Colonel General N.A. Lomov, ed., *Scientific-Technical Progress and the Revolution in Military Affairs*, trans. U.S. Air Force (Moscow: Voenizdat, 1973), pp. 64, 273.

84. Marshal A.A. Grechko, *Guarding Peace and the Building of Communism* (Moscow: Voenizdat, 1971), p. 41.

85. See, for example, Marshal A.A. Grechko, "Guarding Peace and Socialism," *Pravda*, February 23, 1974; Kulikov, in *Partiinaia Zhizn*, December 1972, p. 40; General of the Army I.G. Pavlovskii, "The Economy and the Armed Forces of the USSR," *Planovoye Khoziaistvo*, no. 2 (February 1973), p. 20; Colonel I. Forofonov, "The 24th Party Congress on the Missions of the Soviet Armed Forces at the Current Stage," *Kommunist Vooruzhennykh Sil*, no. 15 (August 1972), p. 77.

86. Cited in Gouré et al., *The Role of Nuclear Forces in Current Soviet Strategy*, p. 110.

87. Even though hard-site defense of missile silos would place less demand on an ABM system than defense of urban areas, it should be noted that the difficulties are by no means trivial. See Ruina, in *SALT: The Moscow Agreements and Beyond*, pp. 62-63.

88. See Chapter 3, pp. 61, 74.

89. See Wolfe, "The Convergence Issue and Soviet Strategic Policy," p. 149.

90. As it was expressed in February 1978 by Secretary of Defense Harold Brown: "Since 1964 we have witnessed a particularly impressive growth and qualitative improvement in the Soviet strategic nuclear forces. If these forces are dedicated simply to pure deterrence, or even to large-scale, second-strike assumed destruction—conservatively designed—we must still wonder whether they are not excessive in quantity and mismatched in characteristics to either of these purposes." *Department of Defense Annual Report FY 1979, Harold Brown, Secretary of Defense*, February 2, 1978, p. 34.

91. Colin S. Gray, "Soviet Rocket Forces: Military Capability, Political Utility," *Air Force Magazine*, March 1978, pp. 50-54.

92. Lambeth, in *Current History*, October 1975, pp. 125, 152.

## NOTES TO CHAPTER 6
## EVOLUTION OF THE SOVIET STRATEGIC
## POSTURE IN THE SALT ERA

1. See Thomas W. Wolfe, "Military Power and Soviet Policy," in William E. Griffith, ed., *The Soviet Empire: Expansion & Détente* (Lexington, Mass.: Lexington Books, 1976), pp. 145-46.

2. A definition of detente as a tactical "breathing spell" preparatory to dealing decisively with the West from a superior power position purportedly had been passed along by Brezhnev to East European Communist leaders in 1973. The report's authenticity, however, has not been established. See John W. Finney, "U.S. Hears of Brezhnev Reassurance to Bloc That Accords Are a Tactic," *New York Times*, September 17, 1973.

3. The "Rocket Troops of Strategic Designation," as they are called in the Soviet Union, came into being in late 1959 and early 1960. In the West they are generally known as the Strategic Rocket Forces. In addition to its ICBM units, the SRF also controls medium- and intermediate-range ballistic missiles (M/IRBM), which have a "strategic" mission against Eurasian targets. The SRF does not control missiles with ranges less than 1000 kilometers (600 miles), which are attached to the ground forces.

4. These were the SS-7 and SS-8, deployed before 1964, and the SS-9, SS-11, and SS-13, deployed after 1964. All were liquid-fueled except the SS-13, the Soviet Union's first ICBM in the solid-fuel category.

5. Alton H. Quanbeck and Barry M. Blechman, *Strategic Forces: Issues for the Mid-Seventies* (Washington, D.C.: Brookings Institution, 1973), p. 20. See also Thomas W. Wolfe, in Kurt London, ed., *The Soviet Impact on World Politics* (New York: Hawthorn Books, Inc., 1974), p. 245.

6. It may be noted that there were disputed reports in the fall of 1974 alleging that the Soviets had begun to build new silos in excess of the limits imposed by the May 1972 accords. U.S. defense officials, however, denied that the Soviet Union was "failing to abide by the agreements," thus accepting as a public position the assumption that the structures in question were underground launch control facilities, while asking privately for explanation from the Soviet side in the Standing Consultative Commission. Subsequently, a February 1978 ACDA report to Congress on issues taken up in the SCC disclosed further details concerning this matter. See Chapter 10, pp. 209-11.

7. Except for SLBMs, deployment of the Soviet third-generation strategic missile force had indeed slowed down notably by 1970, at which time the numerical level of deployed ICBMs already came close to the number incorporated in the Interim Agreement two years later. With regard to the quantitative tapering off of the Soviet strategic buildup during SALT I prior to the shift to a new fourth generation of improved ICBMs, some observers believe that this was meant as a "signal" of Soviet restraint for SALT purposes. For an argument along this line, see Raymond Garthoff, "SALT and the Soviet Military," *Problems of Communism*, January-February 1975, p. 30. For the ceilings set by the Interim Agreement, see Chapter 1, p. 13.

8. See Chapter 5, p. 98.

9. On the assumption that Soviet military programming is tied closely to the planning cycle for the Five-Year Plans, it would be logical to suppose that deployment decisions for the new fourth-generation missile programs observed after SALT I had been made not later than 1970—the year in which the Ninth Five-Year Plan (1971-1975) was formulated. By the same logic, R&D decisions for these missiles probably had been made in connection with the previous Five-Year Plan, formulated in 1965. The first flight testing of missiles of the fourth-generation family began in the latter part of 1972.

10. Admiral Thomas H. Moorer, chairman, JCS, *U.S. Military Posture for FY 1975*, 1974, p. 7; *Report of Secretary of Defense James R. Schlesinger to the Congress on the FY 1975 Budget and FY 1975-1979 Defense Program*, March 4, 1974, p. 45 (hereafter cited as *Schlesinger FY 1975 Report*).

11. An on-board digital computer was an important advance, not only for contributing to improved guidance accuracy, but also in terms of targeting flexibility and reprogramming. See *Report of Secretary of Defense James R. Schlesinger to the Congress on the FY 1976 and Transition Budgets and FY 1976-1980 Defense Program*, February 5, 1975, p. II-12 (hereafter cited as *Schlesinger FY 1976 Report*).

12. See Chapter 1, p. 12. About twenty-five of the new silos were located at SS-9 complexes and were somewhat larger than about sixty-six other silos constructed at SS-11 complexes. As it turned out, the larger silos were used to house the SS-18 "heavy" ICBM, while the others were used for SS-17s or SS-19s. See *Statement by General George S. Brown, USAF, Chairman, Joint Chiefs of Staff, to the Congress on the Defense Posture of the United States for FY 1978*, January 20, 1977, p. 10 (hereafter cited as *General Brown FY 1978 Posture Statement*).

13. The cold-launch technique of popping a missile out of its silo by a gas generator before firing of the main booster engines had the advantage both of allowing a larger throwweight missile to be fired from a given-size silo and of permitting relatively rapid reloads. Soviet tests of the technique were first reported in 1974, and subsequently it was confirmed that deployed SS-18 and SS-17 ICBMs were configured for cold launch, while the customary hot-launch method continued to apply in the case of the SS-19. John W. Finney, "Pentagon Says 'Pop-Up' Missile Gives Soviet Heavier Warhead," *New York Times*, September 19, 1974; Clarence A. Robinson, Jr., "Soviets Test Cold-Launch ICBM Firings," *Aviation Week & Space Technology*, September 24, 1973, p. 20. See also, *Report of Secretary of Defense Donald H. Rumsfeld to the Congress on the FY 1977 Budget . . . and the FY 1977-1981 Defense Programs*, January 27, 1976, p. 65 (hereafter cited as *Rumsfeld FY 1977 Report*).

14. See Chapter 5, p. 95f.

15. *Department of Defense Annual Report FY 1970, Harold Brown, Secretary of Defense*, February 2, 1978, p. 49 (hereafter cited as *Brown FY 1979 Report*). Several variants or "mods" of the new fourth-generation ICBMs, providing both single-shot and MIRV capabilities, were developed and tested, but mainly the MIRVed variants were deployed. Because SALT verification procedures would probably require counting any basic missile that had been tested in a MIRV mode as part of the MIRVed-missile quota, it was expected

that the Soviets would continue to deploy mainly MIRVed versions of the SS-17, SS-18, and SS-19, reserving deployment of a single warhead ICBM to an oncoming fifth missile generation. See *General Brown FY 1978 Posture Statement*, p. 10; Colin Gray, in *Air Force Magazine*, March 1978, p. 52. See also Chapter 6, p. 123.

16. *Brown FY 1979 Report*, p. 49.

17. For further discussion of post-Vladivostok MIRV limits, see Chapter 11, p. 227.

18. The phasing out included both obsolescent SS-7 and SS-8 ICBMs being "exchanged" for SLBMs, and some SS-9 and SS-11 ICBMs being replaced by follow-on fourth-generation systems. At the same time, the possibility that a considerable number of improved SS-11 missiles might be retained in the force for some years was suggested by a program for modernizing a "substantial number of SS-11 silos." See *General Brown FY 1978 Posture Statement*, pp. 9-10.

19. The SS-16 was considered to be a likely candidate for a mobile role after being associated with mobile launcher equipment in 1974. However, the initial test program for the SS-16 was from fixed sites. See Michael Getler, "Soviets Reported Stepping Up Flight Testing of New Missile," *Washington Post*, July 27, 1974. Although no deployment of the SS-16 could be confirmed, some sources reported that the Soviets had put at least 100 SS-16 land-mobile models in storage between 1975-1978. See John M. Collins, *American and Soviet Military Trends Since the Cuban Missile Crisis* (Washington D.C.: Center for Strategic and International Studies, Georgetown University, 1978), p. 88.

20. *General Brown FY 1978 Posture Statement*, p. 11. See also Gray, in *Air Force Magazine*, March 1978, p. 51.

21. Schlesinger press conference, August 17, 1973, *Washington Post*, August 18, 1973.

22. *US-USSR Strategic Policies*, Testimony by Secretary of Defense James R. Schlesinger on March 4, 1974, in Hearing before the Subcommittee on Arms Control, International Law and Organization, Committee on Foreign Relations, Senate, sanitized and released April 4, 1974, p. 5. (Hereafter cited as *Schlesinger Testimony, March 4, 1974.*) It should be noted that the throwweight comparison in this instance applied only to ICBM forces. However, the inclusion of SLBM forces would still leave a disparity greatly favoring the USSR. See Chapter 6, p. 97. For more on throwweight, see also Chapter 9, pp. 187, 190-91.

23. The maximum Soviet potential estimated by Secretary Schlesinger was "something like 33,000 RVs." However, he also stated: "We do not believe they [the Soviets] would go in that direction." Ibid., p. 6.

24. Ibid., p. 7.

25. *Schlesinger FY 1975 Report*, p. 6.

26. *Brown FY 1979 Report*, p. 5; *Rumsfeld FY 1977 Report*, pp. 5, 56.

27. See Chapter 5, p. 110f. and note 79.

28. See John W. Finney, "Pentagon Aides Say Soviet Is Developing New Missiles for Use in the 1980's," *New York Times*, July 26, 1974. Other accounts estimated that perhaps only six to eight years would be needed for significant Soviet accuracy improvements. See Edger Ulsamer, "Soviet Objective: Technological Supremacy," *Air Force Magazine*, June 1974, p. 23.

29. For a persuasive analysis showing consistent underestimation of the numerical levels of future Soviet offensive deployments, see Albert Wohlstetter, "Is There a Strategic Arms Race?" *Foreign Policy*, Summer 1974, especially pp. 10-20. This analysis, however, did not bring out the parallel point that new strategic technologies had often replaced older ones at a slower pace than anticipated.

30. *Aviation Week & Space Technology*, September 24, 1973, p. 20.

31. *Briefing on Counterforce Attacks, Hearing*, before the subcommittee on Arms Control, International Law and Organization, Committee on Foreign Relations, Senate (held September 11, 1974; sanitized and made public January 10, 1975), p. 10.

32. *Schlesinger FY 1976 Report*, p. II-8.

33. The officers in question were not identified in press accounts. See Getler, in the *Washington Post*, July 27, 1974.

34. It was, of course, highly unusual for the Russians to disclose such information about the performance of their weapons. Why it was done in this case invites speculation. One explanation might be that the Soviets wished to convey the message that withholding technology transfer of such items as computers would not really prevent them from fielding more accurate missiles.

35. This follows from the $K = \dfrac{Y^{2/3}}{(CEP)^2}$ used in standard equations for calculating single-shot kill probability. Since Y (yield) is raised to the 2/3 power while CEP is squared, kill probability proves much more sensitive to increases in the accuracy than in the yield of warheads. On the other hand, because the range of uncertainties affecting yield is much less than that for CEP, higher yield weapons may help compensate for unexpected operational inaccuracy. See note 37, below.

36. See Gray, in *Air Force Magazine*, March 1978, pp. 52-53; Collins, *American and Soviet Military Trends*, p. 93. According to at least one unconfirmed report, in Soviet tests in early 1978 the SS-18 and SS-19 had achieved CEPs of 0.1 nautical miles or better. See Clarence Robinson, "Soviets Boost ICBM Accuracy," *Aviation Week & Space Technology*, April 3, 1978, pp. 14-16.

37. *Brown FY 1979 Report*, p. 63. The point that the substantially greater yield of Soviet warheads also represented an important factor, along with accuracy improvements, that would help to compensate for operational uncertainties and that contributed to growth of the Soviet threat to U.S. missiles, was made by Schlesinger in February 1975. See *Schlesinger FY 1976 Report*, p. II-8. See also Michael Nacht, "The Vladivostok Accord and American Technological Options," *Survival*, May-June 1975, p. 110.

38. Finney, in the *New York Times*, July 26, 1974. See also Collins, *American and Soviet Military Trends*, p. 94.

39. *Brown FY 1979 Report*, p. 50. With respect to accuracy improvements, CEPs of 0.1 nautical miles (600 feet) might be achieved by inertial guidance methods, after which use of other techniques, including satellite navigation systems, might, in the opinion of some analysts, permit lowering CEPs still more. See Jan Lodal, "Assuring Strategic Stability: An Alternative View," *Foreign Affairs*, April 1976, pp. 466, 479.

40. The predecessors of the Y-class were small numbers of G-, Z-, and H-class submarines, fitted with either SS-N-4 or SS-N-5 ballistic missiles of less than 700-mile range. Only the H-class was nuclear-powered. For more detail on the Soviet effort in the SLBM field, see Thomas W. Wolfe, "Soviet Naval Interaction with the United States and Its Influence on Soviet Naval Development," in Michael MccGwire, ed., *Soviet Naval Developments: Capability and Context* (New York: Praeger Publishers, 1973), pp. 255-57, 262-65; Norman Polmar, *Soviet Naval Power* (New York: National Strategy Information Center, 1972), pp. 31-40; *Understanding Soviet Naval Developments*, Office of the Chief of Naval Operations, Washington, D.C., April 1975, pp. 25-26.

41. See Admiral Thomas H. Moorer, *U.S. Military Posture for FY 1974*, March 23, 1973, p. 8.

42. The Delta-I class, an extended version of the Y-class, was 450 feet long, compared with the U.S. Poseidon of 425 feet.

43. In a rare departure from the customary Soviet practice of not revealing force statistics, the Soviet negotiators maintained that the USSR had forty-eight boats completed or building, with a total capacity of 768 SLBMs. For negotiating purposes, two compromise "baseline" figures of 740 or 710 SLBMs were adopted, but no figure for the number of submarines then possessed by the Soviet Union was mutually agreed upon. See transcript of Kissinger's May 27, 1972, press conference, in *Military Implications of the Treaty on the Limitation of Anti-Ballistic Missile Systems and the Interim Agreement on Limitation of Strategic Offensive Arms, Hearing*, before the Committee on Armed Services, Senate, 92d Cong., 2d session, 1972, p. 107.

44. The SALT I ceilings for the Soviets were 950 SLBMs on sixty-two "modern" SSBN submarines. See Chapter 1, p. 13.

45. *Schlesinger FY 1975 Report*, p. 50; Moorer, *U.S. Military Posture for FY 1975*, p. 22.

46. *General Brown FY 1978 Posture Statement*, p. 13. See also note 42, above.

47. See *Brown FY 1979 Report*, p. 50; Norman Polmar, "The Soviet SLBM Force," *Air Force Magazine*, March 1978, p. 46. In spring 1978, it was reported that the Soviets had reached sixty-four modern SLBM subs, which would exceed the sixty-two boat limit of the SALT I Interim Agreement. See "Subs Raise SALT Observance Question," *Aviation Week & Space Technology*, April 3, 1978, p. 17. It should be noted, incidentally, that the SALT I limits on SSBNs and SLBMs had formally expired on October 3, 1977, but had been informally extended until a SALT II agreement should be reached. For further discussion, see Chapter 11, p. 226.

48. Collins, *American and Soviet Military Trends*, p. 100. The Delta-II was a 500-foot SSBN equipped with sixteen SS-N-8 launchers, while the Delta-III, of approximately the same size, was equipped with a still newer launcher system, the SS-NX-18.

49. Ibid., p. 103; Polmar, in *Air Force Magazine*, March 1978, p. 46. The U.S. Trident, the first unit of which was scheduled to become operational in 1979-1980, would be 560 feet long, mounting twenty-four C-4 launchers with about ten MIRVs each.

50. *General Brown FY 1978 Posture Statement*, pp. 13-14; Collins, *American and Soviet Military Trends*, p. 103.

51. The Trident C-4 missile will have a range of 4000 nautical miles. However, the warhead technology under development for Trident, going beyond MIRV to a more advanced type of multiple warhead, MARV (maneuverable reentry vehicles that can change course on final approach to the target), will be much superior to the Soviet SS-N-8. See Moorer, *U.S. Military Posture for FY 1975*, p. 9; John W. Finney, "Maneuverable Warhead Being Developed by U.S.," *New York Times*, January 19, 1974.

52. *General Brown FY 1978 Posture Statement*, p. 13. The initial deployment of Delta-class SSBNs was to northern (Barents Sea) waters, where they could be covered less easily by Western surveillance. See George C. Wilson, "Soviets Change Sub Tactics," *Washington Post*, April 28, 1975.

53. The Poseidon C-3 missile with about ten MIRVs was retrofitted into all thirty-one Lafayette-class SSBNs by 1978. The Polaris A-3 missile with three MRVs was intended to remain on the ten earliest U.S. SSBNs of the George Washington and Ethan Allen classes until their phasing out for Trident, beginning in 1979.

54. A variant of the SS-N-6, labeled Mod 3, with a MRV capability, had been tested and brought close to operational readiness by 1974, but this missile lacked the attributes of a true MIRV. See Moorer, *U.S. Military Posture for FY 1975*, p. 21; Collins, *American and Soviet Military Trends*, p. 101.

55. There was also a possibility that the SS-NX-17 might be designed for MRV rather than the MIRV delivery. See *General Brown FY 1978 Posture Statement*, p. 13; Polmar, in *Air Force Magazine*, March 1978, p. 46.

56. *Brown FY 1979 Report*, p. 50. Another Soviet seaborne missile that was at one time thought to be a candidate for retrofitting into Y-class submarines was the SS-N-13. This was a ballistic missile incorporating rather advanced technology, but it was of relatively short range and thus unlikely to be for strategic use. Apparently, no decision was made to deploy it in the Y-class or other SSBNs, although some analysts felt it might appear eventually aboard Y-class boats as an antiship or antisub weapon.

57. *General Brown FY 1978 Posture Statement*, p. 13; Polmar, in *Air Force Magazine*, March 1978, p. 46.

58. Ibid. See also Collins, *American and Soviet Military Trends*, p. 100.

59. See Chapter 5, p. 101.

60. For a discussion of the transaction at the Vladivostok summit, see Chapter 9.

61. Precisely what the peak strength of the Long Range Aviation (LRA) heavy bomber force was prior to leveling off at about 140 after the mid-sixties is not entirely clear. Some sources put the figure at about 200 to 210. See Collins, *American and Soviet Military Trends*, p. 108. In the present study, as indicated by Table 6-1 on p. 117, we have shown the force at 160 heavy bombers in 1964, before it bottomed out at 140. It should be noted, of course, that the LRA has also included a sizable force of some hundreds of medium bombers (TU-16 Badger and TU-22 Blinder), which are configured primarily for missions over or peripheral to the Eurasian land mass, but which could be employed against U.S. targets under extreme conditions warranting one-way missions.

62. See Thomas W. Wolfe, *Soviet Power and Europe: 1945-1970* (Baltimore: The Johns Hopkins Press, 1970), p. 181; Malcolm MacKintosh, *Juggernaut, the Russian Forces 1918-1966* (New York: Macmillan Co., 1967), p. 306; J.I. Coffey, *Strategic Power and National Security* (Pittsburgh: University of Pittsburgh Press, 1971), p. 10.

63. George Wilson, "Russia Testing New Bomber," *Washington Post*, October 19, 1969; Tad Szulc, "Soviet Said to Fly Big New Bomber; Policy Shift Seen," *New York Times*, September 5, 1971.

64. Moorer, *U.S. Military Posture for 1975*, p. 24; Collins, *American and Soviet Military Trends*, p. 107.

65. For an informative discussion of the wide range of estimates of the Backfire's performance, see Collins, *American and Soviet Military Trends*, pp. 16, 19, 108.

66. Ibid., p. 108. See also Ulsamer, in *Air Force Magazine*, June 1974, p. 23.

67. *General Brown FY 1978 Posture Statement*, p. 20.

68. Norman Polmar, "Soviet Naval Aviation," *Air Force Magazine*, March 1978, p. 70.

69. See Chapters 10, pp. 201-02, 212-13; 222-23, 225f, 228f.

70. *General Brown FY 1978 Posture Statement*, p. 19; *Brown FY 1979 Report*, p. 51.

71. See Chapter 5, pp. 110-13.

72. *Schlesinger FY 1976 Report*, p. II-6. This SA-3 was designed to provide low-altitude protection against bombers, while the SA-5, or Tallin system, whose characteristics had led some Western analysts to suspect that it might be convertible into ABM defenses, was a long-range, high-altitude system possibly intended to counter missile-launching aircraft before they could reach their target areas. Incidentally, Article VI of the ABM Treaty, pushed by the U.S. side, was aimed at preventing the conversion of such systems as the SA-5 into ABM defenses. See *Arms Control and Disarmament Agreements*, 1977 edition, U.S. Arms Control and Disarmament Agency, Washington, D.C., p. 133.

73. Some of these launchers had multiple rails, making it possible for them to accommodate a total of about 12,000 surface-to-air missiles before reload. See *Brown FY 1979 Report*, p. 47.

74. Organizationally, the PVO-S (Russian acronym for "Anti-Air Defense of the Country") has at its disposal only surface-to-air missile and interception aircraft units earmarked for strategic defense of the country. In addition, however, there are numerous "nonstrategic" mobile air defense missile units attached to the ground forces. These mobile units under some circumstances could of course augment the strategic defenses, especially for defense against low-level attacks by bombers or cruise missiles. See William F. Scott, "Troops of National Air Defense," *Air Force Magazine*, March 1978, p. 58.

75. However, four battalions of "general purpose" Nike-Hercules SAMs were connected to a standby strategic role (in Alaska and Florida) after deactivation of the strategic units under NORAD. See *General Brown FY 1978 Posture Statement*, p. 28.

76. See Table 5-1, p. 97.

77. Among the newest interceptors introduced into the PVO were the

YAK-28P Firebar; TU-28 Fiddler; SU-15 Flagon A,D,E; and MIG-25 Foxbat A. It was reported in 1978 that another new interceptor, the MIG-29, was entering service. The MIG-23 Flogger also was being modified for an air defense role. The remainder of the PVO interceptor force consisted in 1978 of the SU-11 Fishpot B; MIG-19 Farmer B,E; and the MIG-17 Fresco D. *General Brown FY 1978 Posture Statement*, p. 26. For further details concerning these aircraft, see John W.R. Taylor, "Gallery of Soviet Aerospace Weapons," *Air Force Magazine*, March 1978, pp. 97-99.

78. The U.S. strategic interceptor force, more than half of which was made up of Air National Guard squadrons, consisted in 1978 mainly of the F-101 Voodoo, the F-102 Delta Dagger, and the F-106 Delta Dart, all designs first introduced in the late 1950s. A few F-4 Phantoms of later design were added to the force in 1977 by conversion of some ANG units from older aircraft. *Brown FY 1979 Report*, p. 121. See also Collins, *American and Soviet Military Trends*, pp. 136-37.

79. These aircraft could be diverted to strategic air defense use, but at the expense of their employment elsewhere in a crisis situation.

80. See Chapter 1, pp. 00-00; Chapter 5, pp. 110-11.

81. According to some informed sources, the Soviet Union historically had spent three times as much on its bomber defenses as the United States had spent on its entire bomber force. See Senator John C. Culver, "The Future of the Strategic Bomber," *AEI Defense Review* 2, no. 1 (February 1978):12.

82. *Brown FY 1979 Report*, p. 51.

83. Ibid. See also Collins, *American and Soviet Military Trends*, p. 137.

84. A prior deployment involving a predecessor to the Galosh system, the so-called Griffen, had been started and then abandoned toward the end of the Khrushchev period. A fuller account of the Soviet ABM program may be found in Wolfe, *Soviet Power and Europe*, pp. 186-88, 437-41.

85. These claims had first been made under Khrushchev and were continued in the first years of the Brezhnev-Kosygin regime. Later, more guarded statements began to appear, such as Marshal Malinovskii's comment at the 23rd Party Congress in 1966 that Soviet defenses could cope with "some" but "not all" enemy missiles. *Pravda*, April 3, 1966.

86. For more details on this debate, see Wolfe, *Soviet Power and Europe*, pp. 439-41.

87. See Chapter 4, p. 85.

88. See Chapter 5, pp. 110-11.

89. See Chapter 1, pp. 7f., 14f. and, especially, note 33.

90. For references to the ongoing Soviet R&D program in the ABM field, see: Moorer, *U.S. Military Posture for FY 1975*, p. 33; *General Brown FY 1978 Posture Statement*, p. 24; *Brown FY 1979 Report*, p. 124. The United States, it should be observed, also continued to conduct some research in various advanced technologies, intended, as one secretary of defense put it, to "enable us to maintain our lead in ABM technology." See *Schlesinger FY 1976 Report*, p. II-48. However, on the grounds that the U.S. R&D programs were much less extensive than those of the USSR, and because the United States after SALT I had dismantled its only active ABM site at Grand Forks, while the Soviets had not done likewise, critics held that there was a real asymmetry in this area.

91. See Chapter 1, p. 21. It should be noted that the ABM Treaty barred only defenses "currently consisting" of such components as interceptor missiles and radars (Article II), and did not specifically prohibit possible future systems based on different physical principles, such as lasers, charged particle beams, or other esoterica. The Agreed Interpretations section of the 1972 Protocol to the ABM Treaty stated that in the event that "ABM systems based on other physical principles" were created in the future, limitations on such systems "would be subject to discussion" in accordance with Article XIV on amending the ABM Treaty. See *Arms Control and Disarmament Agreements*, 1977 edition, pp. 132-35, 141.

92. Marshal V.D. Sokolovskii et al., *Voennaia Strategiia*, 2d ed. (Moscow: Voenizdat, 1963), p. 398.

93. Norman Polmar, "Thinking about Soviet ASW," *United States Naval Institute Proceedings*, May 1976, p. 108; Robert R. Soule, *Counterforce Issues for the U.S. Strategic Nuclear Forces*, Background Paper, Congressional Budget Office, U.S. Congress, January 1978, pp. 25-26.

94. Admiral of the Fleet S.G. Gorshkov, "Historical Experience and the Present Day," *Voprosy Filosofii*, no. 5 (May 1975), pp. 30-31.

95. See Thomas W. Wolfe, *Soviet Strategy at the Crossroads* (Cambridge: Harvard University Press, 1965), p. 185. One should note that Gorshkov had also expressed less than sanguine views about the prospects of countering modern nuclear subs with ASW forces, as in his series of *Morskoi Sbornik* articles starting in February 1972. See E.T. Wooldridge, Jr., "The Gorshkov Papers: Soviet Naval Doctrine for the Nuclear Age," *Orbis*, Winter 1975, p. 1161.

96. See Leonard Sullivan, ed., *Securing the Seas*, The Atlantic Council, Washington, D.C., January 1979, Chapter 10.

97. Ibid. For representative Soviet sources on the subject, see: Engineer-Captain V. Mikhailin, "Physics and ASW Defense," *Krasnaia Zvezda*, March 10, 1962; I.M. Sotnikov and N.A. Brusentsev, *Aviatsiia Protiv Podvodnikh Lodok* (Moscow: Voenizdat, 1970), pp. 101-12; Engineer-Captain E. Buzov, "Trends in the Development of Non-Acoustic Means of Detection," *Morskoi Sbornik*, September 1974, pp. 85-89.

98. It is a point of some interest that most of the larger Soviet surface ships built since 1966 have been described by the Russians themselves as "antisubmarine" ships. In particular, the Soviet Navy's three aircraft carriers, the Moskva, Leningrad, and Kiev, are called "large antisubmarine cruisers" (*bolshiye protivolodochniye kreisery*).

99. Norman Polmar, in *Naval Institute Proceedings*, May 1976, pp. 108-29.

100. A belief that invulnerability of the SLBM force could be assured despite Soviet ASW advances rested in large part on the planned introduction of Trident I missiles of 4000-nautical-mile range, which would greatly expand the open ocean area for on-station patrol and thus magnify the problems of detection and attack for ASW.

101. *Rumsfeld FY 1977 Report*, p. 70.

102. *Brown FY 1979 Report*, p. 52.

103. See, for example, Henry S. Bradsher, "Vulnerability Growing for U.S. Sub-Based Missiles?" *Washington Star*, December 12, 1977; Collins, *American and Soviet Military Trends*, pp. 103-4.

104. For comment on the evolving role of Soviet naval forces to protect their own SSBNs from the adversary's ASW forces, see *CNO Report*, Admiral James L. Holloway, Chief of Naval Operations, Washington, D.C., March 1, 1978, p. 35.

105. The assessment by Secretary of Defense Harold Brown that the number of U.S. ICBMs surviving a Soviet attack in the mid-1980s could be reduced to "low levels" (*Brown FY 1979 Report*, p. 63) did not specify what these figures might be. However, there are numerous published analyses, with rather widely varying results. To cite a few examples:

Calculations made for a congressional study for the same time period ranged from about 150 surviving U.S. ICBMs to about 500, depending on weapons accuracy, reliability, target hardness, and other factors posited. The lower figure assumed SS-18 type attack, with 0.1 n mi (600 ft) CEP, 1.5 megaton yield, 0.8 reliability, target hardness 2000 psi, and two shots per target. Surviving SLBMs ranged from 440 to 560, with loss of about 30 percent in the worst case due almost entirely to destruction in port. Surviving bombers ranged from 120 to 312, with the survival rate of about 80 percent in the high case being largely due to advance warning and high alert status. The scenarios yielding the foregoing figures assumed a single Soviet attack. In counterforce exchange scenarios, Soviet first and U.S. second strike, the worst-case calculation left 52 U.S. ICBMs surviving, compared with 1069 for the Soviet Union. See Soule, *Counterforce Issues for U.S. Strategic Forces*, pp. 13-30, 37, 60-73.

By contrast with the above results, a comparative analysis prepared for ACDA by Carl Thorne in 1978, using a different methodology and assumptions, indicated that as of 1978 the second-strike retaliatory capability of U.S. strategic forces would exceed the first-strike capability of the Soviets against both hard and soft targets, while in the mid-1980s U.S. and Soviet forces would have approximately equal capabilities. As explained at a press briefing on this study, although the Soviet first-strike capability could destroy about 90 percent of Minuteman, an alerted U.S. bomber force armed with ALCMs was given the capability to survive and destroy more Soviet targets in retaliation. See *U.S. and Soviet Strategic Capability through the Mid-1980s: A Comparative Analysis*, ACDA, August 1978, and *Transcript of On-the-Record Discussion with Paul C. Warnke, Director, ACDA*, August 29, 1978, especially pp. 6, 8-14.

For a third study presenting calculations on ICBM vulnerability in a variety of hypothetical nuclear exchanges, and arguing that uncertainties of outcome are greater for the first-strike attacker than suggested by standard analytic methods, see John D. Steinbruner and Thomas M. Garwin, "Strategic Vulnerability: The Balance Between Prudence and Paranoia," *International Security*, Summer 1976, pp. 138-81.

106. For the rationale behind "reduced emphasis" on U.S. air defenses, see *Schlesinger FY 1976 Report*, pp. II-41, 42.

107. For discussion of the 1961 reorganization of Soviet civil defense, which placed it under the direction of the Ministry of Defense, see Leon Gouré, *The Resolution of the Soviet Controversy over Civil Defense*, The Rand Corporation, RM-3223-PR, Santa Monica, June 1962, and Harriet Fast Scott, "Civil Defense in the USSR," *Air Force Magazine*, October 1975, p. 30. A Soviet account is given under the item "*Grazhdanskaia Oborona*" (Civil Defense), in *Sovetskaia Voennaia Entsiklopediia* (Moscow: Voenizdat, 1977), 3:23-24.

108. In July 1972, Colonel-General A.T. Altunin, a vigorous 51-year-old army officer with broad combat experience, was made a deputy minister of defense and placed in charge of Soviet Civil Defense. There followed a new phase in a compulsory nationwide civil defense program, characterized among other things by training for preattack dispersal and evacuation of urban residents from potential target areas, as well as additional shelter construction for the country's leadership cadres and a selected portion of its labor force. See Leon Gouré, *Soviet Civil Defense 1965-1970* (Coral Gables: Center for Advanced International Studies, University of Miami, 1972), and *Soviet Civil Defense—Post-Strike Repair and Restoration*, June 1973; Major George Kolt, "The Soviet Civil Defense Program," *Strategic Review*, Spring 1977, pp. 52-62. See also Colonel-General A. Altunin, "The Main Direction," *Voennye Znaniia*, no. 12 (December 1973), pp. 4-5.

109. For concise accounts of this debate, see: Deborah Shapley, "Soviet Civil Defense: Insiders Argue Whether Strategic Balance is Shaken," *Science*, December 10, 1976, pp. 1141-45; Collins, *American and Soviet Military Trends*, pp. 137-41; Henry S. Bradsher, "Civil Defense Plans Compared," *Washington Star*, November 9, 1976.

110. According to some patrons of this viewpoint, Soviet civil defense measures could potentially reduce Soviet fatalities to as low as 4 or 5 percent of the population in a nuclear conflict, compared with estimates of at least 50 percent American fatalities; hence, a "survivability gap." See Joanne S. Gailar and Eugene P. Wigner, "Will Soviet Civil Defense Undermine SALT?" *Human Events*, July 8, 1972, pp. 497-98, and "Civil Defense in the Soviet Union," *Foresight*, May-June 1974, p. 10; Leon Gouré, *War Survival in Soviet Strategy*, (Coral Gables: Center for Advanced International Studies, University of Miami, 1976), pp. 131-60; Paul H. Nitze, "Assuring Strategic Stability in an Era of Détente," *Foreign Affairs*, January 1976, pp. 211-12; "Intensified Soviet Civil Defense Seen Tilting the Strategic Balance," *Aviation Week & Space Technology*, November 22, 1976, p. 17.

111. For representative expressions skeptical of Soviet civil defense capabilities, see: Les Aspin, "Soviet Civil Defense: Myth and Reality," *Arms Control Today*, September 1976, pp. 1-4, and "Putting Soviet Power in Perspective," *AEI Defense Review* 2, no. 3 (1978):6-9; "The New Nuclear Strategy: Battle of the Dead?" *Defense Monitor*, Center for Defense Information, Washington, D.C., July 1976; Sydney Drell and Frank von Hipple, "Limited Nuclear War," *Scientific American*, November 1976, pp. 33-34.

112. See Collins, *American and Soviet Military Trends*, p. 140.

113. *Brown FY 1979 Report*, p. 64.

114. Brown proposed to deal with the problem of Soviet perceptions and expectations by ensuring that U.S. strategic delivery forces could continue to pose "unacceptable damage" to the Soviet Union, rather than by imitating the Soviet civil defense effort. Ibid., pp. 65-66.

115. *Soviet Civil Defense*, director of Central Intelligence, N178-10003, July 1978, pp. 3, 11. This document, a condensed report reflecting the latest in a series of studies undertaken after Soviet civil defense became a controversial issue in the mid-1970s, was released by Senator John C. Culver of Iowa,

chairman of a Senate subcommittee concerned with U.S. civil defense programs. Among salient aspects of the Soviet civil defense effort brought out in the report were: (1) Hardened shelter protection for about 110,000 leadership cadres and from 24 to 48 percent of the essential labor force existed, but no more than 20 percent of the total population could be accommodated in blast-resistant shelters; (2) Under the most favorable conditions for the USSR, including several days for urban evacuation, casualties could be reduced to the "low tens of millions," but under the worst conditions could be more than 100 million; (3) The number of full-time personnel engaged in civil defense activity was about 100,000, with upwards of 16 million auxiliaries.

116. Interview by V. Aleksandrov with General of the Army A.I. Radziyevskiy, "A Provocative Campaign," *Literaturnaia Gazeta*, January 19, 1977, p. 9. For other Soviet writing on civil defense, see P.T. Yegorov, I.A. Shlyakov, and N.I. Alabin, *Grazhdanskaia Oborona* (Moscow: Vysshaya Shkola, 1970), translated and published under the auspices of the U.S. Air Force as *Civil Defense: A Soviet View*, in the series Soviet Military Thought, no. 10 (Washington, D.C.: Government Printing Office). See also Major General A.S. Milovidov and Colonel V.G. Kozlov, eds., *The Philosophical Heritage of V.I. Lenin and Problems of Contemporary War*, (Moscow: Voenizdat, 1972), p. 337.

117. Henry (G.A.) Trofimenko, "The 'Theology of Strategy,'" *Orbis*, Fall 1977, pp. 506-10.

## NOTES TO CHAPTER 7
## SHIFTS IN U.S. STRATEGIC POLICY

1. Force-size ceilings that had been established by Secretary McNamara in 1964-65 had survived essentially intact through the next decade and beyond. See Chapter 1, p. 6.

2. See Chapter 1, pp. 7-8. The First ten MIRVed Minuteman III deployments, replacing Minuteman I, were completed in 1970. The first Poseidon-equipped conversion of the Polaris SSBN became operational in January 1971.

3. Lynn Etheridge Davis, *Limited Nuclear Options: Deterrence and the New American Doctrine*, Adelphi Papers, no. 121, International Institute for Strategic Studies, London, 1976, p. 3. This paper gives one of the most useful accounts available of the origins of the strategic revisions that later came to be rather widely called the "Schlesinger Doctrine."

4. For previous discussion of how the NSC apparatus was revamped under Dr. Kissinger, see Chapter 2, pp. 26-27.

5. *U.S. Foreign Policy for the 1970s, A New Strategy for Peace*, A Report to the Congress by Richard M. Nixon, President of the United States, February 18, 1970, p. 122.

6. *U.S. Foreign Policy for the 1970s: The Emerging Structure of Peace*, A Report to the Congress by Richard M. Nixon, President of the United States, February 9, 1972, p. 158. The pertinent references in the 1971 message may be found on pp. 170-71 of that document.

7. See Davis, *Limited Nuclear Options*, pp. 2-3.

8. Ibid., pp. 1-4. As noted by another analyst, the new doctrine of flexibility did not displace assured destruction as the fundamental deterrent to general nuclear war. However, assured destruction was modified to replace its prior criterion of inflicting unacceptable punishment on an attacker (generally defined since McNamara's day as destroying 20-25 percent of the enemy's population and 50 to 75 percent of his industrial capacity) with a criterion according to which SIOP targets would be specifically selected to delay Soviet recovery indefinitely. See John M. Collins, *American and Soviet Military Trends Since the Cuban Missile Crisis*, (Washington, D.C.: Georgetown University Center for Strategic and International Studies, 1978), p. 80; Senator John C. Culver, "The Future of the Strategic Bomber," *AEI Defense Review* 2, no. 1 (February 1978): 11. See also note 88, below.

9. *U.S.-USSR Strategic Policies*, Testimony by Secretary of Defense James R. Schlesinger on March 4, 1974, in Hearing before the Subcommittee on Arms Control, International Law and Organization, Committee on Foreign Relations, Senate, sanitized and released April 4, 1974, p. 26. (Hereafter cited as *Schlesinger Testimony, March 4, 1974*.)

10. See Chapter 5, pp. 110-11.

11. Schlesinger's specific program proposals and the reasons for amending U.S. strategic policy and doctrine were expounded in his first annual report to Congress in March 1974. See *Report of Secretary of Defense James R. Schlesinger to the Congress on the FY 1975 Budget and FY 1975-1979 Defense Program*, March 4, 1974, especially pp. 26, 30, 41, 44 (cited hereafter as *Schlesinger FY 1975 Report*). His strategic ideas also had been given a prior airing in remarks at the Overseas Writers Association luncheon in Washington, D.C., January 10, 1974, and at a Pentagon press conference January 24, 1974. Further development of the rationale and programs associated with Schlesinger's strategic approach was contained in his *Report to the Congress on the FY 1976 and Transition Budgets and FY 1976-1980 Defense Program*, February 5, 1975, especially pp. I-3-22, II-1-53 (hereafter cited as *Schlesinger FY 1976 Report*).

12. *Schlesinger FY 1975 Report*, pp. 4, 5, 38.

13. Ibid., p. 38; *Schlesinger Testimony, March 4, 1974*, p. 55.

14. *Schlesinger Testimony, March 4, 1974*, p. 9.

15. Ibid., p. 8.

16. Ibid. See also *Schlesinger FY 1975 Report*, p. 35.

17. *Schlesinger Testimony, March 4, 1974*, p. 9.

18. Ibid., p. 8; *Schlesinger FY 1975 Report*, p. 38.

19. See Chapter 5, p. 111, especially note 79; and 6, p. 121.

20. *Schlesinger Testimony, March 4, 1974*, p. 10.

21. Ibid., pp. 42, 55.

22. Ibid., p. 55.

23. *Schlesinger FY 1975 Report*, pp. 28, 29, 43, 44.

24. Ibid., p. 30. See also Chapter 6, pp. 120-21.

25. Ibid., p. 6.

26. Ibid., p. 42.

27. Ibid., p. 27.

28. *Schlesinger Testimony, March 4, 1974*, p. 7.

29. *Schlesinger FY 1975 Report*, p. 26.

30. Ibid., pp. 43-44. See also Chapter 6, p. 120.

31. Ibid., pp. 28, 43-44.

32. Ibid., pp. 6, 26, 30.

33. The Trident program, first known as ULMs (for Undersea Long Range Missile System) had been initiated in 1969. The first design contract for the B-1, which had grown out of conceptual studies in the mid-1960s for an "Advanced Manned Strategic Aircraft (AMSA)," was let in 1970. The continuation of these two programs, together with silo upgrading and procurement of Minuteman III, constituted by far the largest items in the FY 1975 and FY 1976 budgets for strategic force modernization.

34. *Schlesinger FY 1975 Report*, pp. 52-55.

35. See Section 5, of H.J. Res-1227, of September 30, 1972. A copy of this Joint Congressional Resolution may be found in Mason Willrich and John B. Rhinelander, eds., *SALT: The Moscow Agreements and Beyond* (New York: The Free Press, 1974), p. 315.

36. *Schlesinger FY 1975 Report*, pp. 4, 42.

37. *Schlesinger Testimony, March 4, 1974*, p. 38.

38. *Schlesinger FY 1975 Report*, pp. 40-41.

39. Ibid., pp. 40-42; *Schlesinger Testimony, March 4, 1974*, p. 18.

40. Ted Greenwood and Michael L. Nacht, "The New Nuclear Debate: Sense or Nonsense?" *Foreign Affairs*, July 1974, pp. 761-62. This article gave a good account of the pros and cons on the main strategic issues, though its authors tended to come down on the side of the debate critical of the Schlesinger approach.

41. Dr. Iklé, who became director of the U.S. Arms Control and Disarmament Agency in April 1973, had argued earlier that year and again in early 1974 that a policy of "naked deterrence" must be supplemented by changes in strategic doctrine and weaponry that would, among other things, "introduce a last chance—should something go wrong—to prevent the utmost catastrophe." His views may be found in "Can Nuclear Deterrence Last Out the Century?" *Foreign Affairs*, January 1973, pp. 267-85, and "The Prevention of Nuclear War in a World of Uncertainty," speech at the Joint Harvard-MIT Arms Control Seminar, February 20, 1974. Dr. Panovsky, director of the Stanford Linear Accelerator Center, though recognizing the shortcomings of a mutual assured destruction doctrine, argued essentially that it offered the best chance of preventing nuclear war in the face of technological and strategic factors that had locked the United States and the USSR into a mutual-hostage relationship. His views may be found in "The Mutual-Hostage Relationship between America and Russia," *Foreign Affairs*, October 1973, pp. 109-18.

42. Barry Carter, "Nuclear Strategy and Nuclear Weapons," *Scientific American*, May 1974, pp. 20-31; Kosta Tsipis, *Offensive Missiles*, Stockholm Paper no. 5, Stockholm International Peace Research Institute, August 1974, pp. 25-29.

43. Herbert Scoville, Jr., "Flexible Madness," *Foreign Policy*, Spring 1974, pp. 170-71; Jack Ruina, "SALT in a Mad World," *New York Times Magazine*, June 30, 1974, p. 51.

44. Carter, in *Scientific American*, May 1974, p. 30. See also comments by Senators Edmund S. Muskie and Claiborne Pell, in *Schlesinger Testimony, March 4, 1974*, pp. 42, 55.

45. Greenwood and Nacht, in *Foreign Affairs*, July 1974, pp. 766, 771. While noting such arguments that targeting flexibility might make nuclear war more likely, the authors of this article concluded that the uncertain risks of escalation would probably keep political leaders from precipitant recourse to nuclear weapons.

46. Tsipis, *Offensive Missiles*, pp. 9, 29.

47. Greenwood and Nacht, in *Foreign Affairs*, July 1974, p. 780. See also panelist comments by Senator J.W. Fulbright and McGeorge Bundy, in "Dealing with Moscow: East-West Experts View Value and Risks," *New York Times*, August 7, 1974.

48. Carter, in *Scientific American*, May 1974, pp. 25, 27; Tsipis, *Offensive Missiles*, pp. 26-28, 33. See also *Federation of Atomic Scientists Public Interest Report*, Special Issue on Counterforce and SALT, Chicago, Illinois, February 1974.

49. Scoville, in *Foreign Policy*, Spring 1974, pp. 170-71; Carter, in *Scientific American*, May 1974, pp. 27-28; John C. Baker and Robert E. Berman, "Evaluating Counterforce Strategy," *New York Times*, February 22, 1974; Senator Thomas J. McIntyre, "Increasing the Nuclear Danger," ibid., June 4, 1974.

50. Tsipis, *Offensive Missiles*, pp. 30-32; Carter, in *Scientific American*, May 1974, pp. 28-29; Baker and Berman, *New York Times*, February 22, 1974.

51. Tsipis, *Offensive Missiles*, p. 28.

52. Carter, in *Scientific American*, May 1974, p. 29. See also Greenwood and Nacht, in *Foreign Affairs*, July 1974, p. 778.

53. Carter, in *Scientific American*, May 1974, p. 25.

54. Ibid., pp. 25-26. See also Greenwood and Nacht, in *Foreign Affairs*, July 1974, p. 771.

55. McIntyre, in the *New York Times*, June 4, 1974.

56. See, for example, Greenwood and Nacht, in *Foreign Affairs*, July 1974, p. 773.

57. Editorial, "A Counter Military Capability," *Strategic Review*, U.S. Strategic Institute, Washington, D.C., Spring 1974, pp. 9-10. See also Arthur G.B. Metcalf, "A Strategic Doctrine for the United States: Secretary Schlesinger's Report," ibid., pp. 4-6.

58. Ibid., p. 10. The editors of this journal, one might note, later opened its pages to a critical rebuttal of their own advocacy of a vigorous U.S. counterforce program. See Robert Sherman, "The Fallacies of Counterforce," *Strategic Review*, Spring 1975.

59. Edward N. Luttwak, "Nuclear Strategy: The New Debate," *Commentary*, April 1974, p. 57. See also Colin S. Gray, "From Superiority to Sub-Parity," *Orbis*, Spring 1974, p. 297.

60. Mark B. Schneider, "Nuclear Flexibility and Parity," *Air Force Magazine*, September 1974, p. 77.

61. Ibid., p. 76.

62. Luttwak, in *Commentary*, April 1974, p. 59; Colin S. Gray, *The Soviet-American Arms Race* (Lexington, Mass.: Lexington Books, 1976), p. 164. See also Michael May, "Some Advantages of a Counterforce Deterrence," *Orbis*, Summer 1970, pp. 271-83.

63. Luttwak, in *Commentary*, April 1974, p. 59; Schneider, in *Air Force Magazine*, September 1974, p. 28. Soviet reaction to the Schlesinger strategic program is discussed in Chapter 8, pp. 162-66.

64. Senator McIntyre had introduced an amendment to the military procurement bill on June 4, 1974, that would have deferred counterforce development programs until the president had notified Congress that it was impossible to get an agreement with the Soviet Union in SALT to limit multiple warheads for missiles. See John W. Finney, "Missile Debate Sought in Senate," *New York Times*, June 5, 1974.

65. John W. Finney, "Senate Endorses New Nixon Policy on Better ICBMs," *New York Times*, June 11, 1974.

66. See Chapter 5, pp. 94 98. The failure to make progress in SALT at the July 1974 Moscow summit evidently did not hurt Schlesinger's case in the Congress, if only because of the general impression that the Russians—and not the Pentagon programs espoused by Schlesinger—were mainly responsible for not reaching agreement. On this point, see Joseph Kraft, "Time Out for Henry Kissinger," *Washington Post*, July 11, 1974. See also Henry T. Simmons, "U.S. Strategic Power: New U.S. Initiatives," *The Retired Officer*, August 1974.

67. The April 1975 recommendation of the McIntyre subcommittee to delete $110 million in research funds to improve the counterforce capability of U.S. strategic systems was rejected by the Senate in June 1975, by a vote of 52 to 42. See Richard L. Madden, "Senate Rejects a $1.2-Billion Cut in Arms Budget," *New York Times*, June 5, 1975.

68. See Chapter 2, p. 27f, and note 23.

69. These basic elements, in addition to such doctrinal criteria as selective nuclear options and essential equivalence, included programs for Trident, B-1, Minuteman upgrade, cruise missile development, advanced ICBM technology (MX), advanced reentry systems, and improved space surveillance, communications, and airborne command systems. See *Schlesinger FY 1976 Report*, pp. II-1-67; *Report of Secretary of Defense Donald H. Rumsfeld to the Congress on the FY 1977 Budget and FY 1977-1981 Defense Programs*, January 27, 1976, pp. 50-97 (hereafter cited as *Rumsfeld FY 1977 Report*); and his similar annual report of the following year, dated January 17, 1977, pp. 58-78, 105-7, 121-43 (hereafter cited as *Rumsfeld FY 1978 Report*).

70. See Leslie H. Gelb, "Senators Clash with Schlesinger," *New York Times*, April 5, 1974.

71. *Rumsfeld FY 1977 Report*, p. 60.

72. Ibid., p. 63; *Rumsfeld FY 1978 Report*, p. 122.

73. *Rumsfeld FY 1977 Report*, p. 63.

74. *Rumsfeld FY 1978 Report*, p. 125.

75. Ibid., p. 126. For an informative discussion of alternative land-mobile ICBM basing modes, see Colin S. Gray, *The Future of Land-Based Missile Forces*, Adelphi Papers no. 140, International Institute for Strategic Studies, London, 1978, pp. 18-24.

76. *Rumsfeld FY 1978 Report*, p. 130.

77. The United States had originally proposed that the deployment of mobile land-based ICBM launchers be specifically prohibited, but it eventually had to be satisfied with a unilateral statement on the subject on May 20, 1972. *Arms Control and Disarmament Agreements*, 1977 edition, U.S. Arms Control and Disarmament Agency, p. 145. See also Chapter 1, p. 13.

78. Further discussion of the land-mobile deployment issue and its implications may be found in Chapters 8, pp. 176-77, 192-94; 11, pp. 222, 223, 225, 227f.

79. *Rumsfeld FY 1978 Report*, pp. 108, 126.

80. Ibid., p. 131. The original IOC of the Trident system had been set for the fall of 1978. See *Schlesinger FY 1975 Report*, p. 59.

81. *Rumsfeld FY 1978 Report*, p. 134.

82. See Charles Mohr, "Carter Orders Steps to Increase Ability to Meet War Threats," *New York Times*, August 26, 1977. The 3 percent increase was to be in "real" terms, with inflation discounted.

83. For useful background on the buildup of Soviet theater force capabilities in Europe, see: *The Growing Dimensions of Security*, Atlantic Council Policy Paper, Washington, D.C., November 1977, pp. 31-49; Phillip A. Karber, *The Tactical Revolution in Soviet Military Doctrine*, BDM Corporation, McLean, Va., March 2, 1977; Jeffrey Record, "Theater Nuclear Weapons: Begging the Soviet Union to Pre-empt," *Survival*, September-October 1977, pp. 208-11.

84. See *Fiscal Year 1978 Budget Revisions*, February 1977, Executive Office of the President, p. 31. The total authority request for the defense portion of the revised budget was down $2.7 billion from the $122.8 billion Ford budget. The 3 percent "real" increase mentioned in note 82, above, came only with the FY 1979 budget, the first one fully prepared by the Carter administration. See *Department of Defense Annual Report FY 1979, Harold Brown, Secretary of Defense*, February 2, 1978, p. 12 (hereafter cited as *Brown FY 1979 Report*).

85. *Fiscal Year 1978 Budget Revisions*, p. 30.

86. Secretary of Defense Harold Brown, Briefing on Budget, February 21, 1977, in *Selected Statements*, Department of the Air Force, March 1, 1977, pp. 6-7.

87. Described as a comprehensive net assessment and military force posture review that was originally intended to provide a "grand design" for U.S. foreign and military policy in the Carter administration, PRM-10 was prepared by a number of interagency teams under the general supervision of Prof. Samuel Huntington of the NSC staff and Dr. Lynn Davis, a deputy assistant secretary of defense in ISA. Reportedly, the study became a subject of dispute within the administration and went through several revisions giving varying assessments of relative U.S.-Soviet strength. See Robert G. Kaiser, "Memo Sets Stage in Assessing U.S., Soviet Strength," *Washington Post*, July 6, 1977; Richard Burt, "U.S. Analysis Doubts There Can Be Victor in Major Nuclear War," *New York Times*, January 6, 1978.

88. Among other findings of PRM-10 reportedly were that U.S. strategic forces must maintain a capability to inflict "unacceptable damage" on the Soviet

Union, defined as 70 percent of Soviet "recovery resources," and that in the event of a strategic nuclear war, neither the U.S. nor the USSR could emerge a winner. Burt, in the *New York Times*, January 6, 1978. This article was based on a supposed copy of the PRM-10 study obtained by the *New York Times*, but since—see note 87, above—the study went through various revisions, it is possible that the *Times* did not acquire the final version. Other sources have claimed that the final version gave an assessment of the military balance much more favorable to the U.S. than earlier drafts, and that the Joint Chiefs of Staff had found the ultimate conclusions "too optimistic." See Kingsbury Smith, "Joint Chiefs Blast Study of Soviet Arms Buildup," *Baltimore News American*, July 19, 1977.

89. President Carter's cancellation announcement was greeted as a "surprise" in the press because he had given the impression to a number of visiting congressmen that he would approve production of at least a limited number of the 244 B-1s originally wanted by the Air Force. The president's decision to cancel B-1 production did not, incidentally, cut off R&D funding (approximately $200 million). Some interpreted this as a genuine move to keep a penetrating bomber option open to hedge against problems with other strategic systems, as the president said, but others saw it simply as a sop to the B-1's proponents. See Bernard Weinraub, "Carter Turns Down B-1 As Expensive and Unneeded; Existing Weapons Stressed," *Washington Post*, July 1, 1977; Charles W. Corddry, "Carter Aborts B-1; Unmanned Missile Favored," *Baltimore Sun*, July 1, 1977; "B-1 No, Cruise Yes," *Newsweek*, July 11, 1977, p. 14.

90. See, for example, Senator Culver, "The Future of the Strategic Bomber," pp. 3-6; Editorial, "Courage on the B-1," *Chicago Sun-Times*, July 1, 1977; Bernard Weinraub, "Defense Chief Sees a Saving of Billions by Dropping the B-1," *New York Times*, July 2, 1977; Tom Wicker, "A-1 or the B-1," ibid., July 3, 1977.

91. For a range of critical comment on the B-1 cancellation, see: "Ford Calls B-1 Ruling a Mistaken Gamble," *New York Times*, July 1, 1977; Editorial, "Carter Shoots Down B-1: Domestic Politics Blamed for His Risk to Security," *Detroit News*, July 1, 1977; Edgar Ulsamer, "U.S. Strategic Deterrence at the Crossroads," *Air Force Magazine*, December 1977, pp. 43-45; "Jane's Editor Says B-1 Decision May Doom the West," *New York Times*, December 8, 1977.

92. Although the Senate went along in 1977 with the Carter administration's revocation of production funds for the B-1, the House refused to cancel $462 million previously appropriated to build the first two production models, apart from the first four prototype B-1s. At the end of January 1978, the issue remained unresolved, with the president having declared that rescission of the B-1 funds was among his legislative priorities for the year. See Paul Houston, "House Refuses to Cancel Funds for 2 B-1 Planes," *Los Angeles Times*, December 7, 1977; *Aerospace Daily*, January 26, 1978, p. 131.

93. Transcript of President's News Conference, June 30, 1977, *New York Times*, July 1, 1977. In addition to its internal "political" function of compensating for the B-1, the president's new emphasis on cruise missiles also had the external function, as he put it a month later in a speech in Charleston, S.C., of "compensating for the growing threat to our deterrent capability represented by the buildup of Soviet strategic offensive weapons forces." The

Russians, incidentally, gave Carter no credit for the B-1 cancellation as a unilateral example of "strategic restraint." Rather, they charged that his decision would add a formidable "fourth component" to the U.S. strategic triad. V. Matveev, "Commentary on One White House Decision," *Izvestiia*, July 7, 1977. See Hedrick Smith, "Carter Bids Soviet Limit Big Missiles in Response to U.S.," *New York Times*, July 21, 1977.

94. The cruise missile technology of the 1970s, based on advances in guidance, electronics miniaturization, small turbine engine design, and high energy fuels, combined with miniaturized warhead technology, had greatly altered the strategic delivery potential associated with earlier generations of long-range aerodynamic cruise missiles, such as the Snark and Navaho of the 1950s. The new cruise missiles were essentially small drone aircraft whose terrain-matching guidance system and very low altitude flight pattern gave them great accuracy (a few hundred feet) and made defense against them difficult. The new cruise missiles also promised to be very versatile, carrying either nuclear or conventional warheads, and performing either strategic or tactical roles. Credit for re-establishing a cruise missile development program in the early 1970s has usually been given to Dr. Henry Kissinger and Secretary of Defense Melvin Laird, who purportedly broached the idea in order to win JCS support for the SALT I agreements. See John W. Finney, "New U.S. Missile Snags Arms Talks," *New York Times*, June 16, 1975. For relevant background on the technical, operational and arms control significance of the new cruise missiles, see: Kosta Tsipis, "The Long-Range Cruise Missile," *Bulletin of the Atomic Scientists*, April 1975, pp. 15-26; Richard Burt, "The Cruise Missile and Arms Control," *Survival*, January-February 1976, pp. 10-17; Colin S. Gray, "Who's Afraid of the Cruise Missile?" *Orbis*, Fall 1977, pp. 517-32; Robert L. Pfaltzgraff, Jr., and Jacquelyn K. Davis, *The Cruise Missile: Bargaining Chip or Defense Bargain?*, Institute for Foreign Policy Analysis, Cambridge, Mass., January 1977.

95. Although the last B-52H bomber had been built in 1962, by appropriate modifications and employment the useful life of the B-52 could probably be extended to "1990 or beyond," according to expert testimony. See remarks of General Richard H. Ellis, commander of SAC, in *Fiscal Year 1978 Supplemental Military Authorization, Hearings*, before the Subcommittee on Research and Development, Committee on Armed Services, Senate, 95th Cong., August 24, 1977, p. 191.

96. *Brown FY 1979 Report*, pp. 37, 114-19. According to Brown, analysis had indicated that a B-1 force would be 40 percent more expensive than a B-52/ALCM force of comparable capability. During the season of controversy following the president's June 1977 decision, Rockwell International, maker of the B-1, announced that its studies showed that the B-1 modified for cruise missile delivery would be more cost-effective than either a B-52/ALCM combination or any of the other potential ALCM platforms that had been proposed, such as the "stretched" FB-111H bomber or wide-body transports. This contention in turn was challenged by Senator William Proxmire, who said he had been informed by the Defense Department that the cost of the B-1 as a cruise missile carrier would be 60 percent higher than for a wide-body transport and 22

percent higher than for a B-52 carrier. See Donald E. Fink, "B-1 Cost Effectiveness Claimed," *Aviation Week & Space Technology*, December 12, 1977, p. 14; "Proxmire Says Pentagon Rejects B-1 Cruise Missile Claims," *Defense/Space Daily*, January 5, 1978, p. 14.

97. *Brown FY 1979 Report*, p. 119. The Air Force and the Navy had been directed in early 1977 by Brown to consolidate their cruise missile development efforts into a single program headed by a Navy officer.

98. Force levels under discussion in 1977-1978 included use of 70 to 120 B-52G bombers with twenty ALCMs each, for a force of 1400 to 2400 long-range cruise missiles launchable from outside the Soviet air defense perimeter. If all of the 150 B-52Gs available were to be used as missile platforms, the number of ALCMs, 3000, would add about one-third to the nuclear weapon force loadings in U.S. strategic forces. See Senator Culver, "The Future of the Strategic Bomber," pp. 7, 12.

99. As pointed out by some observers disturbed by the B-1 cancellation, the issue of ALCM range limits acquired added significance as the likelihood of a new penetrating bomber decreased. See Ulsamer, in *Air Force Magazine*, December 1977, p. 46.

100. See, for example, editorial, "The B-1: Still Wondering," *Los Angeles Times*, December 19, 1977.

101. See Chapters 10, pp. 201-02, 212-16; and 11, p. 226f., 228f.

102. *Brown Fy 1979 Report*, p. 58.

103. Ibid., pp. 59, 62-66. See also Chapter 6, pp. 122, 132.

104. *Brown FY 1979 Report*, p. 65. In addition to continuing R&D on the B-1 as a hedge, Brown also said it was planned to "explore a number of possible options for other penetrating bombers." See also note 89, above.

105. *Brown FY 1979 Report*, pp. 110-13. The first Poseidon submarine backfitted with the Trident I (C-4) missile was scheduled for deployment in October 1979. For previous comment on Trident performance, see Chapter 6, notes 49 and 51.

106. Bernard Weinraub, "Defense Chief Backs Start on a System of Mobile Missiles," *New York Times*, October 6, 1977.

107. *Brown FY 1979 Report*, p. 109, Reportedly, the late 1977 decision to rescind came after the Office of Management and Budget had told the president in December 1977 that further research on the MX basing mode was required.

108. Ibid., p. 59.

109. Among studies giving a negative evaluation of the trench-basing mode reportedly were an assessment of the U.S. strategic posture initiated in December 1977 by the Pentagon's Office of Program Evaluation and Analysis; a missile deployment study completed at M.I.T. in March 1978; and a report to Secretary Brown by the Defense Science Board. See Richard Burt, "M.I.T. Team Is Critical of Proposal to Base Mobile Missiles in Tunnels," *New York Times*, March 25, 1978, and "Sea-and-Land Missile Sought by Pentagon," ibid., April 24, 1978; Bernard Weinraub, "New Missile Project with Mobile Bases Being Slowed by U.S.," ibid., June 12, 1978.

110. See Richard Burt, "U.S. Aides Push New Plan for Random Deploying of Mobile Missiles," *New York Times*, June 18, 1978; Robert G. Kaiser and Walter

Pincus, "U.S. Seen Favoring Extra Missile Holes," *Washington Post*, July 9, 1978; George C. Wilson, "Joint Chiefs Chairman Says U.S. Needs a Mobile Missile," ibid., July 26, 1978; Don Oberdorfer, "U.S. to Retain 'Shell Game' Mobile Missile Option, Brown Says," ibid., August 23, 1978. In November 1978, Secretary Brown again asked for funds to begin full-scale development of the MX, although it was stated that a decision on how the missile would be based might be deferred for another year. See Richard Burt, "Pentagon Includes Two New Missiles In Its 1979 Budget," *New York Times*, November 14, 1978.

111. See, for example, Paul H. Nitze, "The Comparative Costs of MAPS/ ALPS Incremental Aim Points Additions Versus Soviet Warhead Fractionization" (Arlington, Va., August 16, 1978.) (Mimeo.)

112. See Chapters 9, p. 192f; 11, pp. 228, 231f.

113. *Brown FY 1979 Report*, p. 63.

114. Ibid. See also Chapter 7, pp. 142f., 146.

115. See Chapter 7, pp. 145-46; see also Chapter 6, p. 120f.

116. *Brown FY 1979 Report*, p. 53. However, it was reported in late November 1978 that tentative moves toward enhancing U.S. capabilities for limited nuclear conflict were under discussion within the administration, as part of a revision of U.S. strategic doctrine. See Richard Burt, "U.S. Moving Toward Vast Revision of Its Strategy on Nuclear Warfare," *New York Times*, November 29, 1978.

117. Ibid., p. 55.

118. Ibid., pp. 79, 108.

119. See Bernard Weinraub, "Brown Says Soviet Can· Fell Satellites," *New York Times*, October 5, 1977.

120. *Brown FY 1979 Report*, pp. 125, 129.

121. See Chapter 6, pp. 133-34.

122. See *Rumsfeld FY 1977 Report*, p. 95.

123. Henry S. Bradsher, "U.S. Scraps Effort to Curb Soviet Civil Defense as It Seeks to Match It," *Washington Star*, November 22, 1978; Richard Burt, "Carter Adopts a Program to Bolster Civil Defense in a Nuclear Attack," *New York Times*, November 13, 1978.

124. Richard Burt, "Carter Uncommitted on Money For Plan to Bolster Civil Defense," *New York Times*, December 2, 1978.

125. See *Schlesinger FY 1975 Report*, p. 26; *Rumsfeld FY 1978 Report*, p. 64; *Brown FY 1979 Report*, p. 62.

126. *Brown FY 1979 Report*, p. 62.

127. Ibid., p. 45.


NOTES TO CHAPTER 8
SALT POLICY DEVELOPMENTS IN THE
PERIOD PRIOR TO VLADIVOSTOK

1. Rowland Evans and Robert Novak, "Kissinger or Schlesinger?" *Washington Post*, September 19, 1974. See also Victor Zorza, "Worrying about Kissinger," ibid., October 8, 1974. See also Chapter 2, pp. 27-28.

2. Ibid. In this connection, following Gerald Ford's succession to the

presidency in August 1974, there were rumors that Schlesinger might soon be replaced or that Kissinger might lose his "second hat" as head of the National Security Council apparatus. In both cases, the White House reaffirmed that the two men remained secure in their respective posts for the time being, though before the next year was out, Schlesinger would lose his. See: L. Edgar Prina, "Doubts Erased, Schlesinger to Stay," *San Diego Union*, August 13, 1974; "White House Denies Any Plans to Take a Job from Kissinger," *New York Times*, September 18, 1974.

3. See Stephen S. Rosenfeld, "Kissinger and Schlesinger," *Washington Post*, February 3, 1974.

4. See, for example, James Reston, "Kissinger and the Joint Chiefs of Staff," *New York Times*, June 23, 1974.

5. Leslie H. Gelb, "Schlesinger for Defense, Defense for Detente," *New York Times Magazine*, August 4, 1974, p. 35.

6. Ibid.

7. Rosenfeld, in the *Washington Post*, February 3, 1974.

8. Murrey Marder, "Kissinger: Ford Firm on Detente," *Washington Post*, September 20, 1974.

9. For an illuminating list of similarities and differences in the positions of the two, see Leslie H. Gelb, "Debate on U.S. Nuclear Policy: Just What Is Strategic Superiority?" *New York Times*, July 30, 1974.

10. Ibid.

11. *Secretary Kissinger's Statement on U.S.-Soviet Relations*, before the Senate Foreign Relations Committee, September 19, 1974, Department of State, Office of Media Services, p. 11.

12. Kissinger Press Conference in Moscow, July 3, 1974, in *Department of State Bulletin*, July 29, 1974, p. 215 (hereafter cited as *Kissinger Moscow Press Conference, July 1974*).

13. *Secretary Kissinger's Statement on U.S.-Soviet Relations*, September 19, 1974.

14. Secretary Kissinger's address, "Constancy and Strength in U.S. Foreign Policy," August 20, 1974, Department of State, Office of Media Services, p. 3.

15. Ibid.

16. *Secretary Kissinger's Statement on U.S.-Soviet Relations*, September 19, 1974.

17. Ibid., p. 10.

18. Ibid., p. 12.

19. See Gelb, in the *New York Times*, July 30, 1974.

20. Ibid.

21. See *Secretary Kissinger's Press Conference*, March 21, 1974, Department of State, Office of Media Services, p. 9; *Secretary Kissinger's Statement on U.S.-Soviet Relations*, September 19, 1974, p. 10.

22. *Secretary Kissinger's Press Conference*, March 21, 1974, p. 9.

23. Gelb, in the *New York Times*, July 30, 1974.

24. Gelb, in *New York Times Magazine*, August 4, 1974, p. 44; Joseph Kraft, "Letter from Moscow," *The New Yorker*, July 29, 1974, p. 70. For previous discussion of the MIRV and other issues at the mid-1974 summit, see Chapter 5, pp. 101-102.

25. *RN: The Memoirs of Richard Nixon* (New York: Grosset & Dunlap, 1978), pp. 1024-25. Nixon's account, which gave a very disparaging picture of the attitude displayed by Schlesinger and the Joint Chiefs, said nothing explicit about how an acceptable proposal was to be worked out. According to other unconfirmed accounts, however, irreconcilable differences led to excluding Pentagon inputs into the final drafting of a U.S. position for the summit meeting. See Clarence A. Robinson, Jr., "Ten MIRV Proposals Prepared," *Aviation Week & Space Technology*, July 1, 1974, p. 12.

26. *Kissinger Moscow Press Conference, July 1974*, p. 210. See also Chapter 3, pp. 72-73.

27. See Leslie H. Gelb, "Schlesinger Rebuts Kissinger Remark, Denies Pentagon Impeded Arms Talks," *New York Times*, July 4, 1974; Michael Getler and Thomas O'Toole, "Military Supports Accords," *Washington Post*, July 4, 1974.

28. See Chapter 4, p. 82f.

29. Leslie H. Gelb, "How U.S. Made Ready for Talk at Vladivostok," *New York Times*, December 3, 1974; "Background Briefing by Henry Kissinger, 3 December 1974," in *Survival*, July-August 1975, p. 192 (hereafter cited as *Kissinger Background Briefing, December 3, 1974*). See also Chapter 2, p. 31.

30. Gelb, in the *New York Times*, December 3, 1974.

31. Ibid.

32. Ibid. See also Victor Zorza, "The SALT Bargain with the Military," *Washington Post*, December 12, 1974; Chapter 2, p. 42.

33. Gelb, in the *New York Times*, December 3, 1974.

34. Ibid.

35. See Alton Frye, "Kissinger and Arms Limitation," *Washington Post*, August 17, 1974.

36. For an interpretation along these lines, see the two-part commentary by Chalmers M. Roberts, "How Much Detente?" *Washington Post*, August 19 and September 7, 1974.

37. Ibid. See also Gelb, in *New York Times Magazine*, August 4, 1974, pp. 9, 43.

38. See Chapter 7, especially pp. 136-45.

39. See Observer article, "Strange Position of J. Schlesinger," *Pravda*, July 12, 1975. See also Christopher S. Wren, "Soviet Assails Schlesinger on Nuclear Arms Remark," *New York Times*, July 13, 1975.

40. For typical commentary along these lines, see: B. Svetlov, "Despite the Spirit of the Times," *Izvestiia*, January 4, 1974; A. Platonov and L. Alekseyev, "A Responsible Task," *Pravda*, February 14, 1974; V. Vinograd, "An Increase for the Pentagon," *Krasnaia Zvezda*, August 28, 1974; A. Grigoryants, "Those Who Are against Detente," *Nedelya*, no. 35 (August-September 1974), pp. 2-3.

41. V.A. Matveyev, "Fresh Gains in the Struggle against Opponents of Detente," *Za Rubezhom*, no. 22 (August 1974), p. 9; Grigoryants, in *Nedelya*, August-September 1974.

42. V. Larionov, "Arms Limitation and Its Enemies," *Pravda*, April 17, 1974.

43. See Chapter 5, p. 34f.

44. A. Karenin, "On Restraining Strategic Arms," *Mezhdunarodnaia Zhizn*, no. 9 (September 1974), p. 19.

45. Ibid., pp. 14, 20. The point concerning the ABM Treaty, while not linked with Karenin's discussion of the Schlesinger doctrine, is of interest because it had not been previously advanced as part of the Soviet rationale for the treaty.

46. G.A. Trofimenko, "Problems of Strengthening Peace and Security in Soviet-American Relations," *SShA: Ekonomika, Politika, Ideologiia*, no. 9 (September 1974), p. 17.

47. Note the repetition of this charge that "public" and "real" U.S. strategies are quite different in a later essay that Trofimenko was invited to write for an American journal. See "The 'Theology of Strategy,' " *Orbis*, Fall 1977, p. 500.

48. Ibid., p. 18.

49. See Chapter 5, p. 98.

50. See Genrik Trofimenko, "Double Standards and SALT II," *Washington Star-News*, November 10, 1974.

51. One may note the correspondence between this Soviet concern about the Schlesinger doctrine's being focused on the lower part of the nuclear spectrum and the Schlesinger rationale (see Chapter 7, p. 136f.) that the real problem with which the U.S. targeting revision was meant to deal was the deterrence of lower-level attacks and provocations that might escalate. The pertinent difference, of course, is that what represented a bolstering of deterrence from Schlesinger's viewpoint was labeled intimidation from the Soviet viewpoint. Objectively, this amounts to saying that "deterrence" and "intimidation" are opposite sides of the same coin.

52. G.A. Trofimenko, "USSR-USA: Peaceful Coexistence as a Norm of Mutual Relations," *SShA: Ekonomika, Politika, Ideologiia*, no. 2 (February 1974), p. 17. For other expressions of a similar viewpoint, see: M.A. Milshteyn and L.S. Semeiko, "Strategic Arms Limitation: Problems and Prospects," ibid., no. 12 (December 1973), pp. 3-12; G.A. Arbatov, "The Impasses of the Policy of Force," *Problemy Mira i Sotsializma*, no. 2 (February 1974), pp. 41-47; Aleksandr Bovin, "Peace and Social Progress," *Izvestiia*, September 11, 1973; G.A. Arbatov, ed., *USA: The Scientific-Technical Revolution and Trends in Foreign Policy* (Moscow: Mezhdunarodnye otnosheniya, 1974), pp. 69-70.

53. Rear Admiral Professor V. Shelyag, "Two World Outlooks—Two Views on War," *Krasnaia Zvezda*, February 7, 1974; General of the Army Ye. Maltsev, "Lenin's Ideas of the Defense of Socialism," ibid., February 14, 1974; Colonel Ye. Rybkin, "Leninist Conception of War and the Present," *Kommunist Vooruzhennykh Sil*, no. 20 (October 1973), pp. 21-28. (In this article, Rybkin took the unusual step of criticizing another Soviet spokesman, Aleksandr Bovin, by name.) For other military arguments for maintaining Soviet defense preparations at a high level, see Colonel A. Pozmogov, "The Building of Socialism and Communism in the USSR—The Embodiment of Lenin's Ideas," ibid., no. 3 (February 1974), p. 78; General of the Army A. Yepishev, "Soviet Army's Historic Mission," *Soviet Military Review*, no. 2, Moscow (February 1974), p. 5.

54. For discussion of this earlier debate, see Thomas W. Wolfe, *Soviet*

*Strategy at the Crossroads* (Cambridge: Harvard University Press, 1965), pp. 70-78; *Soviet Power and Europe: 1945-1970* (Baltimore: John Hopkins Press, 1970), pp. 437, 503-9.

55. See Thomas W. Wolfe, *The Military Dimension in the Making of Soviet Foreign and Defense Policy*, The Rand Corporation, P-6024, Santa Monica, October 1977, p. 35.

56. For previous discussion of this point, see Chapter 5, pp. 110-12.

57. The Soviet leadership failed to confirm Dobrynin's optimistic response to a U.S. MIRV proposal given to him through the "back channel" by Kissinger before the latter's March 1974 visit to Moscow, which might suggest either that there had been a reversal of position within the top Kremlin leadership or that Dobrynin was out of tune with Moscow on the issue. See Chapter 4, p. 82f.

58. See Chapter 5, p. 42. See also Hedrick Smith, "Brezhnev Listened to His Military-Industrial Complex," *New York Times*, July 7, 1974.

59. A quite different interpretation of Brezhnev's motives with respect to MIRV at the mid-1974 summit has been offered, incidentally, by some observers. Joseph Kraft, for example, noted that Brezhnev might have been "giving American negotiators the impression that he wanted to make a deal but that his hands were tied by his own military men. It was, after all, standard practice for both Stalin and Khrushchev to blame their subordinates for disagreements while themselves coming on as the good guys." See Kraft, in *The New Yorker*, July 29, 1974, p. 70.

60. On this point, Nixon in his *Memoirs*, discussing the conditions under which the mid-1974 summit was to take place, notes the following: "For the first time since the Watergate break-in, Brezhnev expressed concern about my ability to make decisions domestically . . . and he was understandably concerned that my sudden or unexpected departure from office would leave him in an embarrassing and exposed position within his own hierarchy." *RN: The Memoirs of Richard Nixon*, p. 1026.

61. "Brain of the Army," *Pravda*, November, 13, 1974.

62. See Victor Zorza, "The SALT Bargain with the Military," *Washington Post*, December 12, 1974.

63. See Chapter 8, p. 160f.

64. Gelb, in the *New York Times*, December 3, 1974.

65. *Kissinger Background Briefing, December 3, 1974*, p. 192.

66. Ibid., pp. 192-93.

67. Gelb, in the *New York Times*, December 3, 1974.

68. Peter Osnos, "Soviets Sounding Rhapsodic on Virtues of Arms Accord," *Washington Post*, December 6, 1974.

69. It may be noted that the idea of having a summit meeting in November 1974, according to Nixon, had been discussed by him with Brezhnev during the mid-1974 summit. Vladivostok, however, had not been mentioned as the site, and of course no basis for agreement was then in sight either. See *RN: The Memoirs of Richard Nixon*, p. 1034.

70. See Chapter 5, pp. 101-02.

71. If this were the case, incidentally, then the proposition that the Schlesinger doctrine was to blame for stiffening the Soviet position at the mid-1974 summit (see above, p. 169-70) would hold less water.

72. A somewhat more byzantine hypothesis concerning the Soviet interest to which Kissinger might have appealed has been ventured by Victor Zorza. According to Zorza, a hint could have been dropped that the best way for the Kremlin to box in its favorite bogeyman, Senator Jackson, would be to conclude a "breakthrough" agreement in SALT with President Ford—thus serving both the immediate cause of detente and helping to keep out of the White House in 1976 the man whom the Kremlin itself had so often accused of trying to dismantle detente. See Zorza, "Kissinger's Breakthrough," *Washington Post*, November 28, 1975.

## NOTES TO CHAPTER 9
## VLADIVOSTOK: A PIVOTAL SALT
## II TRANSACTION

1. During much of the time spent on SALT issues at the two-day Vladivostok summit (which by varying accounts was from seven and a half to nine and a half hours), the four principals reportedly were closeted alone, with their advisers standing by. In the Soviet entourage, which included Ambassador A.F. Dobrynin, G.M. Korniyenko, and A.M. Aleksandrov, the ranking military man was Colonel-General M.M. Kozlov, head of the Main Operations Directorate of the General Staff. Marshal Grechko, who usually had been the top Soviet military figure in evidence at summit meetings in the Soviet Union, was not on hand at Vladivostok. On the American side, the chief advisers present were Ambassador Walter J. Stoessel, Helmut Sonnenfeldt, Arthur A. Hartman, and William Hyland of the State Department and Lieutenant General Brent Scowcroft. As customary at summit talks up to that time, no ranking officials of either the Department of Defense or the Joint Chiefs of Staff attended the Vladivostok meeting. General Scowcroft was present in his NSC capacity as Dr. Kissinger's deputy for national security affairs.

2. Bernard Gwertzman, "Ford Says Accord Gives a Basis for Cut in Arms," *New York Times*, December 3, 1974.

3. For further discussion of steps toward completion of a SALT II accord, see Chapters 10 and 11.

4. Although initially indicated to be in the zone of agreement, this was one of the Vladivostok points that subsequently became contentious. See Chapter 10, p. 200f.

5. The assumption here was that the new accord would be completed well before the expiration of the Interim Agreement in October 1977, which did not prove to be the case. At Vladivostok, incidentally, it was not decided whether a SALT II agreement would be converted into a treaty or take some other form. See Gerard C. Smith, "SALT after Vladivostok," *Journal of International Affairs* 9, no. 1 (January 1975): 7.

6. This provision too was later altered. See Chapter 9, pp. 178-80.

7. See "Text of the Nuclear Arms Agreement," *New York Times*, November 25, 1974.

8. See Chapter 9, p. 179f. The actual texts of these aide-mémoire have not been published with other official documents on arms control agreements.

9. See Peter Osnos, "Soviets Sounding Rhapsodic on Virtues of Arms Accord," *Washington Post*, December 6, 1974. See also Chapter 9, pp. 181-82.

10. Leslie H. Gelb, "How U.S. Made Ready for Talk at Vladivostok," *New York Times*, December 3, 1974.

11. "Press Conference of the Secretary of State," Bureau of Public Affairs, Department of State, December 7, 1974, p. 4.

12. See Chapter 5, p. 100f.

13. See Smith, in *Journal of International Affairs*, January 1975, p. 8. The mid-1974 summit's upper figure was about 1000 MIRVed launchers. See Chapter 5, pp. 102-03.

14. "Press Conference of the Secretary of State," December 7, 1974, p. 3.

15. Gelb, in the *New York Times*, December 3, 1974. Both the U.S. MIRV and overall proposed ceilings evidently had been upped by 100 between October 1974 and Vladivostok—advance movement toward the higher Soviet preference, as it were.

16. "Kissinger Sums Up '74," interview in *Newsweek*, December 30, 1974, p. 29.

17. See Bernard Gwertzman, "Kissinger Warns Arms Pact Foes Imperil Detente," *New York Times*, December 8, 1974.

18. See Clarence A. Robinson, Jr., "SALT Proposals Facing Hurdles," *Aviation Week & Space Technology*, December 9, 1974, p. 12.

19. For further discussion of this question, see Chapter 10, p. 200f.

20. See Michael Getler, "High MIRV Levels May Reduce Spy Satellites' Verification Role," *Washington Post*, November 28, 1974; Robinson, in *Aviation Week & Space Technology*, December 9, 1974, p. 12.

21. Michael Getler, "U.S. Halts Installation of MIRVs in Montana," *Washington Post*, February 1, 1975.

22. See Chapter 7, pp. 139, 146.

23. According to one account, it was felt by American officials that U.S. surveillance capabilities would permit detection of Soviet mobile systems with about "80 percent effectiveness." See Robinson, in *Aviation Week & Space Technology*, December 9, 1974, p. 14.

24. See Michael Getler, "Exclusions in Arms Pact Stir Controversy," *Washington Post*, December 4, 1974.

25. See John Herbers, "Kissinger Describes Vladivostok Accord as 'Breakthrough,' " *New York Times*, November 25, 1974.

26. See Robinson, in *Aviation Week & Space Technology*, December 9, 1974, p. 13, and by the same author, "U.S. Weighs SALT Proposals," ibid., June 23, 1975, p. 13. See also Paul H. Nitze, "The Vladivostok Accord and SALT II," *The Review of Politics*, April 1975, p. 135.

27. Robinson, in *Aviation Week & Space Technology*, December 9, 1974, p. 14. Further discussion of the Backfire issue will be found in Chapter 10, pp. 201-02, 212-14, 215.

28. Robinson, in *Aviation Week & Space Technology*, December 9, 1974, p. 13. This apparently represented some shift from a previous Soviet argument that a bomber, because of its multiple bomb load, should not be equated with a single missile launcher.

29. See Richard Burt, "Technological Change and Arms Control: The Cruise Missile Case," in Johan J. Holst and Uwe Nerlich, eds., *Beyond Nuclear*

*Deterrence: New Aims, New Arms* (New York: Crane, Russak & Company, 1977), p. 180.

30. Ibid., p. 185; Bernard Gwertzman, "Kissinger, after Senate Briefing, Calls Criticism of Arms Accord Surprising," *New York Times*, December 5, 1974. Which interpretation—the U.S. or Soviet—most accurately reflected what transpired at Vladivostok with regard to the air-launched missile question is probably not clarifiable. It has been suggested that the potential of the new long-range cruise missile technology (see Chapter 7, note 94) was not fully appreciated by the Soviets, and possibly by the U.S. negotiators, at Vladivostok, which might account for the imprecision in handling cruise missiles there. See Richard Burt, "The Cruise Missile and Arms Control," *Survival*, January-February 1976, p. 13. Further discussion of the cruise missile issue will be found in Chapter 10, pp. 201-02, 212-16.

31. Editorial, "Summit at Vladivostok," *Washington Post*, November 26, 1974.

32. See Herbers, in the *New York Times*, November 25, 1974.

33. See Chapter 10, p. 200. See also Colin S. Gray, "A Problem Guide to SALT II," *Survival*, September-October 1975, p. 233.

34. See Peter Osnos, "Detente Gets Boost at Summit," *Washington Post*, November 25, 1974.

35. "The Arms Pact Reduces Neither Terror Nor Costs," *New York Times*, December 1, 1974.

36. As quoted by John Herbers, in the *New York Times*, November 25, 1974.

37. See, for example: Editorial, "The Vladivostok Accord," *Washington Post*, December 6, 1974; Joseph Kraft, "The High Price of Detente," ibid., November 26, 1974; editorial, "New Chance for SALT," *New York Times*, December 26, 1974; Paul Nitze, "Vladivostok and Crisis Stability," *Wall Street Journal*, January 24, 1975. See also the extensive testimony on Vladivostok given by various individuals in *The Vladivostok Accord: Implications to U.S. Security, Arms Control, and World Peace, Hearings*, before the Subcommittee on International Security and Scientific Affairs, Committee on International Relations, House of Representatives, 94th Cong., 1st session, June 24, 25, and July 8, 1975. (Cited hereafter as *Hearings on the Vladivostok Accord*.)

38. William Chapman, "Senator Jackson Asks Further Arms Limits," *Washington Post*, December 9, 1974; "Jackson Disputes Kissinger on Arms," *New York Times*, December 9, 1974.

39. Bernard Gwertzman, "Three Senators Back Soviet Arms Deal," *New York Times*, December 13, 1974. The same resolution was reintroduced in the 94th Congress, on January 17, 1975, but remained in committee until its close. See Leslie H. Gelb, "Three Senators for Arms Pact: Kissinger Welcomes Move," *New York Times*, January 18, 1975; *Congressional Record*, January 17, 1975, pp. S462-S464; May 6, 1975, p. S7502.

40. Robert Keatley and Richard Levine, "Dismayed Kissinger Defends Arms Pact from Charges of High Costs, Soviet Gains," *Wall Street Journal*, December 9, 1974; Gwertzman, in the *New York Times*, December 8, 1974.

41. *Newsweek*, December 30, 1974, p. 29.

42. See Murrey Marder, "Vladivostok Pact Modified in Anticipation of Hill Fight," *Washington Post*, December 29, 1974.

43. Michael Getler, "Stennis, Gen. Brown Endorse Proposed Nuclear Arms Pact," *Washington Post*, December 6, 1974.

44. John W. Finney, "Pentagon Chief Sees Pact Leading to Arms Buildup," *New York Times*, December 7, 1974.

45. Ibid. See also, Michael Getler, "Schlesinger Backs Pact, Sees Some Rise in Arms," *Washington Post*, December 7, 1974.

46. For a summary discussion reflecting both points of view, see "The Vladivostok Arms Control Agreement," *Bulletin of The American Academy of Arts and Sciences*, February 1975, pp. 4-15.

47. Murrey Marder, "Arms Group Gives Nod to A-Pact," *Washington Post*, December 12, 1974; Walter Slocombe and Andrew Hamilton, "Promising Reasonable Arms Accord," ibid., December 16, 1974; Gwertzman, in *New York Times*, December 13, 1974.

48. Herbert Scoville, Jr., "Moving Backward on Arms Curbs," *New York Times*, December 12, 1974; *Hearings on the Vladivostok Accord*, pp. 71-72.

49. George W. Rathgens, as quoted by Gwertzman, in the *New York Times*, December 13, 1974.

50. Robert Hotz, editorial: "A New Taste of SALT," *Aviation Week & Space Technology*, December 9, 1974.

51. Michael Parks, "Moscow Hails Arms Pact as 'Major Turning Point,' " *Baltimore Sun*, November 26, 1974. See also, Osnos, in the *Washington Post*, December 6, 1974.

52. "Results of the Meeting of General Secretary L.I. Brezhnev with U.S. President G. Ford," *Pravda*, November 29, 1974. Brezhnev's penchant for consensus leadership and for covering his flanks if something should go wrong could be seen in this action, which put the whole Soviet leadership on record in approval of his negotiations with President Ford.

53. Editorial, "A Big Contribution to the Cause of Peace," *Pravda*, December 1, 1974; Yu. Nikolaev, "Vladivostok Meeting: Important Results," *Mezhdunarodnaia Zhizn*, no. 1 (January 1975), p. 4.

54. Editorial, "An Efficient Peace Policy," *Pravda*, December 30, 1974.

55. V. Matveyev, "Developing What Has Been Achieved," *Izvestiia*, November 29, 1974.

56. Interview with N. Polyanov, deputy editor of *Izvestiia*, Moscow Radio, December 2, 1974.

57. *Pravda*, November 29, 1974; Editorial, "Great Success of the Vladivostok Meeting," *Izvestiia*, November 27, 1974.

58. Nikolaev, in *Mezhdunarodnaia Zhizn*, January 1975, pp. 7-8. See also, "Soviet Uneasy at Arms Pact Criticism," *New York Times*, November 29, 1974.

59. V. Osipov, "Common Sense and Ulterior Motives," *Izvestiia*, December 5, 1974.

60. See Osnos, in the *Washington Post*, December 6, 1974.

61. Colonel A. Leontiev, "Oil Smells of Blood," *Krasnaia Zvezda*, December 1, 1974. It may be noted that Leontiev's article was published a month before Dr. Kissinger's much-publicized comment in a *Business Week* interview on the

possibility of military intervention over oil, hence ruling out any connection between the two.

62. See "Soviet Military Hints at Dissent on Arms Issue," *New York Times*, December 2, 1974.

63. Interview in *Newsweek*, December 30, 1974, p. 29.

64. This assumes that estimates of existing Soviet forces, as distinct from future projections, are relatively unequivocal. By the time of Vladivostok, the overall Soviet force level apparently had increased slightly over the level of 2375 given in U.S. estimates as of mid-1974. By mid-1975, the Soviets had reached 2450, exceeding the agreed level, by U.S. estimates. See Table 5-1, Chapter 5, p. 97.

65. A prime example of this could be seen in the Soviets' hanging on to soft-site versions of early SS-7 and SS-8 ICBMs long after hardening of the ICBM force became the rule. See Richard Burt, "SALT II and Offensive Force Levels," *Orbis*, no. 2 (Summer 1974), p. 475.

66. The cumulative process envisaged here presumably would have been constrained with regard to ICBM and SLBM numbers by the May 1972 Interim Agreement ceiling of 2358. After expiration of the Interim Agreement in October 1977, however, and in the absence of the Vladivostok ceilings, the process would have been free to operate at its own pace.

67. That is, the levels to be attained in the five-year life of the Interim Agreement up to October 1977 had been set to accommodate Soviet proposals and thus presumably bore some relation to what Soviet planners considered the proper numerical margin to be maintained over the United States.

68. See Chapter 9, p. 175.

69. These deployment rates correspond to figures given by Secretary Schlesinger in closed testimony in September 1974, later declassified. See *Briefing on Counterforce Attacks, Hearing*, before the Subcommittee on Arms Control, International Law and Organization, Committee on Foreign Relations, Senate, September 11, 1974, sanitized and made public on January 10, 1975, pp. 9-10.

70. See Chapter 6, p. 119f.

71. See Chapter 11, pp. 226, 227.

72. "Press Conference of the Secretary of State," December 7, 1974, p. 2.

73. Among assumptions that could affect the figures somewhat, for example, are that the Soviets would choose to use 300 of their MIRV quota for SLBMs, and that each SLBM would have only three RVs. Should the Soviets either use their MIRV quota mostly for ICBMs, or develop a MIRVed SLBM with as many RVs (ten) as an American SLBM, they could have from about 1000 to 2000 more warheads than shown in Table 9-1.

74. Schlesinger had testified in March 1974 that the Soviets had the potential of translating their throwweight into "15,000 warheads or more," but he thought they might not choose to go beyond 7000 to 8000 RVs. See Chapter 6, p. 120f.

75. As indicated by Table 5-1, p. 97, the Soviets were estimated to have had about 8.5 million pounds of throwweight in mid-1978. While under the projected Vladivostok regime they would have increased this to 11 million

pounds by the early 1980s, the U.S. throwweight would remain almost unchanged.

76. Interview in *Newsweek*, December 30, 1974, p. 29.

77. See Chapter 9, p. 185.

78. Compare, for example, Kissinger's remarks on January 16, 1975, on the Bill Moyers TV show, to the effect that those critical of the high ceilings had "never negotiated with the Soviet Union."

79. In this connection, incidentally, it is a matter of some interest that throughout the SALT I and II negotiations the Soviet side apparently never specified China by name as justification for larger Soviet forces, although U.S. allies in NATO were singled out as grounds for compensating the Soviet Union with more SLBMs. Perhaps reluctance to bring the sensitive subject of Soviet relations with another communist power into the negotiations accounted for the Soviets' not openly adverting to a Chinese threat to buttress their claims for larger forces. Another factor might also have been Soviet realization that the China case was double-edged, permitting the U.S. side as well to assert that it should be compensated for a Chinese threat if the subject were laid on the table.

80. "Press Conference of the Secretary of State," December 7, 1974, p. 2.

81. Yields of fourth-generation Soviet MIRVed warheads ranged from 500 kilotons to 2 megatons per RV, compared with 40 to 300 kilotons for U.S. MIRVs. See John M. Collins, *American and Soviet Military Trends Since the Cuban Missile Crisis* (Washington, D.C.: Georgetown University Center for Strategic and International Studies, 1978), pp. 93, 101; Edward Luttwak, *The US-USSR Nuclear Weapons Balance*, The Washington Papers (Beverly Hills: Sage Publications, 1974), pp. 27, 62.

82. *Report of Secretary of Defense James R. Schlesinger to the Congress on the FY 1976 and Transition Budgets and FY 1976-1980 Defense Program*, February 5, 1975, p. II-8. (Cited hereafter as *Schlesinger FY 1976 Report*.) See also Michael Nacht, "The Vladivostok Accord and American Technological Options," *Survival*, May-June 1975, p. 110.

83. See previous comment on this point, Chapter 5, p. 98.

84. An articulate exponent of this viewpoint was Paul H. Nitze. See his "Vladivostok and Crisis Stability," *Wall Street Journal*, January 24, 1975; "The Vladivostok Accord and SALT II, *Review of Politics*, April 1975, p. 160; "Assuring Strategic Stability in an Era of Détente," *Foreign Affairs*, January 1976, pp. 220-21. For an answering argument that missile throwweight is a misleading indicator of relative strategic capability, and that the Soviet advantage deriving from greater throwweight has therefore been exaggerated, see Jan M. Lodal, "Assuring Strategic Stability: An Alternative View," *Foreign Affairs*, April 1976, pp. 464-67.

85. "Press Conference of the Secretary of State," December 7, 1974, p. 2. As an example of a step that would increase U.S. throwweight, if "cold launching" were adopted for Minuteman, the additional usable silo space would translate into a missile diameter providing at least a tripling of Minuteman throwweight. See Nacht, in *Survival*, May-June 1975, p. 112.

86. See Finney, in the *New York Times*, December 7, 1974.

87. *Schlesinger FY 1976 Report*, pp. II-8, 9.

88. For informative discussion of the subject, see: Lynn E. Davis and Warner R. Schilling, "All You Ever Wanted to Know about MIRV and ICBM Calculations but Were Not Cleared to Ask," *Journal of Conflict Resolution*, June 1973, pp. 207-42; D.C. Kephart, *Some Aids for Estimating Damage Probabilities or Attacks against Targets with P and Q Vulnerability Numbers*, The Rand Corporation, R-1168/1-PR, Santa Monica, November, 1973; *Strategic Survey 1969* (London: International Institute for Strategic Studies, 1970), pp. 30-33; Luttwak, *The US-USSR Nuclear Weapons Balance*, pp. 40, 62; Thomas A. Brown, "Number Mysticism, Rationality and the Strategic Balance," *Orbis*, Fall 1977, pp. 479-94. See also previous reference to the contrasting outcomes of various vulnerability calculations, Chapter 6, pp. 127-34, especially note 105.

89. Assuming a yield per warhead of 1.2 MT and a .25-mile CEP, and with an assumed kill probability of $P_k$ .55 against 1000-psi targets, 5200 Soviet warheads could theoretically destroy from 90 to 95 percent of a force of 1000 Minuteman. Such calculations using the standard counterforce formula do not, however, reflect other factors involved in arsenal exchanges, such as the "fratricide" effects of incoming warheads on each other and various operational and targeting considerations, all of which could alter the theoretical outcome. For an illuminating discussion of fratricide and other factors that tend to make the advantage of accuracy compared to yield less one-sided than the standard static formula of damage expectancy would indicate, see Nacht, in *Survival*, May-June 1975, pp. 109-10.

90. The range of development options for improvement of U.S. hard-target kill capabilities included both short-term and long-term programs. As pointed out by Schlesinger, the near-term options (up to the early 1980s) were limited to Minuteman III improvements. The longer-term options such as the large MX ICBM and terminally guided MARV payloads for the MX and Trident II SLBM required development time, placing their availability for deployment in the mid-1980 period and beyond. See *Schlesinger FY 1976 Report*, p. II-20.

91. For example, even though the yield of U.S. weapons might remain well below that of Soviet warheads, with accuracies on the order of a few hundred feet or less possible with terminally guided MARV or map-matching cruise missiles, lethality would be very high. See Kosta Tsipis, *Offensive Missiles*, Stockholm Paper no. 5, Stockholm International Peace Research Institute, August 1974, p. 27; *Strategic Survey 1973* (London: International Institute for Strategic Studies, 1974), p. 59.

92. For some representative statements along this line by senior Air Force officers, see Edgar Ulsamer, "Our ICBM Force—The Vulnerability Myth," *Air Force Magazine*, August 1974, pp. 65-69.

93. *Schlesinger FY 1976 Report*, p. I-14.

94. Ibid., p. II-9. See also Chapter 6, p. 120f., Chapter 7, pp. 146, 149f.

95. See Chapter 7, pp. 127f., 150.

96. See Chapter 7, pp. 148-49.

97. *Schlesinger FY 1976 Report*, p. I-16; *Strategic Survey 1974* (London: International Institute for Strategic Studies, 1975), p. 64.

98. Besides accuracy, other advantages of fixed systems include good two-way communications, responsiveness to central control, and low operating costs. See *Schlesinger FY 1976 Report*, p. II-27.

99. "Loss of Bases May Slow SALT," *Washington Star*, August 4, 1975.

100. See Chapter 5, pp. 103-06.

101. See Raymond Garthoff, "SALT and the Soviet Military," *Problems of Communism*, January-February 1975, p. 35.

## NOTES TO CHAPTER 10
## STALEMATE IN THE POST-VLADIVOSTOK
## NEGOTIATIONS

1. See Bernard Gwertzman, "Brezhnev, Ford Agree to Delay Talks till Fall," *New York Times*, April 27, 1975; Christopher S. Wren, "Brezhnev Hints Further Delay in U.S. Visit for Summit Talks," ibid., June 6, 1975; Peter Osnos, "Soviets: No Summit Soon," *Washington Post*, November 12, 1975.

2. See Murrey Marder, "U.S., Soviets to Focus on Arms Limits," *Washington Post*, May 19, 1975. Kissinger's first meeting with Gromyko after Vladivostok had been in Geneva in mid-February 1975, at which time issues relating to the Middle East and Cyprus received more attention than SALT. See "Kissinger Meets Gromyko to Talk about Relations," *New York Times*, February 17, 1975.

3. The Soviet side submitted its draft version of a SALT II treaty based on the Vladivostok guidelines shortly after negotiations resumed in January 1975, followed by the United States a few weeks later.

4. In SALT I, the United States had proposed that the volumetric threshold for a heavy missile be 70 cubic meters. The new Soviet SS-19 was around 100 cubic meters. For previous discussion of the heavy-missile issue, see Chapter 1, pp. 12-13.

5. Although the new cruise missile technology promised to provide a relatively cheap delivery system (estimated less than $1 million per copy) with long-range, high accuracy, and good low-altitude penetration characteristics, the cruise missile was by no means a wonder weapon and could eventually become vulnerable to improved low-altitude defenses. Moreover, the Air Force ALCM-B and the Navy Tomahawk were only under development, and would not become available for deployment before the early 1980s. For previous reference to the new cruise missile technology and citations of the literature, see Chapter 7, p. 149 and note 94.

6. See editorial, "The SALT Deadlock," *Wall Street Journal*, May 19, 1975.

7. See Murrey Marder, "Ford-Brezhnev Arms Talks Gain, but Obstacles Remain," *Washington Post*, August 3, 1975.

8. Henry S. Bradsher, "Missile Pact Foundering on Numbers," *Washington Star*, May 2, 1975. See also Flora Lewis, "U.S.-Soviet Talks on Nuclear Arms Reported in Peril," *New York Times*, July 11, 1975.

9. See editorial, "SALT II Progress," *New York Times*, May 23, 1975.

10. Ibid. See also Leslie H. Gelb, "Atomic Arms Talk Opened by Gromyko and Kissinger," *New York Times*, May 30, 1975; Henry S. Bradsher, "U.S. Easing Stand on Soviet Missiles to Promote Pact," *Washington Star*, May 23, 1975; Clarence A. Robinson, Jr., "U.S. Weighs SALT Proposals," *Aviation Week & Space Technology*, June 23, 1975, pp. 12-14.

11. See statement by Senator James L. Buckley, "The Score on SALT," in *Aviation Week & Space Technology*, September 8, 1975, p. 11.

12. According to remarks by Paul Warnke, Soviet agreement to "each of the basic elements of the American position on verification" of MIRVed missiles and their launchers was completed in the period from May 1977 to July 1978. See his speech of July 25, 1978, "SALT: Its Contribution to U.S. Security and World Peace," in *Current Policy*, no. 27, Department of State, August 1978, p. 3.

13. See Chapter 9, p. 177f. and note 30.

14. See Murrey Marder, "Arms Problems Still Exist, Gromyko Says," *Washington Post*, September 19, 1978.

15. See Chapter 6, pp. 117, 126.

16. See Clarence A. Robinson, Jr., "Backfire Draws Focus in SALT," *Aviation Week & Space Technology*, August 25, 1975, pp. 14-15; Buckley statement, ibid., September 8, 1975, p. 11; Colin S. Gray, "Major Issues of SALT II," *Air Force Magazine*, August 1975, p. 72. The Soviet rationale for excluding Backfire apparently had shifted from an earlier argument in SALT II that the U.S. B-1 should be banned but the Backfire should be exempted because it was already in production and hence not a new program like the B-1.

17. Some analysts have contended that Backfire would not have arisen as a post-Vladivostok issue had not the United States been looking for a makeweight to balance against its own desire to exclude cruise missiles from the ceiling. While there is perhaps something to be said for this view, it would appear to go much too far in attributing the post-Vladivostok stalemate almost exclusively to unreasonable American demands. See Alexander R. Vershbow, "The Cruise Missile: The End of Arms Control?" *Foreign Affairs*, October 1976, p. 143.

18. See John W. Finney, "The Soviet Backfire Bomber and the U.S. Cruise Missile," *New York Times*, December 3, 1975. According to some accounts, Kissinger's efforts in 1975 to resolve the Backfire and cruise missile issues had been carried out mainly through the back channel, rather than through the Geneva delegation. See Robinson, in *Aviation Week & Space Technology*, August 25, 1975, p. 14.

19. See Marilyn Berger, "Kissinger Says Soviets Must End SALT Deadlock," *Washington Post*, November 11, 1975. See also Richard Burt, "The Cruise Missile and Arms Control," *Survival*, January-February 1976, p. 13.

20. Berger, in the *Washington Post*, November 11, 1975.

21. See Chapter 9, p. 177f.

22. See Burt, in *Survival*, January-February 1976, p. 13.

23. The range threshold of 372 miles is in statute miles. This amounts to about 324 nautical miles. The principal Soviet cruise missile launched from some surface ships and Echo-class nuclear-propelled submarines was the SS-N-3 (Shaddock), with a range of about 225 nautical miles (260 statute miles). The AS-4 and AS-6 air-launched cruise missiles had ranges of about 150 nautical miles (170 statute). These were larger and much less sophisticated vehicles than the small precision-guided cruise missiles under development by the United States. For previous reference to the Soviet Navy's cruise missile capability, see Chapter 5, p. 104. According to some reports in early 1976, the Soviets were

then developing a longer-range version of their AS-4 ALCM for launching from the Backfire. It would have a range of about 425 nautical miles. A longer-range version of the SS-N-3 was also reported under development. See Clarence A. Robinson, Jr., "Soviets Make New SALT Bid," *Aviation Week & Space Technology*, February 2, 1976, p. 12.

24. Among the reported grounds on which the United States opposed the Soviet cruise missile proposals were the difficulty of verifying a sweeping deployment ban; the encroachment of such a ban on potential tactical use of cruise missiles—where their most interesting potential was believed by many defense planners to lie; and the inroads upon the established apportionment of strategic vehicles among ICBM, SLBM, and bomber forces that inclusion of strategic cruise missiles would entail. See Burt, in *Survival*, January-February 1976, p. 13. See also Robert Kennedy, "The Cruise Missile and the Strategic Balance," *Parameters*, March 1978, pp. 53-57.

25. For statements of the official U.S. view at the time, see: *The Meaning of Detente*, General Foreign Policy Series 280, Department of State, June 1974, and "An Assessment of Detente," in *Secretary Kissinger's Statement on U.S.-Soviet Relations*, Special Report no. 6, Department of State, September 19, 1974, pp. 12-15. For useful discussion of critical attitudes toward detente, see Richard Rosecrance, "Detente or Entente?" *Foreign Affairs*, April 1975, especially pp. 465-69; "The Superpowers and Detente," in *Strategic Survey 1974*, pp. 57-60.

26. For a perceptive analysis of Soviet detente policy around the beginning of 1975, see Vladimir Petrov, *U.S.-Soviet Detente: Past and Future*, American Enterprise Institute for Public Policy Research, Washington, D.C., April 1975. See also Robert Conquest et al., "Detente: An Evaluation," *International Review*, Spring 1974, and Rosecrance, in *Foreign Affairs*, April 1975, pp. 469-77.

27. See, for example, V. Razmerov, "Socialist International Relations," *Mirovaia Ekonomika i Mezhdunarodnye Otnosheniia*, no. 12 (December 1974), p. 13. See also, "The Dialectics of International Detente," *Problemy Mira i Sotsializma*, no. 9 (September 1974), pp. 83-86.

28. See Chapter 5, p. 110.

29. It is to be noted, of course, that the Soviet concept of "correlation of forces" takes in political, social, and economic factors, as well as military power. For a Soviet description of this concept, see G. Shakhnazarov, "On the Problem of the Correlation of Forces in the World," *Kommunist*, no. 3 (February 1974), pp. 77-89. For a more concise explanation of the concept, see Foy D. Kohler and Mose L. Harvey, eds., *The Soviet Union: Yesterday, Today, Tomorrow* (Coral Gables: Center for Advanced International Studies, University of Miami, 1975), p. 10.

30. James Reston, "A Time for Reflection," *New York Times*, May 2, 1975.

31. See text of President Ford's speech before a joint session of Congress, Department of State News Release, April 10, 1975, p. 6.

32. Ibid. See also: James M. Naughton, "Standing by Commitments, Ford Assures U.S. Allies," *New York Times*, May 7, 1975; "Schlesinger Affirms U.S. Vow to Honor Defense Obligations," ibid., April 16, 1975; Robert Keatley,

"Kissinger Raps China and Soviet Union for Aid to Hanoi, U.S. Allies for 'Silence,' " *Wall Street Journal*, April 18, 1975.

33. See Marilyn Berger, "Kissinger Sees Danger to Soviet Detente," *Washington Post*, May 13, 1975.

34. *New York Times*, April 16, 1975.

35. See, for example, George C. Wilson, "Fallout from Vietnam: Hill Leaders See Challenge to Military Programs," *Washington Post*, April 21, 1975; Robert Kleiman, "U.S. Defenses Abroad," *New York Times*, April 30, 1975; "Pentagon Hit for Strategy on A-War," ibid., May 6, 1975.

36. In this connection, the military contribution to the communist victory in South Vietnam has been spelled out at length by the North Vietnamese themselves. See the account of an analysis on this subject in July 1975 by General Vo Nguyen Giap, North Vietnam's defense minister, and his deputy, General Van Tien Dung: "Giap Analyzes Vietnam Victory," *New York Times*, July 11, 1975.

37. For a concise expression of this concern, see the article by Admiral Elmo R. Zumwalt, Jr., former chief of Naval Operations, "Uncle Sam: No More Mr. Nice Guy," *New York Times*, April 11, 1975.

38. This assessment reportedly was given to the French Socialist leader, François Mitterrand, by N.N. Inozemtsev in late April 1975. See Flora Lewis, "Moscow Courts Paris Socialist," *New York Times*, May 8, 1975.

39. See, for example, Peter Osnos, "Soviets Circumspect: No Public Gloating over U.S. Reverses," *Washington Post*, April 6, 1975; Christopher S. Wren, "Soviet Adheres to Detente Despite Shifts in World," *New York Times*, April 7, 1975; "Brezhnev Says End of Conflict in Indochina Will Help Detente," ibid., May 9, 1975.

40. Christopher S. Wren, "Moscow Sees the Chance to Fill a Diplomatic Void," *New York Times*, May 4, 1975.

41. "Hanoi Top Power in Corner of Asia," *New York Times*, May 11, 1975.

42. See, for example, "Irate Khmer Rouge Beat Soviet Newsman," *Washington Post*, May 9, 1975; "Cambodians Praise China: No Mention of Soviet Union," ibid., May 12, 1975. For signs of Chinese opposition to what Peking's propagandists have described as a Soviet attempt to "swallow Southeast Asia," see also Fox Butterfield, "China Increases Soviet Criticism," *New York Times*, July 11, 1975.

43. See Flora Lewis, in the *New York Times*, May 8, 1975.

44. See *Pravda*, April 17, 1975, and editorial, ibid., April 18, 1975. In addition to the April plenum's approval, the detente line was conspicuously endorsed the following month in a combined statement on May 9 by the Politburo, the Council of Ministers, and the Supreme Soviet, as well as in a major VE-Day commemorative speech by Brezhnev. See *Pravda*, May 8, 9, 1975.

45. See "A Plunge into Oblivion," *Time*, April 28, 1975, p. 36.

46. Ibid. See also Victor Zorza, "Kremlin Differences on Detente," *Washington Post*, April 17, 1975, and "The Soviet Succession Struggle," ibid., April 24, 1975.

47. Any such Soviet belief in the need to soothe the United States might well have been reinforced by the display of American resolution given dramatic

emphasis in President Ford's prompt response to Cambodian seizure of the freighter *Mayaguez* in mid-May.

48. The most specific sets of particulars were to be found in three articles that appeared between June and August 1975, all highly critical of Kissinger's negotiating style. One was by Tad Szulc, "Soviet Violations of the SALT Deal: Have We Been Had?" *The New Republic*, June 7, 1975, pp. 11-15. Another was by Elmo R. Zumwalt, Jr., and Worth Bagley, "Zumwalt-Bagley on the Kissinger Legacy: Soviets Cheat and We Turn Our Backs," *Washington Star*, August 10, 1975. The third was by Melvin R. Laird, "Is This Detente?" *The Reader's Digest*, July 1975, pp. 54-55.

49. See Szulc, in *The New Republic*, June 7, 1975, p. 13; Zumwalt and Bagley, in the *Washington Star*, August 10, 1975.

50. Szulc, in *The New Republic*, June 7, 1975, pp. 13-15. Editorial, "SALT II: The Verification Problem," *Baltimore Sun*, June 22, 1975. See also, Interim Agreement, Article V, in *Arms Control and Disarmament Agreements: Texts and History of Negotiations*, U.S. Arms Control and Disarmament Agency, Washington, D.C., February 1974, p. 140.

51. Szulc, in *The New Republic*, June 7, 1975, pp. 14, 15.

52. See, for example, Michael Getler, "Soviets Said to Ease U.S. Suspicions of Arms Violations," *Washington Post*, May 20, 1975.

53. Interview with Henry Kissinger, "We Are Moving into a New World," *U.S. News & World Report*, June 23, 1975, p. 23.

54. Transcript of President's News Conference on Foreign and Domestic Matters, *New York Times*, June 26, 1975.

55. *New York Times*, June 26, 1975. See also Zumwalt and Bagley, in the *Washington Star*, August 10, 1975.

56. *New York Times*, July 2, 1975.

57. See Chapter 2, p. 35.

58. See *SALT ONE: Compliance*, Selected Documents no. 7, Department of State, February 1978, pp. 3-10. For a summary comparison of the principal alleged Soviet violations, and the response given in the February 1978 report, see Appendix D.

59. See Chapter 10, p. 201f.

60. Murrey Marder, "Kissinger Plans New Arms Talks," *Washington Post*, December 5, 1975.

61. "Report Says U.S., Soviets Agree on Key SALT Clause," *Washington Post*, January 13, 1976. Up to this time, official Washington sources had not suggested that an agreement was in sight.

62. Sources include Robert L. Pfaltzgraff, Jr., and Jacquelyn Davis, *SALT II: Promise or Precipice?* (Coral Gables: Center for Advanced International Studies, University of Miami, 1976), pp. 18-25, and by the same authors, *The Cruise Missile: Bargaining Chip or Defense Bargain?* (Cambridge: Institute for Foreign Policy Analysis, Inc., 1977), pp. 45-53; Clarence A. Robinson, Jr., in *Aviation Week & Space Technology*, February 2, 1976, pp. 12-13; Murrey Marder, in the *Washington Post*, February 8, 1976; Section on "Arms Control Negotiations," in *Analysis of Arms Control Impact Statements Submitted in Connection with the Fiscal Year 1978 Budget Request*, Senate Committee on

Foreign Relations, April 1977, pp. 294-304 (cited hereafter as *FY 1978 Arms Control Impact Statements*).

63. Some accounts indicate that both ALCMs and SRAMs were to be included in the twelve to twenty missiles per bomber. The range of SRAMs (short-range attack missiles, mainly for air defense suppression), however, was considerably less than 372 miles.

64. One pair of critics (see Pfaltzgraff and Davis, *SALT II, Promise or Precipice?*, p. 19) averred that this exchange would have favored the Soviets because it would have allowed them 250 non-SALT-accountable Backfires in which they would carry ten ALCMs each, whereas the United States would have emerged with only 250 SLCMs in return, and its own ALCM-carrying bombers would be SALT-accountable. This interpretation, it may be noted, did not jibe with a later SALT impact statement to Congress, in which it was said: ". . . if the Soviet Union deployed ALCMs with over 600-km range on the new Backfire bomber, those Backfires so equipped would be counted in the SALT aggregate limits and in the sublimit of MIRVed missile launchers." See *Fiscal Year 1979 Arms Control Impact Statements*, Statements Submitted to the Congress by the President Pursuant to Section 36 of the Arms Control and Disarmament Act (Washington, D.C.: Government Printing Office, June 1978), p. 67.

65. See Robinson, in *Aviation Week & Space Technology*, February 1976, p. 12. See also Chapter 9, pp. 175, 179f., 187f. for previous discussion of the reduction question at Vladivostok.

66. See Pfaltzgraff and Davis, *SALT II: Promise or Precipice?*, p. 23.

67. According to some accounts, the Soviets dropped any range limitations on ALCMs in their January proposal. According to other accounts, the Soviets at the Ford-Brezhnev meeting in Helsinki in August 1975 had suggested that all cruise missiles with ranges up to 3500 miles be excluded from counting in SALT, but had subsequently called this suggestion a "mistake" and retracted it. Whatever the case, the Soviets at some point returned to a range-limitation position, for the ALCM range issue was a contentious one during the 1977-78 negotiations. See Vershbow, in *Foreign Affairs*, October 1976, p. 143; *FY 1978 Arms Control Impact Statements*, pp. 281, 296; William Beecher, "US Weighs New SALT Initiative," *Boston Globe*, July 7, 1976.

68. See Pfaltzgraff and Davis, *The Cruise Missile: Bargaining Chip or Defense Bargain?*, p. 48.

69. In addition to various specific points noted in our discussion, one line of criticism was that the January proposals, at least on the U.S. side, lacked any clear concept of the relationship between arms control agreements and U.S. national security interests. See Pfaltzgraff and Davis, *SALT II: Promise or Precipice?*, p. 18.

70. See Bernard Gwertzman, "Kissinger Expects Arms Accord Soon," *New York Times*, October 13, 1975; Marilyn Berger, "Kissinger Says Soviet Must End SALT Deadlock," *Washington Post*, November 11, 1975.

71. See *FY 1978 Arms Control Impact Statements*, pp. 298, 324-25.

72. Ibid., pp. 282-89.

73. For a range of views asserting that the United States should unilaterally eschew further development of cruise missiles because of their "potentially

devastating impact" on strategic stability and arms control," and because existing U.S. forces were already adequate for deterrence without adding such weapons, see: Vershbow, in *Foreign Affairs*, October 1976, pp. 133-46; Thomas A. Halsted, "Should We Deploy Cruise Missiles?" *Baltimore Sun*, January 17, 1976; Townsend Hoopes, "There Is No Objective Need for the Cruise Missile," *New York Times*, December 30, 1975.

74. Engineer-Captain N. Shaskolskii, "One More Guided Missile," *Krasnaia Zvezda*, September 10, 1975.

75. Some analysts believed the Soviets were bound to take up a "cruise missile race," if for prestige reasons only. Subsequently, the Soviets did warn that they too could build cruise missiles if agreement on curbs were not reached. See *FY 1978 Arms Control Impact Statements*, pp. 284-85. For the Soviet view, see Marshal D.F. Ustinov, "Guardian of Peaceful Labor, Bulwark of Universal Peace," *Kommunist*, February 1977, p. 18.

76. See *FY 1978 Arms Control Impact Statements*, pp. 296-97.

77. See Pfaltzgraff and Davis, *The Cruise Missile: Bargaining Chip or Defense Bargain?*, p. 49.

78. See Halsted, in the *Baltimore Sun*, January 17, 1976.

79. See Kennedy, in *Parameters*, March 1978, p. 55.

80. Burt, in *Survival*, January-February 1976, p. 13.

81. See Bernard Gwertzman, "U.S. and Soviet Union Resume Arms Talks," *New York Times*, September 30, 1976.

82. Although election year pressures not to make concessions to the Russians had to be reckoned with, Ford was also under some pressure from other quarters to move closer to the Soviet position for the sake of reaching an agreement. An example was Senate Resolution 399 introduced by Senator Edward Kennedy in early 1976, which urged the president to seek range limitations on cruise missiles essentially along lines of the Soviet proposal for land- and sea-launched cruise missiles, and pending an agreement, also urged the president to offer the USSR an immediate moratorium on flight testing of all strategic-range cruise missiles. *Congressional Record*, February 25, 1976, pp. S2288-2291.

83. Gwertzman, in the *New York Times*, September 30, 1976.

84. Ibid. On the matter of solutions for the Backfire and cruise missile issues, Dr. Fred C. Iklé, then the director of ACDA, testified before the Senate Foreign Relations Committee on January 14, 1977, that "we offered five different solutions within as many months. Yet the Soviet Union made no effort to come up with counterproposals of its own which could help to resolve those issues." See editorial, "Mr. Carter and SALT," *Chicago Tribune*, January 27, 1977.

85. Beecher, in the *Boston Globe*, July 7, 1976.

86. "Speech of Comrade L.I. Brezhnev," *Pravda*, June 30, 1976. See also Michael Getler, "Brezhnev: U.S. Election Stalls Arms Agreement," *Washington Post*, June 30, 1976.

87. Author's conversations with members of the Ford administration. It might be noted, as reported by William Beecher in the *Boston Globe*, July 7, 1976, that senior U.S. officials had been rankled by Brezhnev's public move to

blame the United States for the SALT stalemate, particularly after Brezhnev's having allegedly said at Helsinki that he would do what he could to help Ford's election prospects.

88. John W. Finney, "U.S.-Soviet Talks on Strategic Arms Resume in Geneva, but Progress During Election Campaign Is Doubted," *New York Times*, September 22, 1976.

89. "U.S.-Soviet Arms Talks to End till Carter Inaugural," *New York Times*, November 20, 1976.

## NOTES TO CHAPTER 11
## RENEWED SEARCH FOR A SALT II ACCORD

1. Charles Mohr, "Carter Would Defer Issue of Russian Bomber and U.S. Cruise Missile," *New York Times*, February 9, 1977. At this news conference, Carter also brought up the "gray area" case of the Soviet SS-20 land-mobile missile, suggesting that if the Soviets would cease deploying it, the United States would be prepared to drop its mobile missile development, presumably meaning the MX ICBM. For previous discussion of these missile programs, see Chapters 6, pp. 119-21, and 7, pp. 146-47, 150f.

2. "Text of Inaugural Address," *Washington Star*, January 20, 1977. See also "Carter and Brezhnev: The Game Begins," *Time*, February 7, 1977, pp. 40-42.

3. See earlier discussion of changes in the policy mechanism for SALT under the Carter administration, Chapter 2, pp. 28, 36-39, 42-44.

4. See Chapter 10, p. 216.

5. *The SALT Process*, remarks, January 19, 1978, by Paul C. Warnke, director of ACDA, before the National Foreign Policy Conference for Editors and Broadcasters, Department of State News Release, p. 2 (hereafter cited as Warnke, *The SALT Process*).

6. "Speech of Comrade L.I. Brezhnev," *Izvestiia*, January 19, 1977. In this speech, Brezhnev also dismissed what he termed "unfounded assertions" that the Soviet Union was "striving for military superiority with the aim of delivering a 'first-strike.' " At the same time, he told his audience: "Of course, comrades, we are perfecting our defenses. It cannot be otherwise."

7. Bernard Gwertzman, "Carter Looks to New Arms Talks with Russians within Three Months," *New York Times*, January 28, 1977.

8. Debate in the United States over implications of the ongoing Soviet military buildup and the extended stalemates in both SALT and MBFR negotiations had been fueled at about the turn of administrations by leaked results of what was known as the Team A and B intelligence exercise, in which Soviet affairs specialists from outside the governmental intelligence community prepared a "Team B report," taking a more sombre view of the implications than had previous national intelligence estimates (NIEs). For discussion of this and other background on the debate, see: Murrey Marder, "Carter to Inherit Intense Dispute on Soviet Intentions," *Washington Post*, January 2, 1977; William Greider, "U.S.-Russian Arms Debate at Crossroads," ibid., February 20, 1977; Daniel Southerland, "Great Debate on U.S.-Soviet Arms Rages," *Christian*

*Science Monitor*, February 16, 1977; Daniel O. Graham, "Intelligence: Realities and Myth," *Wall Street Journal*, March 11, 1977; *The National Intelligence Estimates A-B Team Episode Concerning Soviet Strategic Capability and Objectives*, Report, Senate, Select Committee on Intelligence, February 16, 1978. For earlier references in the present study to some aspects of the debate, see Chapters 6, pp. 115-16, 132, 133; and 7, 148-49.

9. For previous comment on the controversy that arose during extended confirmation hearings on Warnke's appointment, see Chapter 2, p. 44.

10. Hedrick Smith, "U.S. Policy on Soviet: A Two-Edged Attitude," *New York Times*, January 29, 1977. See also Robert R. Bowie, "Carter and the Kremlin," *Christian Science Monitor*, February 2, 1977.

11. See, for example, Vladimir Bolshakov, "International Week: Review," *Pravda*, March 13, 1977; David K. Shipler, "Pravda Cautions U.S. on Rights Criticism," *New York Times*, March 13, 1977; David K. Willis, "Soviets Criticize Carter by Name on Many Issues," *Christian Science Monitor*, March 14, 1977; Interview with Georgi Arbatov: "On 'Human Rights' A Soviet Official Tells U.S.—Don't Push the Issue Too Far," *U.S. News & World Report*, March 14, 1977, p. 24; Peter Osnos, "Angry Mood in the Kremlin: Soviet Irritation with Carter Complicates Vance Visit," *Washington Post*, March 25, 1977.

12. "Speech of Comrade L.I. Brezhnev," *Pravda*, March 22, 1977.

13. One Soviet commentator, for example, borrowing points from several Brezhnev speeches, charged that it was no secret that the U.S. military-industrial complex opposed realization of the Vladivostok accord, that "final work" on the accord had been "dragged out" an "unpardonably long time" through "no fault of ours," and "that already more than two months of the new administration in Washington" had passed with "no constructive steps yet in sight." Sergei Vishnevskii, "International Week: Review," *Pravda*, March 27, 1977.

14. See Murrey Marder and Peter Osnos, "Soviets Criticize U.S. on SALT, Human Rights," *Washington Post*, March 28, 1977.

15. Bernard Gwertzman, "Carter Encouraged by Soviet on Arms: Adamant on Rights," *New York Times*, March 23, 1977.

16. Bernard Gwertzman, "Carter Says Vance, in Soviet, Will Seek Deep Weapons Cuts," *New York Times*, March 25, 1977.

17. Secretary Vance's party of some fourteen officials from the Departments of State and Defense and ACDA included Paul Warnke, who had finally been sworn in less than two weeks earlier as director of ACDA and chief SALT negotiator. For a list of others in the party, see ibid.

18. Murrey Marder, "Vance Arrives in Moscow to Push for Cuts in Arms," *Washington Post*, March 27, 1977. See also Bernard Gwertzman, "Vance Is In Moscow To Affirm Detente and Seek Arms Cuts," *New York Times*, March 27, 1977.

19. The details of the proposals are drawn largely from the analysis of Paul H. Nitze, "An Analysis of the Two US/Moscow SALT Proposals of March 1977," in *The Carter Disarmament Proposals: Some Basic Questions and Cautions* (Coral Gables: Center for Advanced International Studies, University of Miami, 1977), pp. 10-11 (hereafter cited as *Basic Questions on March 1977 SALT Proposals*). See also "Excerpts From Secretary Vance's Press Conference

on Arms Talks in Moscow," *New York Times*, March 31, 1977; Richard Burt, "The Scope and Limits of SALT," *Foreign Affairs*, July 1978, p. 755.

20. There was considerable confusion about whether this provision—which had been discussed in prior negotiations—was included in this form in the March 1977 comprehensive package. See Nitze, in *Basic Questions on March 1977 SALT Proposals*, p. 11, and Bernard Gwertzman, "Technical Issue in Arms Proposal Stirs Controversy in Washington," *New York Times*, May 3, 1977.

21. It was not clear whether the U.S. side had specified the various kinds of "collateral constraints"—such as restrictions on Arctic basing, training, and colocation with tankers—that would provide "assurances" against strategic use of Backfire. See Henry S. Bradsher, "What U.S. Sought on SALT," *Washington Star*, April 10, 1977.

22. As Paul Warnke expressed it some months later, the "comprehensive" approach had been an attempt "to shortcut the arms control negotiating process and move in one single giant step toward very significant reductions in numbers and toward a whole series of qualitative restraints. It went too far for the Soviet Union." Warnke, *The SALT Process*, p. 3. The most detailed explanation of the rationale behind the March 1977 package was given by Zbigniew Brzezinski at a press conference in early April, in which he stressed that greater "stability" was the primary strategic and political aim of the proposal. Among other things, he said it had been proposed to the Russians that they "forego those elements in their strategic posture which threaten us the most," particularly MIRVed, land-based ICBMs, in return for constraint upon U.S. systems most threatening to the Soviets, such as giving up a highly accurate MX, foregoing strategic cruise missiles, and reducing total MIRVed missiles. Brzezinski indicated that the negative Soviet reaction to the comprehensive package came as no surprise, and comparing it with Kosygin's initial negative reaction to the Glassboro ABM proposal in 1967, suggested that the Soviets might eventually come around to seeing the merit in the U.S. March 1977 package. A full account of the Brzezinski interview may be found in "Brzezinski Details Administration's Position," *Aviation Week & Space Technology*, April 18, 1977, pp. 34-39.

23. See Richard Burt, "Behind the SALT Impasse," *Washington Post*, April 10, 1977. For discussion of verification problems related to the comprehensive proposal, see John F. Lehman, "The Carter Comprehensive SALT Proposal: Verification and Gray Area Systems," in *Basic Questions on March 1977 SALT Proposals*, pp. 17-24. For an informed argument about the reduction proposals of the March 1977 package see Amoretta Hoeber, Patrick Parker, and William Van Cleave, "Reality and SALT," *Journal of International Relations*, Summer 1977, pp. 10-11. The authors' assertion is that though the proposals were a step in the right direction in attempting to reduce Soviet throwweight to more stable levels, other aspects of the package disallowed key survivability measures, such as ICBM mobility, and therefore the net effect might not be to enhance stability.

24. See Nitze, in *Basic Questions on March 1977 SALT Proposals*, pp. 11-12. According to Nitze's calculations, the 150 SS-18s and 400 SS-19s and -17s permitted the Soviets would leave them an ICBM throwweight of about 5.2 million lbs, compared with about 1.25 million lbs for the U.S. force of 550 Minuteman.

25. Among other things, the Soviets would have had to destroy half of their existing heavy missiles, and to cut back most of their fourth-generation deployment programs to stay within the 550 MIRVed ICBM limit, not to mention having to scrap their fifth-generation missile development programs.

26. Brezhnev, whose physical appearance had worsened since he was last seen by American visitors, did not show up for the opening day's afternoon session at which Vance presented the comprehensive U.S. proposal, although he had been present at the morning session when he delivered a stern lecture on the principle of "non-interference in internal affairs." See Murrey Marder and Peter Osnos, "Vance and Soviets Are Far Apart on Arms, Rights," *Washington Post*, March 29, 1977; Hal Piper, "Brezhnev Complaint Starts Talks," *Baltimore Sun*, March 29, 1977.

27. See Chapter 10, pp. 213-14.

28. See Murrey Marder and Peter Osnos, "U.S., Soviets at Impasse on Arms Negotiations," *Washington Post*, March 31, 1977; Bernard Gwertzman, "Arms Talks Break Off As Soviet Repeats Two Key Proposals by U.S.; Carter Says He Isn't Discouraged," *New York Times*, March 31, 1977.

29. A.A. Gromyko, *Statement At a Press Conference on the Results of the Talks Held by Leonid Brezhnev and Andrei Gromyko with US Secretary of State Cyrus Vance, March 31, 1977*, Pamphlet, Novosti Press Agency Publishing House, Moscow, 1977, p. 14 (cited hereafter as *Gromyko March 31, 1977 Statement*). See also David K. Shipler, "Gromyko Charges U.S. Seeks Own Gain in Arms Proposals," *New York Times*, April 1, 1977.

30. *Gromyko March 31, 1977 Statement*, p. 11.

31. Ibid., p. 24. Among other points in Gromyko's gravamen were: the USA had adopted a policy of revising the Vladivostok accords (p. 6); "no green light was given to cruise missiles" at Vladivostok (p. 5); Brezhnev had "personally" explained to both Ford and Carter that Backfire is a "medium-range and not a strategic bomber" (p. 3); the Soviet Union deserves the credit for a long list of disarmament initiatives over the past years, and not "the country which today all but declares itself to be a champion of general and complete disarmament" (p. 19).

32. Failure to communicate the specifics of the comprehensive proposal prior to its unveiling was said to have angered the Russians, though it was not clear how much they had been told before Vance's arrival in Moscow. According to some accounts, the Soviets got a week's private notice on the basic shape of the new package, but key numbers—which had been worked out in Washington in exceptional secrecy and closely held—were not disclosed to the Russians until Vance himself presented them in Moscow. See Robert G. Kaiser and Murrey Marder, "In Pursuit of a SALT II Agreement: The Secretive Birth of Carter's New Plan for Arms Reductions," *Washington Post*, April 11, 1977. See also Chapter 4, p. 83f. According to Dr. Brzezinski, detailed figures had not been sent in advance in order to get "the top Soviet leaders to focus" on the proposal, rather than having them respond on the basis of a "categorical critique" prepared ahead of time in the Soviet Defense Ministry. See interview, in *Aviation Week & Space Technology*, April 18, 1977, p. 38.

33. See note 31, above.

34. "Excerpts from Remarks by President," *New York Times*, March 31, 1977. See also "Carter Warns He May Add Arms If Moscow Balks in Further Talks," ibid.; Edward Walsh, "Carter Says He Will 'Hang Tough,' " *Washington Post*, March 31, 1977.

35. "Text of US-Soviet Communiqué, *New York Times*, April 1, 1977.

36. Bernard Gwertzman, "Dobrynin Consults with Vance to Seek a New Arms Parley," *New York Times*, April 8, 1977, and "Carter and Dobrynin Meet on Arms Issue," ibid., April 13, 1977.

37. See Bernard Gwertzman, "After Two-Year Stalemate, U.S. and Soviet Now Have Agreed on New Blueprint for Arms Negotiations," *New York Times*, May 24, 1977.

38. See *The Strategic Arms Limitation Talks*, Special Report no. 46, The Department of State, July 1978, p. 7.

39. See, for example, editorial, "A Problem That Can and Must Be Resolved," *Pravda*, April 14, 1977. See also, "Moscow Is Adamant on Arms Negotiation," *New York Times*, April 15, 1977.

40. Bernard Gwertzman, "U.S. and Soviet Agree on a Formula to End Arms Pact Impasse," *New York Times*, May 21, 1977. It might be noted that Soviet commentary subsequently described the revised SALT approach worked out in the May and September 1977 meetings as having turned back "toward the essential direction jointly determined in Vladivostok." See editorial, "The Task of Limiting Strategic Arms: Prospects and Problems," *Pravda*, February 11, 1978.

41. Gwertzman, in the *New York Times*, May 24, 1977. Gromyko was quoted when leaving Geneva airport that progress had not necessarily been made toward "solution of the main problems," and that the United States had "not given up its attempts to achieve unilateral advantages." See "Major Snags Remain As Parley in Geneva on Arms Accords Ends," ibid., May 22, 1977.

42. See "Prospects Diminish for New Arms Pact," *New York Times*, June 16, 1977; Graham Hovey, "U.S. and Soviet Defer Arms Talks Two Weeks," ibid., September 1, 1977; Bernard Gwertzman, "SALT Just Isn't Going Anywhere," ibid., September 4, 1977.

43. Burt, in *Foreign Affairs*, July 1978, p. 756.

44. Warnke, *The SALT Process*, p. 3.

45. See, for example: Eugene Kozicharow, "Options Studied for Expiration of SALT," *Aviation Week & Space Technology*, August 1, 1977, p. 16; Robert G. Bell, *Implications of Extending the SALT I Interim Agreement*, Congressional Research Service, Library of Congress, May 16, 1977.

46. See Chapter 2, p. 47.

47. Warnke, *The SALT Process*, p. 3.

48. See, in particular, Richard Burt, "Major Concessions by U.S. and Soviet on Arms Reported," *New York Times*, October 11, 1977; Edgar Ulsamer, "The Equal Sign in the SALT II Equation," *Air Force Magazine*, January 1978, pp. 27-31.

49. Ibid.

50. Ibid. The precise numbers in each of these two sublimit categories were not settled until some time in the first part of 1978, but when finally agreed,

they came out closer to the lower figure understood to have been proposed by the United States.

51. *The Strategic Arms Limitations Talks*, p. 8. For previous comment on Soviet reluctance to furnish relevant data in SALT, see Chapters 1, p. 9f.; 3, p. 70. The exchange of data that was finally agreed to in SALT, apparently in December 1977, was limited in the Soviet case essentially to numbers of constrained strategic systems and their Soviet designations. One of the side effects of this was the gradual appearance in the U.S. press of designations like the RSM-50 and RSM-52 in place of the NATO descriptive system customarily used. (The Soviet designations are for two SLBMs—one called by NATO the SS-N-18, the other the Typhoon missile.) See Clarence A. Robinson, Jr., "SALT Stance Allows New Missiles," *Aviation Week & Space Technology*, April 24, 1978, p. 16.

52. Burt, in *Foreign Affairs*, July 1978, p. 758.

53. *The Strategic Arms Limitation Talks*, p. 8. See also Chapter 10, p. 200 and note 12.

54. See Burt, in the *New York Times*, October 11, 1977; *The Strategic Arms Limitation Talks*, p. 8.

55. See Burt, in *Foreign Affairs*, July 1978, pp. 757-58.

56. Ibid., p. 759; Robinson, in *Aviation Week & Space Technology*, April 24, 1978, p. 16.

57. *The Strategic Arms Limitation Talks*, p. 8; Don Oberdorfer, "Vance, Gromyko Resume SALT Talks," *Washington Post*, September 28, 1978.

58. See Burt, in the *New York Times*, October 11, 1977; Warnke, *The SALT Process*, p. 5; Oberdorfer, in the *Washington Post*, September 28, 1978.

59. See Burt, in *Foreign Affairs*, July 1978, pp. 757-58.

60. See Kurt Birrenbach, "European Security: NATO, SALT and Equilibrium," *Orbis*, Summer 1978, pp. 297-308; Colin S. Gray, "The End of SALT? Purpose and Strategy in U.S.-U.S.S.R. Negotiations," *Policy Review*, Fall 1977, p. 40; Fred Charles Iklé, "SALT and Nuclear Balance in Europe," *Strategic Review*, Spring 1978, pp. 21-23; Colonel Joel M. McKean, *SALT Two Ratification Issues*, National Security Affairs Monograph 78-2, National Defense University, Washington, D.C., March 1978, pp. 10-11.

61. Burt, in *Foreign Affairs*, July 1978, pp. 755-60. See also Don Oberdorfer, "U.S. and Soviets Report Progress on Arms Treaty," *Washington Post*, October 1, 1978.

62. "The Task of Limiting Strategic Arms: Prospects and Problems," *Pravda*, February 11, 1978.

63. G. Arbatov, "Time for Crucial Decisions," *Pravda*, March 28, 1978.

64. Arbatov's article made note that similar "vacillations" had cost the chance of reaching an agreement in 1976 under the Ford administration.

65. See Chapter 3, pp. 68-69.

66. A partial account of the Congressional group's session with Ogarkov is given by David K. Shipler, "Soviet Said to Agree on Satellite Talks," *New York Times*, April 3, 1978.

67. "Visit by L.I. Brezhnev to the Pacific Fleet: Speech of Comrade L.I. Brezhnev," *Pravda*, April 8, 1978.

68. See *SALT TWO: Verification*, Selected Documents No. 7, The Department of State, February 1978, p. 12.

69. See Rowland Evans and Robert Novak, ". . . No Rubber-Stamping," *Washington Post*, March 16, 1978.

70. Henry L. Trewhitt, "The Senate Looms Large Now As an Obstacle to SALT," *Baltimore Sun*, June 11, 1978.

71. Rowland Evans and Robert Novak, "The Coming SALT Battle," *Washington Post*, April 21, 1978. See also Burt, in *Foreign Affairs*, July 1978, p. 763, and Harry Gelber, "SALT and the Strategic Future," *Orbis*, Summer 1978, p. 286.

72. See Chapter 2, p. 47. See also Meg Greenfield, "SALT in the Wounds," *Washington Post*, May 3, 1978; Murrey Marder, "US-Soviet Tension Seen on Rise: Political Climate Darkens for Talks on Arms Reductions," ibid., May 25, 1978; Robert G. Kaiser, "Selling SALT to the Senate," ibid., May 28, 1978.

73. Robert G. Kaiser and Walter Pincus, "White House Imposing Freeze on Strategic Arms Talks," *Washington Post*, June 2, 1978.

74. Editorial, "SALT: 'Freeze,' " *Washington Post*, June 3, 1978.

75. On this occasion, Vance met with Brezhnev and Gromyko accompanied only by Ambassador Malcolm Toon and interpreter William Krimer.

76. Bernard Gwertzman, "U.S. and Soviet Said to Resolve a Key Issue Blocking Arms Pact," *New York Times*, April 25, 1978; Richard Burt, "U.S. Agreed with Soviet to Limit Cooperation with Allies on Arms," ibid., May 2, 1978.

77. "Carter and Gromyko Report Some Gains on Strategic Arms," *New York Times*, May 28, 1978; Richard Burt, "Soviet Proposal Blamed in Delay on Arms Talks," ibid., June 4, 1978. The proposal in question—to ban all new Soviet and U.S. ICBMs through 1985—reportedly was rejected so as not to foreclose the U.S. option of a mobile MX land-based missile.

78. See Dusko Doder, "Kremlin Showing Alarm As Sino-US Ties Grow," *Washington Post*, August 24, 1978; Craig R. Whitney, "Soviet Leadership Worried Over China's Re-emergence," *New York Times*, November 30, 1978.

79. See Bernard Gwertzman, "Vance and Gromyko, in Geneva, Seek Agreement on Arms Treaty," *New York Times*, July 13, 1978.

80. Don Oberdorfer, "Moscow Mission Is Further Step in Treaty Quest," *Washington Post*, September 6, 1978; Bernard Gwertzman, "Warnke Carries Ideas on SALT to Moscow," *Washington Star*, September 6, 1978. One of the ideas carried to Moscow later was reported to have been a proposal, adopted by President Carter at the suggestion of Congressmen Bob Carr of Michigan and Thomas Downey of New York, to add to the SALT II Treaty a ban on testing of "depressed trajectory" SLBMs. Such a ban would prevent reduction of warning time from SLBMs fired from offshore against U.S. bomber bases. How this proposal was received by the Russians was not reported. See Charles W. Corddry, "U.S. Brings Up New Issue for SALT II Talks," *Baltimore Sun*, September 16, 1978.

81. Don Oberdorfer, "U.S. and Soviets Report Progress on Arms Treaty," *Washington Post*, October 1, 1978.

82. Don Oberdorfer, "Arms Talks Recess: Resume in Moscow Later This Month," *Washington Post*, October 2, 1978.

83. "SALT's Last (Big) 5%," *Time*, November 6, 1978, p. 36.

84. Robert G. Kaiser and Don Oberdorfer, "U.S. and Soviets Reported on Verge of SALT II Pact," *Washington Post*, October 6, 1978. This account also broke the news that Paul Warnke had decided to resign upon completion of a SALT II agreement.

85. Bernard Gwertzman and Henry S. Bradsher, "SALT: Caution Signaled on New Pact," *Washington Star*, October 19, 1978; Don Oberdorfer, "U.S. Cautious on Arms Pact on Eve of Moscow Talks," *Washington Post*, October 21, 1978.

86. See William Beecher, "SALT Reported Inching Along," *Boston Globe*, October 24, 1978. The Soviet press also reported that differences had been narrowed "in some respects." See Boris Averchenko, "International Week: Review," *Pravda*, October 29, 1978.

87. Don Oberdorfer, "Moscow Talks Begin with Four Issues Pending," *Washington Post*, October 22, 1978.

88. *Time*, November 6, 1978, p. 36.

89. William Beecher, "Russians Offer New Proposal for SALT Pact," *Boston Globe*, October 18, 1978; Henry S. Bradsher, "SALT Narrows Down to a Few Sticky Issues," *Washington Star*, October 15, 1978.

90. Walter Pincus, "U.S. Is Pressing to Limit Warheads on Each ICBM," *Washington Post*, October 26, 1978; Edgar Ulsamer, "In Focus," *Air Force Magazine*, November 1978, p. 12.

91. Pincus, in the *Washington Post*, October 26, 1978.

92. Oberdorfer, in the *Washington Post*, October 22, 1978.

93. Henry S. Bradsher, "Soviet Bomber Still Thorn in SALT Talks," *Washington Star*, October 21, 1978.

94. Don Oberdorfer, "SALT Negotiations End; New Round of Talks Expected," *Washington Post*, October 21, 1978; Beecher, in the *Boston Globe*, October 18, 1978; "Detente: SALT's Last Stage," *Newsweek*, October 30, 1978, pp. 49-50.

95. The U.S. estimate of the production rate was about thirty per year, according to Beecher, in the *Boston Globe*, October 18, 1978. A reported new plant adjacent to the Backfire assembly plant was said to have given concern that the Soviets might be planning to increase Backfire production, which would, of course, increase the sensitivity of any "loophole" suspicion. See Bonner Day, "Soviet Bombers: A Growing Threat," *Air Force Magazine*, November 1978, p. 85.

96. Beecher, in the *Boston Globe*, October 18, 1978.

97. See Senator Frank Church, *Strategic Arms Limitation Talks and Comprehensive Test Ban Negotiations*, Report to the Committee on Foreign Relations, Senate, August 11, 1978, p. 5 (sanitized and made public, September 1978). See also Chapter 11, p. 227f.

98. Church, in *Strategic Arms Limitation Talks*, p. 5. See also Henry S. Bradsher, "SALT Treaty Closer, Problems Remain After Moscow Talks," *Washington Star*, October 23, 1978.

99. TASS interview with Foreign Minister Andrei Gromyko, October 6, 1978. See also Oberdorfer, in the *Washington Post*, October 21, 1978.

100. Among verification problems, apparently, was Soviet adoption of encoded telemetry from testing of the SS-18. Although not a violation under SALT I terms, this practice could impede verification of qualitative limitations under the SALT II accord, and hence could become a very contentious issue. See Richard Burt, in the *New York Times*, November 7, 1978. See also Bradsher, in the *Washington Star*, October 20, 23, 1978.

The logic behind the American argument that MAP would be SALT-compatible was given by Paul Warnke in answer to a question at a press conference in August 1978. He said: "In SALT, what is limited is strategic launchers, whether they're ballistic missile submarine tubes, ICBM launchers, or heavy bombers. You don't have to verify where that launcher is at any particular time. Obviously, you don't know where a ballistic missile submarine is. You can move a heavy bomber around from place to place, and that doesn't interfere with SALT. Similarly, you can hypothesize the sort of mobile ICBM launching system which is in fact verifiable in that you know what the launchers are and how many of them there are." Transcript of On-the-Record Discussion with Paul C. Warnke . . . , August 29, 1978, p. 18. See also Don Oberdorfer, "Warnke: SALT Doesn't Preclude 'Shell Game' Idea," *Washington Post*, August 25, 1978.

101. Church, *Strategic Arms Limitation Talks*, pp. 8-9. Although few proponents claimed that a SALT II accord would reduce defense spending, some argued that it would contribute to "future cost avoidance," since in its absence, "each side would escalate military expenditures." See Stanley Hoffman, "Dealing With Moscow," *New York Times*, November 8, 1978, and Roger George, "SALT and the Defense Budget," *Arms Control Today*, November 1978, p. 4.

102. Paul C. Warnke, *SALT Two—The Home Stretch* (Address to Foreign Policy Association, New York, August 23, 1978), ACDA release, p. 6.

103. Ibid.

104. Senator Edward M. Kennedy, "SALT II and the Vulnerability of Minuteman," *Washington Star*, October 8, 1978.

105. Paul Warnke, *SALT: Its Contribution to U.S. Security and World Peace* (Remarks before Conference on U.S. Security and the Soviet Challenge, Hartford, Conn., July 25, 1978), State Department Release No. 27, August 1978, p. 4. (Hereafter cited as Warnke, *SALT: Its Contribution.*)

106. Ibid.

107. Ibid., p. 6. See also Church, *Strategic Arms Limitation Talks*, p. 7.

108. As noted in Chapter 11, p. 233, one of the last major sticking points was the Soviet attempt to extend the restriction on long-range GLCMs and SLCMs. Should it have become necessary for the U.S. to give in on this issue in order to get an agreement, this argument of SALT II's supporters would, of course, be vitiated.

109. Warnke, *SALT: Its Contribution*, p. 6.

110. Senator Charles McC. Mathias, Jr., "SALT II: Will Carter Make the Strong Case There Is?", *Christian Science Monitor*, September 21, 1978.

111. See McKean, *SALT Two Ratification Issues*, p. 20.

112. Church, *Strategic Arms Limitation Talks*, p. 8. See also Herbert Scoville, Jr., "U.S., Soviets May Have Ups and Downs but SALT Must March On," *Los Angeles Times*, September 10, 1978.

113. Vernon A. Guidry, Jr., "Warnke Warns on 'Bribing' SALT Critics," *Washington Star*, December 6, 1978.

114. See Gelber, in *Orbis*, Summer 1978, p. 284; McKean, *SALT Two Ratification Issues*, p. 5; Burt, in *Foreign Affairs*, July 1978, pp. 760-61; *Is America Becoming Number 2?: Current Trends In the U.S.-Soviet Military Balance*, Committee on the Present Danger, Washington, D.C., October 5, 1978, pp. 12-13.

115. See Burt, in *Foreign Affairs*, July 1978, p. 760; Eugene V. Rostow, "SALT II—A Soft Bargain, A Hard Sell," speech at Conference on U.S. Security and the Soviet Challenge, at Hartford, Conn., July 25, 1978; Paul H. Nitze, *Considerations Bearing on the Merits of an Agreement*, Arlington, Va., December 4, 1978, pp. 3-4. (Mimeograph.)

116. William R. Van Cleave and Seymour Weiss, "National Intelligence and the USSR," *National Review*, June 23, 1978, pp. 777-80. See also "Criteria For Evaluating SALT," *National Security Record*, The Heritage Foundation, November 1978, p. 1.

117. Richard Pipes, "Rethinking Our Nuclear Strategy," *Wall Street Journal*, October 12, 1978.

118. See sources cited in note 60, above. See also Vernon A. Guidry, Jr., "SALT Will Hurt Security, Jackson Tells NATO Panel," *Washington Star*, November 28, 1978.

119. Senator Lloyd M. Bentsen, Jr., "Do We Really Need SALT II?", *Dallas Morning News*, October 17, 1978; Constantine C. Menges, "Closing the Loopholes, SALT II: Truth or Consequences," *The New Leader*, September 25, 1978.

120. Burt, in *Foreign Affairs*, July 1978, p. 767.

121. The campaign to sell SALT, overseen by the Office of the Counselor of the State Department, Matthew Nimetz, included a speakers' program, organizing of conferences in various states on U.S.-Soviet relations and SALT, as well as intensive congressional liaison activities, reportedly even more extensive than the "mobilization" for the Panama Canal treaties. The effort to win support in Congress included invitations to every senator to travel to Geneva to take part in a negotiating session as a regular member of the SALT delegation. See Richard L. Strout, "Carter's Crucial Push for SALT Ratification," *Christian Science Monitor*, October 10, 1978; editorial, "The SALT Salesmen," *Wall Street Journal*, October 24, 1978. The author is also indebted for the information given above to research done by Rose Gottemoeller.

122. Warnke's intention to resign in order to return to his law practice first became known on October 6, 1978 (see note 84, above), his resignation becoming effective on October 31. Departure of the controversial ACDA head, regretted by his supporters and received with satisfaction by his opponents, deprived SALT of its most vigorous and competent advocate within the administration. Whatever criticism might be made of Warnke's policy preferences, he had by all accounts been a tough and able negotiator in SALT encounters with the Russians.

123. See Kenneth H. Bacon, "Warnke Quits Arms Control Post in Move Seen Prelude to Conclusion of SALT Pact," *Wall Street Journal*, October 11, 1978; Joseph Kraft, "Warnke: Pulled, Not Pushed," *Washington Post*, October 19, 1978.

124. "Carter Names Retired General As ACDA Chief," *Washington Post*, October 21, 1978. See also Chapter 2, note 61. During his military career, General Seignious had been director of the JCS Joint Staff, and head of the Defense Security Assistance Agency.

125. See editorial, "The Wrong Man for Disarmament," *New York Times*, November 24, 1978; Alton Frye, "ACDA's General: Time for Strategic Withdrawal," *Washington Post*, December 6, 1978.

126. "Earle, Veteran of Arms Talks, Named Chief SALT Negotiator," *Washington Post*, October 27, 1978.

127. For previous discussion of the ACDA organizational role in SALT, which was written prior to Warnke's departure, see Chapter 2, pp. 43-45.

128. Semenov's impending departure from SALT to take up a diplomatic post in Bonn was first disclosed by Warnke at his farewell press conference on October 30, 1978. No official announcement by the Soviet government had been made up to that time. See George C. Wilson, "Arms Curb Protocol Praised by Warnke," *Washington Post*, October 31, 1978. See also, Chapter 3, pp. 60f., 68.

129. See Chapter 3, p. 70f.

130. Gromyko, for example, had said during a press conference in Paris at the end of October: "It seems as though we still need a number of meetings." On the American side, no suggestions were offered as to how many meetings might be needed; in fact, it was indicated by anonymous Washington officials that the United States was reluctant to schedule any new meetings until there were indications that Moscow might budge from its set positions. See "Gromyko Urges Talks among All Nuclear Powers," *Los Angeles Times*, October 29, 1978.

131. Spokesmen on both sides appeared to acknowledge that the time had come when political decisions, and not further exchanges between arms control negotiators, would be required to resolve the remaining differences. See Craig Whitney, "Moscow Aide Concedes Differences in the Soviet Leadership over Arms Pact," and Richard Burt, "Hopes for Early Arms Accord Fade in Washington," *New York Times*, November 7, 1978.

132. Senator John G. Tower of Texas, as quoted by Don Lewis, "SALT 'Tilts' toward Soviets, May Not Pass Senate—Tower," *New Orleans Times-Picayune*, October 20, 1978.

133. In this connection, see the unusual comment to American reporters by Valentin M. Falin, a Central Committee functionary, suggesting that there were differences to be ironed out on a treaty among the Defense Ministry, the Foreign Ministry, and the Defense Council. See Whitney, in the *New York Times*, November 7, 1978.

134. Bernard Gwertzman, " 'Now-or-Never' Session in SALT Talks Approaches," *Washington Star*, September 24, 1978.

135. David K. Shipler, "Senators' Soviet Trip Points Up Misunderstandings," *New York Times*, November 19, 1978; Kevin Klose, "Soviets' Outlook Baffles Senators On Moscow Visit," *Washington Post*, November 19, 1978.

136. A revival within the Carter administration of cautious optimism that agreement might be near followed remarks on December 7 by the president that remaining differences were "minor" compared with earlier ones, and that "if the Soviets are adequately forthcoming, I would guess that any further delay would

be minimal." Washington officials indicated a couple of days later that another Vance-Gromyko meeting would be held before the end of the year to conclude the SALT II accord and arrange for a summit signing ceremony between Carter and Brezhnev as early as January 1979. See Don Oberdorfer, "President Carter on Two Fronts For SALT Accord," *Washington Post*, December 8, 1978; Richard Burt, "Strides in Arms Talks With Soviet Said to Bring Summit Session Near," The *New York Times*, December 11, 1978. Richard Burt, "President Cites 'Good Progress' In Arms Parley," ibid., December 13, 1978.

NOTES TO CHAPTER 12
CONCLUDING REFLECTIONS ON THE
SALT EXPERIENCE

1. For a representative statement reflecting this school of thought, see Senator Frank Church, *Strategic Arms Limitation Talks and Comprehensive Test Ban Negotiations*, Report to the Committee on Foreign Relations, Senate, August 11, 1978, sanitized and made public, September 1978.

2. For articulate expressions of this school of thought, see Edward N. Luttwak, "Why Arms Control Has Failed," *Commentary*, January 1978, pp. 19-28; Colin S. Gray, "The End of SALT? Purpose and Strategy in US-USSR Negotiations," *Policy Review*, Fall 1977, pp. 31-46.

3. An able expositor of this school of thought is Richard Burt. See his "The Risks of Asking SALT to Do Too Much," *The Washington Review*, January 1978, pp. 19-33, and "The Scope and Limits of SALT," *Foreign Affairs*, July 1978, pp. 751-70.

4. Burt, in *The Washington Review*, January 1978, p. 19.

5. Remarks by Professor Vernon Aspaturian, during arms control seminar at the annual convention of the American Association for the Advancement of Slavic Studies, Washington, D.C., October 14, 1977. From the author's notes.

6. See Chapter 6, p. 130f.

7. See Chapter 5, pp. 108-09.

8. See Chapter 1, p. 7.

9. See Burt, in *The Washington Review*, January 1978, p. 32; Stanley Sienkiewicz, "SALT and Soviet Nuclear Doctrine," *International Security*, Spring 1978, p. 100.

10. Burt, in *The Washington Review*, January 1978, p. 32.

11. Gray, in *Policy Review*, Fall 1977, p. 39.

12. See Thomas W. Wolfe, *The Military Dimension in the Making of Soviet Foreign and Defense Policy*, The Rand Corporation, Santa Monica, P-6024, October 1977, p. 44.

13. See comments by Raymond L. Garthoff, cited in Chapter 4, p. 88.

14. For an analysis covering various bargaining chip examples in SALT, with generally critical findings, see Robert J. Bresler and Robert C. Gray, "The Bargaining Chip and SALT," *Political Science Quarterly*, Spring 1977, pp. 65-88.

15. See Chapter 11, p. 237f. See also Paul H. Nitze, *Consequences of an Agreement*, Arlington, Va., October 30, 1978, pp. 2-6. (Mimeograph.)

16. See Chapter 8, pp. 159-166.

17. See Chapter 2, p. 47.

18. See Chapter 11, p. 229f.

19. Should failure to resolve the last two or three sticking points have prevented final agreement on a SALT II accord, this too could be a source of doubt about the continuation of SALT. At the time of writing in December 1978, it was not clear whether chances of a last-minute compromise or a hopeless deadlock then existed.

20. U.S.-Soviet talks separate from SALT, on banning antisatellite systems, had begun in Helsinki in June 1978. It was possible that any wider consideration of military activities in space might be kept in that forum also.

21. See Chapter 11, pp. 223-224.

22. On the point that one of the paradoxes of arms control is that its very success in reducing numbers of weapons could create a situation of dangerous instability, see Luttwak, in *Commentary*, January 1978, p. 22.

23. Harry Gelber, "SALT and the Strategic Future," *Orbis*, Summer 1978, p. 289; Jack H. Harris and William D. Bajusz, "Arms Control And Gray-Area Systems," *Air Force Magazine*, February 1978, p. 36. See also Burt, in *Foreign Affairs*, July 1978, p. 770.

24. Deborah Shapley, "Technology Creep and the Arms Race: Two Future Arms Control Problems," *Science*, October 20, 1978, pp. 289, 291. This is the third of a three-part series on "technology creep"—defined as incremental, often cheap, and usually inconspicuous advances in technology that can sometimes radically transform the capabilities of weapons systems before top policy leaders have become aware of the change.

25. It should be noted that there is considerable question whether missile site defense would in fact turn out to be a substantially cheaper "solution" to the vulnerability problem.

26. Deborah Shapley, "Technology Creep and the Arms Race: A World of Absolute Accuracy," *Science*, September 29, 1978, p. 1196.

27. The rapid transition to a new technological era, it has been pointed out, poses the problem that new classes of weapons "may very well not fit into traditional categories of strategic or tactical, nuclear or conventional, Earth-based or space-based." Such categories, however, have formed "the conceptual framework of current arms-limitation negotiating strategies." See Kosta Tsipis, "Science And The Military," *Bulletin of the Atomic Scientists*, January 1977, p. 10.

28. For a survey of particle beam weapons development in the United States and the Soviet Union, see the series by Clarence A. Robinson, Jr., "The Beam Weapons Race," "U.S. Pushes Development of Beam Weapons," "Key Beam Weapons Tests Slated," in *Aviation Week & Space Technology*, October 2, 1978, pp. 1-48, October 9, pp. 42-46. See also Richard Burt, "Debate on Missile-Destroyer Arms Picks Up Heat Over Soviet Moves," *New York Times*, December 5, 1978.

29. See Chapter 1, p. 4f.

30. See Gelber, in *Orbis*, Summer 1978, p. 295.

31. Burt, in *The Washington Review*, January 1978, pp. 32-33.

32. See Chapter 11, p. 227f, and note 51, on the limited character of the data base exchange.

33. For previous discussion of the SCC and its functions, see Chapters 2, pp. 34-35, 39; and 3, pp. 70-71.

34. *Congressional Record*, 92d Cong., 2d session, August 3, 1972, p. S26692. It may be noted that most U.S. arms control officials have not stressed a requirement for mutual trust. The emphasis has usually been that SALT agreements rely on verification measures, not "on trust of the Soviet Union." See Paul C. Warnke, "Strengthening United States Security Through SALT," address in Racine, Wisconsin, June 29, 1978, U.S. Arms Control and Disarmament Agency release, p. 6.

# Index

✳

# Selected Rand Books

Leites, Nathan. *The Operational Code of the Politburo.* New York: McGraw-Hill Book Company, Inc., 1951.

Mead, Margaret. *Soviet Attitudes toward Authority: An Interdisciplinary Approach to Problems of Soviet Character.* New York: McGraw-Hill Book Company, Inc., 1951.

Garthoff, Raymond L. *Soviet Military Doctrine.* Glencoe, Illinois: The Free Press, 1953.

Bergson, Abram, and Hans Heymann, Jr. *Soviet National Income and Product, 1940-1948.* New York: Columbia University Press, 1954.

Davison, W. Phillips. *The Berlin Blockade: A Study in Cold War Politics.* Princeton, New Jersey: Princeton University Press, 1958.

Fainsod, Merle. *Smolensk Under Soviet Rule.* Cambridge, Mass.: Harvard University Press, 1958.

Dinerstein, H.S. *War and the Soviet Union: Nuclear Weapons and the Revolution in Soviet Military and Political Thinking.* New York: Frederick A. Praeger, Inc., 1959.

Brodie, Bernard. *Strategy in the Missile Age.* Princeton, New Jersey: Princeton University Press, 1959.

Hitch, Charles J., and Roland McKean. *The Economics of Defense in the Nuclear Age.* Cambridge, Mass.: Harvard University Press, 1960.

Speier, Hans. *Divided Berlin: The Anatomy of Soviet Political Blackmail.* New York: Frederick A. Praeger, Inc., 1961.

Tanham, George K. *Communist Revolutionary Warfare: The Vietminh in Indochina.* New York: Frederick A. Praeger, Inc., 1961.

Gouré, Leon. *Civil Defense in the Soviet Union.* Los Angeles, California: University of California Press, 1962.

Hsieh, Alice Langley. *Communist China's Strategy in the Nuclear Era*. Englewood Cliffs, New Jersey: Prentice-Hall, Inc., 1962.

Dole, Stephen H., and Isaac Asimov. *Planets for Man*. New York: Random House, Inc., 1964.

Wolfe, Thomas W. *Soviet Strategy at the Crossroads*. Cambridge, Mass.: Harvard University Press, 1964.

Rush, Myron. *Political Succession in the USSR*. New York: Columbia University Press, 1965.

Horelick, Arnold L., and Myron Rush. *Strategic Power and Soviet Foreign Policy*. Chicago, Illinois: University of Chicago Press, 1966.

Kolkowicz, Roman. *The Soviet Military and the Communist Party*. Princeton, New Jersey: Princeton University Press, 1967.

Marschak, Thomas A., Thomas K. Glennan, Jr., and Robert Summers. *Strategy for R&D*. New York: Springer-Verlag, 1967.

Quade, E.S., and W.I. Boucher. *Systems Analysis and Policy Planning: Applications in Defense*. New York: American Elsevier Publishing Company, 1968.

Hosmer, Stephen T. *Viet Cong Repression and Its Implications for the Future*. Lexington, Mass.: D.C. Heath and Company, 1970.

Wolfe, Thomas W. *Soviet Power and Europe 1945-1970*. Baltimore, Maryland: The Johns Hopkins Press, 1970.

Levien, Roger E. (ed.). *The Emerging Technology: Instructional Uses of the Computer in Higher Education*. New York: McGraw-Hill Book Company, 1972.

Quandt, William B. (ed.). *The Politics of Palestinian Nationalism*. Berkeley, Calif.: University of California Press, 1973.

Novick, David (ed.). *Current Practice in Program Budgeting (PPBS): Analysis and Case Studies Covering Government and Business*. New York: Crane, Russak & Company, Inc., 1973.

Einaudi, Luigi R. (ed.). *Beyond Cuba: Latin America Takes Charge of Its Future*. New York: Crane, Russak & Company, Inc., 1974.

Becker, Abraham S., Bent Hansen, and Malcolm H. Kerr. *The Economics and Politics of the Middle East*. New York: American Elsevier Publishing Company, 1975.

Quade, E.S. *Analysis for Public Decisions*. New York: American Elsevier Publishing Company, 1975.

Goldhamer, Herbert. *The Soviet Soldier: Soviet Military Management at the Troop Level*. New York: Crane, Russak & Company, Inc., 1975.

Becker, Abraham S. *Military Expenditure Limitation for Arms Control: Problems and Prospects. With a Documentary History of Recent Proposals*. Cambridge, Mass.: Ballinger Publishing Company, 1977.

# About the Author

**Thomas W. Wolfe,** a political scientist and retired military officer, is a senior staff member of The Rand Corporation and a faculty member of George Washington University's Institute for Sino-Soviet Studies. Widely known as an authority on Soviet national security and arms control policy, he has served as air attache at the American Embassy in Moscow and as an arms control negotiator. Dr. Wolfe is the author of *Soviet Strategy at the Crossroads* and *Soviet Power and Europe: 1945-1970,* and a contributing author to more than a dozen other books on Soviet military and foreign policy matters.